MODELING AND SIMULATION CONCEPTS

MODELING AND SIMULATION CONCEPTS

By

Rajendra Kumar
Assistant Professor
Vidya College of Engineering
Meerut (U.P.)

Vikesh Kumar
Associate Professor
Vidya College of Engineering
Meerut (U.P.)

Anil Kumar Kapil
Professor
M.M. Maulana University
Ambala, Haryana

Chandra Sekhar Yadav
Associate Professor
Noida Institute of Engineering Technology
Greater Noida, (U.P.)

UNIVERSITY SCIENCE PRESS
(An Imprint of Laxmi Publications Pvt. Ltd.)
An ISO 9001:2015 Company
BENGALURU • CHENNAI • GUWAHATI • HYDERABAD • JALANDHAR
KOCHI • KOLKATA • LUCKNOW • MUMBAI • RANCHI
NEW DELHI

MODELING AND SIMULATION CONCEPTS

Printed and bound in India
Typeset at Kalyani computer Service, Delhi
First Edition: 2011, Edition: 2017
ISBN 978-81-318-0696-8

Branches

©	Bengaluru	080-26 75 69 30	
©	Chennai	044-24 34 47 26,	24 35 95 07
©	Guwahati	0361-254 36 69,	251 38 81
©	Hyderabad	040-27 55 53 83,	27 55 53 93
©	Jalandhar	0181-222 12 72	
©	Kochi	0484-237 70 04,	405 13 03
©	Kolkata	033-22 27 43 84	
©	Lucknow	0522-220 99 16	
©	Mumbai	022-24 93 12 61	
©	Ranchi	0651-220 44 64	

Published in India by

UNIVERSITY SCIENCE PRESS
(An Imprint of Laxmi Publications Pvt.Ltd.)
An ISO 9001:2015 Company
113, GOLDEN HOUSE, DARYAGANJ,
NEW DELHI - 110002, INDIA
Telephone : 91-11-4353 2500, 4353 2501
Fax : 91-11-2325 2572, 4353 2528
www.laxmipublications.com info@laxmipublications.com

C—
Printed at:

Dedicated
to
Shreya, Devanshi, Preesha, Paridhi, Anand, Aman
and
Akash

CONTENTS

PREFACE

This book outlines the considerable and promising work that is being conducted to counter the problems of uncertainty surrounding the methods used to approach these new applications in the field of modeling and simulation. The book aims to stimulate the reader into seeking out new packages and languages for modeling and simulation.

Modeling and Simulation is a discipline for developing a level of understanding of the interaction of the parts of a system, and of the system as a whole. The level of understanding which may be developed via this discipline is seldom achievable via any other discipline. Software tools for simulation and modeling can help verify the design of hydraulic motion control systems. Model-based control provides an accurate tool for indicating when a hydraulic system will not work and offers advanced techniques for using simulation technology in the development, testing and application of software. A number of modeling and simulation tools have been developed and more are being developed for incident management applications. Each of these tools has focused on a specific aspect of the selected problem.

Modeling and simulation applications have many information representation challenges. Some of the major challenges are discussed in the text.

Chapter 1 describes the concept of system and modeling. It shows, why do we need of modeling and simulation.

Chapter 2 describes simulation preliminaries and important facts about simulation. This chapter represents some simulations using MatLab. A detailed discussion on Monte-Carlo simulation is presented in this chapter.

Chapter 3 describes the simulation and modeling of some physical systems including. Chapter 4 describes a detailed modeling and simulation of Queuing system. Chapter 5 describes a detailed modeling and simulation of Inventory system.

Chapter 6 describes design and evaluation of simulation experiments. A detailed discussion on various factors that affect verification and validation of a simulation model is also presented in this chapter.

Chapter 7 describes a detailed discussion on various charts and PERT networks.

Chapter 8 describes a detailed discussion on GPSS, SIMULA and some other simulation languages along with various simulation packages.

We have taken considerable care to ensure that this text is as error free and effective as possible and will be grateful if any error remains behind being printed out with other suggestions for further improvement of this book.

—Authors

ACKNOWLEDGEMENT

We acknowledge Dr. B P Sharma, Mr. Dinesh Shrma, Dr. Vinod Kumar, Dr. Aditya Gautam, Mr. S K Jain, Mr. Pradeep Jain, Mr. Saurabh Jain, Dr. O P Agarwal who always motivated us for such projects.

We are indebted to Dr. P K Singh of MMMEC Gorakhpur, Dr. Divakar Singh Yadav of IET, Lucknow, Dr. Vikram Singh Yadav, Dr. Yash Pal Singh and Dr. A. K. Solanki of BIET, Jhansi for their encouragement and motivation time to time.

We sincerely thank to Dr. Phalguni Gupta of I1T Kanpur, Dr. Kamal Jain of 11T Roorkee, Dr. Raghu Raj Singh of HBT1 Kanpur, Dr. A K Sahu of DCE Delhi, Dr. Manu Pratap Singh of Dr. B R Ambedkar University Agra for their valuable suggestions.

We are very thankful to all our colleagues. It is a very long list; we specially acknowledge Dr. Mahendra Aswal, Mr. Shwetank Arya, Mr. K. P Tomar, Mr. Rohit Khokhar, Mr. Saurabh Sharma, Ms. Priya Sharma, Mr. Ajay Kumar Chaudhary, Mr. Dilip Singh, Mr. Abhilash, Mr. PR Tripathi, Mr. Jay Prakash.

—Authors

Chapter 1

Systems Concepts and Modeling

1.1 INTRODUCTION

The objective of this subject is to learn about heavy construction equipment, methods, modeling, and simulation. In this text readers will learn how to choose and configure equipment for different purposes such pure pursuit problem, reservoir, inventory control, queueing system, etc.

Computer system users, administrators, and designers usually have a goal of highest performance at lowest cost in least time. Modeling and simulation of system design trade off is good preparation for design and engineering decisions in real-world jobs. In this subject we study modeling and simulation of a variety of systems.

Simulation is one of the most powerful tools available to decision-makers responsible for the design and operation of complex processes and systems. It makes possible the study, analysis and evaluation of situations that would not be otherwise possible. In an increasingly competitive world, simulation has become an indispensable problem solving methodology for engineers, designers and managers. The simulation discipline has now expanded to include modeling of systems that are human-centered (like commercial, economical, and social) thus, containing a large amount of uncertainty. Those new fields of applications make modeling and simulation a dynamically expanding discipline. However, there is a growing gap between the new problems and the methodology. In particular, more robust research is required in the area of continuous simulation methodology and numerical methods. Another important point is model validation: it is difficult to prove that the model used is absolutely valid. Through examining the system dynamics methodology, which is over fifty years old, and it is still used in many application fields. However, less attention is given to the model validity. Modeling and simulation lies somewhere between science and art, frequently resembling the art of misapprehension.

Modeling and Simulation is a discipline, it is also very much a form of art. One can learn about riding a bicycle from reading a book. To really learn to ride a bicycle one must become actively engaged with a bicycle. Modeling and Simulation follows much the same reality. One can learn much about modeling and simulation from reading books and talking with other people. Skill and talent in developing models and performing simulations is only developed through the building of models and simulating them. From the interaction of the developer, the modeling emerges an understanding of what makes sense and what does not.

The terms model and system are key components of simulation. By a model we mean a representation of a group of objects or ideas in some form other than that of the entity itself. By a system we mean a group or collection of interrelated elements that cooperate to accomplish some stated objective. One of the real strengths of simulation is the fact that we can simulate systems that already exist as well as those that are capable of being brought into existence, *i.e.,* those in the preliminary or planning stage of development. Dynamic modeling in organizations is the collective ability to understand the implications of change overtime. This skill lies at the heart of successful strategic decision process. The availability of effective visual modeling and simulation enables the analysts and the decision-makers to boost their dynamic decision by rehearsing strategy to avoid hidden pitfalls.

System Simulation is the mimicking of the operation of a real system, such as the day-to-day operation of a bank, or the running of an assembly line in a factory, or the value of a stock portfolio over a time period, or the staff assignment of a hospital or a security company, in a computer. Instead of building extensive mathematical models by experts, the readily available simulation software has made it possible to model and analyze the operation of a real system by non-experts, who are managers but not programmers.

Simulation is nothing but the execution of a model, represented by a computer program that gives information about the system being investigated. The simulation approach of analyzing a model is opposed to the analytical approach, where the method of analyzing the system is purely theoretical. As this approach is more reliable, the simulation approach gives more flexibility and convenience. The activities of the model consist of events, which are activated at certain points in time and in this way affect the overall state of the system. The points in time that an event is activated are randomized, so no input from outside the system is required. Events exist autonomously and they are discrete so between the executions of two events nothing happens. The SIMSCRIPT (a simulation language) provides a process-based approach of writing a simulation program. With this approach, the components of the program consist of entities, which combine several related events into one process.

In the field of simulation, the concept of principle of computational equivalence has beneficial implications for the decision-maker. Simulated experimentation accelerates and replaces effectively the wait and watch anxieties in discovering new insight and explanations of future behavior of the real system.

With the integration of artificial intelligence, agents and other modeling techniques, simulation has become an effective and appropriate decision support for the managers. For example, in a consumer retail environment it can be used to find out how the roles of consumers and employees can be simulated to achieve peak performance. It is apparent that there are many problems of real-life that cannot be represented mathematically due to the stochastic nature of the problem, the conflicting ideas needed to properly describe the problem under study, or the complexity in problem formulation. Therefore under such circumstances simulation is the most often used tool. The analysts and designers of physical systems have long applied the simulation techniques and these now have become important tools for dealing with the complex problems in real-life.

Most but not all digital integrated circuits manufactured today are first extensively simulated before they are manufactured to identify and correct design errors. Simulation early in the design cycle is important because the cost to repair mistakes increases dramatically the later in the product life cycle that the error is detected. Another important application of simulation is in developing virtual environments, for example in training. Simulations generate dynamic environments with which users can interact as if they were really there. Such simulations are used extensively today to train military personnel for battlefield situations, at a fraction of the cost of running exercises involving real tanks, aircraft, etc.

It is assumed that Von Neuman and Stanislaw Ulam developed first important application of simulation for determining the complicated behavior of neutrons in a nuclear shielding problem being to complex for mathematical analysis. Computer simulation provides a means to take off the behaviors of complex real systems both quickly and economically. Simulation models can expeditiously compare the outcomes of alternatives before selecting a course of action. Simulation models can also provide a dynamic virtual environment for training. All simulation models require the mathematical representation of a real system that exists, or could exist, in time and space. A computational representation of that system then links inputs to outputs through the system architecture.

Computer-based modeling and simulation is used extensively for development of many complex, large-scale systems such as networks, information systems, and physical systems. Modeling concepts, theories, and methods provide a foundation for characterizing structure and behavior of dynamic systems at varying levels of details. These models can be constructed and subsequently simulated. Since dynamical systems can be described using alternative modeling and simulation approaches, it is important to understand their strengths and appropriateness.

It is often said that computers are revolutionizing science and engineering. By using computers we are able to construct complex engineering designs such as space shuttles. We are able to compute the properties of the universe, as it was fractions of a second after the big bang. Our ambitions are ever increasing. We want to create even more complex designs such as better spaceships, cars, medicines, computerized cellular phone systems, etc. We want to understand deeper aspects of nature. These are just a few examples of computer-supported modeling and simulation.

This text presents an object-oriented component-based approach to computer-supported mathematical modeling and simulation through the powerful Modelica language and its associated technology. Modelica can be viewed as an almost-universal approach to high-level computational modeling and simulation, by being able to represent a range of application areas and providing general notation as well as powerful abstractions and efficient implementations.

1.2 MODELING AND SIMULATION PROJECTS

Several projects have been developed so far and several are under progress. The main objectives of the modeling and simulation project being developed are to:

- Learn about the potential of modeling and simulation tools in construction
- Learn how to use simple modeling and simulation software
- Analyze a specific site operation in order to gain insight into its design.

The modeling and simulation project includes the following tasks:

1. Use of modeling and simulation software package to accurately model and simulate an operation from one site to which a field trip was organized. This requires learning about basic modeling approaches, collecting site data, and learning how to use the software. There are usually classic models available. Accuracy of the model must be verified.
2. Suggest possible improvements and/or alternatives to the operation based on analysis.
3. Perform a sensitivity analysis of the operation.
4. Evaluate the software used based on its ease to learn and usefulness for different applications.
5. Documentation of the model, simulating results, sensitivity analysis, final conclusions and recommendations in a project report.

1.3 THE SYSTEM CONCEPT

Before simulation we need a system. Let us define a system first. What is a system? A system can be almost anything. A system can contain subsystems, and the subsystems may again contain sub-systems. A possible definition of systems might be: System is a well-defined object in the Real-world under specific conditions, only considering specific aspects of its structure and behavior, or a system is an object or collection of objects whose properties we want to study. A system can also be defined as the collection of objects that act and interact together toward some logical end. Our wish to study selected properties of objects is central in this definition. The selection and definition of what constitutes a system is somewhat arbitrary and must be guided by what the system is to be used for.

A system can be understood as an entity, which maintains its existence through the interaction of its parts. Model is a simplified representation of the actual system intended to promote understanding. Whether a model is a good model or not depends on the extent to which it promotes understanding. Since all models are simplifications of reality there is always a trade-off as to what level of detail is included in the model. If too little detail is included in the model one runs the risk of missing relevant interactions and the resultant model does not promote understanding. If too much detail is included in the model may become overly complicated and actually exclude the possibility of the development of understanding.

A system is a potential source of data. It can be defined as a list of variables. There are variables that are generated by the environment, and which influence the behavior of the system. These variables are called the *input* of the system. There are some other variables that are determined by the system, and that in turn influence the behavior of its environment. These variables are called *outputs* of the system.

Some other definition of systems can also be adapted. While defining the system, there are certain tasks that must be done. Among these are:

- Divide the system into logical subsystems.
- Define the entities, which will flow through the system.
- For each subsystem, define the stations (locations where something is done to or for the entities).
- Define the basic flow patterns of entities through the stations using flow diagrams.
- Define alternative designs for the system, which are to be considered.
- Develop flow charts to show the routing logic for flexible paths.

1.3.1 System Terminology

We live in a world of systems driven by causes and affects. Those systems include inventory, production, financial, chemical, biological, thermodynamic or workflow. Systems can be modeled as nodes representing system variables and connecting lines representing causal effects. The changing value of one variable can cause another to increase or decrease. Understanding how a system really works is the first step towards using, improving, automating or explaining it to others.

Causal Loop Diagrams (CLDs) are used to model the dynamic systems. It is the simple diagram notation of nodes and lines identifies the important variables in a system and how they interact. Facts about the system are used to parameterize a causal loop diagram. Each node becomes a variable that identifies a quantifiable property of the system that changes overtime. Each line can have equations or rules that formalize how one variable affects another.

The parameterized models must have all the information needed to simulate the dynamic response of the system over a series of time increments. The model is declarative in that the diagram, variables and equations just declare facts about the system. Let us define various factors of a system:

- **State:** Collection of variables and their values necessary to characterize a system at a particular time. It can also be defined as a variable characterizing an attribute in the system such as level of stock in inventory or number of jobs waiting for processing.
- **Event:** A change in system state, or an occurrence at a point in time which may change the state of the system, such as arrival of a customer or start of work on a job.
- **Entity:** An object that passes through the system.
- **Queue:** A queue is not only a physical queue of people, it can also be a task list, a buffer of finished goods waiting for transportation or any place where entities are waiting for something to happen for any reason.
- **Creating:** Creating is causing an arrival of a new entity to the system at some point in time.

- **Scheduling:** Scheduling is the act of assigning a new future event to an existing entity.
- **Random variable:** A random variable is a quantity that is uncertain, such as inter-arrival time between two incoming flights or number of defective parts in a shipment.
- **Random variate:** A random variate is an artificially generated random variable.
- **Distribution:** A distribution is the mathematical law, which governs the probabilistic features of a random variable.

1.3.2 Entity States

Entities migrate from state to state while they work their way through a model. An entity is always in one of five alternative states, as detailed below.

The Active State. The Active State is the state of the currently moving entity. Only one entity moves at any instant of *wall-clock* time. This entity progresses through its operations nonstop until it encounters a delay. It then migrates to an alternative state. Some other entity then becomes the next active entity, and so on.

The Ready State. During an Entity Movement Phase there may be more than one entity ready to move, and yet entities can only move (be in the Active State) one-by-one. The Ready State is the state of entities waiting to enter the Active State during the current Entity Movement Phase.

The Time-delayed State. The Time-delayed state is the state of entities waiting for a known future simulated time to be reached so that they can then (re)enter the ready state. A *part entity* is in a time-delayed state, for example, while waiting for the future simulated time at which an operation being performed on it by a machine will come to an end.

The Condition-delayed State. The Condition-delayed State is the state of entities delayed until some specified condition comes about, *e.g.,* a *part entity* might wait in the condition-delayed state until its turn comes to use a machine. Condition-delayed entities are removed *automatically* from the condition-delayed state when conditions permit.

The Dormant State. Sometimes it is desirable to put entities into a state from which no escape will be triggered automatically by changes in model conditions. It is called state the dormant state. Dormant-state entities rely on modeler-supplied logic to transfer them from the Dormant State back to the Ready State. Job-ticket entities might be put into a Dormant State, for example, until an operator entity decides which job-ticket to pull next.

1.3.3 Entity Management Structures

Simulation software uses the following lists to organize and track entities in the five entity states.

The Active Entity. The active entity forms an unnamed *list* consisting only of the active entity. The Active-State entity moves nonstop until encountering an operation that puts it into another state (transfers it to another list) or removes it from the model. A Ready-State entity then becomes the next Active-State entity. Eventually there is no possibility of further action at the current time. The EMP (Entity Management System) then ends and a Clock Update Phase begin.

The Current Events List. Entities in the Ready-State are kept in a single list here called the *current events list* (CEL). Entities migrate to the current events list from the future events list, from delay lists, and from user-managed lists. In addition, entities cloned from the Active-State entity usually start their existence on the current events list.

The Future Events List. Entities in the Time-Delayed State belong to a single list into which they are inserted at the beginning of their time-based delay. This list, called the *future events list* (FEL) here, is usually ranked by increasing entity move time. Move time is the simulated time at which an entity is scheduled to try to move again. At the time of entity insertion into the FEL, the entity's move time is calculated by adding the value of the simulation clock to the known (sampled) duration of the time-based delay.

After an Entity Movement Phase is over, the Clock Update Phase sets the clock's value to the move time of the FEL's highest ranked (smallest move time) entity. This entity is then transferred from the FEL to the CEL, migrating from the Time-Delayed State to the Ready State and setting the stage for the next EMP to begin.

The preceding statement assumes there are not other entities on the FEL whose move time matches the clock's updated value. In the case of move-time ties, some tools will transfer all the time-tied entities from the FEL to the CEL during a single CUP, whereas other tools take a "one entity transfer per CUP" approach. Languages that work with internal entities usually use the FEL to support the timing requirements of these entities. The FEL is typically composed both of external and internal entities in such languages.

Delay Lists. Delay lists are lists of entities in the Condition-Delayed State. These entities are waiting for a condition to come about (*e.g.,* waiting their turn to use a machine) so they can be transferred automatically into the Ready State on the current events list. Delay lists, which are generally created automatically by the simulation software, are managed by using related waiting or polled waiting.

If a delay can be related easily to events in the model that might resolve the condition, then related waiting can be used to manage the delay list. For example, suppose a machine's status changes from busy to idle. In response, the software can automatically remove the next machine-using entity from the appropriate delay list and put it in the Ready-State on the current events list. Related waiting is the prevalent approach used to manage conditional delays. If the delay condition is too complex to be related easily to events that might resolve it, polled waiting can be used. With polled waiting the software checks routinely to see if entities can be transferred from one or more delay lists to the Ready-State. Complex delay conditions for which polled waiting can be useful include Boolean combinations of state changes, *e.g.,* a part supply runs low or an output bin needs to be emptied.

User-Managed Lists. User-managed lists are lists of entities in the Dormant State. The modeler must take steps to establish such lists and provide the logic needed to transfer entities to and from the lists.

1.3.4 A Simple Example

Let us consider building a simulation fuel station with a single pump served by a single service man. Assume that arrival of vehicles as well their service times are random. At first identify the:

- **States:** number of vehicles waiting for service and number of vehicles served at any moment
- **Events:** arrival of vehicles, start of service, and end of service
- **Entities:** these are the vehicles in this example
- **Queue:** the queue of vehicles in front of the pump, waiting for service
- **Random realizations:** inter-arrival times, service times, etc.
- **Distributions:** we shall assume exponential distributions for both the inter-arrival time and service time.

Next, specify what to do at each event. The above example would look like this, at event of entity arrival, Create next arrival. If the server is free, send entity for start of service. Otherwise it joins the queue. At event of service start, Server becomes occupied. At event of service end, Server becomes free. If any entities waiting in queue then: (*i*) remove first entity from the queue; and (*ii*) send it for start of service.

Some initiation is still required, for example, the creation of the first arrival. Lastly, the above is translated into code. This is easy with an appropriate library that has subroutines for creation, scheduling, proper timing of events, queue manipulations, random variate generation, and statistics collection.

How to simulate? Besides the above, the simulation program records the number of vehicles in the system before and after every change, together with the length of each event.

1.3.5 Systems and Experiments

Experimentation is the physical act of carrying out an experiment. An experiment may interfere with system operation (influence its input and parameters) or it may not. As such, the experimentation environment may be seen as a system in its own right (which may in turn be modeled by a lumped model). Also, experimentation involves observation. Observation yields measurements. A system is given, what reasons can there be to study a system? There are many answers to this question but we can distinguish two major motivations:

- Study a system to understand it in order to build it. This is the engineering point of view.
- Satisfy human interest, *e.g.,* to understand more about nature.
- **System:** That which is to be described, analyzed and controlled, anything of interest, which is to be described in detail. Often defined as a collection of

objects enclosed by a boundary, but this is not essential and the boundary may be conceptual rather than tangible.

- **Environment:** All that is external to the system. Everything else of interest, but which will not be described in detail. Commonly conceived, as external to the system, but again, this is not essential.
- **Open and closed systems:** The behavior of an open system may depend upon its environment; *i.e.,* the two interact. A closed system does not interact with its environment.
- **System variable:** A quantity, used to describe the system, which may change with time or space.
- **System input:** A quantity that is prescribed or imposed on the system by the environment; *i.e.,* an independent variable.
- **System output:** *Any* system variable of interest is system's output.
- **State determined systems (SDS):** A class of systems fully determined by a finite set of *state variables.*
- **State:** A minimal, complete and independent set of state variables that uniquely describe the system.
- **State equations:** To describe a state-determined system's behavior uniquely for all $t > t_0$ it is sufficient to have:
  (i) Value of a finite set of variables ($x_1, x_2, x_3, \ldots\ldots, x_n$) at t_0,
  (ii) Value of a finite set system inputs ($u_1, u_2, u_3, \ldots\ldots, u_n$) for all $t > t_0$, and
  (iii) A set of state equations: $y_m = g_m(x_1, x_2, \ldots\ldots, x_n, u_1, u_2, u_3, \ldots\ldots u_r, t)$

$$dx_1 / dt = f_1(x_1, x_2, \ldots\ldots, x_n, u_1, u_2, u_3, \ldots\ldots u_r, t)$$
$$dx_2 / dt = f_2(x_1, x_2, \ldots\ldots, x_n, u_1, u_2, u_3, \ldots\ldots u_r, t)$$
$$dx_3 / dt = f_3(x_1, x_2, \ldots\ldots, x_n, u_1, u_2, u_3, \ldots\ldots u_r, t)$$
$$\vdots$$
$$dx_n / dt = f_n(x_1, x_2, \ldots\ldots, x_n, u_1, u_2, u_3, \ldots\ldots u_r, t)$$

- **Output equations:** Any output variables of a state-determined system may be expressed as functions of its state and input variables:

$$y_1 = g_1(x_1, x_2, \ldots\ldots, x_n, u_1, u_2, u_3, \ldots\ldots u_r, t)$$
$$y_2 = g_2(x_1, x_2, \ldots\ldots, x_n, u_1, u_2, u_3, \ldots\ldots u_r, t)$$
$$y_3 = g_3(x_1, x_2, \ldots\ldots, x_n, u_1, u_2, u_3, \ldots\ldots u_r, t)$$
$$\vdots$$
$$y_m = g_m(x_1, x_2, \ldots\ldots, x_n, u_1, u_2, u_3, \ldots\ldots u_r, t)$$

1.3.6 Vector Notation

A more compact notation in terms of vectors is given as follows:

- **State space:** An abstract n-dimensional space defined by the state variables.
- **State vector:** A point in state space defined by a complete set of state variables.
- **Input space:** An abstract r-dimensional space defined by the input variables.
- **Input vector:** A point in input space defined by a complete set of input variables.
- **Output space:** An abstract m-dimensional space defined by the output variables.
- **Output vector:** A point in output space defined by a complete set of output variables.

1.3.7 Natural and Artificial Systems

As, a system, can be described as orderly interconnections of parts into a meaningful whole. As we are concerned with the classifications of systems, we can easily recognize three broad categories of systems:

Natural Systems—The systems whose operation is beyond the man's control are called natural systems, like solar system.

Man-made Systems—The systems, which are devised and operated by human, like aircraft flight control system.

Hybrid System—The systems, which are only partially controllable by human being, like artificial rain production system.

A system can occur naturally, *e.g.,* the universe, and it can also be artificial such as a space shuttle, or a mix of both (hybrid). For example, the house in with solar-heated valve warm water is an artificial system, *i.e.,* manufactured by humans. If we also include the sun and clouds in the system it becomes a combination of natural and artificial components.

Here, we must be clear about how a system is to be defined for specific simulation. Our first impulse is to point at the pendulum and to say "the system is that thing there." This method, however, has a fundamental disadvantage: every material object contains no less than infinity of variables, and therefore, of possible systems. The real pendulum, for instance, has not only length and position; it has also mass, temperature, electric conductivity, chemical impurities, crystalline structure, radioactivity, velocity, reflecting power, tensile strength, a surface film of moisture, bacterial contamination, an optical absorption, elasticity, shape, specific gravity, etc. Any suggestion that we should study all the facts is unrealistic, and actually the attempt is never made. The necessary point is that we should pick out and study the facts that are relevant to some main interest that is already given.

Let us consider, if the system is completely artificial, we must be highly selective in its definition depending on what aspects we want to study for the moment. An important property of systems is that they should be *observable*. Some systems, but not large natural systems like the universe, are also *controllable* in the sense that we can influence their behavior through inputs:

- The *inputs* of a system are variables of the environment that influence the behavior of the system. These inputs may or may not be controllable by us.
- The *outputs* of a system are variables that are determined by the system and may influence the surrounding environment.

In many systems the same variables act as both inputs and outputs. We talk about a *causal* behavior if the relationships or influences between variables do not have a causal direction, which is the case for relationships described by equations. For example, in a mechanical system the forces from the environment influence the displacement of an object, but on the other hand, the displacement of the object influences the forces between the object and environment. What is input and what output is in this case, is primarily a choice by the observer, guided by what is interesting to study, rather than a property of the system itself.

1.3.8 Experiment with System

An experiment can be defined as a process of extracting data from system by exerting it through its inputs. Experimenting with a system thus means to make use of its property of being controllable and observable. To perform an experiment on the system means to apply a set of external conditions to the accessible inputs, and to observe the reaction of the system to these inputs by considering the route behavior of the accessible outputs.

Observation is essential in order to study a system according to our definition of system. We must at least be able to observe some outputs of a system. We can learn even more if it is possible to exercise a system by controlling its inputs. This process is called *experimentation*, like the definition below says:

An *experiment* is the process of extracting information from a system by exercising its inputs. To perform an experiment on a system it must be both controllable and observable. We apply a set of external conditions to the accessible inputs and observe the reaction of the system by measuring the accessible outputs.

One of the disadvantages of the experimental method is that for a large number of systems many inputs are not accessible and controllable. These systems are under the influence of inaccessible inputs, sometimes called *disturbance inputs*. Likewise, it is often the case that many really useful possible outputs are not accessible for measurements; these are sometimes called *internal states* of the system. There are also a number of practical problems associated with performing an experiment, like:

- *The experiment might be too expensive*: investigating ship durability by building ships and letting them collide is a very expensive method of gaining information.
- *The experiment might be too dangerous*: training nuclear plant operators in handling dangerous situations by letting the nuclear reactor enter hazardous states is not advisable.
- *The system needed for the experiment might not yet exist*: This is typical of systems to be designed or manufactured.

The shortcomings of the experimental method lead us over to the model concept. If we make a model of a system, this model can be investigated and may answer many questions regarding the real system if the model is realistic enough. One of the major disadvantages of experimenting with real or actual system is that the systems are under the influence of a large number of additional inaccessible inputs and a number of real useful outputs, which are not accessible through measurements either.

1.3.9 Preliminary Data Preparation and Experimental Design

We can define simulation as being experimentation via a model to gain information about a real world process or system. It then can follow that we must concern ourselves with the strategic planning of how to design experiments that will yield the desired information at the lowest cost. The design of experiments comes into play at two different stages of a simulation study. It first comes into play very early in the study, before the first line of code has been written and before the finalization of the design of the model. As early as possible, we want to select the measures of effectiveness to be used in the study, what factors we are going to vary, how many levels of each of those factors we will investigate and the number of samples we will need in order to carry out the entire experiment. We can calculate ahead of time the sample sizes needed. If the number is large then we know that the model must run very fast and let this influence the design of the model. Having this fairly detailed idea of the experimental plan early, allows the model to be better planned to provide efficient generation of the desired data.

We need data to drive our simulation model. Every simulation study involves input data gathering and analysis. Stochastic systems contain numerous sources of randomness. The analyst must therefore be concerned about what data to use for input to the model for things such as the inter-arrival rate of entities to the system, processing times required at various stations, time between breakdowns of equipment, rejection rates, travel times between stations etc. Having good data to drive a model is just as important as having sound model logic and structure. Data gathering is usually interpreted to mean gathering numbers, but gathering numbers is only one aspect of the problem. The analyst must also decide what data is needed, what data are available and whether it is pertinent, whether existing data are valid for the required purpose, and how to gather the data.

In real-world simulation studies, the gathering and evaluation of input data is very time consuming and difficult. Up to one third of the total time used in the study is often consumed by this task. Depending upon the situation, there are several potential sources of data. These include:

- Historical records
- Observational data
- Similar systems
- Operator estimates
- Vendor's claims
- Designer estimates
- Theoretical considerations.

Each of these sources has potential problems. Even when we have copious data, it may not be relevant. For example, we may have sales data when we need demand data.

In other cases we may have only summary statistics. When historical data does not exist, the problem is even more difficult. In such cases we must estimate both the probability distribution and the parameters based upon theoretical considerations.

1.4 CONCEPT OF MODEL

The essence of the art of modeling is abstraction and simplification. We want to design a model of the real system that neither oversimplifies the system to the point where the model becomes trivial (or worse misleading) nor carries so much detail that it becomes clumsy and prohibitively expensive to build and run. The tendency among inexperienced modelers is to try to include too much detail. One should always design the model around the questions to be answered rather than try to imitate the real system exactly. In every group or collection of entities, there exists a vital few and a trivial many. In fact 80% of the behavior can be explained by the action of 20% of the components. Our problem in designing the simulation model is to make sure that we correctly identify the vital few components and include them in our model.

Modeling is used to represent/re-use/exchange knowledge about system structure and behavior. According to definitions of model:

A model is a simplified representation of a system at some particular point in time or space intended to promote understanding of the real system.

A model (M) for a system (S) and an experiment (E) is anything to which experiment (E) can be applied in order to answer questions about system (S).

These definitions do not imply that a model is a computer program. It can also be a piece of hardware or simply an understanding of how a particular system works. Given the previous definitions of system and experiment, we can now attempt to define the notion of model:

A *model* of a system is anything an experiment can be applied to in order to answer questions about that *system*. This implies that a model can be used to answer questions about a system without doing experiments on the real system. Instead we perform a kind of simplified experiments on the model, which in turn can be regarded as a kind of simplified system that reflects properties of the real system. In the simplest case a model can just be a piece of information that is used to answer questions about the system.

Given this definition, any model also qualifies as a system. Models, just like systems, are hierarchical in nature. We can cut out a piece of a model, which becomes a new model that is valid for a subset of the experiments for which the original model is valid. A model is always related to the system it models and the experiments it can be subject to. A statement such as "a model of a system is invalid" is meaningless without mentioning the associated system and the experiment. A model of a system might be valid for one experiment on the model and invalid for another. The term model *validation* always refers to an experiment or a class of experiment to be performed.

We talk about different kinds of models depending on how the model is represented:

- ***Physical* model:** This is a physical object that mimics some properties of a real system, to help us answer questions about that system. For example, during design of artifacts such as buildings, reservoirs, airplanes, etc., it is common to construct small physical models with same shape and appearance as the real objects to be studied, *e.g.,* with respect to their smooth properties and aesthetics.

- ***Mathematical* model:** A description of a system where the relationships between variables of the system are expressed in mathematical form. Variables can be measurable quantities such as size, length, weight, volume, temperature, unemployment level, bit rate, information flow, etc. Most laws of nature are mathematical models in this sense. For example, Ohm's law describes the relationship between current and voltage for a resistor; Newton's laws describe relationships between velocity, acceleration, mass, force, etc.
- ***Mental* model:** A statement like "a person is reliable" helps us answer questions about that person's behavior in various situations, such kinds of models are mental models.
- ***Verbal* model:** This kind of model is expressed in words. For example, the sentence "More accidents will occur if the speed limit is increased" is an example of a verbal model. Expert systems is a technology for formalizing verbal models.

The kinds of models that we primarily deal with in this text are mathematical models represented in various ways, *e.g.,* as equations, functions, simulation programs, etc. Artifacts represented by mathematical models in a computer are often called virtual prototypes. The process of constructing and investigating such models is virtual prototyping. Sometimes the term physical modeling is used also for the process of building mathematical models of physical systems in the computer if the structuring and synthesis process is the same as when building real physical models.

1.4.1 Why Models

The use of models is an essential part of the decision-making process. These models range from the mental models buried in the mind of the decision-maker and not necessarily visible, to the explicit large scale models used to explore the consequences of specific decisions or phenomena affecting outcomes of a given model. To some extent perceived utility of the model will be influenced by the complexity of the model and it then follows that the drive for increased utility and complexity in the model will lead to the situation where the person making the decision is unable to understand the processes followed by the model in producing its outcomes. The need to establish validity and the process of model verification have been debated in the simulation area for many years, and with the development of animated interfaces it is now possible to adopt more comprehensive processes of validation and verification to be followed leading to higher levels of credibility for the model. Simulation therefore could occupy a more prominent position in the tool-kit of decision-makers as the animation interface and ease of model development continues to advance over the next ten years. Development of simpler and more powerful interfaces, often referred to as simulators, has led to the situation where simulation is no longer the technique of last resort but is a technique which is available to engineers, designers and managers.

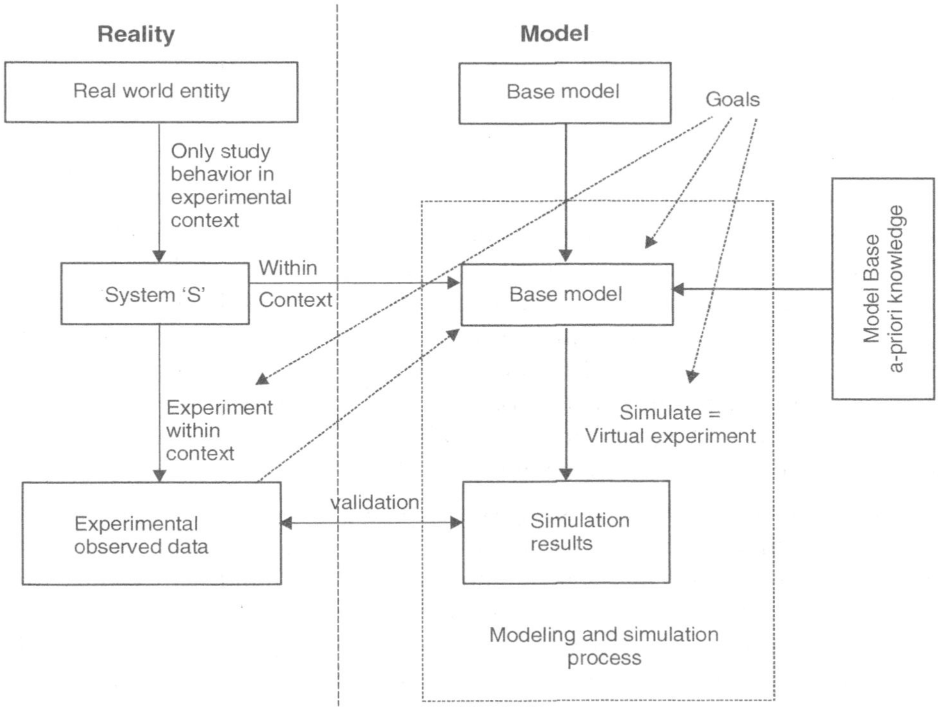

Fig. 1.1 Relation in reality and model

In this section we would like to discuss simulation as the process of designing a computer based model of a reference system, which may be real or proposed, and conducting experiments with this model for the purpose of understanding the behavior of the reference system and/or evaluating various strategies for the design or operation of the reference system. The specific area of simulation which is the focus of this study is discrete-event simulation (DES) which is the modeling of systems in which the state of variable changes only at a discrete set of points of time. The relation in reality and the developed model is explained in figure 1.1.

1.5 PRINCIPLES USED IN MODELING

Methods. Lack of adequate modeling methods is one of the most serious shortfalls in using Modeling and Simulation. In order to maximize the potential of modeling and simulation technologies for commercial manufacturing and defense acquisition, basic research must be undertaken to improve understanding of modeling methods and characteristics, including scalability, multi-resolution modeling, semantic consistency, modeling complexity, fundamental limits of modeling and computation, and uncertainty. Scalability is the attribute of a system's architecture that pertains to the behavior and performance of the system as the size, complexity, and interdependence of its elements or applications increase. Difficulties in dealing with large-scale software systems are well documented. Techniques that work for small systems often fail markedly when the scale is increased significantly. To be upwardly scalable, a system must assure consistency in both the functionality and the quality of the services it provides as the number of its users increases indefinitely.

To scale by a million, an application's storage and processing capacity would have to be able to grow by a factor of 1 million just by adding more resources.

Components. Traditional modeling and simulation have focused on micro level components rather than on macro level integration of these components. However, with the advent of large-scale systems such as extended enterprises and distributed mission training, it is necessary to develop approaches for designing scalable Modeling and Simulation system architectures, including process specifications, linguistic support, granularity, and levels of abstraction to support system architecture design. This effort includes modularization, interconnectivity, and integration platforms as well as the standardization of application programs, automatic installation of modules, and verification. Metrics for such designs include robustness, reliability, flexibility, and the ability of the system to adapt dynamically to changing conditions when simulating large numbers of agents, determining an adequate level of fidelity for individual agents' behavior, validating agent-based models, and avoiding ad hoc assumptions during model development.

Semantic Consistency. Semantic Consistency, also known as substantive interoperability, refers to consistent phenomenological representations of modeling of real-world systems and processes among interacting distributed simulations. For example, two combat simulations must have consistent models of inter-visibility or they will be unable to interoperate meaningfully in a distributed simulation. Research into semantic consistency and a general mathematical language for expressing models are recommended. Dealing with complexity and errors abstraction is the process of extracting a relatively sparse set of entities and relationships from a complex reality to produce a valid simplification of that reality. Abstraction is a general process; it includes simplification approaches such as aggregation, omission of variables and interactions, linearization, replacing stochastic processes by deterministic ones (and conversely), and changing the formalism in which models are expressed.

Complexity. The complexity of a model is measured in terms of the time and space required to execute it as a simulation. The more detail included in a model, the greater the resources required of the development team to build it and to execute it as a simulation once it is built. Validity is preserved through appropriate morphism mappings at desired levels of specification. Thus, abstraction methods, such as aggregation, will be framed in terms of their ability to reduce the complexity of a model while retaining its validity relative to the given modeling objectives inevitable resource constraints require working with models at various levels of abstraction. The complexity of a model depends on the level of detail, which in turn depends on the size/resolution product. The size/resolution product reflects the fact that increasing the size, or number of components, and resolution, or number of states per component, leads to increasing complexity. Since complexity depends on the size/resolution product, complexity can be reduced by reducing the size of the model or its resolution or both.

Several new approaches to modeling complexity are being developed. One of them is the notion of coordinated families of simulations at different levels of resolution. This approach presupposes the existence of effective ways to develop and correlate the underlying abstractions. A second approach, exploratory analysis, attempts to overcome computational complexity by addressing the issue of optimization, or searching through large spaces of alternatives for best solutions to a problem. This approach uses low-resolution models with a wide scope intended to capture the main features of an overall system or scenario. The approach seeks to exploit the reduction in the large space of alternatives that low-resolution, or highly abstracted model structures, may provide. A third approach fundamentally reconsiders the issue of optimization as a search for the best among many alternatives. The fast, frugal and accurate (FFA) perspective on real-world intelligence provides a framework for insight into this issue. FFA is taken from the domain of human decision-making in which full optimization is associated with unbounded rationality. This perspective recognizes that the real-world is a threatening environment in which knowledge is limited, computational resources are bounded, and little time is available for sophisticated reasoning. Simple building blocks that steer attention to informative cues, terminate search processing, and make final decisions can be put together to form classes of heuristics that perform at least as well as more complex algorithms.

Fundamental Limits of Modeling and Computation. In order to satisfy the needs of simulation for increasingly complex systems and processes, an integration of the statistics-oriented approach and simulation research must be emphasized by the academic community and the computer-science-oriented approach in acquisition and manufacturing. The statistics-oriented approach deals with prediction and management of uncertainty, whereas the computer-science-oriented approach deals with interoperability, reusability, integration, distributed operation, and human/machine interfaces. The computer-science-oriented approach is necessary for the future operational success of defense acquisition and commercial manufacturing, but as processes and systems become increasingly complex, estimation and management of uncertainties will become increasingly important. Some fundamental limitations in computation in dealing with complex systems must be recognized. The performance of any future complex system will be unavoidably stated in probabilistic terms. A suite of software and a collection of databases may be technically interoperable and can be used to calculate system performance under a given set of operating environments, but there is no way that these tools can estimate the percentage of time that the system will perform satisfactorily under different circumstances, what the expected performance will be under uncertainty, or what the confidence level of the estimate is.

Performance Estimate. In addition, in order to improve the system performance estimate by adjusting or tuning various parameters in different phases of the acquisition process, dimensionality, or combinatorial explosion, must be dealt with. The first fundamental limitation in computation states that each system performance evaluation via simulation is time consuming. The second limitation states that a very large number of such evaluations may be necessary. These difficulties are multiplicative. Finally, there is a third limitation is "No Free Lunch Theorem". Without specific structural assumptions, there exists no optimization or search algorithm that can perform better on the average than blind search in dealing with the first and second limitation. These three limitations are fundamental limits on computation in dealing with complex systems. No amount of theoretical, hardware, or software advances can overcome them. Consequently, a strategic redirection is called for in dealing with them.

Therefore, to deal with the large search spaces imposed by the second and third computational limitations, the structure of specific problems must be learned along the way. A number of automated learning theories currently in trend in artificial intelligence research, such as knowledge discovery, data mining, Bayesian networks, and Tabu search, may be significant for developing modeling capabilities. Tabu search is a heuristic technique for search in combinatorial optimization problems.

Errors. Errors in Distributed Simulations fix resources and a model complexity that exceeds these resources, a trade-off must be made between size and resolution. If some aspects of a system are represented very accurately, only a few components will be representable. Alternatively, a comprehensive view of the entire system can be provided, but only at a low resolution. Such resolution may introduce errors that may pose particular problems in distributed simulations. In such complex, networked systems of models, owing to low resolution each model will typically be in error to some degree. Therefore, it is natural to expect that in a complex system of many linked models, even if individual inaccuracies are small, such errors can accumulate, propagate, and reinforce each other, rendering the behavior of the aggregate significantly different from the behavior of the real system. Error propagation in distributed simulations plays an important role in verification, validation, and accreditation, and therefore is an important area of research that needs to be strengthened. In the current state of the art, it is possible to suggest that such error propagation may, or may not be, a significant issue in distributed simulations. On other hand, modeling errors in complex systems can be like noises that are more or less statistically independent. The cumulative effect of many independent errors behaves according to the central limit theorem and decrease with increasing complexity under some reasonable assumptions. A simple case is the law of large numbers, which improves accuracy by averaging many measurements. A second mitigating factor is the theory of ordinal optimization, mentioned above. Research here has shown that for the purpose of comparison (for example, which is better?), very crude models are quite sufficient.

Model Correctness. Model correctness is the fundamental requirement of ensuring that the predictions of a simulation model can be relied upon. The correctness of simulation requires the development of accurate and reliable models of real-world systems. A prerequisite to this is an understanding of the real-world systems and objects to be modeled, their contextual domains, and the phenomenology of their operations and interactions, all at a level of detail sufficient to justify the model. Once the models have been implemented as simulations, their correctness must be rigorously evaluated. Domain Knowledge Improved understanding of the real-world basis for models is needed in the areas of phenomenology of warfare, physics-based modeling, and human behavior modeling. Phenomenology of Warfare the military domain is of special importance because it is the primary focus of SBA and because it is the domain in which human lives are most likely to be risked on the basis of decisions made using modeling and simulation.

Human Behavior Modeling. Computer-generated forces are often used in training simulations to provide both opposing forces and supplemental friendly forces for human participants in a simulation. They are also often used to generate all of the entities in battlefield simulations being used for non-training purposes, such as analysis and experimentation. Automated or semi-automated entities are created, and their behavior is controlled by the computer system, perhaps assisted by a human operator, rather than by human participants in a simulator. These automated behaviors are produced by algorithms based on models of human behavior. The reliability of the results depends on the validity of the behavior-generation methods. While current behavior-generation methods are reasonably effective at producing behavior that is in accordance with straightforward strategic policy, they fall far short of producing realistically human behavior with all its unpredictability and sophistication. Several studies have concluded that a need exists for improvement in human behavior modeling.

1.6 MODEL VERIFICATION AND VALIDATION

A key area of the model development process in the simulation area is the development of verification and validation stages in the process. Management scientists have very little to say about how one goes about "verifying" a simulation model or the data generated that the modeling process has the following five steps:

1. **Systems Analysis:** The study of a system in order to ascertain its salient elements and to outline their interactions and behavior mechanisms;
2. **System Synthesis:** The construction of a complete, logical structure in order to provide a reasonable symbolic mimicry, or model of the system's elements and interactions, including the determination and collection of data required to support the model's structure;
3. **Verification:** Verification is concerned with building the model right. It is utilized in the comparison of the conceptual model to the computer representation that implements that conception. Simulation models can be run interactively or in batch mode. Interactive runs are of use in checking out (verifying) model's logic during model-building and in troubleshooting a model when execution errors occur. Batch mode is then used to make production runs. Interactive runs put a magnifying glass on a simulation model while it executes. The modeler can follow the active entity step by step and display the current and future events lists and the delay and user-managed lists as well as other aspects of the model. These activities yield valuable insights into model behavior for the modeler who knows the underlying concepts. Without such knowledge, the modeler might not take full advantage of the interactive tools provided by the software or, worse yet, might even avoid using the tools.
4. **Validation:** Validation is concerned with building the right model. It is utilized to determine that a model is an accurate representation of the real system. The validation is process of comparison of responses emanating from the verified model with available information regarding the corresponding behavior of the simulated system; and
5. **Model Analysis:** The process of contrasting of model responses under alternative environmental specifications (or input conditions).

The general level of agreement on the definition of verification and validation should not however be taken as evidence to suggest that this part of the model development process is either simple or straightforward.

1.7 TYPES OF MODELS

1.7.1 Continuous and Discrete-time Models

Continuous-time Models

Continuous-time models are the models used for continuous time simulations. In these cases, state or the variables of the system change with time. Continuous-time models are created and recognized by the property `'Ts' = 0`. You can create and analyze all the objects as continuous-time models by setting `'Ts'` equal to zero at the time of creation, by using the following MATLAB statement:

$$m = \text{idpoly}(1,\ [0\ 2\ 1],\ 1,\ 1,\ [1\ 3\ 4],\ \text{'Ts'},\ 0)$$

$$\text{for the model } y = \frac{2s+1}{s^2+3s+4}u + e$$

where all model characteristics are then computed and graphed for the continuous-time representation. Time and frequency scales are determined based on the dynamics of the system (the pole/zero locations). For simulation and prediction, the continuous-time models are first converted to discrete time, using the sampling interval and inter sample behavior of the data.

Estimating Continuous-time Models

The estimation routines support the estimation of continuous-time state-space models in several different ways. The major reason for identifying continuous-time models is to secure a particular structure of the continuous-time state-space matrices. This would typically reflect a physical interpretation or some gray-box modeling work done, as for the process models, described.

Transformations

Transformations between continuous-time and discrete-time model representations are performed by `c2d` and `d2c`. Note that it is not sufficient just to assign a new value of `Ts` to the model object. The corresponding uncertainty measure (the estimated covariance matrix of the internal parameters) is also transformed in most cases. The syntax is :

`modc = d2c(modd)` for discrete to continuous

`modd = c2d(mc,T)` for continuous to discrete

The transformation `c2d` also offers an optional output argument that describes how the initial state should be transformed.

If the discrete-time model has some pure time delays, the default command removes them before forming the continuous-time model, and appends them using the property `InputDelay` in model `modc`. This property is used to add appropriate phase lag and shift the data whenever the model is used. The command `D2C` also offers an option to approximate the dead time by a finite dimensional system. Note that the disturbance properties are translated by the somewhat questionable formula.

The covariance matrix is translated by the Gauss approximation formula using numerical derivatives. Here is an example that compares the promise plots of an estimated model and its continuous-time counterpart.

- `m = armax(Data,[2 3 1 2]);`
- `mc = d2c(m); bode(m,mc)`

The transformations between discrete and continuous time depend on the inter sample behavior of the input. The formulas are different if the input is assumed to be piecewise constant or piecewise linear between samples (`'zoh'` or `'foh'`). For estimated discrete-time models, the input properties of the estimation data are used for this purpose, by default. To override this, add an extra argument, as described in the reference pages for `c2d` and `d2c`.

Discrete-time Model

Such models are used for discrete-time simulations. Discrete-time simulation is commonly used by the operations research work to study large, complex systems which do not lend themselves to a conventional analytic approach. A well-known example of discrete-time simulations is inventory model simulation. Airports, telephone exchanges, production line, stock of goods are some other examples of discrete-time models.

This kind of model setup allows us to directly assess the structural inter-dependencies among the shocks to returns and the two different volatility components. The model estimates suggest that the leverage effect, or asymmetry between returns and volatility, works primarily through the continuous volatility component. The excellent fit of the model makes it an ideal candidate for an easy-to-implement auxiliary model in the context of indirect estimation of empirically more realistic continuous-time jump diffusion effectively incorporating the relevant information in the high-frequency data.

1.7.2 Continuous and Discrete-event Models

System or models in which changes are predominantly discontinuous are Discrete Simulation Models. Discrete-event simulation concerns the modeling of a system as it evolves overtime by a representation in which state variables change instantaneously at separate points in time. The amount of data that must be stored and manipulated for most real-world systems dictates that discrete-event simulation is done on a digital computer.

Continuous simulation concerns the modeling overtime of a system by representation in which the state variables change continuously with respect to time. Continuous simulation models involve differential equations that give relationships of the rates for change of the state variables with time. If the differential equations are particularly simple, they can be solved analytically to give the values of the state variables for all values of time as a function of the values of the state variable at time 0. For most continuous models analytic solutions are not possible and numerical analysis techniques as Runge-Kutta integration are used to integrate the differential equations numerically, given specific values for the state variables at time 0.

Discrete-event models use discrete-events as a set of circumstances that cause instantaneous changes in one or more system state descriptions. Since some systems are neither completely discrete nor completely continuous, the need may arise to construct a model with aspects of both discrete-event and continuous simulation resulting in a combined discrete-continuous simulation. The three fundamental types of interactions that can occur between discretely changing and continuously changing state variables:

- A discrete-event may cause a discrete change in the value of continuous state variables.
- A discrete-event may cause the relationship governing a continuous state variable to change at a particular time.

A continuous state variable achieving a threshold value may cause a discrete-event to occur or to be scheduled.

1.7.3 Deterministic and Stochastic Models

Deterministic models produce deterministic results. If a simulation model does not contain any probabilistic or random components, it is called deterministic. In deterministic models, the output is 'determined' once the set of input quantities and relationships in the model have been specified. It takes a lot of compute time to evaluate what this output can be. When a system is modeled with at least some random input components then it is stochastic simulation model. The output produced by stochastic model is random. The outputs only estimate the true characteristics of model. This is the main disadvantage of stochastic simulation model. Stochastic or probabilistic models are subject to random effects:

- Typically, they have one or more random inputs *e.g.,* arrival of customers, service time etc.
- Outputs from stochastic models are "estimates" of the true characteristics of the system
- Need to repeat experiments number of times
- Need to have confidence in the results.

1.7.4 Static and Dynamic Models

Static models—If the system state is independent of time. A static simulation model is a representation of a system at a particular time. These models may be used to represent a system in which time simply plays no role, for example, Monte Carlo Models.

Dynamic models—A model is called dynamic model if the system state changes with time. A dynamic simulation model represents a system as it evolves overtime, for example, Conveyor system in a factory.

1.7.5 Linear and Non-linear Models

- *Linear model*—The model in which output is a linear function of input parameters.
- *Non-Linear Model*—A model can be non-linear in its parameters, non-linear in its observed variables, or non-linear in both its parameters and variables. Non-

linear in the parameters means that the mathematical relationship between the variables and parameters is not required to have a linear form. A linear model is a special case of a non-linear model.

1.8 THE MODELING

The way of creating or developing a model is called modeling. Modeling means the process of organizing knowledge about a given system. A model is a pattern, plan, representation, or description designed to show the structure or workings of an object, system, or concept.

Problem Formulation: Problem formulation is concerned with:

- Identification of controllable and uncontrollable inputs.
- Identification of constraints on the decision variables.
- Definition of measure of system performance and an objective function.
- Development of a preliminary model structure to interrelate the inputs and the measure of performance.

Data Collection and Analysis: Regardless of the method used to collect the data, it is concerned with the decision of how much to collect be a trade-off between cost and accuracy.

Simulation Model Development: Acquiring sufficient understanding of the system to develop an appropriate conceptual, logical and then simulation model is one of the most difficult tasks in simulation analysis.

Model Calibration: The process of parameter estimation for a model. Calibration is a tuning of existing parameters and usually does not involve the introduction of new ones, changing the model structure. In the context of optimization, calibration is an optimization procedure involved in system identification or during experimental design.

Input and Output Analysis: Discrete-event simulation models typically have stochastic components that mimic the probabilistic nature of the system under consideration. Successful input modeling requires a close match between the input model and the true underlying probabilistic mechanism associated with the system. The input data analysis is to model an element (like arrival process, service times, etc.) in a discrete-event simulation given a data set collected on the element of interest. This stage performs intensive error checking on the input data, including external, policy, random and deterministic variables. System simulation experiment is to learn about its behavior. Careful planning, or designing, of simulation experiments is generally a great help, saving time and effort by providing efficient ways to estimate the effects of changes in the model's inputs on its outputs. Statistical experimental-design methods are mostly used in the context of simulation experiments.

Sensitivity Estimation: For sensitivity analysis, users must be provided with affordable techniques if they are to understand which relationships are meaningful in complicated models.

Optimization: The traditional optimization techniques require gradient estimation. As with sensitivity analysis, the current approach for optimization requires intensive simulation to construct an approximate surface response function.

1.8.1 Stochastic Modeling

Stochastic means being or having a random variable. A stochastic model is a tool for estimating probability distributions of potential outcomes by allowing for random variation in one or more inputs overtime. The random variation is usually based on fluctuations observed in historical data for a selected period using standard time-series techniques. Distributions of potential outcomes are derived from a large number of simulations (stochastic projections) which reflect the random variation in the input provided to the system.

A stochastic model can be used to set-up a projection model which looks at a single policy, an entire portfolio or an entire company. But rather than setting investment returns according to their most likely estimate, for example, the model uses random variations to look at what investment conditions might be like.

Based on a set of random outcomes, the experience of the policy/portfolio/organization is projected, and the outcome is noted. Then this is done again with a new set of random variables. In fact, this process is repeated thousands of times. At the end, a distribution of outcomes is available which shows not only what the most likely estimate, but what ranges are reasonable too. Stochastic modeling builds volatility and variability (randomness) into the simulation and therefore provides a more accurate representation of real life.

1.8.2 Stochastic Processes

A stochastic process is a probabilistic model of a system that evolves randomly in time and space. Formally, a stochastic process is a collection of random variables $\{X(t), t \in T\}$ all defined on a common probability space. The $X(t)$ is the state while time t is the index that is a member of set T.

Examples are the delay $\{D(i), i = 1, 2, ...\}$ of the ith customer and number of customers $\{Q(t), t \geq 0\}$ in the queue at time t in an M/M/1 queue. In the first example, we have a discrete-time, continuous state, while in the second example the state is discrete and time is continuous.

The man made systems have mostly discrete state. Monte Carlo simulation deals with discrete-time while in discrete even system simulation the time dimension is continuous.

Simulation Output Data and Stochastic Processes. To perform statistical analysis of the simulation output we need to establish some conditions, *e.g.,* output data must be a covariance stationary process (*e.g.,* the data collected over n simulation runs).

Stationary Process (strictly stationary). A stationary stochastic process is a stochastic process with the property that the joint distribution all vectors of h dimension remain the same for any fixed h.

First Order Stationary. A stochastic process is a first order stationary if expected of X(t) remains the same for all t. For example, in economic time series, a process is first order stationary when we remove any kinds of trend by some mechanisms such as differencing.

Second Order Stationary. A stochastic process is a second order stationary if it is first order stationary and covariance between X(t) and X(s) is function of t's only. Again, a process is second order stationary when we stabilize also its variance by some kind of transformations such as taking square root. Clearly, a stationary process is a second order stationary, however the reverse may not hold. In simulation output statistical analysis we are satisfied if the output is covariance stationary.

Covariance Stationary. A covariance stationary process is a stochastic process {X(t), $t \leq T$} having finite second moments, *i.e.*, expected of $[X(t)]^2$ be finite. Clearly, any stationary process with finite second moment is covariance stationary. A stationary process may have no finite moment whatsoever. Since a Gaussian process needs a mean and covariance matrix only, it is stationary (strictly) if it is covariance stationary.

Two Contrasting Stationary Process. Consider the following two extreme stochastic processes:

- A sequence Y_0, Y_1,....., of independent identically distributed, random-value sequence is a stationary process, if its common distribution has a finite variance then the process is covariance stationary.
- Let Z be a single random variable with known distribution function, and set $Z_0 = Z_1 = ...Z_i$. Note that in a realization of this process, the first element, Z_0, may be random but after that there is no randomness. The process {Z_i, i = 0, 1, 2, ..} is stationary if Z has a finite variance.

Output data in simulation lies between these two types of process. Simulation outputs are identical and mildly correlated. It depends on a queueing system how large is the traffic intensity. An example could be the delay process of the customers in a queueing system.

1.9 SYSTEM ENGINEERING

Modeling and simulation is the field closely related with system engineering. Systems engineering often involves the modeling or simulation of some aspects of the proposed system in order to validate assumptions or explore theories. For example, highly complex systems such as aircraft are usually modeled and simulated before flight. In this way the initial aero-elastic engineering and control equations can be drafted and improved upon before any physical system is ever constructed or developed. Since aircraft are often very expensive, this reduces the expense and difficulty of debugging the controls and reduces the risk of crashing real aircraft. Careful initial testing and flight envelope expansion are typically still required to reach acceptable levels of safety and performance in advanced aircraft.

The role of the system engineer is especially important when systems must have especially predictable and reliable behavior. For example, medical machinery, power plants, and spacecraft usually consist of many individually engineered and manufactured parts, by different companies. System engineering provides the assurance that normal operations, including parts failures, will not provide a hazard for the user or anyone else in the community. The application of systems engineering processes may also result in significant cost savings, as well as providing a reasonable assurance of the eventual success of the project.

Systems Engineering (SE) is an interdisciplinary approach and means for enabling the realization and deployment of successful systems. It can be viewed as the application of engineering techniques to the engineering of systems, as well as the application of a systems approach to engineering efforts. Systems engineering integrates other disciplines and specialty groups into a team effort, forming a structured development process that proceeds from concept to production to operation and disposal. Systems engineering considers both the business and the technical needs of all customers, with the goal of providing a quality product that meets the user needs.

System development often requires contribution from diverse technical disciplines. Each of these disciplines is normally focused on their own particular contribution to the system (for example, jet engine designers would not be focused on the aircraft's hydraulic subsystem). System engineering's advantage point is a holistic perspective of the system and from this perspective integrates all of these technical efforts to ensure that their various subsystems work with one another. By providing a systems view of the development effort, System Engineering helps meld all the technical contributors into a unified team effort, forming a structured development process that proceeds from concept to production to operation and, in some cases, through to termination and disposal. System Engineering is usually directly responsible for any engineering function that is not deemed sufficiently necessary on a project to require a full-time, specialist engineer, although consultants may be enlisted as needed.

Ideally, Systems Engineering considers both the business and the technical needs of all customers with the goal of providing a quality product that meets the user needs. However, the reality in any very large project is often that user needs exceed what the sponsor is willing to pay for; and the schedule to satisfy those needs generally exceeds what either of them is willing to live with. As a result, 'satisfaction of all technical requirements' is subject to the usual constraints of cost, schedule, and producibility.

Taking an interdisciplinary approach to engineering systems is inherently complex, since the behavior of and interaction among system components are not always well-defined or understood. Defining and characterizing such systems and subsystems, and the interactions among them, is the primary aim of systems engineering. On very large programs, a systems architect may be designated to serve as an interface between the user/sponsor and systems engineer.

There are several methods and tools that are frequently used by systems engineers: requirements capture, systems architecture and design, functional analysis, interface design and specification, communications protocol design and specification, simulation and modeling, verification and validation/acceptance testing, fault modeling.

SUMMARY

Simulation is a discipline, not a software package; it requires detailed formulation of the problem, careful translation or coding of the system logic into the simulation procedural language (regardless of the interface type), and thorough testing of the resulting model and results. There are at least two different skills required to be successful at simulation. The first skill required is the ability to understand a complex system and its interrelationships. The second skill required is the ability to translate this understanding into an appropriate logical representation recognized by the simulation software.

Recently, industry in general has begun to accept that the engineering of systems, both large and small, can lead to unpredictable behavior and the emergence of unforeseen system characteristics or emergent properties. Decisions made at the beginning of a project whose consequences are not clearly understood can have enormous implications later in the life of a system, and it is the task of the modern systems engineer to explore these issues and make critical decisions. There is no method which guarantees that decisions made today will still be valid when a system goes into service years or decades after it is first conceived but there are techniques to support the process of systems engineering. Examples include the use of soft systems methodology, the Unified Modeling Language etc., each of which are currently being explored, evaluated and developed to support the engineering decision making process.

EXERCISE QUESTIONS

1. Explain the need of modeling and simulation.
2. In what kind of projects modeling and simulation is preferred?
3. Explain the fields where simulation and modeling is used very effectively.
4. Explain the difference between reality and the model in terms of modeling and simulation.
5. Explain the difference between simulation and experiment. Explain the parameters used for experiments with a system.
6. Write short notes on:

   (*i*) Natural System (*ii*) Artificial System

   (*iii*) Hybrid System (*iv*) Model
7. What are different types of models? Give the difference between discrete and continuous models.
8. Explain the difference between mental model and mathematical model.
9. Explain the difference between static and dynamic model.
10. What do you understand by model validation, verification and calibration?
11. What do you mean by stochastic process and stochastic modeling?
12. Explain the principles used in modeling of a system.

Chapter 2

SIMULATION CONCEPTS

2.1 INTRODUCTION

Simulation modeling is similar to other engineering disciplines. It requires training and experience to become competent, and is not really as easy as some people might have you believe. It is an art as well as a science. Simulation is one of the most powerful tools available to decision-makers responsible for the design and operation of complex processes and systems. It makes possible the study, analysis and evaluation of situations that would not be otherwise possible. In an increasingly competitive world, simulation has become an indispensable problem solving methodology for engineers, designers and managers. Simulation is the imitation of the operation of a real-world process or system overtime. Simulation involves the generation of an artificial history of the system, and the observation of that artificial history to draw inferences concerning the operating characteristics of the real system that is represented. Simulation is an indispensable problem-solving methodology for the solution of many real-world problems. Simulation is used to describe and analyze the behavior of a system. Both existing and conceptual systems can be modeled with simulation.

Recent advances in modeling and simulation technologies make them increasingly appealing as a means of improving commercial manufacturing and defense acquisition. However, in order for these technologies to support the desired applications in commercial manufacturing and defense acquisition, additional research and development is needed. As challenge, the organizations involved in simulation and modeling are often asked to investigate emerging modeling and simulation technologies, efforts to develop them, and identify gaps that would have to be filled in order to make these emerging technologies a reality. The organizations rephrase this task and require determining those topics requiring research and development to be effectively used in commercial manufacturing and defense acquisition. The topics requiring research and development are identified by the committee on the basis of the challenges in the real-world.

A framework for the modeling and simulation of hybrid analog/digital systems has long been needed. Today, the need to design mixed-signal chips to support the growth in wireless devices and next-generation automotive electronics has brought this problem to the foreground. Mixed-Signal Chips (MSCs) have been implemented as custom-Application-Specific Integrated Circuits (ASICs), but must now be mass-produced for use in wireless technology. MSCs receive analog signals, process and manipulate them mainly in digital form, and reconvert them back to analog form. The challenge for systems design is the high level of functionality of an MSC.

It is useful to distinguish between two broad classes of simulations. The first is product modeling or engineering simulations, which simulate the physics of products or systems being designed with a high degree of detail and physical fidelity. The intent of these simulations is to assist design engineers in understanding the physical performance of the product or system as designed. They often simulate only one system or subsystem at a time and run slower than read time. They can be loosely defined as using modeling and simulation to determine how to build a system. The second class of simulations is performance modeling or effectiveness simulations, which simulate products or systems that are assumed to exist and operate as designed. The intent of these simulations is to determine how effective the systems would be in use or what performance parameters the systems must have in order to be effective in use. They often simulate scenarios involving many simulated systems and run in real time or faster. They can be loosely defined as using modeling and simulation to determine which system to build. The ability to link these two types of simulations is necessary for achieving the goals of defense acquisition. The ability to reuse engineering models and simulations in effectiveness simulations would save time and money.

Physics-based flight dynamics models use aerodynamics equations rather than look-up tables to model the flight characteristics of a simulated aircraft. The physics of failure and assessment of a potential system's durability and operational availability is of special interest. Such assessments would greatly benefit from accurate physical models that support predictions of the modes and times of failure of physical systems. Several studies have concluded the need for improvements in physics-based modeling. Physics-based modeling is arguably more important for defense manufacturing and acquisition than for other simulation applications such as training.

2.2 SIMULATION

Before we proceed further, it becomes necessary to define the term simulation in more suitable forms. We define simulation as the process of designing a model of a real system and conducting experiments with this model for the purpose of understanding the behavior of the system and evaluating various strategies for the operation of the system. Thus it is critical that the model be designed in such a way that the model behavior mimics the response behavior of the real system to events that take place overtime. The terms model and system are key components of our definition of simulation. By a model we mean a representation of a group of objects or ideas in some form other than that of the entity itself. By a system we mean a group or collection of interrelated elements that cooperate to accomplish some stated objective. One of the real strengths of simulation is the fact that we can simulate systems that already exist as well as those that are capable of being brought into existence, *i.e.,* those in the preliminary or planning stage of development.

Some other important definitions are:

Definition 1: *Simulation is the use of system model that has the designed characteristics of reality in order to produce the essence of actual operation.*

Definition 2: *Simulation is representation of reality through the use of a model or other device, which will react in the same manner as reality under a given set of conditions.*

Definition 3: *A Simulation model may be defined as one which depicts the working of a large scale system of men, machine, materials and information operating over a period of time in a simulated environment of the actual real- world conditions.*

Definition 4: *According to Churchman, Simulation is defined as,*

"A simulates B" is true if and only if:

(*a*) A and B are formal systems;

(*b*) B is taken to be a real systems;

(*c*) A is taken to be an approximation to the real system; and

(*d*) The rule of validity in A are non-error-free, otherwise A will become the real system.

Thus, simulation is the manipulation of a model in such a way that it operates on time or space to compress it, thus enabling one to recognize the interactions that would not otherwise be apparent because of their separation in time or space.

Simulation in general is to pretend that one deals with a real thing while really working with an imitation. In operations research the imitation is a computer model of the simulated reality. A flight simulator on a personal computer is also a computer model of some aspects of the flight: it shows on the screen the controls and what the "pilot" is supposed to see from the cockpit.

To fly a simulator is safer and cheaper than the real airplane. For precisely this reason, models are used in industry commerce and military: it is very costly, dangerous and often impossible to make experiments with real systems. Provided that models are adequate descriptions of reality (they are valid), experimenting with them can save money, suffering and even time.

Modeling and Simulation is a discipline for developing a level of understanding of the interaction of the parts of a system, and of the system as a whole. The level of understanding, which may be developed via this discipline, is seldom achievable via any other discipline.

2.3 WHY GO FOR SIMULATION

At the most general level, simulation is considered as a form of cognition. Cognition is the action or process of acquiring knowledge. There are three basic methods how to get information (knowledge) of objective reality: Experiment, Analysis, and Simulation. Let us take one practical example to demonstrate the nature of these three methods.

Experiment: Common example of experiment can be seen as, take stopwatches and measure the time every train spends in the railway station. Count the trains, at the end sum all times and divide them by the number of trains. *Experiment is always the most* *accurate method that should be used whenever it is feasible*. Unfortunately very often the experiment is:

- Too dangerous (behavior of a nuclear reactor in critical situations, landing with a plane with one jet off, etc.)
- Too expensive (all cases that cause a damage, long experiments studying throughput of a data network using leased phone lines, etc.)
- Not possible at all if the system being investigated is not available (evaluation of more possible alternatives in the design stage.)

Analysis: Common example of analysis can be seen as, use a formula of the Queuing Theory to compute the average time spent in the system directly. To use a formula you will have to assume certain queuing model, which means a considerable simplification of the real system, and you will need some quantitative parameters.

Analysis (mostly mathematical) is typically based on strong assumptions that are rarely true in practical life. Another possible drawback of analytical methods is too complicated apparatus used and/or too time consuming computation. An example of this is analysis of Queuing Networks. On the other hand, using formulae gives mostly fast results and it is possible to check a large number of alternatives by simply inserting different values of parameters to the formulae. Experimental methods are mostly much more time consuming. Another problem of analysis is availability of necessary parameters. Their exact measuring is also not necessarily feasible or it is impossible in the design stage. Using estimated data or data taken from other similar systems decreases credibility of results.

Simulation: Simulations may be performed manually. Most often, however, the system model is written either as a computer program or as some kind of input into simulator software. A simulation generally refers to a computerized version of the model, which is run overtime to study the implications of the defined interactions. Simulations are generally iterative in their development. One develops a model, simulates it, learns from the simulation, revises the model, and continues the iterations until an adequate level of understanding is developed. Simulation is also an experimental method. Instead of experimenting with the real system the experiments are performed with the simulation model (whose design is thus the key point of simulation studies). Also simulation has many drawbacks. Here are the most important ones:

- Too demanding creation of simulation models.
- Programming simulation models in general languages (like Pascal, Fortran) is too difficult.
- There are efficient simulation languages but their mastering represents a big initial investment not always justified.
- There are simulation-tools based typically on some graphical technique that simplify or even automate creation of simulation models of certain class of systems.
- Only, limited knowledge of the system being simulated, and some quantitative parameters must be known.

These methods cannot be ranked because all of them have advantages and disadvantages. They can be compared only in the context of certain particular case taking into account various criteria.

Simulation could be much more flexible than analysis because simulation languages support generation of random numbers with practically any distribution. In the above example both random figures can be based on any distributions obtained experimentally. Nevertheless any distribution needs either several parameters (if it is a theoretical one) or directly the Distribution Function *i.e.,* the distribution is obtained by measuring. There can be also things in the system (typically in the design stage) that cannot be quantified and often it is necessary to accept the fact that there might be aspects we are not aware of at all, like to much time consuming computation. An example is analysis of large-scale systems with many components working in parallel. Because application of real parallelism is still not common, a program performed by a single processor simulates such systems. Parallel activities are then performed one at a time. The result of this is the fact that simulation could be much slower than the real time. In general 1 second of the model time takes 10 minutes of the CPU time. This of course disables application of simulation in real time control.

A general rule of thumb could be like that: *"If the experiment is feasible, use it. It is always the best method because all the aspects are taken into account. Even if other methods were used during the design stage, experiment can serve as a final evaluation of the system. If the experiment is not feasible try to find an appropriate analytical method. If it is not available, simulation can be used."*

Simulation is not only the last option as it looks like in the above rule. Simulation can contribute very much to understanding of the system being analyzed not only by supplying answers to the questions that were originally given. Very often creation of the simulation model is the first occasion where certain things are taken into account. Specification of the simulated system can (and often it does) reveal errors or ambiguities in the system design. So simulation can help very much by avoiding future very expensive updating of the ready system. A simulation is an experiment performed on a model. A mathematical simulation is a coded description of an experiment with a reference to the model to which this experiment is to be applied. Simulation is imitation of the operation of a facility or process, usually using a computer.

2.4 WHY IS SIMULATION IMPORTANT?

Simulation is the next best thing to observing a real system in operation since it allows us to study the situation even though we are unable to experiment directly with the real system, either because the system does not yet exist or because it is too difficult or expensive to directly manipulate it. We consider simulation to include both the construction of the model and the experimental use of the model for studying a problem. Thus, we can think of simulation modeling as an experimental and applied methodology, which seeks to:

- Describe the behavior of a system.
- Use the model to predict future behavior, *i.e.,* the effects that will be produced by changes in the system or in its method of operation.

Except by experimenting with the real system, simulation is the only way available for the analysis of arbitrary system behavior. Analytical techniques are just perfect, but they usually require a set of simplifying assumptions to be made before they become applicable. Reasons to use simulation:

- The physical system is not available.
- The experiment may be dangerous.
- The cost of experimentation is too high.
- Control variable, state variable and system parameter may be inaccessible.
- The time constants of the system are not compatible with those of experimenter.
- Suppression of disturbance.
- Suppression of second order effect.

2.5 WHEN TO USE SIMULATIONS?

Systems that change with time, such as a fuel filling center where vehicles come and go and involve randomness are required to simulate. Nobody can guess at exactly which time the next vehicle should arrive at the filling center, are good conditions for simulation. Modeling complex dynamic systems theoretically need too many simplifications and the emerging models may not be therefore valid. Simulation does not require so many simplifying assumptions, making it the only tool even in absence of randomness. Simulations are appropriate tool in following conditions:

- The knowledge gained in the designing of a model may be very helpful towards suggesting improvements in the system under investigation.
- Simulation enables the study of, and experimentation with, the internal interaction of the complex systems or subsystems.
- To study the effect of alterations to an existing system. Simulation compares design alternatives for a system that does not exist.
- Informational, organizational, and environmental changes can be simulated, and the effect of these changes on the models behavior can be observed.
- By changing simulation inputs and observing the results of output, valuable insights may be obtained into which variable are most important and how these variables interact.
- Simulation can be used as instructive device to support analytic solution methodologies.
- Simulation can be used to experiment with the new designs or policies prior to implementation, so as to prepare for what may happen.
- Simulation can be used to verify analytical solution.
- Requirements can be determined by simulating different capabilities for a machine.
- Simulation can be used to study complex system, where analytic solutions are infeasible. Some modern systems are so complex that the interactions can be organized only through simulation.

A simulation is not appropriate in following conditions:

- If model assumptions are simple such that mathematical methods can be used to obtain exact answers (analytical solutions), or a common sense can be used to solve it.
- Simulation should not be used if the problem can be solved analytically.
- Simulation should not be used if it is easier to perform direct experiments.
- Simulation should not be used if the cost exceeds the savings.
- Simulation should not be used if the resources and time are not available.
- Simulation takes data, sometimes a large amount of data. If no data is available, not even estimates, simulation is not advised.
- Simulation should not be used if there is no ability to verify and validate the model.
- Simulation should not be used if the persons involved in simulation have unreasonable expectations.
- Simulation should not be used if the system behavior is too complex or cannot be defined.

2.6 HOW TO SIMULATE?

System simulation is done to see its real life effect before its development. When the decision is made for simulation a proper study of the system is must. In approaching a system study, it is essential to consider first what mathematical techniques might be applied to drive analytical solution. It is matter of judgment to decide whether the degree of analysis is sufficient for simulation. When the decision is made for simulation in order to use a more realistic system, it is still important to limit the amount the detail in the model to the minimum level necessary. The step by step nature of the simulation technique means that the amount of computation increases very rapidly as the amount of detail increases.

Suppose we are interested in a vehicle fuel filling center. We may describe the behavior of this system graphically by plotting the number of vehicles in the filling center as the state of the system. Every time a vehicle arrives the graph increases by one unit while a departing vehicle causes the graph to drop one unit. This graph, could be obtained from observation of a real station, but could also be artificially constructed. Such artificial construction and the analysis of the resulting sample path (or more sample paths in more complex cases) consist of the simulation.

2.6.1 Final Experimental Design

If we have developed the model, verified its correctness, and validated its adequacy, we again need to consider the final strategic and tactical plans for the execution of the experiments. We must update project constraints on time (schedule) and costs to reflect current conditions. Even though we have exercised careful planning and budget control from the beginning of the project, we must now take a hard, realistic look at what resources remain and how best to use them. We will also have learned more about the system in the process of designing, building, verifying and validating the model which we will want to incorporate into the final plans. The design of a computer simulation experiment is essentially a plan for purchasing a quantity of information that costs more or less depending upon how it was acquired. Design profoundly affects the effective use of experimental resources because:

- The design of the experiments largely determines the form of statistical analysis that can be applied to the data.
- The success of the experiments in answering the desired questions is largely a function of choosing the right design.

Simulation experiments are expensive both in terms of the analyst's time and labor and in some cases, in terms of computer time. We must therefore carefully plan and design not only the model but also its use.

2.6.2 Experimentation and Analysis

Next we come to the actual running of the experiments and the analysis of the results. We now have to deal with issues such as how long to run the model (*i.e.,* sample size), what to do about starting conditions, whether the output data are correlated, and what statistical tests are valid on the data. Before addressing these concerns, we must first ascertain whether the real system is terminating or non-terminating because this characteristic determines the running and analysis methods to be used. In a terminating system, the simulation ends when a critical event occurs. For example, a bank opens in the morning empty and idle. At the end of the day it is once again empty and idle. Another example would be a duel where one or both participants are killed or the weapons are empty. In other words, a system is considered to be terminating if the events driving the system naturally cease at some point in time. In a non-terminating system, no such critical event occurs and the system continues indefinitely (*e.g.,* a telephone exchange or a hospital). A second system characteristic of interest is whether the system is stationary or non-stationary. A system is stationary if the distribution of its response variable (and hence it is mean and variance) does not change overtime. With such systems we are generally concerned with finding the steady state conditions, *i.e.,* the value which is the limit of the response variable if the length of the simulation went to infinity without termination. Whether the system is terminating or non-terminating, we must decide how long to run the simulation model *i.e.,* we must determine sample size. But first we must precisely define what constitutes a single sample. There are several possibilities:

1. Each transaction considered a separate sample. For example, turn-around time for each job or total time in the system for each customer.
2. A complete run of the model. This may entail considering the mean or average value of the response variable for the entire run as being a datum point. Multiple runs are referred to as replication.
3. A fixed time period in terms of simulated time. Thus a simulation may be run for n time periods, where a time period is an hour or a day or a month.

4. Transactions aggregated into groups of fixed size. For example, we might take the time in the system for each 10 jobs flowing through and then use the mean time of the group as a single datum point. This is usually referred to as batching.

If the system is a non-terminating, steady-state system we must be concerned with starting conditions, *i.e.,* the status of the system when we begin to gather statistics or data. If we have an empty and idle system *i.e.,* no customers present, we may not have typical steady state conditions. Therefore, we must either wait until the system reaches steady-state before we begin to gather data (warm-up period), or we must start with more realistic starting conditions. Both of these approaches require that we be able to identify when the system has reached steady-state.

Finally, most statistical tests require that the data points in the sample be independent *i.e.,* not correlated. Since many of the systems we model are queueing networks, they do not meet this condition because they are auto-correlated. Therefore, very often we must do something to assure that the data points are independent before we can proceed with the analysis.

2.6.3 Implementation and Documentation

At this point we have completed all the steps for the design, programming and running of the model as well as the analysis of the results. The final two elements that must be included in any simulation study are implementation and documentation. No simulation study can be considered successfully completed until its results have been understood, accepted and used. It is remarkable how often modelers will spend a great deal of time trying to find the most elegant and efficient ways to model a system and then throw together a report to the sponsor or user at the last minute. If the results are not used, the project was a failure. If the results are not clearly, concisely and convincingly presented, they will not be used. The presentation of the results of the study is a critical and important part of the study and must be as carefully planned as any other part of the project. Among the issues to be addressed in the documentation of the model and study are:

- Choosing an appropriate vocabulary (no technical jargon).
- Length and format of both written and verbal reports (short and concise).
- Timeliness.
- Must address the issues that the sponsor or user consider important.

2.6.4 Paths to Failure

Not all simulation studies are unqualified successes. In fact, unfortunately, too many fail to deliver as promised. When we look at the reasons that projects fail, we find that it is usually traceable to the same reasons over and over. Most failures occur on early projects *i.e.,* the first or second project undertaken by an organization. Many inexperienced modelers bite off more than they can chew. This is not surprising since in most cases they have learned the science but not the art of simulation. This is why it is advisable to begin with small projects that are not of critical significance to the parent organization. Almost all other failures can be traced to one of the following:

- Failure to define a clear and achievable goal.
- Inadequate planning and underestimating the resources needed.
- Inadequate user participation.
- Writing code too soon before the system is really understood.
- Inappropriate level of included detail (usually too much).
- Wrong mix of team skills.
- Lack of trust, confidence and backing by management.

2.6.5 Paths to Success

Just as we can learn from studying projects that fail, we can also learn from those that. Obviously the first thing we want to do is avoid the errors of those who fail. Thus we want to:

- Have clearly defined and achievable goals.
- Be sure we have adequate resources available to successfully complete the project on time.
- Have management's support and have it known to those who must cooperate with us in supplying information and data.
- Assure that we have all the necessary skills required available for the duration of the project.
- Be sure that there are adequate communication channels to the sponsor and end users.
- Have a clear understanding with the sponsor and end users as to the scope and goals of the project as well as schedules.
- Have good documentation of all planning and modeling efforts.

2.7 BENEFITS AND PITFALLS IN SIMULATIONS

Simulation has a number of advantages over analytical or mathematical models for analyzing systems. First of all, the basic concept of simulation is easy to comprehend and hence often easier to justify to management or customers than some of the analytical models. In addition, a simulation model may be more credible because its behavior has been compared to that of the real system or because it requires fewer simplifying assumptions and hence captures more of the true characteristics of the system under study.

The basic concept of simulation is easy to comprehend and hence often easier to justify to management or customers than some of the analytical models. In addition, a simulation model may be more credible because its behavior has been compared to that of the real system or because it requires fewer simplifying assumptions and hence captures more of the true characteristics of the system under study. Every concept in itself has its advantages and disadvantages. Sometimes developing a complete system without simulating its behavior may be a risky task. If the system is not feasible then there is need to design the system again with different parameters. This could play an important role and save money to be wasted with wrong design. Here are some benefits and pitfalls of simulation:

- We can test new designs, layouts, etc., without committing resources to their implementation.
- We can test new designs, layouts, etc., without committing resources to their implementation.
- It can be used to explore new staffing policies, operating procedures, decision rules, organizational structures, information flows, etc., without disrupting the ongoing operations.
- Simulation allows us to identify bottlenecks in information, material and product flows and test options for increasing the flow rates.
- Simulation allows us to test hypothesis about how or why certain phenomena occur in the system.
- Simulation can be used to explore new staffing policies, operating procedures, decision rules, organizational structures, information flows, etc., without disrupting the ongoing operations.
- Simulation allows us to identify bottlenecks in information, material and product flows and test options for increasing the flow rates.
- Simulation allows us to test hypothesis about how or why certain phenomena occur in the system.
- New policies, operating procedures, decision rules, flow of information, etc., can be explored without disrupting ongoing operations of the real system.
- New hardware design, transportation system, physical layout, etc., can be tested without committing resources for their acquisition.
- Time can be expanded or compressed allowing for a slowdown or speedup of the phenomenon under investigation.
- Simulation allows us to control time. Thus we can operate the system for several months or years of experience in a matter of seconds allowing us to quickly look at long time horizons or we can slow down phenomena for study.
- Simulation allows us to gain insights into how a modeled system actually works and understanding of which variables are most important to performance.
- Simulation's great strength is its ability to let us experiment with new and unfamiliar situations and to answer "what if" questions.
- Simulation modeling is an art that requires specialized training and therefore skill levels of practitioners vary widely. The utility of the study depends upon the quality of the model and the skill of the modeler.
- Gathering highly reliable input data can be time consuming and the resulting data is sometimes highly questionable. Simulation cannot compensate for inadequate data or poor management decisions.

- Simulation models are input-output models, *i.e.,* they yield the probable output of a system for a given input.

Even though simulation has many strengths and advantages, it is not without drawbacks. Among these are:

- Simulation modeling is an art that requires specialized training and therefore skill levels of practitioners vary widely. The utility of the study depends upon the quality of the model and the skill of the modeler.
- Gathering highly reliable input data can be time consuming and the resulting data is sometimes highly questionable. Simulation cannot compensate for inadequate data or poor management decisions.
- Simulation models are input-output models, *i.e.,* they yield the probable output of a system for a given input. They are therefore "run" rather than solved. They do not yield an optimal solution; rather they serve as a tool for analysis of the behavior of a system under conditions specified by the experimenter.

2.8 SIMULATION AND ANALYTICAL METHODS

Extensive development has been made out in both the fields ever since the beginning of quantitative science. Development of computing machines is evolved as substitute for labor of human computers. Computers lower cost of approximations as compared to analytical results. This can even lead to simply throwing it on the computer even when analytical results are obtainable; even, indeed, when analytical results are well-known in the literature.

Comparisons. In approaching a system study, it is essential to consider what mathematical techniques might be applied to derive analytical solutions. Mathematical techniques require that the models should be expressed in some particular format. The system must be approximated or abstracted in order to derive a model that fits the format of a mathematical technique. It is the matter of judgment to decide whether the degree of abstraction required to apply analytical methods is too difficult. To make this judgment consider all questions to be answered in system study and the level to which the accuracy of answers need to be known.

Table 2.1 Comparison between Analytical and Simulation methods

Analytical Methods	*Simulation Methods*
• Analytical Methods produce general solutions.	— Simulation methods give specific solutions.
• In analytical method, all the conditions involved to solve a problem are considered.	— Each execution of a simulation tells only whether a particular set of conditions is successful or not.
• Mathematical solution is preferable, when solution being sought is some maximizing condition.	— Many simulation runs may be needed to find a maximum, and still undecided whether it is a local or global maximum.

• Analytical method produces solutions in a single run.	— To consider all conditions, the simulation process has to be repeated with many different conditions.
• Many analytical results occur in the form of complex series that still require extensive evaluation.	— Simulation is used to obtain results directly from a model with specific values.
• Range of problems to be solved mathematically is limited.	— Simulation is a powerful extension of mathematical solutions.
• Analytical model of a system is fixed.	— Simulation model of the desired system changes as analyst modeling of the system changes.
• Analytical methods employ the dedicated reasoning of mathematics to solve the model.	— Simulation models employ numerical methods; models are run rather than solved.
• Analytical methods are expensive and time consuming.	— Simulation gives results in few minutes at a very low cost.
• Analytical model remains same. of the analyst.	— Simulation model varies with experience

The step-by-step nature of the simulation technique means that the amount of computation increases very rapidly as the amount of details increases. The best way of using simulation is an extension of mathematical solution. This can be achieved at the cost of too much simplification. Simple limitations on the system can easily be removed by simulation. When a solution of the problem is known, then also simulation provides a quick and more convenient way of deriving results.

2.9 BASIC NATURE OF SIMULATION

The simulation techniques make no specific attempt to isolate the relationships between any particular variable, instead it explore the way in which all variables of the model change with time. For a better simulation, the relationship among the variable must be derived from the observations. Following are the main points regarding the nature of simulation:

Simulation imitates the operations of a facility or process, usually via computer:

- *What system is being simulated?*
- *To study system, often make assumptions/approximations, both logical and mathematical operations, about how it works.*

These assumptions form a model of the system to be simulated if model structure is simple enough, we can use mathematical methods to get exact information on questions of interest *i.e.*, analytical solution.

But most complex systems require models that are also complex (to be valid) it must be studied via simulation *i.e.*, evaluate model numerically and collect data to estimate model characteristics.

Example: Manufacturing Company considering extending its plant:

- Build it and see if it works out?
- Simulate current, expanded operations *i.e.*, we can also investigate many other issues along the way, quickly and cheaply.

Some (not all) application areas:

- Designing and analyzing manufacturing systems.
- Evaluating military weapons systems or their logistics requirements.
- Determining hardware requirements or protocols for communications networks.
- Determining hardware and software requirements for a computer system.
- Designing and operating transportation systems such as airports, freeways, ports, and subways.
- Evaluating designs for service organizations such as call centers, hospitals, fast food restaurants, and post offices.
- Reengineering of business processes.
- Determining ordering policies for an inventory system.
- Analyzing financial or economic systems.

Surveys of use of Operations Research/Modeling Simulation techniques:

- Simulation consistently ranked as one of the three most important techniques.
- Simulation was second only to the broad category of "mathematical programming".

Impediments to acceptance, use of simulation:

- Models of large systems are usually very complex.
- But now we have better modeling software *i.e.*, more general, flexible, but still (relatively) easy to use.
- Can consume a lot of computer time.
- But now have faster, bigger, cheaper hardware to allow for much better studies than just a few years ago and this trend will continue.
- However, simulation will also continue to push the envelope on computing power in that we ask more and more of our simulation models.
- Impression that simulation is "just programming".
- There is a lot more to a simulation study than just coding a model in some software and running it to get the answer.
- Require careful design and analysis of simulation models *i.e.*, simulation methodology.

2.10 THE SIMULATION PROCESS

The essence or purpose of simulation modeling is to help the ultimate decision-maker to solve a problem. Therefore, to learn to be a good simulation modeler, one must merge good problem-solving techniques with good software engineering practice. We can identify the following steps, which should be present in any simulation study:

1. **Problem Definition.** Clearly defining the goals of the study so that we know the purpose, *i.e.,* why are we studying this problem and what questions do we hope to answer?
2. **Project Planning.** It is assurance about sufficient and appropriate personnel, management support, computer hardware, and software resources to do the job.
3. **System Definition.** Determining the boundaries and restrictions to be used in defining the system (or process) and investigating how the system works.
4. **Conceptual Model Formulation.** It is developing a preliminary model either graphically (*e.g.,* block diagram or process flow chart), or in pseudo-code to define the components, descriptive variables, and interactions (logic) that constitute the system.
5. **Preliminary Experimental Design.** Selecting the measures of effectiveness to be used, the factors to be varied, and the levels of those factors to be investigated, *i.e.,* what data need to be gathered from the model, in what form, and to what extent.
6. **Input Data Preparation.** Identifying and collecting the input data needed by the model.
7. **Model Translation.** It is formulation of the model in an appropriate simulation language.
8. **Verification and Validation.** Confirming that the model operates the way the analyst intended (debugging) and that the output of the model is believable and representative of the output of the real system.
9. **Final Experimental Design.** Designing an experiment that will yield the desired information and determining how each of the test runs specified in the experimental design is to be executed.
10. **Experimentation.** Executing the simulation to generate the desired data and to perform sensitivity analysis is experimentation.
11. **Analysis and Interpretation.** Drawing inferences from the data generated by the simulation runs.
12. **Implementation and Documentation.** It is the process of reporting the results, putting the results to use, recording the findings, and documenting the model and its use.

The activities and steps in modeling and simulation process are given by figure 2.1.

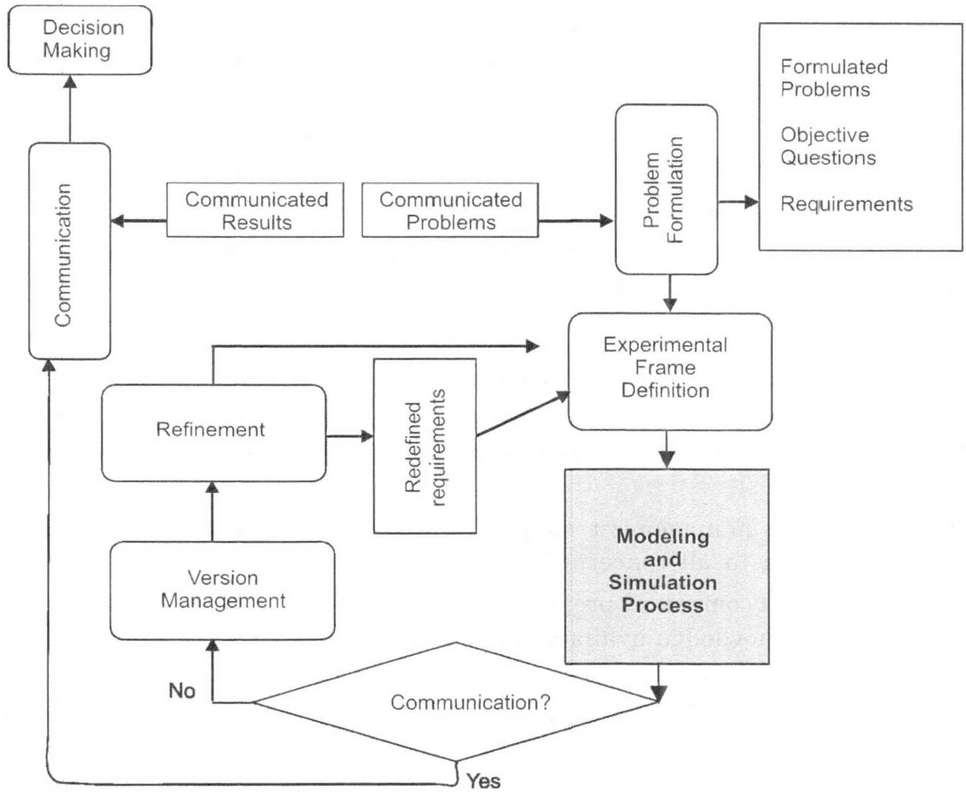

Fig. 2.1 Modeling and simulation process

It is important for the inexperienced modeler to understand that the longer you wait to start step 7, the faster you will complete the model and the project—assuming of course, that you spend that time understanding the problem, designing the model and designing the experiments to be executed. Computer Scientists have devoted a great deal of effort to software engineering and have developed design and management methods aimed at yielding rapid programs while minimizing errors. One of the major ideas that have emerged from this effort is the validity of the "40-20-40 Rule." This rule states that 40 percent of the effort and time in a project should be devoted to Steps 1 through 6, 20 percent to step 7, and the remaining 40 percent to steps 8 through 12.

2.10.1 Problem Definition and Project Planning

Experience indicates that beginning a simulation project properly, may well make a critical difference between success and failure. We begin our analysis by gathering information about the problem. Usually, the project begins with the sponsor describing the situation to the analyst in vague and imprecise terms, such as costs are too high or, "too many jobs are late." We must consider the sponsor's problem description as a set of symptoms requiring diagnosis. The usual flow of events will be:

Diagnosis of symptoms ⇒ Problem definition ⇒ System definition ⇒ Model formulation.

It is important to remember that we do not model a system just for the sake of modeling it. We always model to solve a specific problem. Among the questions to be answered at the beginning of the study are:

- What is the goal of the study *i.e.,* what is the question to be answered or decision to be made?
- What information do we need to make a decision?
- What are the precise criteria we will use to make the decision?
- Who will make the decision?
- Who will be affected by the decision?
- How long do we have to provide an answer?

Once we have those answers we can begin to plan the project in detail. An important aspect of the planning phase is to assure that certain critical factors have been considered. Among these are:

- Do we have management support and has its support for the project been made known to all concerned parties?
- Do we have a competent project manager and team members with the necessary skills and knowledge available for sufficient time to successfully complete the project?
- Do we have sufficient time, computer hardware and software available to do the job?
- Have we established adequate communication channels so that sufficient information is available on project objectives, status, changes in user or client needs etc., to keep everyone (team members, management, and clients) fully informed as the project progresses?

2.10.2 Steps in a Simulation Study

Figure 2.2 shows a set of steps to guide a model builder in a thorough and sound simulation study. The main steps are as following:

1. **Problem Formulation.** Every simulation study begins with a statement of the problem. If the statement is provided by those that have the problem (client), the simulation analyst must take extreme care to insure that the problem is clearly understood. If a problem statement is prepared by the simulation analyst, it is important that the client understand and agree with the formulation. It is suggested that a set of assumptions be prepared by the simulation analyst and agreed to by the client. Even with all of these precautions, it is possible that the problem will need to be reformulated as the simulation study progresses.

2. **Setting of Objectives and Overall Project Plan.** Another way to state this step is prepare a proposal. This step should be accomplished regardless of location of the analyst and client, viz., as an external or internal consultant. The objectives indicate the questions that are to be answered by the simulation study. The project plan should include a statement of the various scenarios that will be investigated. The plans for the study should be indicated in terms of time, which will be required, personnel that will be used, hardware and software requirements if the client wants to run the model and conduct the analysis, stages in the investigation, output at each stage, cost of the study and billing procedures, if any.
3. **Model Conceptualization.** The real-world system under investigation is abstracted by a conceptual model, a series of mathematical and logical relationships concerning the components and the structure of the system. It is recommended that modeling begin simply and that the model grow until a model of appropriate complexity has been developed. For example, consider the model of a manufacturing and material handling system. The basic model with the arrivals, queues and servers is constructed. Then, add the failures and shift schedules. Next, add the material-handling capabilities. Finally, add the special features. Constructing an unduly complex model will add to the cost of the study and the time for its completion without increasing the quality of the output. Maintaining client involvement will enhance the quality of the resulting model and increase the client's confidence in its use.
4. **Data Collection.** Shortly after the proposal is accepted a schedule of data requirements should be submitted to the client. In the best of circumstances, the client has been collecting the kind of data needed in the format required, and can submit these data to the simulation analyst in electronic format. Oftentimes, the client indicates that the required data are indeed available. However, when the data are delivered they are found to be quite different than anticipated. When the study commenced, the data delivered were the average *talk time* of the reservationist for each of the years. Individual values were needed, not summary measures. Model building and data collection are shown as contemporaneous in figure 2.2. This is to indicate that the simulation analyst can readily construct the model while the data collection is progressing.
5. **Model Translation.** The conceptual model constructed in Step 3 is coded into a computer recognizable form, an operational model.
6. **Verification.** Verification concerns the operational model. These models are orders of magnitude smaller than real models (say 50 lines of computer code versus 2,000 lines of computer code). It is highly advisable that verification take place as a continuing process. It is ill advised for the simulation analyst to wait until the entire model is complete to begin the verification process. Also, use of an interactive run controller, or debugger, is highly encouraged as an aid to the verification process.

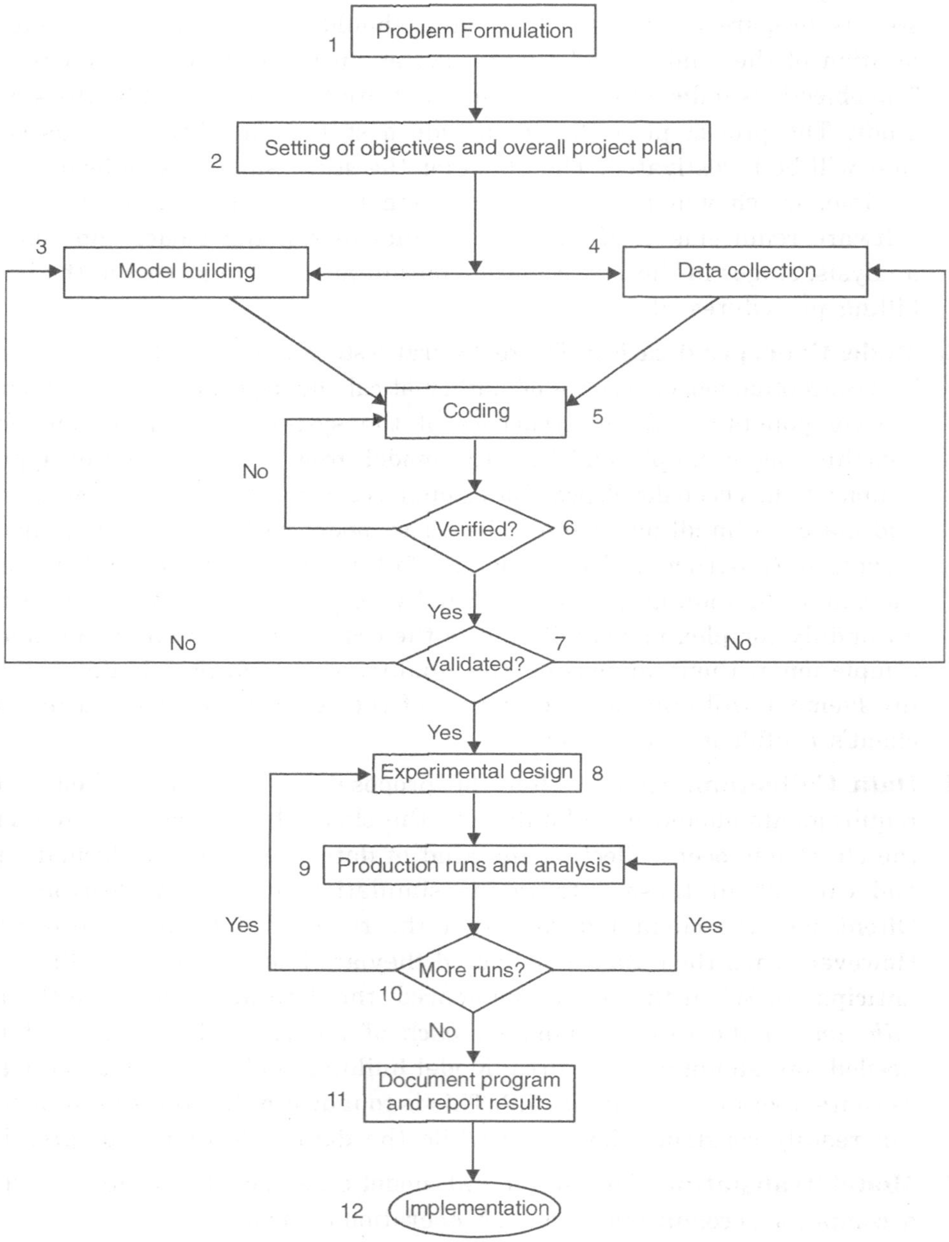

Fig. 2.2 Steps in a simulation study

7. **Validation.** Validation is the determination that the conceptual model is an accurate representation of the real system. Can the model be substituted for the real system for the purposes of experimentation? If there is an existing system, call it the base system, then an ideal way to validate the model is to

compare its output to that of the base system. Unfortunately, there is not always a base system. There are many methods for performing validation.

8. **Experimental Design.** For each scenario that is to be simulated, decisions need to be made concerning the length of the simulation run, the number of runs (or say replications), and the manner of initialization, as required.
9. **Production Runs and Analysis.** Production runs, and their subsequent analysis, are used to estimate measures of performance for the scenarios that are being simulated.
10. **More Runs?** Based on the analysis of runs that have been completed, the simulation analyst determines if additional runs are needed and if any additional scenarios need to be simulated.
11. **Documentation and Reporting.** Documentation is necessary for numerous reasons. If the simulation model is going to be used again by the same or different analysts, it may be necessary to understand how the simulation model operates. This will enable confidence in the simulation model so that the client can make decisions based on the analysis. Also, if the model is to be modified, this can be greatly facilitated by adequate documentation. The result of all the analysis should be reported clearly and concisely. This will enable the client to review the final formulation, the alternatives that were addressed, the criterion by which the alternative systems were compared, the results of the experiments, and analyst recommendations, if any.
12. **Implementation.** The simulation analyst acts as a reporter rather than an advocate. The report prepared in step 11 stands on its merits, and is just additional information that the client uses to make a decision. If the client has been involved throughout the study period, and the simulation analyst has followed all of the steps rigorously, then the likelihood of a successful implementation is increased.

2.11 TYPES OF SYSTEM SIMULATION

Continuous system and discrete system simulation are two main types of system simulation on the basis of continuous and discrete systems.

2.11.1 Continuous System Simulation

Let us first discuss, what are continuous events?

Continuous Events. In Continuous events the state variables change continuously as a function of time, for example airplane flight; the state variables like position, velocity change continuously. The distributed lag model is continuous event model and the simulation of such model is continuous system simulation. This model describes how the attribute of the system are related to each other in the form of linear algebraic equations. In general, in continuous system, the relationships describe the rates at which the attributes change, so that the model contains differential equations.

Continuous System Simulation. Continuous system simulation typically solves sets of differential equations numerically overtime, may involve stochastic elements. Some specialized software available for continuous system simulation. Some discrete-event simulation software can also formulate continuous simulation as well.

Consider the pair of first order ordinary differential equations known as the Lotka-Volterra predator-prey model.

y1′ = (1 – alpha*y2)*y1

y2′ = (–1 + beta*y1)*y2

The functions y1 and y2 measure the sizes of the prey and predator populations respectively. The quadratic cross term accounts for the interactions between the species. Note that the prey population increases when there are no predators, but the predator population decreases when there are no prey. To simulate a system, create a function (or say MATLAB file) that returns a column vector of state derivatives, given state and time values. For this example, we have created a file called LOTKA.M.

type lotka

function yp = lotka(t, y)

%LOTKA Lotka-Volterra predator-prey model. It was developed by Lotka (in 1925) and Volterra (in 1926), independently.

yp = diag([1 - .01*y(2), -1 + .02*y(1)])*y;

To simulate the differential equation defined in LOTKA over the interval 0 < t < 15, invoke ODE23 (Command in Matlab). Use the default relative accuracy of 1e-3 (0.1 percent).

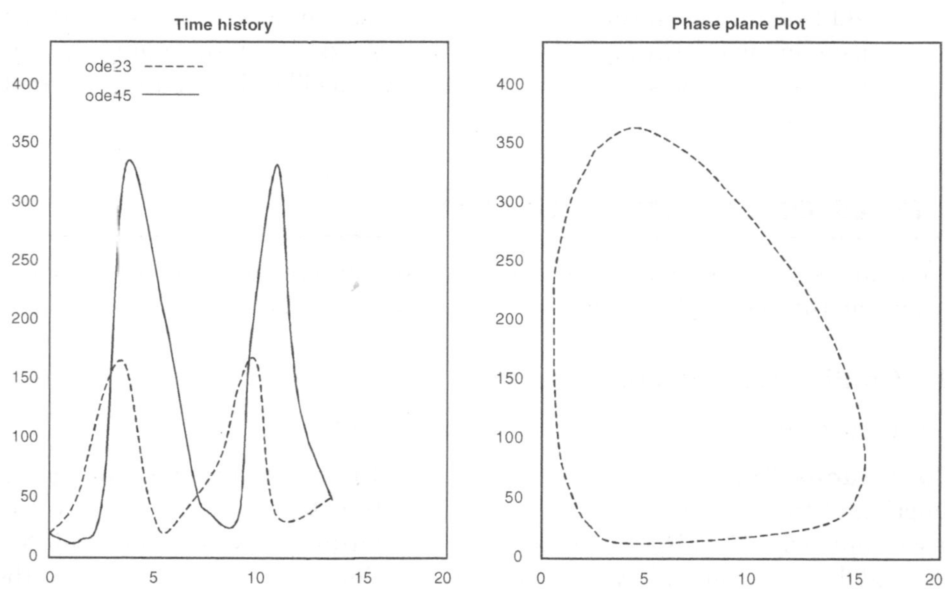

Fig. 2.3 Time history and phase plane plot

% Define initial conditions.

t0 = 0;

```
tfinal = 15;
y0 = [20 20]';
% Simulate the differential equation.
tfinal = tfinal*(1+eps);
[t,y] = ode23('lotka',[t0 tfinal],y0);
%Plot the result of the simulation two different ways.
subplot(1,2,1)
plot(t,y)
title('Time history')
subplot(1,2,2)
plot(y(:,1),y(:,2))
title('Phase plane plot')
```

Now simulate LOTKA using ODE45 (Matlab Command), instead of ODE23. ODE45 takes longer at each step, but also takes larger steps. Nevertheless, the output of ODE45 is smooth because by default the solver uses a continuous extension formula to produce output at 4 equally spaced time points in the span of each step taken. The plot compares this result against the previous.

```
[T,Y] = ode45('lotka',[t0 tfinal],y0);
subplot(1,1,1)
title('Phase plane plot')
plot(y(:,1),y(:,2),'-',Y(:,1),Y(:,2),'-');
legend('ode23','ode45')
```

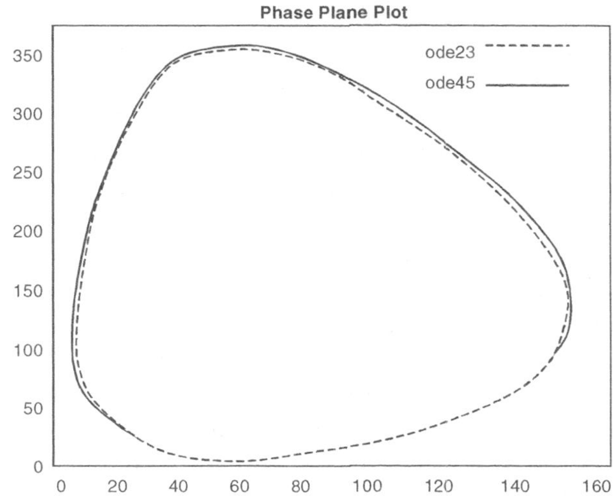

Fig. 2.4 Simulate using ode45 instead of ode23

2.11.2 Discrete System Simulation

Let us discuss first, what are discrete-events?

Discrete-event. Between two consecutive events, nothing happens *i.e.,* the graph is horizontal. When the number of events is finite, we call the events "discrete-events." In some systems the state changes all the time, not just at the time of some discrete-events. For example, the water level in a reservoir with given in and outflows may change all the time. In such cases "continuous simulation" is more appropriate, although discrete-event simulation can serve as an approximation.

A discrete-event simulation is one in which the state of a model changes at only a discrete, but possibly random, set of simulated time points. Two or more traffic units often have to be manipulated at one and the same time point. Such simultaneous movement of traffic at a time point is achieved by manipulating units of traffic serially at that time point. This often leads to logical complexities in discrete-event simulation because it raises questions about the order in which two or more units of traffic are to be manipulated at one time point.

Discrete System Simulation. Discrete-event simulation models typically have stochastic components that mimic the probabilistic nature of the system under consideration. Successful input modeling requires a close match between the input model and the true underlying probabilistic mechanism associated with the system. Discrete simulation deals with systems whose dynamics can be considered as a sequence of events at discrete time points. The key point of a discrete simulation language is the way it controls the proper sequencing of activities in the model. This is also the way a user must view the world when using the language and a base for classification of discrete simulation languages.

The discrete-event simulation formalism fits the general structure of deterministic, causal systems in classical systems theory. Discrete-event simulation allows for the description of system behavior at two levels. At the lowest level, an atomic discrete-event simulation describes the autonomous behavior of a discrete-event system as a sequence of deterministic transitions between sequential states as well as how it reacts to external input (events) and how it generates output (events). At the higher level, a coupled discrete-event simulation describes a system as a network of coupled components. The components can be atomic discrete-event simulation models or coupled discrete-event simulation in their own right. The connections denote how components influence each other. In particular, output events of one component can become, via a network connection, input events of another component. It is shown in how the discrete-event simulation formalism is closed under coupling: for each coupled discrete-event simulation, a resultant atomic discrete-event simulation can be constructed. As such, any discrete-event simulation model, be it atomic or coupled can be replaced by an equivalent atomic discrete-event simulation. The construction procedure of a resultant atomic discrete-event simulation is also the basis for the implementation of an abstract simulator or solver capable of simulating any discrete-event simulation model. As a coupled discrete-event simulation may have coupled discrete-event simulation components, hierarchical modeling is supported.

Discrete-event systems are dynamic systems, which evolve in time by the occurrence of events at possibly irregular time intervals. Discrete-event systems abound in real-world applications. Examples include traffic systems, flexible manufacturing systems, computer-communications systems, production lines, coherent lifetime systems, and flow networks. Most of these systems can be modeled in terms of discrete events whose occurrence causes the system to change from one state to another. In designing, analyzing and operating such complex systems, one is interested not only in performance evaluation but also in sensitivity analysis and optimization.

A typical stochastic system has a large number of control parameters that can have a significant impact on performance of the system. To establish a basic knowledge of the behavior of a system under variation of input parameter values and to estimate the relative importance of the input parameters, sensitivity analysis applies small changes to the nominal values of input parameters. For systems simulation, variations of the input parameter values cannot be made infinitely small. The sensitivity of the performance measure with respect to an input parameter is therefore defined as (partial) derivative.

A discrete-event simulation is one, which employs a next-event technique to control the behavior of the model. Many applications of discrete simulation involve queuing systems of one kind or another. The queuing structure may be obvious as in a queue of jobs waiting to be processed on a batch computer or in a stack of aircraft waiting for landing space at an airport.

As another example, consider customer waiting in a queue in the bank to get service, at grocery store, at red light crossing etc. In the simplest case, the queue would operate with a first-in first-out (FIFO) discipline. The main features of discrete system simulation are as following:

- Study of complex systems.
- Computation of physical times that would occur in real time in a physical system.
- Implementation of sequential simulators.
- Implementation of manufacturing systems.
- Events are processed in time stamp order.
- Unprocessed events are stored in pending event list.

The major limitations in discrete system simulations are:

- A conflict due to simultaneous internal and external events is resolved.
- By ignoring the internal event. It should be possible to explicitly specify behavior in case of conflicts.
- There is limited potential for parallel implementation.

2.11.3 Real-time Simulation

The general process by which a mathematical model of an engineering system is constructed, involves understanding of physical of chemical laws. This includes a number of experiments of measurements to derive the different coefficients of the model. This can be particularly time consuming if the model is not being simplified by assuming linearity.

Detailing of system experiments or measurements and preliminary work could be avoided if an actual device can be used, rather than constructing a model. Real-time simulation uses this approach.

In Real-time simulation, actual devices are used in conjunctions with either digital or hybrid computer to provide simulation of the parts of the system that do not exist or that cannot conveniently be used in an experiment. These actual devices used in experiment should be the part of the desired system. Real-time simulation involves interaction with human being to avoid designing of human model.

Real-time simulation requires computers that can operate in real-time. These computers must be able to respond immediately to signals sent from the physical devices and sent out signals at specific points in time. Real-time simulation is used in many areas such as in aerospace industry. Simulators, provide human beings with a substitute for some environment or situation. Best example of simulators is used in training astronauts. They are suspended in spring harnesses that reduce their apparent weight to that which occurs on the moon surface. Since the main purpose of such devices is to duplicate some sort of sensory stimulus, they cannot properly be classified as computers.

The figure 2.5 shows the variation of real-time simulation from analytical solutions.

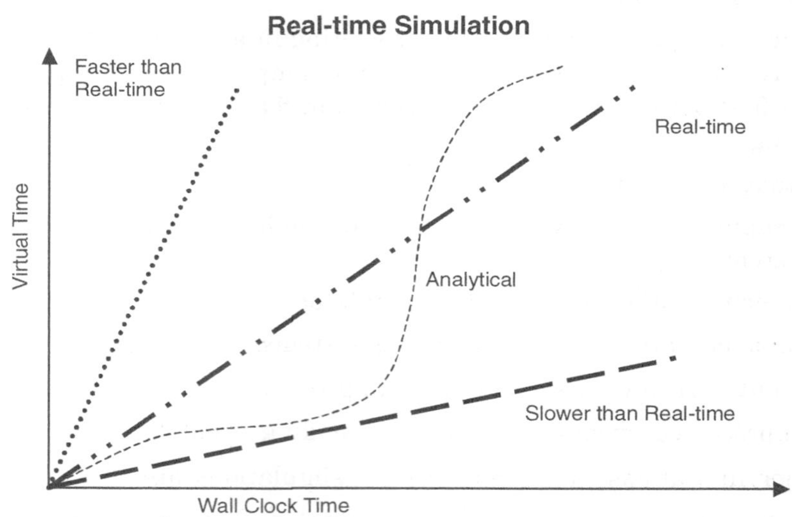

Fig. 2.5 Real-time simulations Vs. Analytical solution

2.11.4 Hybrid Simulation

Hybrid Computer is combination of traditional analog-computer elements, giving smooth, continuous outputs, and elements carrying out some non-linear, digital operations as storing values, switching, and performing logical operations. Integration of analog computer capabilities and special-purposes or specially constructed devices is hybrid computer.

Hybrid computers may be used to simulate systems that are mainly continuous but have some digital element also. Hybrid computers are also useful when a system that can be adequately represented by an analog computer model is the subject of a repetitive study. Hybrid computer can be arranged to carry out large portion of the study without human intervention.

For most of system studies, it is clear that model built can be either continuous or discrete. This factor determines whether analog or digital computers are used for system simulation. This is the time when we have combined discrete-continuous simulation and so we have to combine analog and digital computers to provide hybrid simulation. The arrangement of hybrid simulation depends upon the requirements of the application.

One computer may be simulating the system being studied, whereas the other provides a simulation of the environment in which the system to operate. Simulated system is an interconnection of continuous and discrete subsystems. This system can be modeled best by linkage of an analog computer and a digital computer.

Hybrid simulation has become easier due to the availability of minicomputers, which has lowered the cost and allows dedicated computers for an application. High-speed converters are needed to transform signals from one from of representation to the other. Hybrid simulation is used for the linkage of functionally distinct analog and digital computers done for the purpose of simulation.

2.11.5 Simulation of Stochastic Processes

In simulation of stochastic processes, we model a particular system by studying the flow of *entities* that move through that system. Entities can be customers, job orders, particular parts, information packets, etc. An entity can be any object that enters the system, moves through a series of processes, and then leaves the system. These entities can have individual characteristics which we will call *attributes*. An attribute is associated with the specific, individual entity. Attributes might be such things as name, priority, due date, required CPU time, account number etc. As the entity flows through the system, it will be processed by a series of *resources*. Resources are anything that the entity needs in order to be processed. For example, resources might be workers, material handling equipment, special tools, a hospital bed, access to the CPU, a machine, waiting or storage space, etc. Resources may be fixed in one location (*e.g.*, a heavy machine, bank teller, hospital bed) or moving about the system (*e.g.*, a forklift, repairman, doctor). A simulation model is therefore a computer program which represents the logic of the system as entities with attributes arrive, join queues to await the assignment of required resources, are processed by the resources, released and exit the system. In addition to the logic of how an entity flows through the system, the computer program keeps track of and advances time, as well as keeping track of resource utilization, time spent in queues, time in the system (processing time), and other desired statistics. Much of what happens in the system is probabilistic or stochastic in nature. For example the time between arrivals, the time for a resource to process the entity, the time to travel from one part of the system to another and whether a part passes inspection or not, are usually all random variables. It is these types of data for input to the model that are difficult to obtain.

To perform statistical analysis of the simulation output we need to establish some conditions, *e.g.*, output data must be a covariance stationary process (*e.g.*, the data collected over n simulation runs).

Stationary Process (strictly stationary): A stationary stochastic process is a stochastic process {X(t), $t \in$ T} with the property that the joint distribution all vectors of h dimension remain the same for any fixed h.

First Order Stationary: A stochastic process is a first order stationary if expected of X(t) remains same for all t.

Second Order Stationary: A stochastic process is a second order stationary if it is first order stationary and covariance between X(t) and X(s) is function of t's only.

2.11.6 Social Simulation

Social scientists have always constructed models of social phenomena. Simulation is an important method for modeling social and economic processes. There are different types of computer simulation and their application to social scientific problems. Faster hardware and improved software have made building complex simulations easier. Computer simulation methods can be effective for the development of theories as well as for prediction. For example, macroeconomic models have been used to simulate future changes in the economy; and simulations have been used in psychology to study cognitive mechanisms.

As a general approach in the field, a world is specified with much computational detail. Then the world is simulated to reveal some of the non-trivial implications of the world. When these non-trivial implications are made known in world, apparently it constitutes some added values.

2.11.7 Web-based Simulation

Web-based simulation is quickly emerging as an area of significant interest for both the simulation researchers and simulation practitioners. This interest in web-based simulation is a natural outgrowth of the proliferation of the World Wide Web and its attendant technologies, *e.g.,* HTML, HTTP, CGI, etc. Also the surging popularity of, and reliance upon, computer simulation as a problem solving and decision support systems tools.

The appearance of the network-friendly programming language, Java, and of distributed object technologies like the Common Object Request Broker Architecture (CORBA) and the Object Linking and Embedding/Component Object Model (OLE/COM) have had particularly acute effects on the state of simulation practice.

Currently, the researchers in the field of web-based simulation are interested in dealing with topics such as methodologies for web-based model development, collaborative model development over the Internet, Java-based modeling and simulation, distributed modeling and simulation using web technologies, and new applications.

2.11.8 Parallel and Distributed Simulation

The increasing size of the systems and designs requires more efficient simulation strategies to accelerate the simulation process. Parallel and distributed simulation approaches seem to be a promising approach in this direction. Major topics under such simulations are:

- Synchronization, scheduling, memory management, randomized and reactive/adaptive algorithms, partitioning and load balancing.

- Synchronization in multi-user distributed simulation, virtual reality environments, and interoperability.
- System modeling for parallel simulation, specification, re-use of models/code, and keeping parallel existing simulations.
- Language and implementation issues, models of parallel simulation, execution environments, and libraries.
- Theoretical and empirical studies, prediction and analysis, cost models, benchmarks, and comparative studies.
- Computer architectures, telecommunication networks, VLSI, manufacturing, dynamic systems, and biological/social systems.
- Web based distributed simulation such as multimedia and real-time applications, fault tolerance, implementation issues, use of Java, and CORBA.

2.11.9 Object-oriented Simulation

Object-Oriented Simulation (OOS) can be considered as a special case of Object Oriented Programming (OOP). Some principles of OOP like existence of a varying number of instances of interfering objects have been in standard use in simulation environment for a long time, often using other terminology. The Simula language is the first true object-oriented language. Being more than 38 years old, it still has most (and all important) mechanisms and principles of OOP. Some things like classes, inheritance, virtual methods, etc., have been defined in Simula long time before; they were rediscovered by the Object Oriented Programming boom in recent years.

Object-oriented simulation offers excellent tools for treating models of complex dynamic systems. First of all, we must decide when the system is really complex. Obviously, a system described by a huge set of equations is not necessarily complex. We can solve on a computer set of thousands of simultaneous differential equations, but this does not mean that the model we solve is complex. On the other hand, a system may result to be complex even if the equations are apparently simple, but the system components have very distinct dynamic behavior or if they are of different kind. We say that a dynamic system is complex, if it has multiple components that reveal different dynamic properties. This may occur, for example, when all system components are continuous with concentrated parameters, but the model includes very fast and very slow parts.

Other example is a system where discrete parts interact with continuous sub models of different speed and different kind, for example, an electronic circuit that contains integrated circuits as well as electro-mechanical parts such as relays and motors. In other words, the model complexity has little to do with the model size. Using object-oriented approach we can simulate complex systems creating objects that simulate system sub models and run concurrently. The idea is to launch a set of objects and to coordinate them by other object that only connects the sub models and controls a general (global) interaction rules. Thus, a sub model of very different kind can run and interact in the same simulation program; some of them with integration step thousands of times smaller than others and some of them being discrete or combined.

2.11.10 On-line Simulation

Internet together with Java and JavaScript offers incredible possibilities in problem solving. Instead of time consuming downloading and installation of software packages, it is possible to open directly various solvers, especially for problems that are not frequent and that do not require time consuming computation. Such simulations are available on Internet, for example, Silk, SLX, STARDIS, RT-LAB, JSIM, etc. In the near future it will be more and more difficult to draw a line between web simulation and traditional simulation. Web simulation must allow the simulation and interaction of distributed entities. Not all of the tools are ready for this, but they somehow aim in that direction.

2.11.11 Simulation-based Optimization Techniques

Discrete-event simulation is the primary analysis tool for designing complex systems. Simulation, however, must be linked with optimization techniques to be effectively used for systems design. In this we present several optimization techniques involving both continuous and discrete controllable input parameters subject to a variety of constraints. The aim is to determine the techniques most promising for a given simulation model.

Many man-made systems are modeled as Discrete Event Systems (DES); examples are computer systems, PERT networks, manufacturing systems, nuclear systems, and traffic transportation systems. Discrete Event Systems evolve with the occurrence of discrete events, such as the arrival of a job or the completion of a task, in contrast with continuously variable dynamic processes such as aerospace vehicles, which are primarily governed by differential equations. Owing to the complex dynamics resulting from stochastic interactions of such discrete-events overtime, the performance analysis and optimization of discrete-event systems can be difficult tasks. At the same time, since such systems are becoming more widespread as a result of modern technological advances, it is important to have tools for analyzing and optimizing the parameters of these systems.

Analyzing complex Discrete Event Systems often requires computer simulation. In these systems, the objective function may not be expressible as an explicit function of the input parameters; rather, it involves some performance measures of the system whose values can be found only by running the simulation model or by observing the actual system. On the other hand, due to the increasingly large size and inherent complexity of most man-made systems, purely analytical means are often insufficient for optimization. In these cases, one must resort to simulation, with its chief advantage being its generality, and its primary disadvantage being its cost in terms of time and money. Even though, in principle, some systems are analytically tractable, the analytical effort required to evaluate the solution may be so formidable that computer simulation becomes attractive. While the price for computing resources continues to dramatically decrease, one nevertheless can still obtain only a statistical estimate as opposed to an exact solution. Practically, this is quite sufficient.

These man-made Discrete Event Systems are costly, and therefore it is important to operate them as efficiently as possible. The high cost makes it necessary to find more efficient means of conducting simulation and optimizing its output. We consider optimizing an objective function with respect to a set of continuous and/or discrete controllable parameters subject to some constraints.

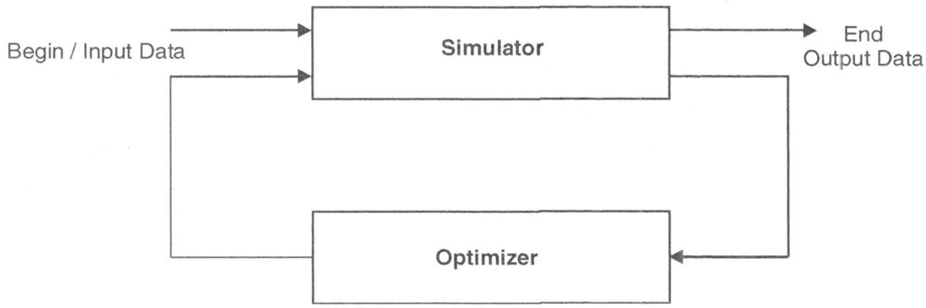

Fig. 2.6 An optimizer support system

2.12 GENERATION OF RANDOM NUMBERS

What we call a Random Number Generator (RNG) is actually a program that produces, a deterministic and periodic sequence of numbers, once its initial state is chosen. In generating sequences of random numbers we wish to duplicate, in effect, a game in which a fair wheel of fortune is spun and the outcome of the game is recorded after each spinning. If the periphery of the wheel of fortune is divided into m equal intervals which are indexed with the integers from 1 to m, this game produces independent random integers which are uniformly distributed in 1 to m range.

There are basically two ways of obtaining sequences of random numbers for a simulation experiment. The first way is simply to read the random numbers from a list of such numbers which has already been compiled by somebody else. For example, a table with 1 million random digits was published in 1955 by the Rand Corporation. Such tables of random numbers have been recorded on magnetic tape and can thus be read quickly by a digital computer.

The second way (the most common) is to have the computer itself generate a sequence of random numbers. This is accomplished by having the computer execute a short program every time a new random number is needed. This computer program essentially uses the last random number produced, say the $(n - 1)$st in the sequence, to produce the next random number, say the nth in the sequence. The specific method employed can be any one of the congruential methods.

For instance, the mixed congruential method uses the expression

$$x_n = ax_{n-1} + c \text{ (modulo } m) \qquad \text{...(2.1)}$$

where x_n and x_{n-1} are the nth and $(n - 1)$st random numbers in the sequence, respectively, and a, c, and m are suitably chosen positive integers with $a < m$ and $c < m$. The indication "modulo m" means that x_n is the remainder of the division of the quantity $ax_{n-1} + c$ by the number m. For example, if $a = 5$, $x_{n-1} = 7$, $c = 3$, and $m = 16$, we have $ax_{n-1} + c = 38$ and $x_n = 38$ (modulo 16) $= 6$.

How many different numbers can we obtain through equation (2.1)? Obviously, *at most*, m, that is all the numbers between 0 and m - 1. For example, with $a = 5$, $c = 3$, $x = 7$, and $m = 16$, we obtain $x_1 = 6$ (as we just saw) and then $x_2 = 1$, $x_3 = 8$, $x_4 = 11$, $x_5 = 10$, $x_6 = 5$, $x_7 = 12$, $x_8 = 15$, $x_9 = 14$, $x_{10} = 91$, $x_{11} = 01$, $x_{12} = 3$, $x_{13} = 2$, $x_{14} = 13$, and $x_{15} = 4$, in all the 16 different numbers in the range from 0 to 15. What is x_{16} in this sequence? We have $a \cdot x_{15} + c = 23$ and $x_{16} = 23$ (modulo m) = 7. Thus, the earlier sequence will now be repeated once again with $x_{17} = 6$, $x_{18} = 1$, and so on.

The example above illustrates two interesting points. First, any sequence of random numbers produced through equation (2.1) is cyclical. Each cycle consists of a necessarily finite number of distinct numbers (at most m). After a cycle has been completed, a new cycle identical to the previous one begins. (In our example each cycle consists of 16 distinct numbers.) The finiteness of the cycles will obviously cause problems in a simulation if the length of a cycle is small: a succession of identical short cycles of numbers definitely does not behave as a sequence of independent random numbers (we have $x_{n+\tau}$ where τ is the length of the cycle). However, if m is a very large number and a and c are chosen with sufficient care to make the length of each cycle comparable to the size of m, the finiteness of the cycles is of no practical significance. Consider the case when m is chosen to be equal to 2^b, where b is the number of bits in a binary computer word. This is the choice of m made in computer-based simulations, since 2^b is the total number of integers that can be expressed in binary form with the number of bits available. When $b = 32$, we have $m = 2^{32}$ distinct numbers. With a cycle length in this order of magnitude, it is an entirely academic matter that the same sequence of numbers will be repeated at some future point.

The second observation concerns the meaning of the word random in the case of sequences produced through equation (2.1). Obviously, if we know a, c, and m we can predict perfectly the complete sequence that will follow any initial number x_0. For this reason, the initial number x_0 used to produce some sequence of numbers is called the seed of this sequence. For the same reason, the sequences of numbers produced through equation (2.1) (as well as through other congruential methods) are also called *pseudo-random* numbers. This, however, is also of academic importance as long as the sequences of numbers produced through equation (2.1) qualify (through passing the appropriate statistical tests) as independent samples from a discrete, uniform probability distribution, that is, as long as the successive numbers appear to an observer to be drawn from a game similar to the spinning wheel game that we described earlier.

In fact, the property of reproducibility for the sequences generated through equation (2.1) is in itself a most desirable one. For, when we wish to perform a simulation experiment under "identical conditions" with some earlier experiment, all we have to do is provide the same seed, x_0, used in the earlier experiment to obtain the same sequence of random (or pseudo-random) phenomena as before.

We have yet to say how the constant positive integers a and c in equation (2.1) are chosen. An unfortunate choice of a and c will unavoidably lead to short cycles of numbers (which are usually anything but uniformly distributed) even for a large m. The branch of mathematics called number theory provides the guidelines for a good choice of a and c. For instance, in the case of digital computers, whereas we have mentioned, we use $m = 2^b$, it can be shown that a should be chosen such that it is equal to 1 in modulo 4 arithmetic (*i.e.*, $a = 1, 5, 9, 13 \ldots$) and that c should be an odd number. The choice of x_0, the seed, is immaterial in this case as far as the length of the cycle is concerned.

The desirable properties of any method for producing sequences of random numbers in a digital computer are:

1. The numbers should appear to be statistically independent of each other (although, strictly speaking, they are perfectly correlated).
2. The numbers should be uniformly distributed over some range.
3. The sequence of numbers should not be self-repeating for any desired length.
4. The random numbers should be producible at very high speed.
5. The method should place minimal requirements on the memory of the computer.
6. Any sequence of random numbers obtained during a given simulation experiment should be reproducible.

The congruential method that we have just described is typical of the techniques used to generate random numbers and possesses all of the properties listed above.

In a practical sense, the important fact is that any modern computer system is preprogrammed to produce sequences of random numbers that possess-at least as all six close approximation of the desirable properties mentioned above. Typically, these numbers are produced by just calling an appropriately named function or subroutine in the computer repertoire (typical names for these mini programs include RAND, RANDU, etc.). All that is required of the programmer is to provide a seed to begin the sequence. The computer subsequently provides automatically the input (*i.e.*, the number x_{n-1} in the mixed congruential. method) needed to produce the next number, $x_{n,}$ in the sequence.

The random numbers produced through these preprogrammed methods are usually presented in the form of numbers uniformly distributed between 0.0 and 1.0. Obviously, the 0 to 1 interval is thus subdivided so finely that, for all practical purposes, it can be assumed that the computer produces statistically independent samples from the continuous uniform probability density function shown on figure 2.7. This, too, will be our assumption from here on, and we shall use the expression independent uniformly distributed over [0, 1] random numbers.

Classical uniform random number generators have some major defects, such as, short period length and lack of higher dimension uniformity. However, nowadays there is a class of rather complex generators, which is as efficient as the classical generators while enjoy the property of a much longer period and of higher dimension uniformity. Computer programs that generate random numbers use an algorithm. That means if you know the algorithm and the seed values you can predict what numbers will result. Because you can predict the numbers they are not truly random they are pseudorandom. For statistical purposes good pseudorandom numbers generators are good enough.

The following figure shows the graph of random variable x with the uniform probability density function over [0, 1].

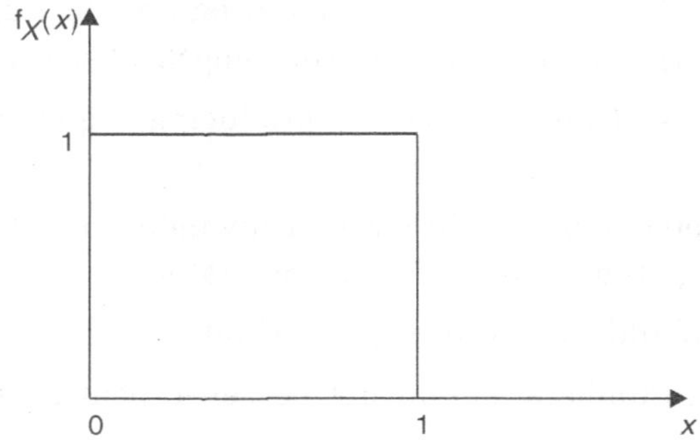

Fig. 2.7 The random variable X with the uniform PDF on [0,1]

real function random()

/* This program returns a pseudo-random numbers with rectangular distribution between 0 and 1. The cycle length is 6.95E+12. IX, IY and IZ should be set to integer values between 1 and 30000 before the first entry. Integer arithmetic up to 30323 is required. */

```
integer ix, iy, iz
     common /randc/ ix, iy, iz
     ix = 171 * mod(ix, 177) - 2 * (ix / 177)
     iy = 172 * mod(iy, 176) - 35 * (iy / 176)
     iz = 170 * mod(iz, 178) - 63 * (iz / 178)
     if (ix .lt. 0) ix = ix + 30269
     if (iy .lt. 0) iy = iy + 30307
     if (iz .lt. 0) iz = iz + 30323
```

/* If integer arithmetic up to 5212632 is available, the preceding 6 statements may be replaced by:

ix = mod(171 * ix, 30269)

iy = mod(172 * iy, 30307)

iz = mod(170 * iz, 30323) */

```
random = mod(float(ix) / 30269. + float(iy) / 30307. + float(iz)
/ 30323., 1.0)
return
end
real function uniform()
```

/*Generate uniformly distributed random numbers using the 32-bit generator. The cycle length is claimed to be 2.30584E+18 Seeds can be set by calling the routine set_uniform.

```
integer*4 z, k, s1, s2
common /unif_seeds/ s1, s2
save /unif_seeds/
k = s1 / 53668
s1 = 40014 * (s1 - k * 53668) - k * 12211

if (s1 .lt. 0) s1 = s1 + 2147483563
k = s2 / 52774
s2 = 40692 * (s2 - k * 52774) - k * 3791
if (s2 .lt. 0) s2 = s2 + 2147483399
z = s1 - s2
if (z .lt. 1) z = z + 2147483562
uniform = z / 2147483563.
return
end
subroutine set_uniform(seed1, seed2)
/* Setting of seeds for the uniform random number generator. */
integer*4 s1, s2, seed1, seed2
common /unif_seeds/ s1, s2
save /unif_seeds/
s1 = seed1
s2 = seed2
return
end
```

2.12.1 Generation of Uniformly Distributed Random Numbers

A FORTRAN code is given below for a generator of uniform random numbers on [0,1]. Given method is multiplicative linear congruential generator suitable for a 16-bit platform. It combines three simple generators. It is constructed for more efficient use by providing for a sequence of such numbers, LEN in total, to be returned in a single call. A set of three non-zero integer seeds can be supplied, failing which a default set is employed. If supplied, these three seeds, in order, should lie in the ranges [1,32362], [1,31726] and [1,31656] respectively.

/* This is the code for portable random number generator for 16-bit computer. It generates a sequence of LEN pseudo-random numbers, returned in variable RVEC. */

```
SUBROUTINE RANECU (RVEC, LEN)
DIMENSION RVEC(*)
SAVE ISEED1, ISEED2, ISEED3
```

```
        DATA ISEED1, ISEED2, ISEED3/1234, 5678, 9876/
/* Default values, used if none supplied via an ENTRY call at RECUIN */
        DO 100 I = 1, LEN
        K=ISEED1/206
        ISEED1 = 157 * (ISEED1 - K * 206) - K * 21
        IF(ISEED1.LT.0) ISEED1=ISEED1+32363
        K=ISEED2/217
        ISEED2 = 146 * (ISEED2 - K*217) - K* 45
        IF(ISEED2.LT.O) ISEED2=ISEED2+31727
        K=ISEED3/222
        ISEED3 = 142 * (ISEED3 - K *222) - K * 133
        IF(ISEED3.LT.0) ISEED3=ISEED3+31657
        IZ=ISEED1-ISEED2
        IF(IZ.GT.706)IZ = Z - 32362
        IZ = 1Z+ISEED3
        IF(IZ.LT.1)IZ = 1Z + 32362
        RVEC(I)=REAL(IZ) * 3.0899E - 5
100 CONTINUE
        RETURN
        ENTRY RECUIN(IS1, IS2, IS3)
        ISEED1=IS1
        ISEED2=IS2
        ISEED3=IS3
        RETURN
        ENTRY RECUUT(IS1,IS2,IS3)
        IS1=ISEED1
        IS2=ISEED2
        IS3=ISEED3
        RETURN
        END
```

2.12.2 Generation of Non-uniformly Distributed Random Numbers

So far we have seen how we can use random number generators to produce numbers in uniform distributions, either discrete, or continuous. However, given a uniform distribution of random numbers in the range [0, 1], we can use easily use this as starting point for more complicated distributions. There are two approaches to generating other distributions, analytical and numeric, using the von Neumanm method.

Analytical Inversion Method. We want to produce random numbers which are distributed according to some arbitrary probability function $f(x)$. In order to be a reasonable probability function, we must have

$$f(x) > 0 \text{ for all } x, \frac{n}{N} = \int_0^{\pi/2} \frac{f(x)dx}{Area\,of\ rect.\ angle\ ABCD} = \int_0^{\pi/2} \frac{f(x)dx}{1\times 1} = \int_0^{\pi/2} f(x)dx \quad ...(2.2)$$

and $$\int_{-\infty}^{\infty} f(x)dx = 1 \quad ...(2.3)$$

We define the cumulative distribution function:

$$F(x) = \int_{-\infty}^{\infty} f(t)dt \text{ and its inverse function } F^{-1}(y) \text{ i.e., } y = F(x) \leftrightarrow x = F^{-1}(y) \quad ...(2.4)$$

The analytical inversing method uses F^{-1} (y). If we have a random number, u, generated from a uniform distribution [0, 1], we can transform it to a random number, in the $f(x)$ distribution by calculating $x = F^{-1}(u)$.

This algorithm is simple, but it requires us to calculate the inverse function of the integral of the function we want, which may not be possible analytically. To show how this works in practice, suppose we want random numbers from an exponential decay function. This would be required if, for example, we were modeling radioactive decays.

The exponential decay probability function is given by:

$$\begin{aligned} f(t) &= \frac{1}{\tau} e^{-t/\tau} \quad for\ x \geq 1 \\ &= 0 \qquad otherwise \end{aligned} \quad ...(2.5)$$

where τ is the average lifetime.

Now we may calculate:

$$F(x) = \int_0^x f(t)dt = \int_0^x \frac{1}{\tau} 1 - e^{-t/\tau} = 1 - e^{-t/\tau} \quad ...(2.6)$$

We can then find the inverse function:

$$u = F(x) = 1 - e^{-x/\tau} \rightarrow x = F^{-1}(u) = -\tau \log(1-u) \quad ...(2.7)$$

But because u is a random number in the range [0, 1], so is $1\text{-}u$ so this reduces to

$$x = F^{-1}(u) = -\tau \log(u) \quad ...(2.8)$$

Some other common random number functions may also be generated using the using analytically derived formulae.

Von Neumann's acceptance-rejection Method. Von Neumann's method is a numerical method which allows random number distributions from any finite interval to be generated.

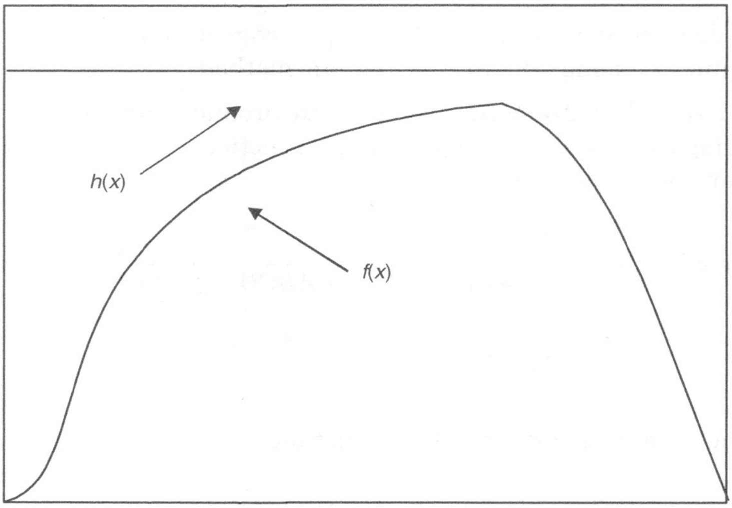

Fig. 2.8 Curve for Von Neumann's method

Assuming the required distribution $f(x)$ is known over some range $[a, b]$ and that one can find a second constant function $h(x) = m$ (parallel line to x axis) such that $M > f(x)$ over the whole range. Then one can generate the distribution of random numbers in the $f(x)$ distribution using the following steps:

(1) Generate a random number, u, from a uniform distribution in the range $[a, b]$

(2) Generate a random number, v, from a uniform distribution in the range $[0, M]$

(3) If $v < f(u)$ we have a *hit* and we accept the random number u else we have a *miss* and we reject the number and go back to step 1.

For example, to generate a random values of in the range of 0 to 5 with a probability distribution of $f(x) = x^2$

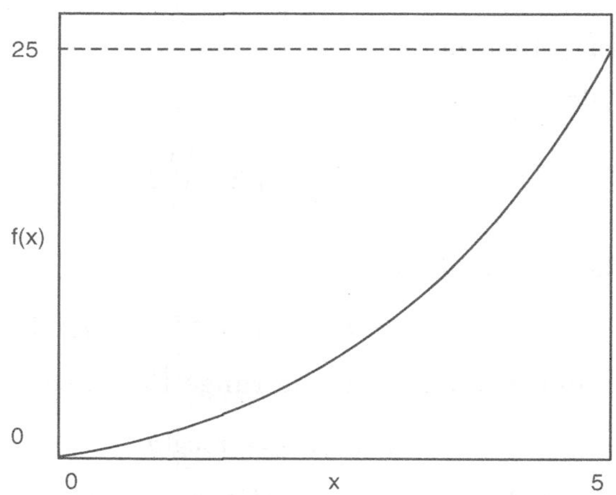

Fig. 2.9 Probability distribution of $f(x) = x^2$

Using Von Neumann's Method we can generate a single random number using a do-while-loop in C language:

```
do {
x = 5.0 * (double)rand()/RAND_MAX ;
prob = 25.0*(double)rand()/RAND_MAX;
        }
while ( prob > x*x );
```

Here we first generate a value of x from a *uniform* distribution. Then a second random number from [0, 25] is used to accept or reject an event, by comparing this probability with the value of x^2.

2.13 MONTE CARLO SIMULATION

Monte Carlo simulation allows using the most convenient distributions to communicate opinions about the randomness in measurements. For example, a measurement process employing N repetitions of a measurement can be handled explicitly as repeated measurements drawn from a Gaussian, or as a single value drawn from a shifted and scaled Student-t distribution. The former approach may facilitate communication with those who are unfamiliar with the proper use of student distributions and who would not really understand the latter approach. The process of Monte Carlo simulation circumvents many complexities of the combination of uncertainty distributions, and only requires combination of the values from the simulated measurements.

It is a simulation in which random statistical sampling techniques are employed such that the result determines estimates for unknown values. Monte Carlo computation (method or technique) was originated during World War II by Ulam and Von Neumann at the Los Alamos Scientific Laboratory. When this approach was applied to problems related to the development of the atomic bombs. In order to design nuclear shields, it was required to know how far neutrons would travel through various materials. The problem was:

(*a*) Too difficult to solve analytically.

(*b*) Too hazardous.

(*c*) Too time consuming to solve experimentally.

Due to above reasons, the experiment was simulated on high-speed computer using random numbers. This technique was called *Monte Carlo technique* based on a gambling-like principle.

Monte Carlo applications are sometimes classified as being simulation and vice versa, presumably because so many simulations involve use of random numbers. Simulation and Monte Carlo are both numerical computational techniques. Simulation applies to dynamic models whereas Monte Carlo technique applies to static models.

Deterministic Problems through Random Numbers

Consider a quadrant of a unit circle (see figure 2.10).

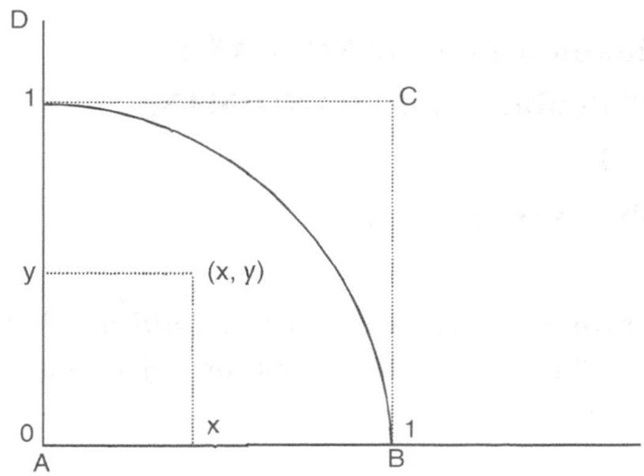

Fig. 2.10 Monte Carlo Evaluation of π

All the points satisfying the equation (2.9) lies in this quadrant

$$x^2 + y^2 \leq 1 \text{ where } x, y \geq 0 \qquad ...(2.9)$$

Equation (2.9) can be rewritten as

...(2.10)

On generating a pair of uniform random number r_1 and r_2 and in the range (0, 1). The pair (r_1, r_2) is acceptable if equation (2.3) becomes else the pair is rejected. Another pair of uniform random number is generated and tested. Clearly, the entire rejected points lie above the curve and those accepted pair lie below the curve.

$$r_2 \leq \sqrt{1 - r_1^2} \qquad ...(2.11)$$

If we generate a large number of random pairs (N) and compute the ratio of the number of pairs accepted (n) to those generated, and if N points are used and n of them fall under the curve, than approximately

$$\frac{n}{N} = \int_0^{\pi/2} \frac{f(x)dx}{Area\ of\ rectangle\ ABCD} = \int_0^{\pi/2} \frac{f(x)dx}{1 \times 1} = \int_0^{\pi/2} f(x)dx \qquad ...(2.12)$$

The accuracy improves as the number N increase limit 0 to $\pi/2$ as curve is starting from x-axis and ending at y-axis. When it is decided that sufficient points have been taken, the value of the integral is estimated by multiplying $\frac{n}{N}$ by the area of rectangle ABCD. The ratio will approach the area under the curve, which is $\pi/4$. Thus by using random number a completely deterministic problem is solved, called Monte Carlo technique. In this example area under the curve was evaluated through rejection technique.

2.13.1 Monte Carlo Methods

The random number generator picks a new random number every time it is called. The numbers are not really random. Actually the numbers are determined by some rule one after another, but they have good statistical properties and can be used for integration and to simulate randomness. The numbers are uniformly distributed integers that fall between *0* and *RAND_MAX* which is 2147483648 in this system. To get a random number that is uniformly distributed between zero and one, we compute

```
double x;
 . . .
x = rand () / 2147483648.0;
```

Program to compute Pi. Here we use the Monte Carlo method to compute the area of the part inside the unit circle relative to the area of the unit square. The value of π is four times this fraction.

```
/* Monte Carlo Pi montecarlopi.c */
# include <stdio.h>
# include <stdlib.h>
# include <math.h>
# include <time.h>
int main ( void )
{
    double x, y, p, s=0.0,  ranmaxpo;
    int i, j, k, n = 1000000;
    ranmaxpo = 1.0 + RAND_MAX;

    srand ( (unsigned int)time ( NULL ) );      /* seed for rand is time */
    printf ( "  n\t\t\t\tMonte Carlo Pi MCP - pi\n" );
    for ( k=1; k<= 10; k++ )
    {
        j=0;
        for ( i=1; i <= n; i=i+1 )
        {
            x = rand () / ranmaxpo;
            y = rand () / ranmaxpo;
            if ( x * x  +  y * y  <= 1 )
                    j++;
        }
        p = 4.0 * j / n;
```

```
        s = s + p;
        printf ( "%4d The approximate for pi is %21.15f %21.15f\n", k, p, p-M_PI);
      }
      p = s / 10.0;
        printf ( " Average approximate for pi is %21.15f %21.15f\n", p,
p-M_PI );
      printf ( " pi = %21.15f \n", M_PI );
      return EXIT_SUCCESS;
}
```

Monte-Carlo method for calculating pi

```
/* Source code montecarlo.c */
#include <stdio.h>
#include <stdlib.h>
#define RANDOM_MAX 2147483648
int main() {
    int i=0, j=0;
    float x, y;
    while(1) {
      x = (double)random()/(double)RANDOM_MAX;
      y = (double)random()/(double)RANDOM_MAX;
    if ((x*x + y*y) < 1)
       j++;
    i++;
   if (i%1000000 == 1)
   printf("%f\n",4*(float)j/(float)i);
   }
}
```

Monte Carlo Method for the integral of *f(x)*. Here is a program that uses the Monte Carlo method to compute the integral of a function. We compute the area that is both under the curve $0 \leq y \leq f(x)$ and in the box $a \leq x \leq b$ and $0 \leq y \leq c$.

/* For Monte Carlo integral, we assume that the function is given between a <= x <= b We compute the area of the { (x,y) : a <= x <= b and 0 <= y <= min(c,f(x)) } by counting the relative number of random points in the rectangle [a,b]x[0,c] that fall in the set. mo_ca_int.c */

```
# include <stdio.h>
# include <stdlib.h>
# include <math.h>
double f( double x );
int main ( void )
{
    double a, b, c, d, x, y, p, q, r, sum=0.0, ans, ranmaxpo;
    int i, j, k, m=15, n=2000000;
    ranmaxpo = 1.0 + RAND_MAX;
    printf ( " Enter the left, right and upper bounds : ");
    scanf ( "%lf %lf %lf", &a, &b, &c );
    a = fabs ( a );
    b = fabs ( b );
    c = fabs ( c );
    if ( b < a )
    {
            d = a;
            a = b;
            c = d;
     }
     printf ( "\n Monte Carlo Integration of min(f(x),%f) over %f <= x <= %f\n", c,
a, b);

     d = pow( c, 1.0 / 3.0 );
     if ( d >= b)
         ans = ( b * b  +  a * a) * ( b * b  -  a * a ) / 4.0;
     else if ( d <= a )
     {
         ans = c * ( b  -  a );
      printf(" Note that here  f(x) > %f  for  %f < x <= %f\n", c, a, b );
     }
     else
     {
      ans = ( d * d + a * a ) * ( d * d - a * a ) / 4.0 + ( b - d ) * c;
      printf(" Note that  here f(x) > %f  for  %f < x <= %f\n", c, d, b );
```

```
    }
    printf( "\n\t n\t Approximate the integral\t\tError\n");
    for(k=1;k<= m; k++)
    {
    j = 0;
    q = c / ranmaxpo;
    r = ( b  -  a ) / ranmaxpo;
        for ( i = 1; i <= n; i = i+1 )
        {
        x = a  +  r * rand ();
        y = q * rand ();
        if ( f(x) > y  )
               j++;
        }
    p = ( b  -  a ) * c * j / n;
    printf ( "%12d%22.15f%22.15f\n", k, p, p  -  ans );
    sum = sum  +  p;
   }
   p = sum / m;
   printf ( "Average int =%21.15f%22.15f\n", p, ans  -  p );
   printf ( "Actual int = %21.15f", ans );
   printf ( " Number of points is %ld\n", (long int)n * (long int)m );
   return EXIT_SUCCESS;
}
double f( double x )
{
       return  x * x * x;
}
```

2.13.2 Random Number Generation through Hill-Wichmann Algorithm

The source code for implementing the Hill-Wichmann algorithm is given below, with comments (indicated by " ' ") for explanation. This is a very short and powerful algorithm which relies on integer arithmetic to generate a very long stream (6.95E+12) of pseudo-random numbers uniformly distributed in the interval between 0 and 1.

```
Public Static Function randHW() As Double
' User VBA function implements the Hill-Wichmann random number generator
' Pseudo-Random Number Generator.
' C IX, IY, IZ SHOULD BE SET TO INTEGER VALUES BETWEEN 1 AND 30000
' C BEFORE FIRST ENTRY (THIS IS THE 'SEEDING' PROCEDURE)
' IX = MOD(171 * IX, 30269)
' IY = MOD(172 * IY, 30307)
' IZ = MOD(170 * IZ, 30323)
' RANDOM = AMOD(FLOAT(IX)/30269# + FLOAT(IY)/30307# + FLOAT(IZ)/30323#, 1#)
'Note: the FORTRAN function AMOD(A,P) = A - (INT(A / P) * P)
' VBA Mod function rounds non-integer values of A,P FIRST, so this cannot be
  used in the last line.
Dim ix As Long, iy As Long, iz As Long
Dim sx As Single, sy As Single, sz As Single
Dim sum As Single
Dim seeded As Boolean 'initialized to 'False'
If seeded = False Then
ix = 123 ' use fixed initial seeds
iy = 234
iz = 345
' iz = CLng(30000.*Time + 1.) ' use random seed (1 <= iz <= 30001)
' based on the current time
seeded = True ' don't re-seed every time!
End If
' the guts of the linear congruential algorithm is only three lines long
ix = 171 * ix Mod 30269
iy = 172 * iy Mod 30307
iz = 170 * iz Mod 30323
' convert the integer values to single precision reals for arithmetic
sx = CSng(ix) / 30269! ' ! ensures denominator is single precision real
sy = CSng(iy) / 30307!
sz = CSng(iz) / 30323!
sum = sx + sy + sz
' take the fractional part of the sum as the random number
randHW = sum - Int(sum)
' some cleaning here to be sure we stay 'inside the lines'
```

```
If randHW <= 0# Then randHW = 0.0000003
If randHW >= 1# Then randHW = 1# - 0.0000003
End Function
```

Another common method for generating high-quality random numbers drawn from a standard Gaussian relies on a simple mathematical transformation originally conceived by Box and Muller. Below is a VBA function that uses the Box-Muller method to transform uniformly distributed random numbers on the interval (0,1), created using the Hill-Wichmann algorithm discussed above and shown, into random numbers drawn from a standard Gaussian distribution, centered on zero and with unit standard deviation.

```
Public Function randBM()
' User function to transform uniform random numbers from randHW (x,y)
' into standard normal variates (r1, r2) using the Box-Muller transformation
Dim x As Double, y As Double, s As Double, r1 As Double, r2 As Double
Const TWO_PI As Double = 2# * 3.14159265358979
x = randHW() ' generate two uniform random numbers, x and y
y = randHW()
s = Sqr(-2# * Log(x)) ' transform to normal random numbers, r1 and r2
r1 = s * Cos(TWO_PI * y)
r2 = s * Sin(TWO_PI * y)
randBM = r1 ' return the cosine term; throw away the sine term
End Function
```

2.14 PENDULUM SIMULATION

2.14.1 Mathematical Presentation

The pendulum is modeled as a point mass at the end of a massless rod. We define the following variables:

- θ = angle of pendulum (0=vertical)
- R = length of rod
- T = tension in rod
- m = mass of pendulum
- g = gravitational constant.

We will derive the equation of motion for the pendulum using the rotational analog of Newton's second law for motion about a fixed axis, which is $\tau = I\alpha$ where

- τ = net torque
- I = rotational inertia
- $\alpha = \theta''$ = angular acceleration.

The rotational inertia about the pivot is $I = mR^2$. Torque can be calculated as the vector cross product of the position vector and the force. The magnitude of the torque due to gravity works out to be $\tau = -Rmg\sin\theta$. So we have $-R\, mg\sin\theta = mR^2\,\alpha$ which simplifies to

$$\theta'' = -\,{}^{g}/_{R}\,\sin\theta$$

This is the equation of motion for the pendulum.

C Language Implementation

```
/* pendulum.c Mimic ODE simulation for the one link pendulum */

#include <stdio.h>
#include <math.h>

#define LENGTH (1.0f)   // length of pendulum
#define WIDTH (0.1f)    // width of pendulum
#define MASS (1.0f)     // mass of link
#define G (9.81f)
#define TIMESTEP 0.01

/* Score parameters */
#define VISCOUS_FRICTION 0.1
#define STATE_PENALTY 0.1

/* servo gains */
double k = 5.0;
double b = 1.0;

// moment of inertia of pendulum around joint.
double I_joint = MASS*(LENGTH*LENGTH + WIDTH*WIDTH)/12 +
MASS*LENGTH*LENGTH/4;
double time = 0.0; // keep track of how much time has passed.
double score = 0; // keep track of the score so far.
FILE *data_file = NULL;

main()
{
  double angle_desired = M_PI;
  double angle = 0;
```

```
    double angular_velocity = 0;
    double new_angular_velocity = 0;
    double angular_acceleration = 0;
    double torque = 0;
    double total_torque = 0;
    double score = 0;
    int count = 0;

    data_file = fopen( "data", "w" );
    if ( data_file == NULL )
      {
        fprintf( stderr, "Cannot open data file.\n" );
        exit( -1 );
      }

  for( ; ; )
      {
        torque = -k*( angle - angle_desired ) - b*angular_velocity;
        total_torque = torque - VISCOUS_FRICTION*angular_velocity
  - MASS*G*LENGTH*0.5*sin(angle);
        angular_acceleration = total_torque/I_joint;
       new_angular_velocity = angular_velocity + angular_acceleration* TIMESTEP;
        angle += (new_angular_velocity + angular_velocity)*TIMESTEP/2;
        angular_velocity = new_angular_velocity;
        time += TIMESTEP;
        score += torque*torque*TIMESTEP + STATE_PENALTY*TIMESTEP* (angle -
angle_desired)* (angle - angle_desired);

        if ( time < 3.0 )
  {
    fprintf( data_file, "%g %g %g %g %g\n", time, angle, angular_velocity, torque, score );
  }
        else
```

```
{
                fclose( data_file );
                        exit( -1 );
}

    // Printing output data
    count++;
    if ( (count % 100) == 0 )
                                {
  printf( "%g %g %g %g %g\n", time, angle, angular_velocity, torque, score );
        }
    }
}
```

2.15 DISTRIBUTED LAG MODELS

When the model is large or more complex then the record keeping becomes troublesome. Then it becomes important, the use of computer and a suitable programming language for simulation. There are some applications of simulation, which are using simple techniques but can be applied without difficulty, even for large models. If all the events occur synchronously, at fixed intervals of time, then the computation remains simple. Distributed lag models are the models which have the following properties:

(*a*) Changing only at fixed intervals of time.

(*b*) Basing current values of the variables on other current values and values that occurred in previous intervals.

These are used extensively in econometric studies where the uniform steps correspond to a time interval, such as a month or a year, over which some economic data are collected. These models consist of linear, algebraic equations. They represent a continuous system, but one in which the data in only available at fixed points in time.

Any variable that appears in the form of the current value and one or more previous intervals is called *lagged variable*. Its value in the previous interval in denoted by attaching the suffix-n to the variable, where n indicates the interval. 1 denotes the previous interval, 2 denotes the one prior to that and so on.

In distributed lag model an initial set of values is given for all variables and values of the variables at the end of one interval can be derived. Taking these values as the new values of the lagged variables, the values can be derived at the end of second interval and so on. Distributed log models are conceptually simple and they can be computed by hand or run extensively on computers. The value of computers is its more conventional data-processing capability.

2.16 COBWEB MODELS

The cobweb model explains why prices in certain markets are subject to periodical fluctuations. It is an economic model of cyclic supply and demand in which there is a lag between responses of producers to a change of price. The basic model of supply and demand, the price adjusts so that quantity supplied and the quantities demanded are equal. The precise mechanism that achieves this equilibrium is not always unambiguous.

The cobweb model shows how achieving supply and demand equilibrium might be so automatic if, as seems reasonable the supplier's set the price and the consumer react with a quantity demanded. For some scopes of the demand and supply changes, the equilibrium can be unstable. The *cobweb model* is a classical demonstration that dynamic behavior by economic agents might not converge to a stable equilibrium with supply equal to demand. This application provides two ways to graph the outcome and let you experiment with the key parameter that determines whether the outcome is stable or not.

The cycle continues to repeat in one of three ways, if the slopes when drawn so that supply was steeper than demand (on price axis), the fluctuation would get wider and wider and fluctuations may become more and more drastic and so a plot of the equilibriums in each period overtime would look like an outward spiral (divergent). Alternatively, fluctuation may become less and less drastic and so a plot of the equilibrium in each period overtime would look like an inward spiral (convergent). Fluctuations may also remain constant (stable), and so a plot of equilibriums would produce a simple, this scenario is unlikely in the short to medium term. In either of the first two scenarios, the combination of the spiral and the supply and demand curves often look like a cobweb hence the name of the theory.

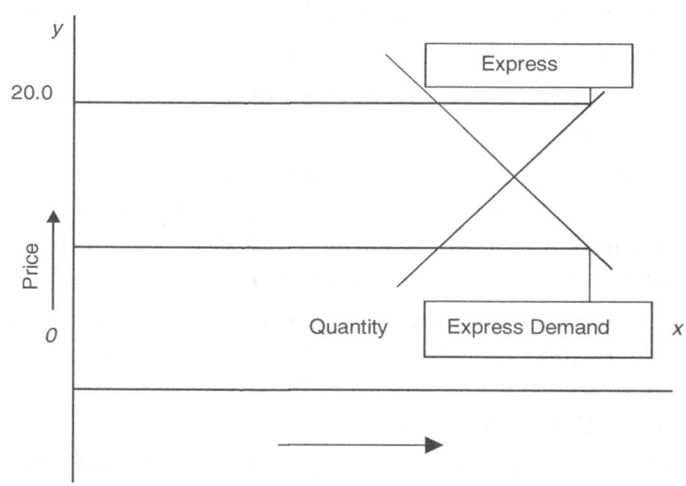

Fig. 2.11 Supply and Demand Curve

The inventory-based price model relaxes the assumption that supply must be equal to demand to consider how maintaining an inventory might moderate the possible instability. For example, Retail stores, very often buy an inventory, set a price, and then wait to see what demand might be.

The inventory base-pricing model illustrates that the cobweb might or might not be a realistic challenge to supply and demand equilibrium. Introducing an inventory buffering the difference between supply and demand and letting prices respond to the level of inventory can be sufficient to eliminate the instability observed for the basic cobweb model. There are two ways to present the cobweb models:

(*a*) **The Traditional Cobweb Model:** This shows the cobweb by alternating between supply and demand.

(*b*) **The Simultaneous Cobweb Model:** This determines supply and demand jointly.

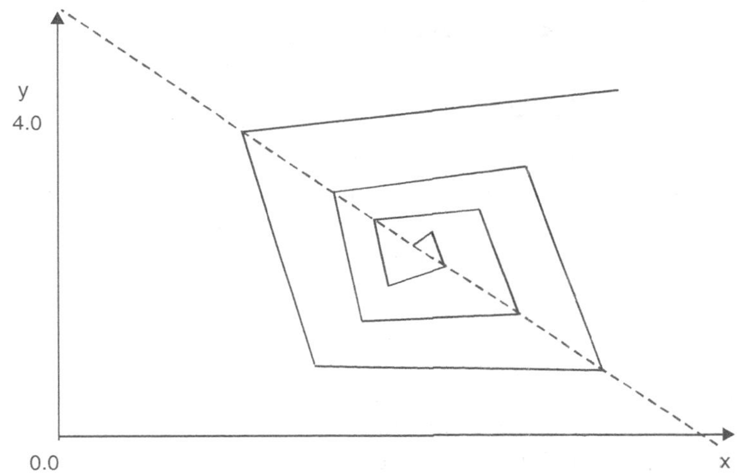

Fig. 2.12 Cobweb of Supply and Demand

One criticism of this model is its assumption that producers are extremely short sighted, they are fundamentally unable to judge market conditions of learn from their pricing mistakes that results in surplus or shortfall cycles. This assumption is seen to be unrealistic.

2.17 OVERVIEW OF MODEL EXECUTION

(1) Experiments, Replications, and Runs. A simulation project is composed of experiments. Experiments are differentiated by the use of alternatives in a model's logic and/or data. An alternate part sequencing rule might be tried, for example, or the quantity of various machines might be varied.

Each experiment consists of one or more replications (trials). A replication is a simulation that uses the experiment's model logic and data but a different set of random numbers, and so produces different statistical results that can then be analyzed across a set of replications. A replication involves initializing the model, running it until a run-ending condition is met, and reporting results. This "running it" phase is called a run.

(2) Inside a Run. During a run the simulation clock (an internally managed, stored data value) tracks the passage of *simulated* time (as distinct from *wall-clock* time). The clock advances in discrete steps (typically of unequal size) during the run. After all possible actions have been taken at a given simulated time; the clock is advanced to the time of the next earliest event. Then the appropriate actions are carried out at this new simulated time, etc.

The execution of a run thus takes the form of a two-phase loop: "carry out all possible actions at the current simulated time," followed by "advance the simulated clock," repeated over and over again until a run-ending condition comes about. The two phases are here respectively called the Entity Movement Phase (EMP) and the Clock Update Phase.

2.18 APPLICATION AREAS OF SIMULATION

2.18.1 Simulation in Healthcare

Simulation is an extremely useful tool for modeling uncertainty, which is a major characteristic of illness and, hence, makes simulation so attractive for modeling healthcare systems. In addition, simulation enables the modeling of complex systems with lots of interacting parts, which is another common feature of healthcare systems. Given the many potential applications of simulation in healthcare, it might be useful to categorize these applications, to help identify the problems amenable to solution by simulation. Healthcare applications tend to fall into two major categories: (1) "analytic" decisions with uncertain components; and (2) comparison of alternative systems for determining resource or scheduling requirements. To focus the discussion of these two types of applications, certain types of simulation models are excluded. The categorization includes stochastic simulation models and excludes deterministic models. Stochastic models contain probabilistic (*i.e.*, random) components, while deterministic models do not. Only stochastic models are included in this discussion, because these types of models generally provide more accurate and informative representations of healthcare systems, given the random nature of illness and its response to treatment. However, the term "simulation" in the broadest sense refers to the operation of a model of a system, and there are many mathematical models of systems that do not include stochastic components. Therefore, readers will see many articles in the healthcare literature in which the term "simulation" is used when it refers to a deterministic model. The categorization also excludes applications for which continuous simulation is used. This type of simulation involves modeling of a system in which the input variables change continuously with respect to time, and these changes are typically defined by differential equations. Continuous simulation is frequently used for modeling biological processes and pharmacokinetic applications, but has also been used for epidemiologic models of disease progression. Continuous simulation models are not included here, since the focus of the discussion is on the application of simulation for improving the organization and delivery of care.

The simulation steps play an important role in a simulation study. The major steps include: (1) problem formulation; (2) setting of objectives and overall project plan; (3) model building; (4) data collection; (5) coding; (6) verification; (7) validation; (8) experimental design; (9) production runs and analysis; (10) repeat of step (9) if necessary; (11) documentation of program and reporting of results; and (12) implementation of proposed system. (Steps

3 and 4 take place concurrently.) The following paragraphs present recommendations for accomplishing some of these steps when developing simulation models. The recommendations are probably applicable to all types of simulation models, not just those in healthcare; but they are based on experience with healthcare projects.

2.18.2 Simulation in Airport Design

Airport design is, by far, the largest practice area for Transsolutions. This is a unique area, with many differences from typical simulation in manufacturing or logistics. Passengers and bags arrive at the airport by the planeload. At the busiest airports the arrivals and departures are coordinated, so that several flights arrive within a short time. Then, after a short time on the ground the aircraft all depart again. A large number of passengers move through the facility during the peak period between the flight arrivals and the departures. After that, the facility will be empty until the next bank of arriving flights. The terminal facilities must be sized to handle these waves of passengers throughout the day. Space within the terminal building is at a premium. Most travelers are aware of the ticket counters, gate lounges, corridors and shops in the public areas. Hidden behind the scenes are the various offices, control rooms, and break areas for the airport and airline employees. The baggage system and various maintenance functions take up most of the space on the ramp level below the passenger areas. The usual question asked by the architects is: "will the facility, as designed, satisfy the needs of the tenant airlines?" This involves comparing the "performance" of the facility to minimum acceptable standards. A typical example is that all passengers connecting from an arriving flight to a departing flight must be able to reach their departure gate within 30 minutes of arrival. Another example all baggage must be delivered to the claim area within 20 minutes of the flight arrival. There may be many other performance requirements, depending on the size and scope of the project.

Airspace/Airfield Capacity. Aircraft are required to maintain separation between other aircraft. As aircraft approach an airport they are funneled closer together with many routes converging into common links. Simulation is useful to evaluate the capacity of the link node network and to evaluate alternative link node structures that could improve capacity. Additionally, ground movements of aircraft represent another link node network. Arriving aircraft move from runways to taxiways to taxi-lanes and eventually to their gates. Aircraft may need to hold on the airfield before reaching to their gate due to general ramp congestion or due to gate unavailability. Departing aircraft follow the reverse process and also usually wait in a departure queue before accessing the runway for take-off. The movement of the aircraft must be carefully planned since many taxi-lanes and taxiways are bidirectional and can only accommodate aircraft movement in one direction at a time. Additionally, aircraft need to be able to stop or park at designated areas on the airfield so that they do not impede the movements of other aircraft. Simulation is frequently used in airfield analyses to determine the benefit (capacity improvements or delay reduction) of adding new runways, taxiways, and taxi-lanes, as well as evaluating how alternative gate allocation strategies impact airfield capacity.

Ramp Operations. Ramp operations are generally much more complicated than most people realize. There are many different functions working in coordination with each other to ensure the efficient utilization of aircraft. Services performed on aircraft include fueling, catering, lavatory cleaning, baggage loading and unloading, cargo loading and unloading. The vehicles performing these services all compete for usage of the same roadways.

Cargo Handling. Airports are large centers for cargo distribution. In addition to planning the pick-up and deliver goods from aircraft, most large airports have main cargo buildings where cargo sortation is performed.

Baggage Handling. Each airline and airport must be able to get a passengers' bag from either the curb or the Airport Ticket Office (ATO) to the departing aircraft. At smaller airports, bag handling is often performed manually, after a bag is delivered to the ramp side of the terminal via a conveyor belt. Larger airports utilize very complex sortation systems to route bags to specific piers or circulating make-up devices. A bag system may also incorporate security screening, early bag storage, and manual encode stations (to identify and manually re-direct bags with missing or unreadable bag tags.) The bag system must ensure that all bags handled throughout the airport can be delivered to their destination gates in time to reach the departing flight. Three technologies dominate airline baggage handling today: conventional conveyor, tilt-tray, and automated guided vehicles.

Passenger Flow. Passenger flow is described in three component sections: general circulation, automated people mover systems, and Federal Inspection Services.

General Circulation. Airport facilities should ensure that passengers experience an acceptable level of service while in the facility. This includes factors such as not having to wait too long in queue at a ticket counter or gate, not having to walk extremely long distances in the terminal, not being crammed into elevators, hallways, or waiting areas where there is little or no ability to circulate. Most importantly all passengers should be able to comfortably reach their gate by either walking or using a moving walkway or airport train. Simulation is frequently used to predict passenger connection times, to determine expected occupancy levels at various locations throughout an airport terminal, or to determine how long passengers will wait at various points throughout the terminal.

Automated People Mover Systems. Most large airports have a light rail system that will connect passengers between terminal buildings. For these systems additional design issues must be considered such as transport time, capacity and station location.

Federal Inspection Services. Passengers arriving to an airport coming from a destination outside of the US and its territories are required to be screened through Immigration, US Customs, and US Agriculture. These facilities must also be properly sized to ensure that all of the passengers using the facility are processed in time to meet connecting flights.

Problem Identification. The first step in any study is to determine a few basic requirements: the system to be studied, the objective of the study, and the timeline for the results. This is never as straightforward as it seems. In some cases the problem identification takes place before a notice to proceed has been given.

Data Collection/Data Analysis/Assumptions Development. Large-scale simulations require a lot of data. Invariably, the information gathering for the model is the longest part of the project. It is typical for the data collection and analysis to take one third to one half of the total project, even more time than the model development. In some cases the required information is readily available, in some form, from existing records provided by the client. The analyst must make the decision whether the available data is sufficient or whether field observations will be necessary. Other parameters may be taken from standard references.

Simulation Design, Development, and Validation. This is probably the most straightforward step in the study. It may be technically challenging, but it is the one step that is probably the easiest to control. Design generally does not start until after the assumptions document has been completed. In reality, there is almost always down during the data collection phase when we start designing the model. There is a risk associated with doing this since anything developed prior to the client acceptance of the assumptions document may be wasted if the assumptions are changed or amended.

Initial Experimentation. Initially, there is need to run some experiment. The initial design of the model generally reflects the baseline scenario. Baseline results should be generated and validated. Project timeline pressures invariably influence or limit the number of replications that can be made.

2.18.3 Validation

Validation is the process off ensuring that the model (with some degree of confidence) represents the true system. Two types of validation are commonly used:

1. If the process being studied already exists, and historical performance data is available, then statistical methods should be used. In most cases simple hypothesis testing techniques can be used to perform the validation.
2. If the process is currently not already in operation then a "Face Validation" needs to be performed. "Face Validation" is the process of reviewing results by experts to determine the reasonableness of the results.

Analysis of Results. After all of the experiments be sure to carefully analyze all of the results. The results from one experiment usually help you determine if other scenarios should also be evaluated.

Develop Report and Present Results. There are many references for the various statistical methods used in the analysis. It is important to provide the results to the client in a format that they will understand. As a general rule architects like information graphically while operations people are more comfortable with numbers in tables. Two types of reports are frequently generated: An Executive Summary (which just focuses on the major results), and a comprehensive summary of the findings from all of the experiments performed. Simulation is not particularly good at providing this type of information, so the analyst should learn to track the results to determine the causes. A statement that the worst case delivery time is 45 minutes is not very informative. Stating that this was caused by the simultaneous unloading of four aircraft on two adjacent belts is much stronger. This second statement explains the unexpected result and suggests possible corrections. Extreme results without explanation are more likely to generate suspicion of the model than of the system being studied. The simulation results represent one of these, operational performance. Cost and projected timeline are other quantifiable factors.

Less quantifiable factors, such as confidence in the supplier, are also considerations. It is rarely necessary to determine whether one alternative is statistically better than another is when the simulation analysis shows that two alternatives are close.

2.19 OTHER APPLICATION AREAS

Following are the other major areas where continuous and discrete simulations are widely used:

- Design and performance evaluation of computer systems—Determining hardware requirements or protocols for communications networks, Studying CPU Scheduling algorithms, Evaluation of Web caching policies.
- Design and analysis of manufacturing systems—Operation of a production line.
- Evaluating designs for service organizations—Study call centers, fast food restaurants, hospitals, and post offices.
- Evaluating military weapons systems or their logistics requirements.
- Designing and operating transportation systems such as airports, freeways, ports, and subways.
- Analyzing financial or economic systems.
- Manufacturing applications.

SUMMARY

A large volume of literature on the theory and success stories has been built-up on this subject during the past decade. On the other hand, it is known from work on numerical analysis, that numerical methods can introduce instabilities that greatly magnify errors even if the underlying models are stable. To obviate error-induced instabilities, criteria that enable choice of time-step size and other controllable factors are well-known for non-distributed simulations. However, the major difference between distributed simulations and their non-distributed counterparts is that control and data are encoded in time stamped messages that travel from one computer to another over a (bandwidth limited) network. Traditional analyses in the design of numerical methods consider trade-offs between accuracy and speed of computation. However, since distributed messaging requires that continuous quantities be coded into discrete packets and sent discontinuously, it is more appropriate to consider discrete event simulation as a natural means to consider accuracy or bandwidth trade-offs. Recent work has shown that significant reductions of message bandwidth demands (number and size of messages) with controllable error and local computation costs are possible. Finally, the issue of numerical stability in complex simulation is related to the problem of sample path continuity with respect to parameter and timing perturbation.

Modeling Simulation and Optimization (MSO) is mature enough to play an important role in the Product Development Process (PDP) in industry. MSO keeps its role as a tool for analysis but can be much more important for synthesis especially in the preliminary design phase. Thus MSO changes the way engineering is performed and where engineers become more involved in the synthesis phase.

In most cases of simulation optimization, we only need to know the order or be able to locate the top one percent of the design. It is not necessary to know the performance value accurately. Approximate simulation models are quite adequate for the former purpose. Once the top one percent has been located with high probability, we can abundant our attention and computing budget on this much smaller subset.

EXERCISE QUESTIONS

1. Why do we go for simulation? Why is simulation important?
2. When do we use simulations? What must we know before simulation?
3. Explain the benefits and pitfalls in simulations.
4. Explain the differences between simulation and analytical methods.
5. Explain the basic nature of simulation.
6. What are important types of system simulation? Explain continuous system simulation.
7. Write short notes on
   (*i*) Discrete System Simulation
   (*ii*) Hybrid Simulation
   (*iii*) Real-time Simulation
   (*iv*) Object-oriented Simulation
   (*v*) Social Simulation
   (*vi*) On-line Simulation
8. Explain web-based simulation and distributed simulation in detail.
9. What do you mean by random numbers? What is the importance of random numbers? Write a high level language program to generate random numbers.
10. Explain the Monte-Carlo method for generating random numbers.
11. Explain the generation of uniformly distributed random numbers.
12. Explain the purpose of generation of non-uniformly distributed random numbers.
13. How random numbers can be used in deterministic problems?
14. Explain the distributed lag models in detail with the help of suitable diagram.
15. Explain cobweb models. In what types of simulation applications it can be used?
16. Explain application areas of system simulation. How simulation can be used in airport design?
17. What do you understand by optimization of modeling simulation?
18. Explain the role of modeling and simulation in product development process?
19. What do you mean by simulation model execution?

Chapter 3

SYSTEM SIMULATION

3.1 INTRODUCTION

Building complex software systems usually begins with addressing the system's architecture. Without a firm impression of how the major components of a software system interact, there is little possibility that the system will perform effectively. One would like to know early in the development cycle that such attributes as reliability, reusability, maintainability, portability, performance, and modifiability are some acceptable level. There are complex dependencies among these attributes. For example, in improving performance, reusability might be sacrificed, or in improving portability, maintainability might require increased effort. Making tradeoffs in this multi-dimensional space is not easy, but if they are not made at a high level of design abstraction, there is little chance that they can be dealt with once coding begins. Simulation is a tool that can be used to examine some of these architectural tradeoff issues. Simulation can provide early insights, for example with timing, resource usage and bottlenecking, and also into usability. In addition, one can rapidly gain insights into the implications of design changes, by running simulations by varying independent parameters.

Computer simulation was developed hand-in-hand with the rapid growth of the computer, following its first large-scale deployment during the World War II to model the process of nuclear detonation. It was a simulation of twelve hard spheres using Monte Carlo method. Computer simulation is often used as an accessory to, or substitution for, modeling systems for which simple closed form analytic solutions are not possible. There are many different types of computer simulation; the common feature they all share is the attempt to generate a sample of representative scenarios for a model in which a complete enumeration of all possible states of the model would be prohibitive or impossible. Computer models were initially used as a supplement for other arguments, but their uses later became rather widespread.

A computer simulation or a computer model is a computer program that attempts to simulate an abstract model of a particular system. Computer simulations have become a useful part of mathematical modeling of many natural systems in computational physics, chemistry and biology, psychology, and social science and in the process of engineering new technology, to gain insight into the operation of those systems. Traditionally, the formal modeling of systems has been via a mathematical model, which attempts to find analytical solutions to problems which enable the prediction of the behavior of the system from a set of parameters and initial conditions. Computer simulations build on, and are a useful adjunct to purely mathematical models in science, technology and entertainment.

Another area where simulation makes considerable sense is in the economic analysis of product lines. In particular, because product line development involves changes in product composition and production, software size measures such as lines of code are not good predictors of productivity improvements. To estimate, track and compare total costs of different assets, adaptation of other cost modeling techniques, particularly activity-based costing to asset-based software production is needed. As mentioned above, some simulation tools incorporate activity-based costing such that, as entities flow through the simulated process, the cost associated with the processing of each entity at each stage can be accumulated. In this way detailed cost predictions can be made with respect to different product line strategies.

The reliability and the trust people put in computer simulations depends on the validity of the simulation model, therefore verification and validation are crucial part in the development of computer simulations. A detailed discussion on verification and validation of simulation experiments is given in chapter 6. Another important aspect of computer simulations is that of reproducibility of the results, meaning that a simulation model should not provide a different answer for each execution. Although this might seem obvious, this is a special point of attention in stochastic simulations, where random numbers should actually be semi-random numbers. An exception to reproducibility is human in the loop simulations such as flight simulations and computer games.

Computer graphics can be used to display the results of a computer simulation. Animations can be used to experience a simulation in real-time *e.g.*, in training simulations. In some cases animations may also be useful in faster than real-time or even slower than real-time modes. For example, faster than real-time animations could be useful in visualizing the build-up of queues in the simulation of human's evacuating a building. Furthermore, simulation results are often aggregated into static images using various ways of scientific visualization. In debugging, simulating a program execution under test can detect far more errors than the hardware itself can detect and, at the same time, log useful debugging information such as instruction trace, memory alterations and instruction counts. This technique can also detect buffer overflow and similar hard to detect errors as well as produce performance information and tuning data.

Simulation can be applied in many critical areas and enables one to address issues before these issues become problems. Simulation is more than just a technology, as it forces one think in global terms, about system behavior, and about the fact that systems are more than the sum of their components. Simulation can provide insights into the designs of, for example, processes, architectures, or product lines before significant time and cost has been invested, and can be of great benefit in support of training. Simulation is being increasingly emphasized in the department of defense community, where there is documented evidence that its impact on costs, quality and schedule is non-trivial. The software engineering community needs to take a stronger role in exploiting the technology.

At an applied level, simulation can support project costing, planning, tracking, and prediction. In a competitive world, accurate prediction provides a significant advantage. If cost estimates are too high, bids are lost, if too low, organizations find themselves in the red. In this context, simulation can provide not only estimates of cost, but also estimates of cost uncertainty. Simulation is a powerful tool to aid activity-based costing, and can incrementally accumulate costs to a very fine degree of resolution. In addition, it can assess the uncertainty of costs based on the interacting uncertainties of independent variables.

A simulation can only be executed if it is supplied with numerical drivers, and this forces the developer to identify points in the model where these drivers are needed. For example, the model may have to know what percentage of design documents pass review and what percentage must be returned for further work. There are many approaches in simulation. Some simulations are based on the need to visualize the airflow across a wing section, while others, such as in combat or flight training, have a need for a virtual reality component. However, the types of simulations we focus in this chapter to use symbolic networks of linked elements that model processes or products. For example, we can model entities flowing through an organization consisting of departments, or model information flowing between a set of integrated software tools. Techniques such as discrete event simulation and systems dynamics are often used here.

Simulation can allow managers to make more accurate predictions about both the schedule and the accumulated costs associated with a project. This approach is inherently more accurate than costing models based on fits to historical data, since it accounts for the dynamics of the specific process. With regard to schedule, simulation can account for dependencies between tasks, finite capacity resources, and delays resulting from probable rework loops. Some simulation tools also allow one to compute the accumulation of costs on an activity-dependent basis. These features are useful for generating proposal that is more accurate in cost and schedule are thus more likely to keep a company in business.

3.2 SIMULATION OF PURE-PURSUIT PROBLEM

A fighter aircraft observes an enemy bomber and flies directly toward it. The main aim of fighter aircraft is to catch the bomber and destroy it. The bomber (or say the target) continues flying (along a specified curve) so that the fighter aircraft (the pursuer) has to change its direction to keep pointed towards the target. Here we determine the course of attack of the fighter and how long it would take for the catch of the bomber. If the target flies along a straight line, the problem can be solved directly with analytic techniques, but the case if the path of the target fly is curved than the problem is much more difficult and normally cannot be solved directly. Simulation is used to solve this problem. Some assumptions for simulation are following:

1. The target and the pursuer are flying in the same horizontal plane. When the fighter first sights the bomber, and both stay in that plane. This makes the pursuit model two-dimensional.
2. The fighter's speed VF is constant (say 20 kilometers/minute).
3. The target's path is specified.

4. After a fixed time span Δt, the fighter changes its direction in order to point itself toward the bomber.

We are considering a rectangular coordinate system in which the two aircrafts are flying. Distances in graph are given in kilometers and the time in minutes. We start measuring the time when the fighter first sees the bomber.

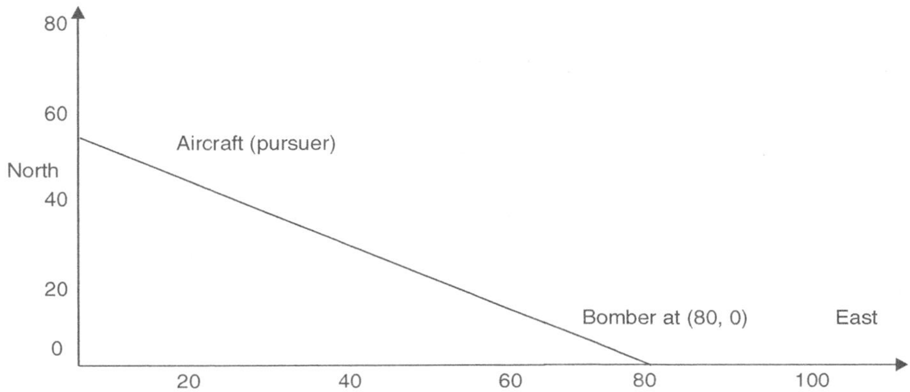

Fig. 3.1 Position of pursuer and target at time zero

We represent the path of the bomber by two arrays XB(t) and YB(t) respectively. Likewise, we shall represent the path of the fighter by two arrays XF(t) and YF(t) respectively. Our aim is to compute the positions of the pursuer *i.e.*, XF(t) and YF(t) for t = 1, 2, 3, . . ., or until the fighter catches the bomber. Assuming that once the fighter is within 10 kilometers of the bomber, the fighter shoots down its target by firing a missile and the pursuit is over.

In case if the target is not caught up within 10 minutes, the pursuit is abandoned and the target is considered escaped. From the time t = 0 till the target is shot down, the attack course is determined as follows:

The distance $D(t)$ at a given time t between the target and the pursuer is given by

$$D(t) = \sqrt{YB(t) - YF(t)^2 + (XB(t) - XF(t)^2} \qquad ...(3.1)$$

The angle θ of the line from the fighter to the target at a given time t is determined by

$$\sin\theta = \frac{YB(t) - YF(t)}{D(t)} \qquad ...(3.2)$$

$$\cos\theta = \frac{XB(t) - XF(t)}{D(t)}$$

...(3.3)

Using this value of the position of the fighter at time (t + 1) is determined by

$$XF(t + 1) = XF(t) + VF\cos\theta \qquad ...(3.4)$$

$$YF(t + 1) = YF(t) + VF\sin\theta \qquad ...(3.5)$$

With these new coordinates of the pursuer, its distance from the target is again calculated using equation (3.1). If this distance is 10 kilometers or less the pursuit is over, otherwise θ is recomputed, and the process continues. The simple strategy of pursuer redirecting him toward the target at fixed intervals of time, while the target goes on its predetermined path without making any effort to evade the pursuer, is called **pure pursuit.** Although in many situations, the strategy used by the pursuer is more sophisticated, this basic approach can be used for any pursuit problems as long as we know the path the pursuer takes and the rule by which the pursuer redirects him.

3.3 EXPONENTIAL GROWTH MODEL

Growth means a rate of change. Consequently, mathematical models describing growth involves differential equations. For example, the growth of population model, if the growth rate coefficient is k, then the rate at which the population grows is k times the current size of the population, is given by

$$x_t = kx \qquad \text{...(3.6)}$$

if $$x = x_0 \text{ at } t = 0$$

x_t is a first order differential equation whose solution is the exponential function. The solution is

$$x = x_0 e^{kt} \qquad \text{...(3.7)}$$

where e is mathematical constant with approximate value 2.71.

If we plot a graph for x with various values of k and initial values of 1, the graph looks like as shown in figure 3.2. From the graph, it can be noted that the population grows indefinitely, for all positive values of k. It can be seen that the population grows faster with greater values of k.

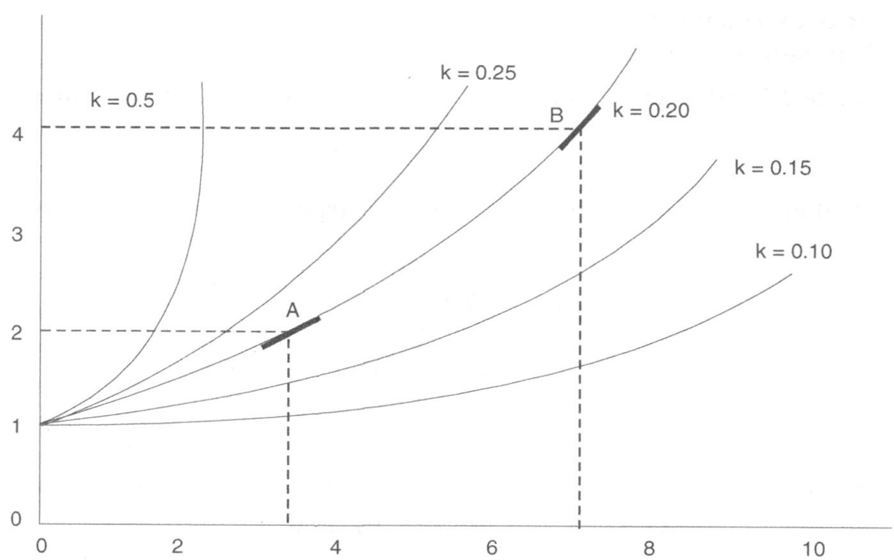

Fig. 3.2 The exponential growth curves.

Assume that $k = 0.2$, $x = 2$, and $x_0 = 1$

We have the equation (3.7) as

$$2 = 1 \times e^{0.21}$$

$$2 = e^{0.21}$$

$$\log 2 = 0.2t$$

$$t = \frac{0.693}{0.2} = 3.46.$$

Let $k = 0.2$, $x = 4$, and $x_0 = 1$, then we have equation (3.7) as

$$4 = e^{0.2t}$$

$$\log 4 = 0.2t$$

$$t = \frac{\log 4}{0.2} = 6.93.$$

On picking the point $x = 2$ at the curve for $k = 0.2$, the corresponding slope at the point 'A' has value 3.46. At point 'B', whose x has become two times *i.e.*, $x = 4$, the slope has become twice as great as at 'A' *i.e.*, 6.93. As the slope is measured as the first order differential coefficient, the growth rate is directly proportional to the current level.

Another way of describing the exponential function is by plotting the logarithms of data against the time and testing whether any particular data represents exponential growth. If the data appears to fall on a straight line, then the growth rate coefficients. It is observed that the logarithm of the variable increases linearly with time. These data can be plotted on semi-logarithmic graph paper where the horizontal lines are placed at logarithmic intervals. Plotting data on such paper is equivalent to taking the logarithm of the data and then plotting on normal linear graph paper. The growth rate coefficient can be estimated by picking two points of the straight line that best fits the data, and then taking the natural logarithm of the ratio of the values. Let the point are x_1 and x_2 at t_1 and t_2 times and $t_2 > t_1$, the result is calculated as:

$$\text{In} \quad \frac{x_2}{x_1} = (t_2 - t_1)k \qquad \text{...(3.8)}$$

For this equation it is possible to derive the value of k when base 10 logarithm are taken for equation (3.8), the corresponding result becomes

$$\log \frac{x_2}{x_1} = 0.434 \ (t_2 - t_1)k \qquad \text{...(3.9)}$$

Sometimes the coefficient k is expressed in the form of T, as

$$k = \frac{1}{T} \qquad \text{...(3.10)}$$

The inverse relationship between k, the growth rate coefficient, and T, the time constant, means that a large coefficient is associated with a small time constant and, therefore, a more rapid rate of increase. The solution for the exponential growth model equation (3.7), takes the form

$$x = x_0 \, e^{t/T} \qquad ...(3.11)$$

The constant T is said to be a *time constant* as it provides a measure of how rapidly the variable x grows. If $t = T$ than equation (3.11) becomes

$$x = ex_0 \qquad ...(3.12)$$

i.e., the variable is exactly e times its initial value x_0

3.3.1 Exponential Decay Model

Exponential decay mode is interpreted as a negative growth model. This is a model in which a variable decays from some initial value x_0, at a rate proportional to the current value. The equation for this model is

$$x = -kx \qquad ...(3.13)$$

If $\quad t = 0$ than $x = x_0 \qquad ...(3.14)$

This is a first-order differential equation whose solution is the exponential function. The solution is

$$x = x_0 \, e^{-kt} \qquad ...(3.15)$$

where e is the mathematical constant with approximate value 2.72.

If we plot a graph for x with various values of k and an initial value of 1, the graph is shown in figure 3.3.

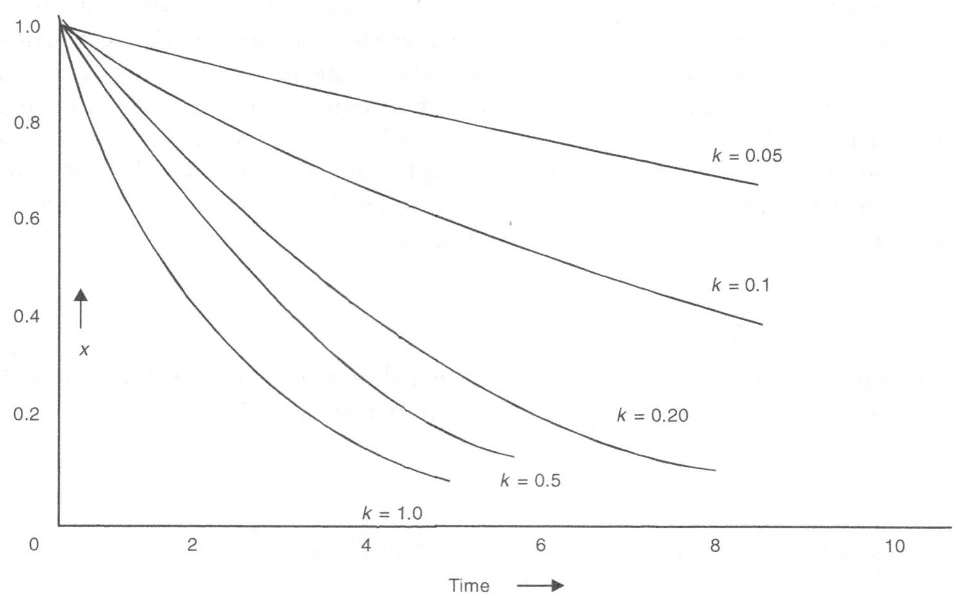

Fig. 3.3 Exponential decay cures

Equation (3.10) in the exponential growth model shows the relation between k and T. The characteristic of the model is that the level x is divided by a constant factor for a given interval of time. In the interval of T time units, the level is divided by e. As $e = 2.72$, the level is reduced by a factor of 0.37. Each successive interval of T reduces the level by the same factor. For example, radioactive material decays. There is nothing significant about the value of e, but comparing values of T for different models measures the relative times they will take to decay by a given fraction.

3.3.2 Modified Exponential Growth Models

The exponential growth model assumes that the rate of growth is proportional to the existing level. This model states an unlimited growth. The exponential growth model cannot be applied to the market model. The market model describes how man items of a product can be sold but there is a limit to the market, if replacement sales are ignored.

A more realistic assumption for a general market model is that the growth rate is proportional to the number of people who have not yet bought the product. Let, the market is limited to some maximum value X, the number of people who might buy the product. Let x be the number of people who buy the product then the number of people who have not purchased the product is $(X - x)$.

The equation of this model can be written as

$$x = k\,(X - x) \qquad \text{...(3.16)}$$

where k is the coefficient of proportionality.

If $\quad t = 0$ than $x = 0 \qquad$ ...(3.17)

This is first-order differential equation whose solution is the exponential function.

The solution is

$$x = X\,(1 - e^{-kt}) \qquad \text{...(3.18)}$$

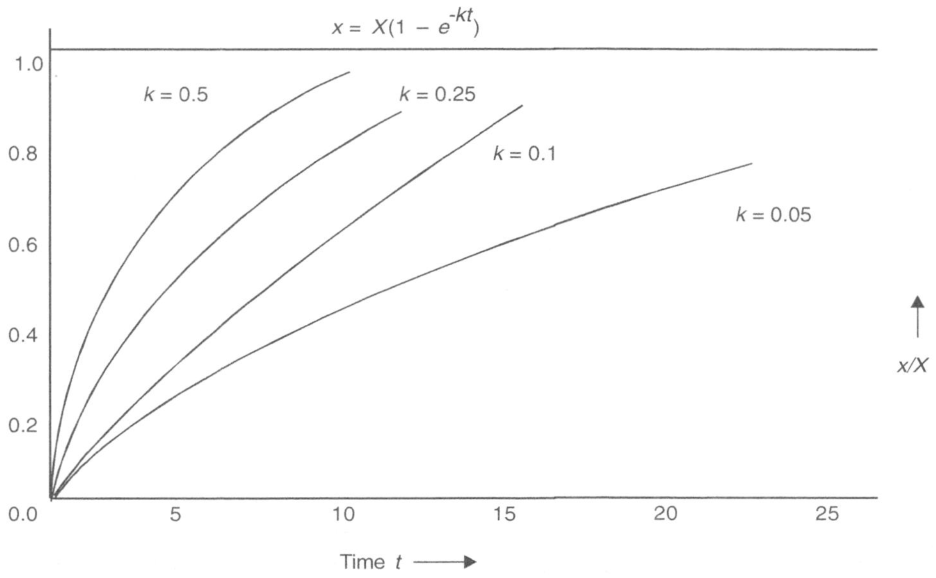

Fig. 3.4 Modified exponential curves

Figure 3.4 plots a graph against x/X and the time for various values of k. The type of curve is known as a *modified exponential curve.* From the graph, it can be noticed that the maximum slope occurs at the origin and slopes steadily decreases as time increases. As a result, the curve approaches the limit more slowly the closer it gets, and never actually reaches the limit.

The constant k plays the same role as the growth rate coefficient in exponential growth model. As k increases, the sales grow rapidly. As with the exponential model, the constant is sometimes expressed in the form $1/T$ in which case, it can be interpreted as a time constant.

3.3.3 Logistic Curves

The most unrealistic feature of the modified exponential curve $x = X\,(-\,e^{-kt})$, is that it shows the maximum slope (variation) at the beginning. In practice, the slope begins at a low value and initially increases as occurs in the exponential growth model. Eventually the slope begins to decline, making the curve of market growth look more like the modified exponential curve. The result is an S-shaped curve as shown in figure 3.5.

Initially the curve turns upwards, looking like the exponential growth model curve. Eventually the curve reaches a point of inflection, where it turns from an increasing to a decreasing slope. From there, the curve resembles a modified exponential curve. For example, when a new product is launched in the market, it is unknown to most. The knowledge of product is spread by advertising and word-of-mouth or by the customers who have actually purchased that product. Under these circumstances, the sales are in proportion to the number of products sold, which is one of the condition governing the exponential growth model. As the number of product sold increases, at a certain point of time the market will be saturated and the condition of the modified exponential model take over.

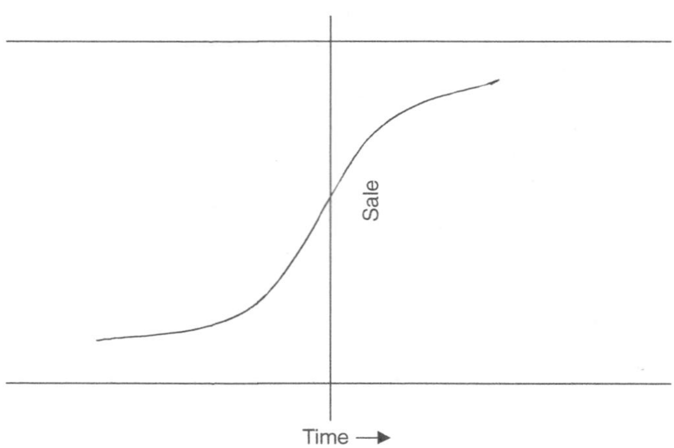

Fig. 3.5 S-shaped growth curve

The logistic function is a combination of the exponential and modified exponential functions, which are used to describe this process mathematically. The differential equation of logistic function is

$$x = kx\ (X - x) \qquad ...(3.19)$$

x = number of people who buy/purchased the product.

X = number of people who might purchase the product or the market limit.

If x is very much small *i.e.,* the product is newly launched essentially at constant value, X. Then the equation (3.19) becomes.

$$x = kxX \qquad ...(3.20)$$

This equation is similar to equation (3.6) of exponential growth model with kX as a constant. If $kX = k$ then equation (3.20) becomes

$$x = k'x \qquad ...(3.21)$$

When the market is almost saturated, the value of x will be very close to X, the market limit, so that it changes very little with time. So the equation (3.21) taken the form

$$x = kX\ (X - x) \qquad ...(3.22)$$

This equation is similar to (3.11) of modified exponential growth model with KX as a constant. If $KX = k''$ then equation (3.22) becomes

$$x = K''\ (X - x) \qquad ...(3.23)$$

This equation (3.23) is similar to equation (3.16). The true equation of logistic function is non-linear in nature, as it contains x^2 as a component on simplifying equation (3.19) we get equation (3.24).

$$x = kx\ X - kx^2 \qquad ...(3.24)$$

The solution is complicated and so omitted. The logistic function can also be applicable to population growth model and the spread of disease. The initial growth corresponds to:

(*a*) The situation in which there are ample resources to support life.

(*b*) The disease being transmitted by contact between infected and uninfected subjects.

The eventual leveling of growth corresponds to:

(*a*) The resources being fully utilized.

(*b*) The number of subjects which are yet uninfected.

3.3.4 Generalization of Growth Models

As we have studied *three* basic growth models:

(*a*) Exponential growth model.

(*b*) Modified exponential growth model.

(*c*) Logistic curves.

Each of these basic models depends upon some coefficients, which are assumed to be constant. But in practice this is not possible. The models can be generalized by removing this assumption. Many other mathematical models could be used as a basis. We are assuming in market model, that the market limit is constant, but it not likely to remain constant. It is going to expand with population growth or fluctuate with economic conditions or respond to both these factors. After finding the best values of the constants to fit in the equation $x = kx\ (X - x)$ of the model, the graph drawn is confined to the upper portion of a logistic curve.

3.4 SIMULATION OF A WATER RESERVOIR SYSTEM

Let us consider the following proposal for constructing a dam across a river to create a reservoir. The reservoir is to be constructed at a specified site. The curve of the projected demand for the water from the reservoir has been determined (from the expected growth pattern and the seasonal fluctuations). The input to the reservoir is from the river inflow and from the rainfall directly over the reservoir. The output consists of the seepage and evaporation (natural) losses, in addition to the water supplied to meet the projected demand. This system (called a simple run-of-river storage demand system) is represented symbolically in figure 3.6.

The amount of seepage loss is not a constant but depends on the volume of the water stored. We have been given a curve showing the seepage loss as a function of volume for the proposed reservoir. Likewise, the evaporation loss depends on the area of the exposed surface and the coefficient of evaporation. We are given another curve showing the surface area as a function of volume as well as the seasonal variation of the coefficient of evaporation. Therefore, for a given volume of water in the reservoir at a particular time of the year we can calculate the two losses.

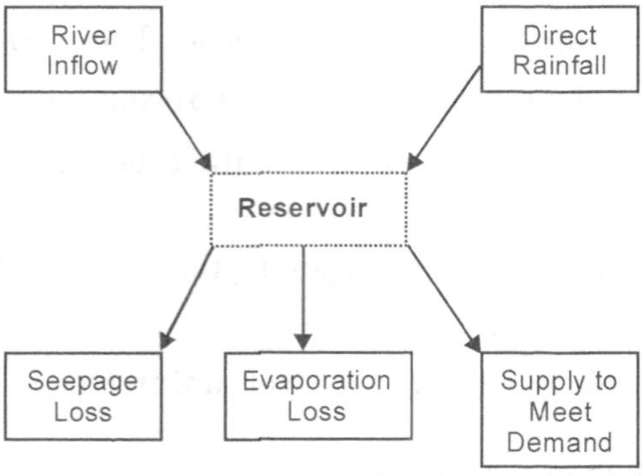

Fig. 3.6 Simple run-of-river storage demand system

In reality no reasonable finite-sized reservoir can provide an absolute guarantee of meeting the demand 100% of the time because the river inflow, the rainfall, the losses, the demand are all random variables. To build such a large dam which will never fail (to meet the demand) through its entire life will generally be uneconomical. Therefore, in practice one determines the reservoir size which will meet the demand with a specified risk of failure (of water shortage). For example, a 2% failure means that once in fifty years the reservoir would become empty before meeting the demand for water. The purpose of the study is to determine the size of the reservoir with a specified risk of failure. There is a single state variable in this system, namely, the volume of water in the reservoir. Since the volume varies continuously with time, we are dealing with a continuous system. It is reasonable to take one month as the basic time interval for the simulation study. Thus, for example, if we wish to simulate the system for 100 years, the simulation run length will be 1200. The simulation will be repeated assuming several different capacities of the reservoir. The output will be in series of ranked shortages for each capacity. The basic procedure, to be repeated for each time step, may be expressed in terms of the following steps:

1. For the current month *M* of the current year *IY* determine the total amount of river inflow and the total rainfall directly over the reservoir. Let the sum of two inputs be denoted by VIN (*i.e.*, R AIN + RFLOW).
2. Add the input volume VIN to the volume left over in the reservoir at the end of the last month VOL (m – 1). This gives us the resultant volume, GROSSV = VIN + VOL (m – 1).
3. On the basis of the last month's volume VOL. (m – 1) calculate this month's seepage and evaporation losses and add them as total loss TLOSS = SEEP + EVAP.
4. From the demand curve (stored as a table in the computer memory) determine the demand of water for the current month DEM.
5. If the TLOSS ≥ GROSSV, then the reservoir runs dry without supplying any water and therefore shortage, SHORT = DEM. The volume of the water left at the end of the current month VOL(m) = 0. Spillage SPILL = 0 and go to Step8; else if TLOSS < GROSSV then the net water volume available to satisfy the demand is VENT = GROSSV – TLOSS.
6. If DEM ≥ VNET the reservoir runs dry and the shortage is given by SHORT = DEM – VNET, and SPILL = 0. Go to Step 8; else if DEM < VNET, then the difference DIFF = VNET – DEM is the water left over.
7. If this leftover water exceeds the capacity CAP of the reservoir there will be a spill over, in other words if DIFF > CAP then SPILL = DIFF – CAP and VOL(m) = CAP; else if DIFF ≤ CAP then SPILL = 0 and VOL(m) = DIFF.
8. Print out SPILL and SHORT for this month, and move to the next month. If the period exceeds the projected simulation length stop, else go to Step 1.

3.5 TRAJECTORY SIMULATION

Simulation has been used in computing trajectories of various types of bullets, rockets, space vehicles, etc. Because of the drag (air-resistance) the equations of motion get sufficiently complex for a closed from mathematical solution. In the case of a rocket the mass itself does not remain constant but reduces as the fuel is used up. Note that in trajectory calculations any refinements, such as:

(*i*) Making the air-resistance more complicated than just proportional to v^2, and also including a non-zero component perpendicular to the velocity vector, and

(*ii*) Taking into account the effects of the earth's rotation, can be easily accommodated. These refinements require only additional computation and not any increased analytical ability. This is one of the fundamental advantages of simulation.

3.6 SUSPENSION SYSTEM

In trajectory problems the external forces (drag and gravity) either remain constant or vary slowly. Consequently the trajectory is a smooth curve. In contrast, the suspension system of an automobile is subjected to abruptly changing forces due to potholes in the road. The purpose of a suspension system is to damp out the effect of vibrations, caused by sudden changes in the road surface.

Each wheel with a mass m in an automobile has an independent suspension system, consisting of a spring and a shock absorber, as shown in figure 3.7. The resistance force of the spring is proportional to the displacement (*i.e.*, compression) and the resistive force of the shock absorber is mostly proportional to the rate of change of displacement. The exact equation of motion for the system is

$$my + k_1 (y - kg\ y) + k_3\ y = k_3 \ . \ F(t) \qquad ...(3.25)$$

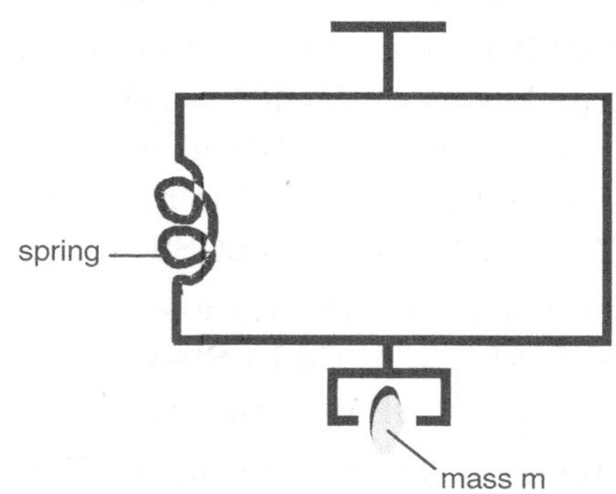

Fig. 3.7 Suspension system

We wish to find the transient behavior of the system with the following values of the constants:

mass $m = 1.0$, $\qquad k_1 = 5.0,\ k_2 = 0.05$

spring stiffness $k_3 = 700$, to two types of forces

(*i*) step function $\qquad F(t) = 0,\ (t \le 0) \qquad ...(3.26)$

$\qquad = a,\ (t > 0)$

(*ii*) ramp function $\qquad F(t) = 0,\ (t \le 0) \qquad ...(3.27)$

$\qquad = a,\ (t > 0)$

3.7 SIMULATION OF AN AUTOPILOT

In order to simulate the action of the autopilot, we first construct a mathematical model of the aircraft system. The error signal, ε, has been defined as the difference between the desired heading, or input, θ_i, and the actual heading, or output, θ_o, We therefore have the following identity:

$$\varepsilon = \theta_i - \theta_o \qquad ...(3.28)$$

We assume the rudder is turned to an angle proportional to the error signal, so that the force changing the aircraft heading is proportional to the error signal. Instead of moving the aircraft sideways, the force applies a torque which will turn the aircraft. The strength of the torque, or turning force, depends on how far back the rudder is placed. However, just as the automobile movement was resisted by a shock absorber, the turning of the aircraft produces a resisting, viscous drag, approximately proportional to the angular velocity of the aircraft. The torque acting on the aircraft can, therefore, be represented by the following equation:

$$\text{Torque} = K\varepsilon - D\theta_o \qquad ...(3.29)$$

where K and D are constants. The first term on the right-hand side is the torque produced by the rudder, and the second is the viscous drag.

In case of differential equations, the fundamental law of mechanics is that the acceleration of a body is proportional to the applied force. That was related to linear motion. The same law, however, applies to a turning motion: the coefficient of proportionality is the inertia of the body, denoted by I. Sine the angular acceleration of the aircraft is the second derivative of its heading, the equation of motion is

$$I\theta_o = \text{torque} \qquad ...(3.30)$$

Substituting from equations (3.28) and (3.29), and transposing terms, the resultant equation is

$$I\theta_o + D\theta_o + K\theta_o = K\theta_i \qquad ...(3.31)$$

If we divide both sides of the equation by I, and make the following substitutions

$$2\xi\omega = \frac{D}{I}, \; \omega^2 = \frac{K}{I},$$

the equation of motion relating output to input then takes the following form:

$$\theta_o + 2\xi\omega\theta_o + \omega^2\theta_o = \omega^2\theta_i$$

Suppose the aircraft is initially flying a steady course which, by definition, we take to be the zero heading. If it is asked to change to a new heading at time zero, this corresponds to a unit step change of input. Because of the correspondence between the equations of motion we have just noted, the results will be the same, which showed the response of the suspension system to a unit the response will be oscillatory if $\xi < 1$.

To simulate how the autopilot can be designed to modify the aircraft response, it is more convenient to leave the model in the form of there individual equations. Using the variables ERROR and TORQUE to represent the error signal and the applied torque, the equations are:

$$\text{ERROR} = \theta_i - \theta_o$$

$$\text{TORQUE} = K \times \text{ERROR} - D \times \theta_o$$

$$\text{I}\theta_o = \text{TORQUE}$$

If we also use the variables HEAD, ANGVEL, and ANGACC to represent the aircraft heading and its first two derivatives, respectively, together with INPUT for the desired heading, the equations can be written

$$\text{ERROR} = \text{INPUT} - \text{HEAD}$$

$$\text{TORQUE} = K \times \text{ERROR} - D \times \text{ANGVEL}$$

$$I \times \text{ANGACC} = \text{TORQUE}$$

A CSMP III program for the system is shown below. Instead of using a step function change of heading, which simply repeats the automobile wheel case, the aircraft is being asked to turn in a circle. The desired heading is then continually increasing at a uniform rate so that

$$\text{INPUT} = A \times \text{TIME}$$

where A is a constant and TIME is a CSMP variable representing the time t^2. The constants K, I, and A have been set to values of 400, 2.00, and 0.0175, respectively. The constant D has been programmed to take different values on five separate runs, so that the damping ratio, ξ, will have the values 0.1, 0.3, 0.7, 1.0, and 2.0. With t expressed in seconds, the equation of motion gives θ_o in radians. The value chosen for A in the simulation makes the input a request for a turn of one degree a second.

```
TITLE AIRCRAFT WITH RATE CONTROL
PARAM D = (5, 656, 16, 968, 39, 592, 56, 56, 113.12)
INPUT = A*TIME
ERROR = INPUT – HEAD
TORQUE = K*ERROR – D*ANGVEL
ANGACC = TORQUE/I
HEAD = INTGRL (0, 0, ANGVEL)
ANGVEL = INTGRAL (0, 0, ANGACC)
CONST I = 2,0, K = 400.0, A = 0.0175
TIMER DELT = 0.005, FINTIM = 10.5, PRDEL = 0.05
PRINT HEAD
```

LABEL HEADING VERSUS TIME

END

The results of the runs are plotted in figure 3.8. They are given in non-dimensional form by plotting $\omega\theta_0/A$ against ωt. The straight line through the origin is the desired heading, which would be followed by the aircraft if it responded perfectly. However, it can be seen that the aircraft lags behind the desired heading and never catches up so long as the turn request remains in effect. The size of the lag increases as the damping ratio increases. The error signal appears as an electrical signal in the autopilot. It can easily be modified by electrical circuits.

The motion of the aircraft can also be measured by instruments giving electrical signals that can be added to the autopilot output. The modifications affect the aircraft response by changing the applied forces. Studies in control theory are concerned with understanding how system behavior can be modified in this way. As an example, suppose it is important to eliminate the lag that builds up as the aircraft's turns. One way this can be done is to add to the error signal a component that is proportional to the integral of the error signal. The applied force is then as follows:

$$F(t) = K\omega + K_i \int \omega \, dt$$

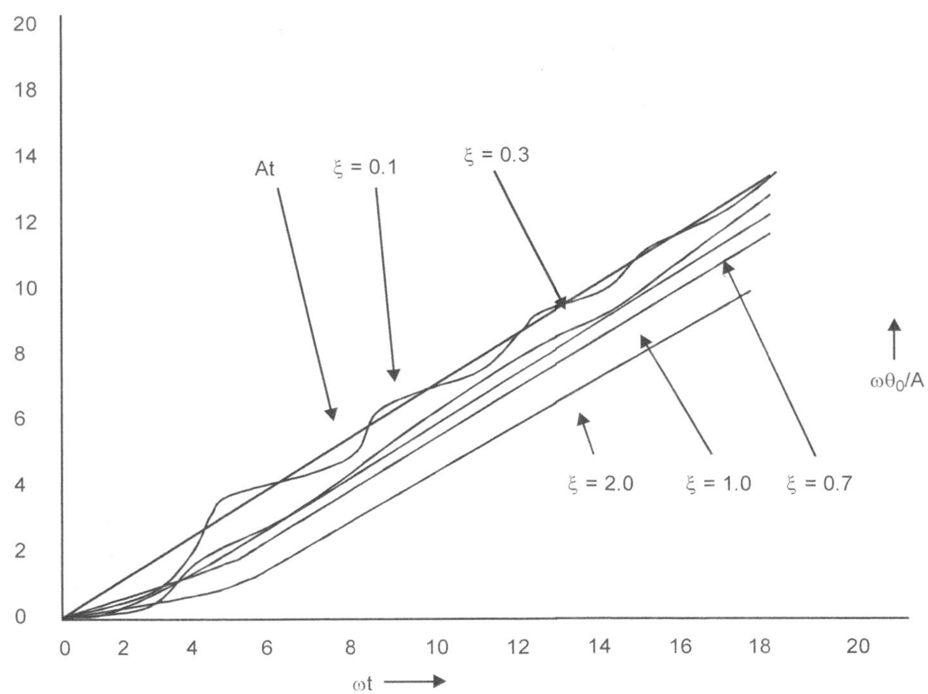

Fig. 3.8 Responses of aircraft flying in a circle with rate control.

With this modification, control theory shows that for the system to remain stable, we must have

$$K_1 < \frac{KD}{I}$$

Figure 3.9 shows the response of the aircraft, under the same conditions as were used before, when this modification is included. In each case, the value of K_1 was Chosen so that $\frac{K_1}{K} = \frac{0.2D}{I}$

The results of figure 3.9 show that the second modification, which is called *integral control,* will eliminate the lag when the aircraft is performing a steady turn.

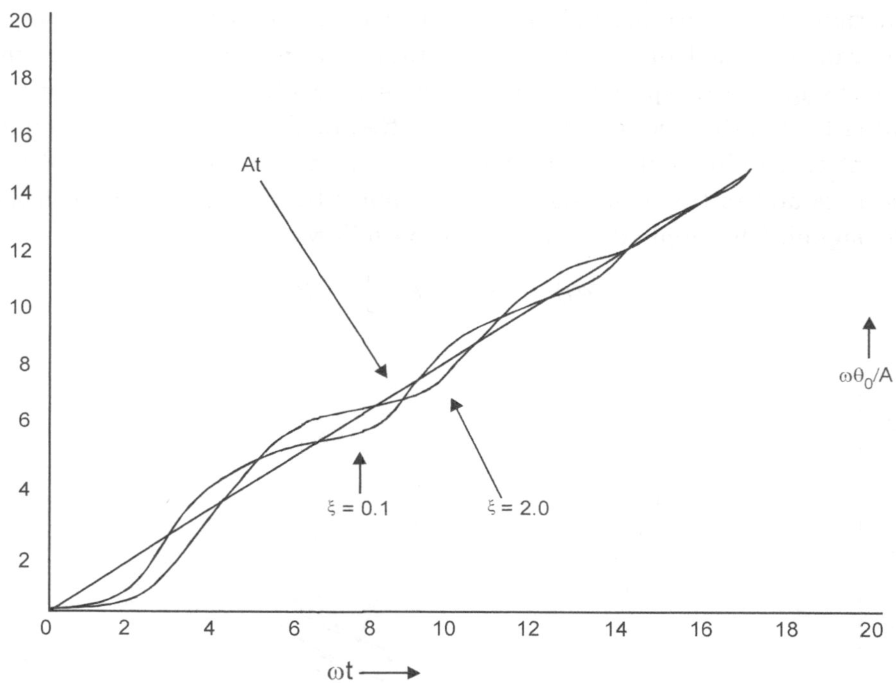

Fig. 3.9 Response of aircraft flying in a circle with integral control

3.8 SIMULATION OF PENDULUM

Here we are presenting MATLAB code to simulate the function of a pendulum under the defined controlled parameters.

3.8.1 Function Pendulum

```
% Inverted pendulum simulation.
% Close all figures.
```

```
close all;

% Set the step size and simulation length.
dt = 0.001;
tf = 1;
thetainit = 0.1; % initial pendulum angle (radians)
m = 0.2; % pendulum mass
M = 1.0; % cart mass
g = 9.81; % acceleration due to gravity
F = 0.1; % coefficient of viscous friction on cart wheels
l = 1; % length of pendulum
r = 0.02; % radius of pendulum mass
J = m * r * r / 2; % moment of inertia of pendulum mass (cylinder)

% Nonlinear simulation.
theta = thetainit;
thetadot = 0;
thetadotdot = 0;
y = 0;
ydot = 0;
ydotdot = 0;
theta_array = [ ];
thetadot_array = [ ];
thetadotdot_array = [ ];
y_array = [ ];
ydot_array = [ ];
ydotdot_array = [ ];

for t = 0 : dt : tf
% Save the old state values.
theta_old = theta;
thetadot_old = thetadot;
thetadotdot_old = thetadotdot;
y_old = y;
ydot_old = ydot;
ydotdot_old = ydotdot;
```

```
    sine = sin(theta);
    cosine = cos(theta);
    % Compute the new state values.
    u = 100*theta;
    theta = theta + thetadot_old * dt;
    thetadot = thetadot + thetadotdot_old * dt;
    thetadotdot = (m*g*l*sine - m*l*cosine*(u +
            m*l*thetadot_old*thetadot_old*sine - F*ydot_old)/(M + m))/
            (J + m*l*l - m*m*l*l*cosine*cosine / (M + m));
    y = y + ydot_old * dt;
    ydot = ydot + ydotdot_old * dt;
    ydotdot = (u - m*l*thetadotdot_old*cosine +
          m*l*thetadot_old*thetadot_old*sine - F*ydot_old)/(M + m);
    % Save the state values in arrays for later plotting.
    theta_array = [theta_array theta];
    thetadot_array = [thetadot_array thetadot];
    thetadotdot_array = [thetadotdot_array thetadotdot];
    y_array = [y_array y];
    ydot_array = [ydot_array ydot];
    ydotdot_array = [ydotdot_array ydotdot];
end

% Linearized simulation.
xdot = zeros(4, 1);
x = zeros(4, 1);
x(3) = thetainit;
A = [0      1       0          0;
     0    -F/M    -m*g/M       0;
     0      0       0          1;
     0    F/M/l  (M+m)*g/M/l   0];
B = [0; 1/M; 0; -1/M/l];
xarray = [ ];

for t = 0 : dt : tf
```

```
    u = 100*x(3);
    xdot = A * x + B * u;
    x = x + xdot * dt;
    xarray = [xarray x];
end
% Comparing the results of the nonlinear and linearized simulations.
t = [0 : dt : tf];
figure;
plot(t, (180 / pi) * theta_array, '-', t, (180 / pi) * xarray(3, :), '--');
title(['Solid = Nonlinear, Dashed = Linearized']);
xlabel('Time');
ylabel('Angle (radians)');
figure;
plot(t, y_array, '-', t, xarray(1, :), '--');
title(['Solid = Nonlinear, Dashed = Linearized']);
xlabel('Time');
ylabel('Position');
```

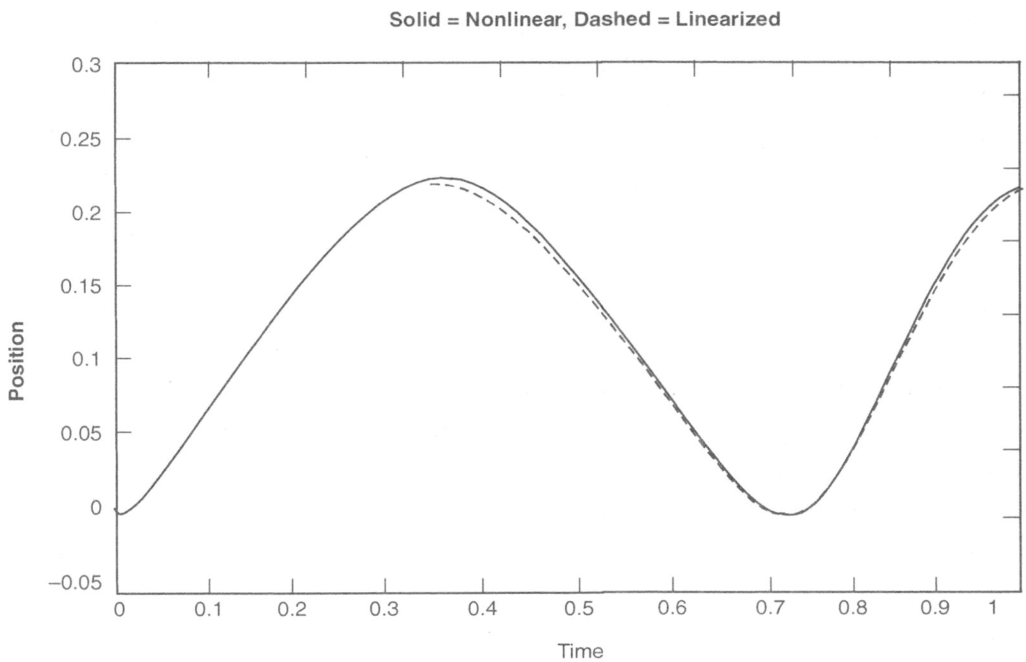

Fig. 3.10 Results of the nonlinear and linear simulations

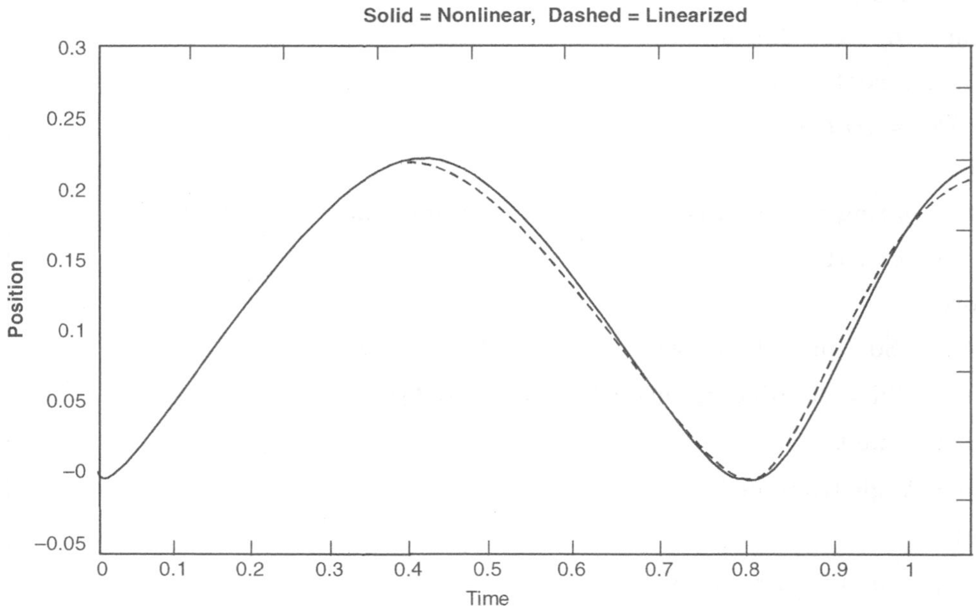

Fig. 3.11 Results of the nonlinear and linear simulations of pendulum

3.8.2 RL Circuit Simulation

A simple series RL circuit simulation is given below that shows how the same results can be obtained numerically and analytically.

```
function [t,yArray,y1Array] = Ex00(dt)
% function [t,yArray,y1Array] = Ex00(dt)
% Series RL circuit simulation
% INPUTS
%  dt = integration step size
% OUTPUTS
%  t = time array
%  yArray = array containing numerical solution
%  y1Array = array containing analytical solution
close all; % Close all figures.
% Set the step size and simulation length.
if ~exist('dt','var')
  dt = 0.1;
end
tf = 10;
% Set the resistor and inductor values.
```

```
R = 1;
L = 1;
% Initialize the simulation.
x0 = -1;
x = x0;
y = 0;
u = 1;
% Initialize some empty arrays for later use.
yArray = [ ];
y1Array = [ ];
for t = 0 : dt : tf % Compute the numerical solution.
  % Compute the output values and save it for later plotting.
  y = R * x;
  yArray = [yArray y];

  xdot = -R * x / L + u / L; % Integrate the state equation.
  x = x + xdot * dt;
end
```

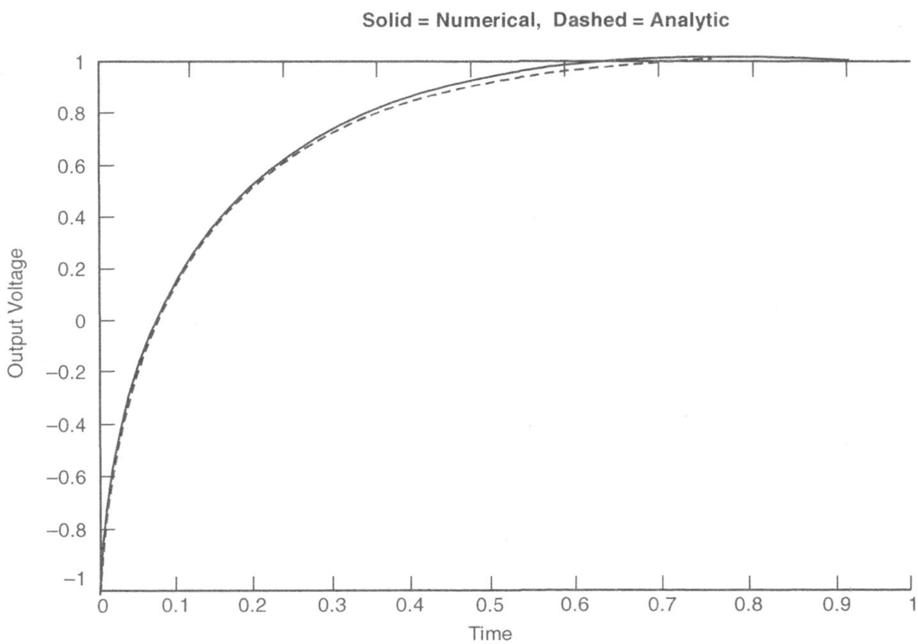

Fig. 3.12 RL circuit simulation

```
% Compute the analytic solution for u = 1.
for t = 0 : dt : tf
```

```
  y1 = 1 + exp(-R*t/L) * (R * x0 - 1);
  y1Array = [y1Array y1];
end
t = 0 : dt : tf;
y1Array = ones(size(t)) + exp(-R*t/L) * (R * x0 - 1);
figure; % Plot the results.
plot(t, yArray, '-', t, y1Array, '--');
title('Solid = Numerical, Dashed = Analytic');
xlabel('Time');
ylabel('Output Voltage');
```

3.8.3 Simulation of Linear Algebra Problem

This following MATLAB code produces solution of a simple linear algebra problem. It then explores some of MATLAB's plotting capabilities. The lines that begin with % are comments to the user.

```
% The linear algebra problem:
%                        | 1 7 -2 6 |
%                    A = | 3 1  1 5 |
%                        | 2 0  6 8 |
%                        | -6 1 9 6 |
% Enter the Matrix A into MATLAB
                     A = [1 7 -2 6; 3 1 1 5; 2 0 6 8; -6 1 9 6]
% Extract all elements of the columns of A into vectors.
% The semicolons following each line suppress the output.
                    A1 = A(:,1);
                    A2 = A(:,2);
                    A3 = A(:,3);
                    A4 = A(:,4);
% Sum the columns to show that the columns are not linearly independent.
  col_sum = A1 + A2 + A3 - A4
  rref(A)


% There are three linearly independent columns in A, and its rank is 3.
% MATLAB could have computed this % directly:
```

rank_of_A = rank(A)

% MATLAB can also find the null space of A.

% The command null(A) returns an orthonormal basis for the null % space of A

null_A = null(A)

% In this case A's null space consists of multiples of this vector. So, by definition, multiplying this vector % by A % should result in zero:

A*null_A

% Since we're doing this with floating point arithmetic, there is some error. We didn't get exactly zero. % Notice % that in double precision (MATLAB's default) the largest error is about 10^(-15).

% Plotting in MATLAB generates a 100 element equally spaced vector from 0 to L

L = 1;

x = linspace(0,L);

% We can create a matrix of eigen functions MATLAB functions often accept vector arguments.

y = zeros(4,length(x));

for count = 1:N,

y(count,:) = sin(count*pi*x/ L);

end

% The n_th row of the 4 x 100 matrix y now contains sin(n*pi*x/L).

% We can plot these against x, using different % line types.

plot(x,y(1,:))

hold on % leave on the previous plot and any other plots until "hold off"

plot(x,y(2,:),'--')

plot(x,y(3,:),'.-')

hold off

% **the next plot command will erase all of these plots**

% add labels, titles, and grid marks

```
xlabel('x (units of L)')
ylabel('f_n(x)')
title('A Multiple Plot')
legend('sin(\pix/ L)','sin(2\pix/ L)','sin(3\pix/ L)',-1)
grid on
```

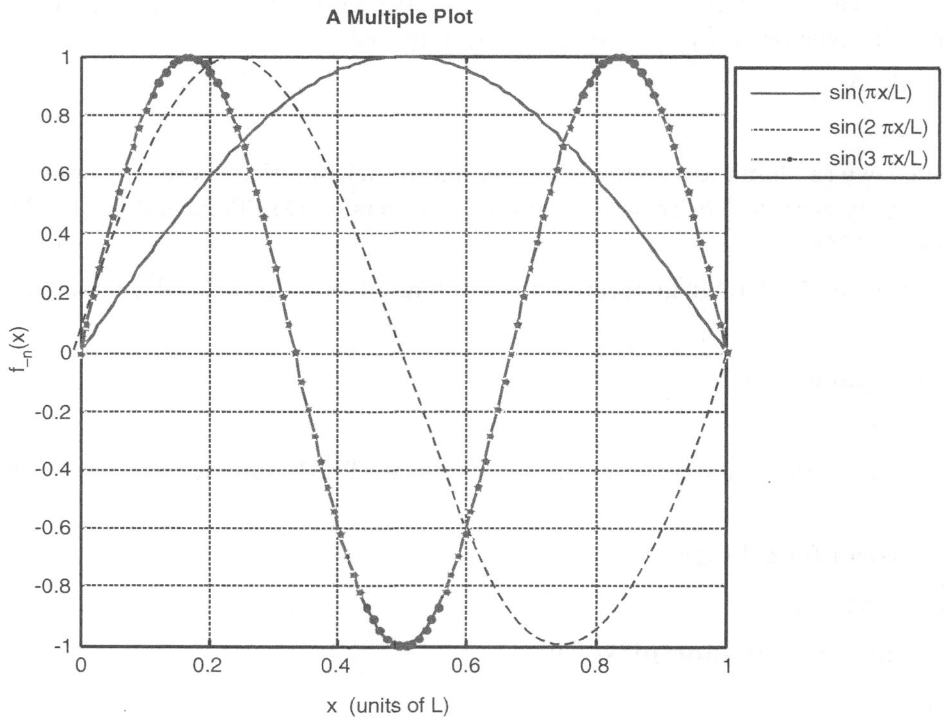

Fig. 3.13 Simulation of Linear Algebra Problem

Simulation of One-dimensional Heat Transfer by Finite Difference Approximation Method

Consider a brick wall which is exposed to the periodic temperature and incident radiation variation as given in table. The other values of wall are:

Thermal conductivity	k	$= 1.5$ W/m °C
Thermal diffusivity	α	$= 8 \times 10^{-7}$ m^2/s
Absorptivity of surface	α	$= 0.8$
Out side wall coefficient	f_o	$= 23$ W/m^2 °C
In side wall coefficient	f_i	$= 7$ W/m^2 °C

Table 3.1 Outside temperature of air and radiation

time	t_o (°C)	I (W/m^2)	time	t_o (°C)	I (W/m^2)
12 midnight	30.0	0	12 Noon	38.5	1000
1	29.5	0	1	39.5	960
2	29.0	0	2	40.5	825
3	28.5	0	3	41.5	645
4	28.5	0	4	39.5	385
5	28.0	0	5	39.0	190
6	28.0	47	6	38.0	47
7	29.0	186	7	36.0	0
8	31.5	390	8	34.5	0
9	33.5	640	9	33.5	0
10	35.5	814	10	33.0	0
11	37.0	954	11	31.5	0

The values of different parameters can be calculated as follows:

$$bio = \frac{f_o}{k}\Delta x$$

$$bii = \frac{f_i}{k}\Delta x$$

$$M = \frac{(\Delta x)^2}{\alpha \Delta \tau}$$

Excess sol air temperature

$$te = (t_o - 25) + \frac{aI}{f_o}$$

Outside surface temperature

$$tso = \frac{bio}{bio+2}te + \frac{2t_1}{bio+2}$$

Inside surface temperature

$$tsi = \frac{bii}{bii+2}ti + \frac{2t_2}{bii+2}$$

Temperature at node 1

$$t/d = \frac{2tso + t_2}{M} + \frac{(M-3)\,t_1}{M}$$

Temperature at node 2

$$t\,2d \;=\; \frac{2tsi + t_1}{M} + \frac{(M-3)\,t_2}{M}$$

Assume initial temperatures are:

Time \ Temp.	*te*	*tso*	*t1d*	*t2d*	*tsi*	*ti*
12 (midnight)	5	7.6	10	10	8.1	0

We have to find the actual temperature values by above method, and then we can calculate maximum heat transfer through the wall.

/*Simulation program of One-Dimensional Heat Transfer by Finite Difference Approximation Method */

```
#include <stdio.h>
#include<conio.h>
void main()
{
int l, time[24] = {0,1,2,3,4,5,6,7,8,9,10,11,12,13,14,15,16,17,18,19,20,21,22,23};
float bio=1.917;
float i[24] = {0, 0, 0, 0, 0, 0, 47, 186, 390, 640, 814, 954, 1000, 960, 825, 645, 385, 190,
47, 0, 0, 0, 0, 0};
float bii = 0.583, m = 5.43, tso = 7.6, te, t1 = 10,ti = 0, t2 = 10, tsi = 8.1, t1d, t2d;
float to[24] = {30, 29.5, 29, 28.5, 28.5, 28, 28, 29, 31.5, 33.5, 35.5, 37, 38.5, 39.5, 40.5,
41.5, 39.5, 39, 38, 36, 34.5, 33.5, 33, 31.5};

clrscr();
printf("\n time  te \t tso \t t1d \t t2d \t tsi");
for(l = 0; l<24;l++)
{
te = (to[l]-25)+0.8*i[l]/23;
tso = bio*te/(bio+2)+2*t1/(bio+2);
tsi = bii*ti/(bii+2)+2*t2/(bii+2);
t1d = (2*tso+t2)/m + (m-3)*t1/m;
t2d = (2*tsi+t1)/m + (m-3)*t2/m;
t1 = t1d;
t2 = t2d;
```

```
printf("\n %d  %3.2f \t %3.2f \t %3.2f \t %3.2f \t %3.2f", time[l], te, tso, t1d, t2d,
tsi);
getch();
}
printf("\n\n SECOND........ CYCLE...........BEGINS\n");
for(l = 0; l<24;l++)
{
te = (to[l]-25)+0.8*i[l]/23;
tso = bio*te/(bio+2)+2*t1/(bio+2);
tsi = bii*ti/(bii+2)+2*t2/(bii+2);
t1d = (2*tso+t2)/m + (m-3)*t1/m;
t2d = (2*tsi+t1)/m + (m-3)*t2/m;
t1 = t1d;
t2 = t2d;
printf("\n %d  %3.2f \t %3.2f \t %3.2f \t %3.2f \t %3.2f", time[l], te, tso, t1d, t2d,
tsi);
getch();
}
printf("\n\n THIRD........ CYCLE...........BEGINS\n");
for(l = 0; l<24;l++)
{
te = (to[l]-25)+0.8*i[l]/23;
tso = bio*te/(bio+2)+2*t1/(bio+2);
tsi = bii*ti/(bii+2)+2*t2/(bii+2);
t1d = (2*tso+t2)/m + (m-3)*t1/m;
t2d = (2*tsi+t1)/m + (m-3)*t2/m;
t1 = t1d;
t2 = t2d;
printf("\n %d  %3.2f \t %3.2f \t %3.2f \t %3.2f \t %3.2f", time[l], te, tso, t1d, t2d,
tsi);
getch();
}
}
```

Results of Simulation

time	te	tso	t1d	t2d	tsi
0	5.00	7.55	9.10	9.17	7.74
1	4.50	6.85	8.28	8.39	7.10
2	4.00	6.19	7.53	7.68	6.50
3	3.50	5.56	6.83	7.01	5.94
4	3.50	5.20	6.26	6.39	5.43
5	3.00	4.67	5.70	5.84	4.95
6	4.63	5.18	5.53	5.33	4.52
7	10.47	7.95	6.39	4.92	4.13
8	20.07	13.08	8.58	4.78	3.81
9	30.76	19.44	11.88	5.08	3.70
10	38.81	25.06	15.48	5.91	3.94
11	45.18	30.02	19.07	7.18	4.58
12	48.28	33.37	22.15	8.78	5.56
13	47.89	34.75	24.33	10.51	6.80
14	44.20	34.05	25.36	12.18	8.14
15	38.93	32.01	25.38	13.60	9.43
16	27.89	26.61	23.66	14.64	10.53
17	20.61	22.17	21.45	15.08	11.33
18	14.63	18.12	19.05	15.00	11.68
19	11.00	15.11	16.85	14.50	11.62
20	9.50	13.25	15.09	13.73	11.23
21	8.50	11.87	13.65	12.84	10.63
22	8.00	10.89	12.48	11.92	9.94
23	6.50	9.56	11.30	11.03	9.23

SECOND........ CYCLE...........BEGINS

time	te	tso	t1d	t2d	tsi
0	5.00	8.22	10.12	10.17	8.54
1	4.50	7.37	9.11	9.31	7.87
2	4.00	6.61	8.23	8.50	7.21
3	3.50	5.91	7.43	7.74	6.58
4	3.50	5.50	6.78	7.04	6.00

5	3.00	4.93	6.14	6.41	5.45
6	4.63	5.41	5.92	5.83	4.96
7	10.47	8.15	6.72	5.36	4.51
8	20.07	13.25	8.88	5.17	4.15
9	30.76	19.59	12.14	5.42	4.00
10	38.81	25.19	15.71	6.21	4.20
11	45.18	30.13	19.27	7.44	4.81
12	48.28	33.47	22.32	9.00	5.76
13	47.89	34.84	24.48	10.71	6.97
14	44.20	34.13	25.50	12.35	8.29
15	38.93	32.07	25.50	13.75	9.56
16	27.89	26.67	23.77	14.77	10.64
17	20.61	22.22	21.54	15.20	11.43
18	14.63	18.16	19.13	15.10	11.77
19	11.00	15.15	16.92	14.59	11.69
20	9.50	13.29	15.15	13.80	11.29
21	8.50	11.90	13.71	12.91	10.69
22	8.00	10.91	12.53	11.98	9.99
23	6.50	9.58	11.34	11.09	9.28
		THIRD........ CYCLE...........BEGINS			
0	5.00	8.24	10.15	10.21	8.58
1	4.50	7.39	9.14	9.35	7.91
2	4.00	6.63	8.25	8.54	7.24
3	3.50	5.93	7.45	7.77	6.61
4	3.50	5.52	6.80	7.07	6.02
5	3.00	4.94	6.16	6.43	5.47
6	4.63	5.41	5.94	5.85	4.98
7	10.47	8.15	6.74	5.38	4.53
8	20.07	13.26	8.89	5.18	4.16
9	30.76	19.59	12.15	5.43	4.01

10	38.81	25.20	15.72	6.22	4.21
11	45.18	30.14	19.28	7.45	4.81
12	48.28	33.47	22.33	9.01	5.77
13	47.89	34.84	24.48	10.71	6.98
14	44.20	34.13	25.50	12.36	8.30
15	38.93	32.08	25.50	13.75	9.57
16	27.89	26.67	23.77	14.77	10.65
17	20.61	22.22	21.54	15.20	11.44
18	14.63	18.16	19.13	15.11	11.77
19	11.00	15.15	16.92	14.59	11.70
20	9.50	13.29	15.16	13.81	11.30
21	8.50	11.90	13.71	12.91	10.69
22	8.00	10.91	12.53	11.98	9.99
23	6.50	9.58	11.34	11.09	9.28

From above results we find that at 9 AM the values of temperature are similar. Therefore we use these temperatures for further calculations.

SUMMARY

Simulation has been applied in many fields, such as aerospace or energy production, but to date it has not seen broad practical application in software engineering. This may be because it is more difficult to accurately model human and organizational behavior than to model physical systems, or it may be that the emphasis on software process is a relatively recent phenomenon. Whatever the reason, this is unfortunate because the rewards from it use are many-fold.

Simulation can be of major help in pinning down software system requirements early in the product life cycle, particularly for examining temporal behavior. Simulation can mimic the performance characteristics of software components and their interactions, the effects of time delays and feedbacks, and of finite capacities and resource bottlenecks. Alternate architectures and designs can be evaluated in a safe environment, prior to implementation. In addition, requirements are rarely static, but evolve as experience grows with product development. Thus simulation is not only a valuable tool in defining the initial requirements, but can be used to test out alternate modifications, prior to their implementation. The processes through which the requirements are managed are also critical. However, as far as modeling is concerned, such processes have much in common with other project management processes (*e.g.*, design, development or testing). Finally, a system simulation can be viewed as a component of the requirements and can provide quantitative measures against which the target software system must comply.

Traditionally, revised or new processes are improved through operational experience. This can be expensive and risky. Simulation can provide considerable insights into how a process will work, prior to its implementation. These insights can help the process designer assess alternatives, and show that a specific process design performs in a manner that meets expectations. In this way, processes can be pre-tested, and buy-in is more likely obtained from management. Subjective criticisms are less likely, since quantitative simulation of validated models can produce very specific and credible answers to perhaps hostile questions.

Simulations work because they allow learners to take the valuable knowledge and skills taught in books, *e*-learning, and the classroom, and practice applying them in an environment that closely approximates the real-world. In addition, well-designed custom business simulations evoke emotions, parallel the learner's job, offer specific feedback from multiple sources, encompass predictable and unpredictable events, promote team interaction, and encourage creative decision-making and discovery. Why are simulations so effective? Simulations, unlike any other learning tool, influence the many different ways adults learn effectively. When simulations are used properly to challenge participants to practice multiple skills, they provide an environment in which participants learn through experience. They succeed because there will be something in a simulation that fits each participant's learning style, no matter what that style is.

Simulations offer a number of value propositions to the three traditional, primary stakeholders in company training programs: training managers, executives, and other business leaders and learning providers. Training managers always are on the lookout for learning solutions that develop multiple skills and quickly improve overall performance. Executives want the same thing but they also want to be certain that the learning solution is tied to improving the business. Learning providers (*e.g.*, training departments or external training vendors) look for solutions that they can develop cost-effectively and that also allow them to meet the goals of both the training managers and business leaders they serve. Simulations meet the requirements of all three stakeholders. Business simulations accelerate performance improvement (or speed to performance), serve as strategic initiative tools are practical learning solutions.

One of the most attractive value propositions of simulations is their ability to shorten the time it takes to turn knowledge into skills. Accelerating Speed to Performance simply means that a learning solution is capable of reducing the cycle time (that is, the elapsed clock or calendar time from start to finish) that it takes for employees to convert new knowledge into skills. For example, a learning solution that allowed an organization to collapse the learning curve for new hires would be highly desirable. Training managers, in particular, see a great deal of value in simulations because of the many skills they force learners to apply and practice. Instead of concentrating on one specific skill for a period of time, simulations force participants to practice several skills at once. This effect accelerates Speed to Performance by allowing trainees to use familiar skills as a base on which to build new knowledge and skills. Simulations also afford participants an opportunity to keep old or seldom-used skills fresh. How else, specifically, do business simulations accelerate Speed to Performance? They teach employees valuable real-world skills, including how to set and achieve goals, receive and give feedback, focus on the major issues and not the irrelevant or minor issues, deal with interruptions and distractions, work individually and collaborating in teams, explore alternative options, deal with stress, have fun.

These experiences are important to training managers and executives alike, because they reinforce the application of multiple skills and the practice of new skills with the goal of accelerating speed to performance. Additionally, these experiences all contribute to the realism of a simulation. They pull participants into the experience, allowing them to take an important and active role in running a company.

EXERCISE QUESTIONS

1. Explain simulation of a water reservoir system and simulation of pure-pursuit problem with suitable model diagrams.
2. Write a program to simulate the suspension system. Observe, in particular, the time required for the wheel to return to normal after it runs over a square pothole and the amount of overshoot.
3. Simulate the suspension system suspension system, with an added requirement that there is a physical stopper that prevents the maximum displacement from exceeding a value of 2 units.
4. Write a computer program to analyze the behavior of the suspension system when it runs over a series of equi-spaced potholes on the road.
5. How will you determine the constants of the spring k_3, and of the shock absorber k_1 (assume k_2 to be one-hundredth of k_1), given m, $F(t)$, the maximum tolerable displacement, and the maximum time allowed to return to normal?
6. Constant c is the drag coefficient for the gun ball. Variables v and θ are the instantaneous velocity and angle of elevation of the cannon ball, and x, y are the coordinates of its instantaneous position, v_0, elevation θ_0 and $x_0 = y_0 = 0$, the program should yield the range.
7. A missile is fired vertically up. It has a rocket, motor that produces a certain constant upward thrust F for as long as the fuel-burning motor is on. The motor burns the fuel at some constant rate b. Assume that the missile does not go so high as to vary the gravity constant g nor does the drag coefficient vary during the flight. Set up the equation of the vertical motion. Write a program which gives the vertical distance y at any time t.
8. Modify the simulation program in exercise (question 6) in order to make it valid for higher altitudes. That is, take into account the reduction in the air resistance and change in the value of the gravitational constant g as the missile rises higher.
9. Suppose a 50 kilogram heat-seeking missile is fired at a jet bomber flying at a constant speed of 1,200 Km/hour. The missile has a rocket motor that produces a thrust of 5000 kilogram for a period of 4 minutes. Simulate the missile system to test its effectiveness and to estimate how close the target should be before a missile is fired. Assume the drag coefficient $c = 0.04$ Kg/Km^2 and the weight of liquid fuel is 20 kilogram (which is burned in 4 minutes at a constant rate).

10. Assuming that the drag force is proportional to the square of the speed and proportional to the cross-sectional area of a moving body, how will you simulate the experiment of the Tower of Pisa by dropping two lead balls of diameter 1 cm and 20 cm from a 500 meter tower?

11. Given a gun that fires spherical balls of a mass *m*, you are asked to produce a range table, *i.e.*, a table that gives ranges for various values of muzzle velocity and gun elevation (firing angle). You are also asked to investigate the sensitivity of range to small changes in muzzle velocity and gun elevation. For simplicity, let us assume that the drag is proportional to the square of the instantaneous velocity of the gun ball, and it is purely along the direction of flight. Making use of the following four equations, write a computer program to produce a range table:

$$m\frac{dy}{dt} + mg\sin\theta + cv^2 = 0$$

12. Explain exponential growth model, exponential decay model, modified exponential growth models in detail.

Chapter 4

QUEUEING SYSTEM

4.1 INTRODUCTION

Queueing system is used to reduce or optimize the total waiting cost. The theory enables mathematical analysis of several related processes, including arriving at the queue, waiting in the queue (essentially a storage process), and being served by the server(s) at the front of the queue. The theory permits the derivation and calculation of several performance measures including the average waiting time in the queue or the system, the expected number waiting or receiving service and the probability of encountering the system in certain states, such as empty, full, having an available server or having to wait a certain time to be served.

The word queue comes, via French, from the Latin *cauda*, meaning tail. Most researchers in the field prefer the spelling 'queueing' over 'queuing', although the latter is somewhat more common in other contexts. Queueing Theory is the study of waiting times in queues (lines). Queueing Theory is used to optimizing systems to reduce wait times. An easy example to understand is looking at wait times in line. For example, if a store has 10 different service lines then any delay at a specific line means all those in that line have to suffer to a greater extent. If, instead, there is one line that feeds all 10 stations then a delay in one line will mean that a delay at one station does not adversely impact the few unlucky enough to choose that line.

Queueing theory, the theory of congestion, is the branch of operations research which explores the relationships between demand on a service system and the delays suffered by the users of that system. Since almost all urban service systems can be viewed as queueing systems. Queueing Theory plays a central role in the analysis of and planning for urban services. This chapter therefore deals with a review of some important results in queueing theory and with an introduction to the applications of these results to the problems on which this book focuses.

Queuing theory is generally considered a branch of operations research because the results are often used when making business decisions about the resources needed to provide service. It is applicable in a wide variety of situations that may be encountered in business, commerce, industry, public service and engineering. Applications are frequently encountered in customer service situations as well as transport and telecommunication and it is occasionally linked to ride theory. Queueing Theory is directly applicable to intelligent transportation systems, call centers, networks, telecommunications, server-queueing, mainframe computer queueing of telecommunications terminals, advanced telecommunications systems, and traffic flow, etc.

Definitions and Notations. Here we are giving definitions of queueing theory/model/system used worldwide.

- A queue is a line of customers waiting to be served.
- We study the phenomena of standing, waiting, and serving, and we call this study Queueing Theory.
- Any system in which arrivals place demands upon a finite capacity resource may be termed a queueing system.
- The term Queueing Theory is often used to describe the more specialized mathematical theory of waiting lines.
- A Queueing System can be described as customers arriving for service, waiting for service if it is not immediate, and if having waited for service, leaving the system after being served. The primary tool for studying these problems (of congestions) is known as Queueing Theory.
- A queue or waiting line is formed when customers arrive at a counter offering certain facilities and demand service.
- A queue, or a waiting line, involves arriving items that wait to be served at the facility which provides the service they seek.
- In Queueing theory, we study situations where units of some kind arrive at a service facility for receiving service of some description, some of the units have to wait for service, and depart after service.
- The theory of queues deals with the investigation of the stochastic law of different processes arising in connection with mass servicing in cases where random fluctuations occur.

The basic phenomenon of queueing arises whenever a shared facility needs to be accessed for service by a large number of jobs or customers. A queue is formed when service requests arrive at a service facility and are forced to wait while the server is busy working on other requests.

In this chapter we shall use the term queueing system to refer to a generic model, which comprises three elements: a user source, a queue, and a service facility that contains one or more (including possibly an infinite number of) identical servers in parallel. Thus, each user of a queueing system is "generated" by a user source, passes through the queue where he/she may remain for a nonnegative period of time (including possibly zero time), and then is processed by a single server-because of the parallel arrangement of servers. Once a user has left any one of the servers in the system, after obtaining service there, the user is considered to have left the queueing system as well.

In view of the description given above, a queueing network can now be defined as a set of interconnected queueing systems. Thus, in a queueing network, the user sources for some of the queueing systems in the network may be other queueing systems in the same network. It can also be inferred that the analysis of models of queueing systems, as we have defined them here, provides the building blocks for the analysis of queueing networks.

To describe a Queueing System fully, information must be supplied to all the three generic elements of the system as we see in figure 4.1:

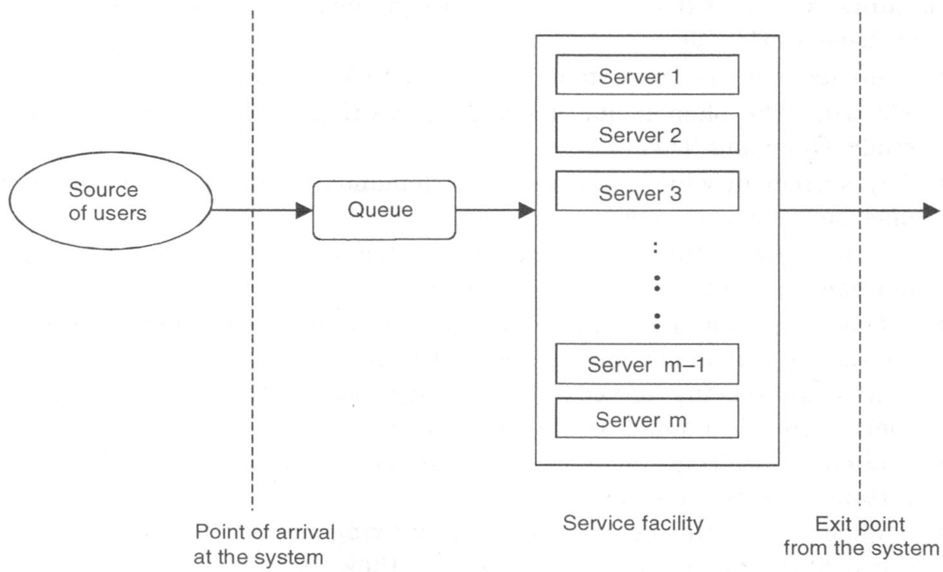

Fig. 4.1 Generic queueing system with m server

- The user generating process (*i.e.,* the arrival process of users at the system).
- The queue discipline (*i.e.,* the order in which users obtain access to the service facility, once they join the queue).
- The service process.

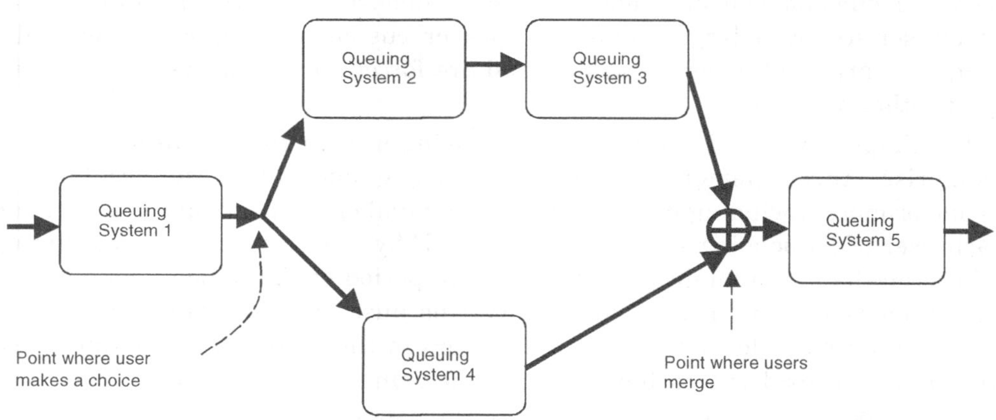

Fig. 4.2 Queuing network considering five queueing systems

To describe a queueing network, further information must be provided (see figure 4.2) on how the queueing systems are interconnected, how they interact, and how users are assigned to the queueing systems. It should be obvious that there exist countless variations of queueing systems and networks. We shall have occasion to refer to some of these variations in following sections. At this point, however, it should be noted that a code has been used in queueing theory for years to describe some of the simplest (and best understood) queueing systems. This code is of the form $A\,|\,B\,|\,m$, where A and B are letter symbols and m is an integer constant. The letters A and B indicate the probability distribution of user inter-arrival times and of service times, respectively, and m is the number of identical parallel servers in the queueing system (thus, m can take values from 1 to ∞).

The standard code letters used for probability distributions in queueing theory are:

- M = Poisson (*i.e.*, negative exponential pdf for user inter-arrival times or for service times; M stands for "memory less")
- D = deterministic (*i.e.*, inter-arrival or service times are constant)
- E_k = kth-order Erlang distribution
- H_k = kth-order hyper-exponential distribution
- G = "general" distribution (*i.e.*, any distribution at all).

The letters A and B can thus be any one of the five symbols above.

Examples of queueing systems that can be defined with this convention are:

- ***M/M/*1:** This is the simplest queueing system to analyze. Here the arrival and service time are negative exponentially distributed (Poisson process). The system consists of only one server. This queueing system can be applied to a wide variety of problems as any system with a very large number of independent customers can be approximated as a Poisson process. Using a Poisson process for service time however is not applicable in many applications and is only a crude approximation.
- ***M/D/n*:** Here the arrival process is Poisson and the service time distribution is deterministic. The system has n servers (for example, a ticket booking counter with n cashiers.) Here the service time can be assumed to be same for all customers).
- ***G/G/n*:** This is the most general queueing system where the arrival and service time processes are both arbitrary. The system has n servers. No analytical solution is known for this queueing system.

To newcomers to queueing theory it always seems strange that, out of all possible probability distributions, only four (M, D, E_k, and H_k) have been assigned special symbols. The simple reason is that only these four distributions offer significant advantages in an abstract analysis, in the sense that when they are present in a queueing model, parts of the mathematical analysis of that model may become more tractable. Thus, all other distributions are lumped under the "general" (G) category (which, of course, also includes the M, D, E, and H_k cases). These comments will become clearer as we make our way through this chapter.

The coded systems also assume independence of successive user arrival times and of successive service times at the queueing system. We shall see several examples of urban service systems where this assumption is not valid in practice. Some more-or-less standard abbreviations are also used to indicate the most commonly encountered queue disciplines. FIFO is used to indicate the first-in-first-out queueing arrangement, also known as FCFS (first come, first served). Similarly, LIFO indicate the situation in which the last user to join the queue becomes the next in line for entering service. The abbreviation SIRO is used to indicate "service in random order."

Another important parameter in the description of a queueing system is the *system capacity*. This indicates the maximum number of users that can at any time be in the service facility *and* in the queue. *Queue capacity*, on the other hand, indicates the maximum number of users that can be in the queue alone.

It is important to emphasize that queueing systems need not adhere to the classical picture of a physically stationary server (a bank teller, a checkout counter, highway toll booths, etc.) where prospective users queue up to be served. It is very common to have systems in which the prospective users remain stationary, possibly at geographically widely separated points, while the server(s) associated with the queueing system visit them according to some (implicit or explicit) priority scheme and provide the requested service.

4.2 WORKING WITH QUEUEING SYSTEM

In working with queueing theory one must, first of all, take the particular real-world system of interest, study the system, and create (or simply select from the list of models in queueing theory) a mathematical model to represent it. Through the analysis of this mathematical model, one then obtains the answers, which supposedly apply to the original system as well. Inherent to the procedure of creating a mathematical model are the notions of simplification and approximation: the analyst must necessarily disregard many details which he or she considers superfluous to the central points of interest. In most cases, approximations must also be made in transforming raw and often incomplete data into mathematical quantities that will make the analysis of the model possible. It is not unusual for an analyst to make many assumptions about certain aspects of the behavior of the real system assumptions based mostly on intuition and experience rather than on any real evidence that the system indeed behaves in this way. Under the circumstances it would then be fair to state that, in most applications, the estimates of quantities of interest which can be obtained through a queueing analysis should only be viewed as approximate indicators of the size of these quantities in the real-world. Consequently, the application of queueing theory is most useful in pointing out the inadequacies of existing operating systems, the directions in which to proceed for improving these systems, and the approximate values that some of the controllable variables of the system must assume to achieve a satisfactory level of performance.

Another major point that should be realized is that queueing theory does not offer a full menu of answers. The state-of-the-art after nearly three decades of intensive research can be summarized roughly as follows:

1. Few closed-form expressions exist for the transient and the non-stationary behavior of queueing systems. Almost all the existing important results of queueing theory are obtained for equilibrium conditions.
2. Even assuming equilibrium conditions, queueing theory runs into enormous mathematical difficulties in all but relatively few types of situations. Quite often, the choice facing an analyst is between, on the one hand, using a realistic mathematical model for which almost no results can be obtained and, on the other, using a simplified model that provides results of questionable validity for the problem at hand.
3. Most of the exact results of queueing theory apply to queueing systems in which the inter-arrival times or the service times or both are negative exponential. Fortunately, there are many real-world systems for which at least the inter-arrival times are negative exponential. The main reason is that many arrival processes observable in practice can be modeled as Poisson processes, which in turn implies negative exponential inter-arrival times. This is especially true when one refers to urban service systems, where Poisson (or nearly Poisson) arrival processes are rich.
4. Queueing theory is very good at estimating the low moments and central moments of such important quantities as the waiting times or the "number of users present" in queueing systems but not nearly as good at computing the probability distributions for these quantities. Indeed, in all but a handful of cases, the only approach available for obtaining probability distributions for most of the quantities of interest in queueing theory is through the use of a combination of transform analysis and numerical analysis techniques.

Points 1–4 above, discouraging as they may sound only mean to provide some perspective and not to detract from the value of the results that queueing theory has generated to date. In fact, some of these results are very powerful. They apply to quite general queueing systems and provide important information about the queueing phenomena that occur, while requiring only a minimum amount of knowledge about the characteristics of inter-arrival times, service times, queue discipline, and so on.

4.3 QUEUEING THEORY BASICS

We have seen that as a system gets congested, the service delay in the system increases. A good understanding of the relationship between congestion and delay is essential for designing effective congestion control algorithms. Queuing Theory provides all the tools needed for this analysis.

4.3.1 Communication Delays

Before we proceed further, let us describe the different components of delay in a messaging system. The total delay experienced by messages can be classified into the following categories:

Table 4.1 Classifications of delays in Queueing System

Processing Delay	• This is the delay between the times of receipt of a packet for transmission to the point of putting it into the transmission queue. • On the receive end, it is the delay between the time of reception of a packet in the receive queue to the point of actual processing of the message. • This delay depends on the CPU speed and CPU load in the system.
Queuing Delay	• This is the delay between the point of entry of a packet in the transmit queue to the actual point of transmission of the message. • This delay depends on the load on the communication link.
Transmission Delay	• This is the delay between the transmissions of first bit of the packet to the transmission of the last bit. • This delay depends on the speed of the communication link.
Propagation Delay	• This is the delay between the points of transmission of the last bit of the packet to the point of reception of last bit of the packet at the other end. • This delay depends on the physical characteristics of the communication link.
Retransmission Delay	• This is the delay that results when a packet is lost and has to be retransmitted. • This delay depends on the error rate on the link and the protocol used for retransmissions.

Little's Theorem. We begin our analysis of queueing systems by understanding Little's Theorem. This theorem states that:

The average number of customers (*N*) can be determined from the following equation:

$$N = \lambda T$$

Here λ is the average customer arrival rate and T is the average service time for a customer. Here we will focus on an intuitive understanding of the result not on proof. Consider the example of a restaurant where the customer arrival rate (λ) doubles but the customers still spend the same amount of time in the restaurant (T). This will double the number of customers in the restaurant (N). By the same logic if the customer arrival rate remains the same but the customers service time doubles, this will also double the total number of customers in the restaurant.

4.3.2 Queueing System Classification

With Little's Theorem, we have some basic understanding of a queueing system. For further understanding we will have to dig deeper into characteristics of a queueing system that impact its performance. For example, queueing requirements of a restaurant will depend upon factors like:

- How do customers arrive in the restaurant? Are customer arrivals more during lunch and dinner time (a regular restaurant)? Or is the customer traffic more uniformly distributed (*e.g.*, a cafe)?
- How much time do customers spend in the restaurant? Do customers typically leave the restaurant in a fixed amount of time? Does the customer service time vary with the type of customer?
- How many tables does the restaurant have for servicing customers?

The above three points correspond to the most important characteristics of a queueing system. They are explained below:

Table 4.2 Characteristics of a Queueing System

Arrival Process	• The probability density distribution that determines the customer arrivals in the system. • In a messaging system, this refers to the message arrival probability distribution.
Service Process	• The probability density distribution that determines the customer service times in the system. • In a messaging system, this refers to the message transmission time distribution. Since message transmission is directly proportional to the length of the message, this parameter indirectly refers to the message length distribution.
Number of Servers	• Number of servers available to service the customers. • In a messaging system, this refers to the number of links between the source and destination nodes.

Based on the above characteristics, queueing systems can be classified by the following convention:

4.3.3 Facts about Queueing System

Queueing Networks. Queues can be chained to form queueing networks where the element departing from one queue enter the next queue. Queueing networks can be classified into two categories: open queueing networks and closed queueing networks. Open queueing networks have an external input and an external final destination. Closed queueing networks are completely contained and the customers circulate continually never leaving the network.

The role of the Poisson process and exponential distributions. To derive a queueing model that represents a real-life system, we prefer a form that is simple or tractable, but require that it be sufficiently realistic. For queueing theory, it has been found convenient to work with probability distributions which exhibit the memory-less property, as this commonly simplifies the mathematics involved. As a result, queueing models are frequently modeled as Poisson processes through the use of the exponential distribution.

Limitations of the Mathematical Approach. Classic queueing theory is often too mathematically restrictive to be able to model all real-world situations exactly. This restriction arises because the underlying assumptions of the theory do not always hold in the real-world. For example; the mathematical models often assume infinite numbers of customers, or queue capacity, or no bounds on inter-arrival or service times, when it is quite apparent that these bounds must exist in reality. Often, although the bounds do exist, they can be safely ignored because the differences between the real-world and theory is not statistically significant, as the probability that such boundary situations might occur is remote compared to the expected normal situation. In other cases the theoretical solution may either prove intractable or insufficiently informative to be useful.

Alternative means of analysis have thus been devised in order to provide some insight into problems which do not fall under the mathematical scope of queueing theory, though they are often scenario-specific since they generally consist of computer simulations and/or of analysis of experimental data.

4.4 THE QUEUEING MODEL

In queueing theory, a queueing model is used to approximate a real queueing situation or system, so the queueing behavior can be analyzed mathematically. Queueing models allow a number of useful steady state performance measures to be determined, including:

- the average number in the queue, or the system,
- the average time spent in the queue, or the system,
- the statistical distribution of those numbers or times,
- the probability the queue is full, or empty, and
- the probability of finding the system in a particular state.

These performance measures are important as issues or problems caused by queueing situations are often related to customer dissatisfaction with service or may be the root cause of economic losses in a business. Analysis of the relevant queueing models allows the cause of queueing issues to be identified and the impact of any changes that might be wanted to be assessed. Queueing models can be represented using Kendall's notation:

$A/B/S/K/N/Disc$

Where:

- A is the inter-arrival time distribution
- B is the service time distribution
- S is the number of servers
- K is the system capacity

- N is the calling population
- *Disc* is the service discipline assumed.

4.4.1 Models Construction and Analysis

Queueing models are generally constructed to represent the steady state of a queueing system, that is, the typical, long run or average state of the system. As a consequence, these are stochastic models that represent the probability that a queueing system will be found in a particular configuration or state. A general procedure for constructing and analyzing such queueing models is:

1. Identify the parameters of the system, such as the arrival rate, service time, queue capacity, and perhaps draw a diagram of the system.
2. Identify the system states. A state will generally represent the integer number of customers, people, jobs, calls, messages, etc., in the system that may or may not be limited.
3. Draw a state transition diagram that represents the possible system states and identify the rates to enter and leave each state. This diagram is a representation of a Markov chain.
4. Because the state transition diagram represents the steady state situation between states there is a balanced flow between states so the probabilities of being in adjacent states can be related mathematically in terms of the arrival and service rates and state probabilities.
5. Express all the state probabilities in terms of the empty state probability, using the interstate transition relationships.
6. Determine the empty state probability by using the fact that all state probabilities always sum to 1.

Whereas specific problems that have small finite state models are often able to be analyzed numerically, analysis of more general models, using calculus, yields useful formulae that can be applied to whole classes of problems. This model not really efficient for the use among the model it has.

4.5 SINGLE SERVER QUEUE SIMULATION

Single server queues are, perhaps, the most commonly encountered queueing situation in real-life. One encounters a queue with a single server in many situations, including business (for example, sales clerk), industry (for example, a production line), transport (for example, a bus, a taxi), telecommunications (for example, telephone line), computing (for example, processor sharing). Even where there are multiple servers handling the situation it is possible to consider each server individually as part of the larger system, in many cases, for example, a shopping mall checkout has several single server queues that the customer can select from.) Consequently, being able to model and analyze a single server queue's behavior is a particularly useful thing to do.

4.5.1 Poisson Arrivals and Services

M/M/1/∞/∞ represents a single server that has unlimited queue capacity and infinite calling population, both arrivals and service are Poisson (or random) processes, meaning the statistical distribution of both the inter-arrival times and the service times follow the exponential distribution. Due to the mathematical nature of the exponential distribution, a number of quite simple relationships are able to be derived for several performance measures based on knowing the arrival rate and service rate. This is fortunate because, an M/M/1 queueing model can be used to approximate many queueing situations.

4.5.2 Poisson Arrivals and General Services

M/G/1/∞/∞ represents a single server that has unlimited queue capacity and infinite calling population, while the arrival is still Poisson process, meaning the statistical distribution of the inter-arrival times still follow the exponential distribution, the distribution of the service time does not. The distribution of the service time may follow any general statistical distribution, not just exponential. Relationships are still able to be derived for a number of performance measures if one knows the arrival rate and the mean and variance of the service rate. However the derivations are generally more complex. A number of special cases of M/G/1 provide specific solutions that give broad insights into the best model to choose for specific queueing situations because they permit the comparison of those solutions to the performance of an M/M/1 model.

A queueing system consists of one or more servers that provide service of some kind to arriving customers. Customers who arrive to find all servers busy (generally) join one or more queues or lines in front of the servers, hence the name queueing system. A large proportion of all discrete-event simulation studies have involved the modeling of a real-world queueing system, or a least some component of the system being simulated was a queueing system.

4.5.3 Components of a Queueing System

A queueing system is characterized by *three* components:

(a) Arrival process

(b) Service mechanism

(c) Queue discipline.

Specifying the arrival process for a queueing system consists of describing how customers arrive to the system. Let A_i be the inter-arrival time between the arrivals of the $(i - 1)$st and ith customers. If A_1, A_2, A_3.... are assumed to be independent and identically distributed (IID) random variables, we shall denote the means (or expected) *inter-arrival time* by *E(A) and call* $\lambda = \frac{1}{E(A)}$ *the arrival rate* of customers.

The *service mechanism* for a queueing system is articulated by specifying the one queue feeding all servers, and the probability distribution of customers, service times. Let S_i be the service time of the lth arriving customer. If S_1, S_2,.... are independent and identically distributed random variables, we shall denote the mean service time of a customer by $E(S)$ and call $\omega = 1/E(S)$ the *service rate* of a server:

(a) **FIFO :** Customers are served in a first-in-first-out manner.

(b) **LIFO :** Customers are served in last-in-first-out manner.

(c) **Priority :** Customers are served in order of their importance or on the basis of their service requirements.

Consider a single-server queueing system as shown in figure 4.3 for which the inter-arrival times A_1, A_2, A_3....are *independent and identically distributed* random variables. A customer who arrives and finds the server idle enters service immediately, and the service times S_1,S_2,.....of the successive customers are IID random variables that are independent of the inter-arrival times. A customer who arrives and finds the server busy joins the end of a single queue. Upon completing service for a customer, the server chooses a customer from the queue (if any) in a first-in-first-out (FIFO) manner.

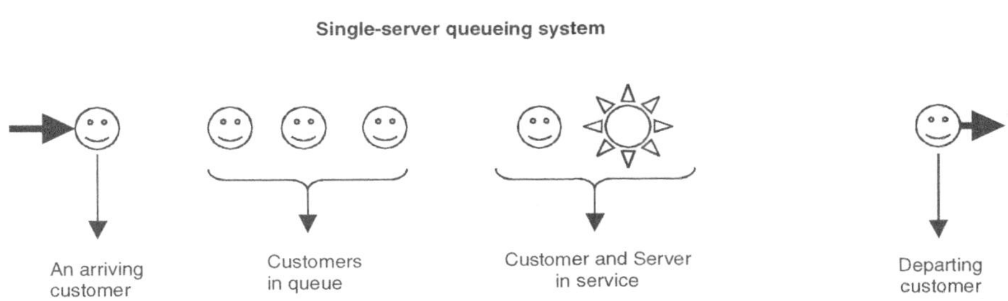

Fig. 4.3 Single-server queueing system

Arrivals and services are described by the distribution of the time between arrivals and service times. The overall effective arrival rate must be less than the maximum service rate, or the waiting line will grow without bound. When queues grow without bound, they are termed "explosive" or unstable. An exceptional situation would be arrival rates that are greater than service rates for short period of time. The *state of the system* is the number of units in the system and the status of the server, busy or idle. An *event* is set of circumstances that cause in instantaneous change in the state of the system. In the single server queueing system there are *two* possible events that can affect the state of the system. They are:

- Entry of unit into the system *i.e.,* the arrival event.
- The completion of service on a unit *i.e.,* the departure event.

The queueing system includes:

- The server
- The unit being serviced
- Units in the queue (if any units are waiting).

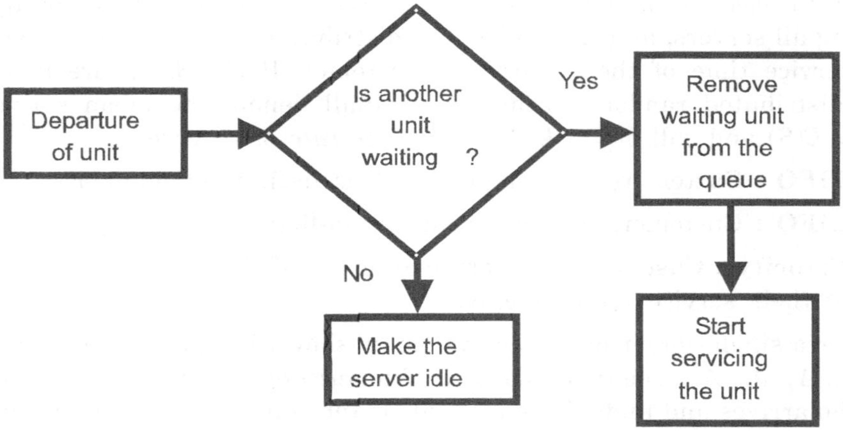

Fig. 4.4 Flow diagram of service just completed

The server can have only *two* possible conditions:

- Busy
- Idle

If service has been completed, the simulation proceeds as shown in figure 4.5.

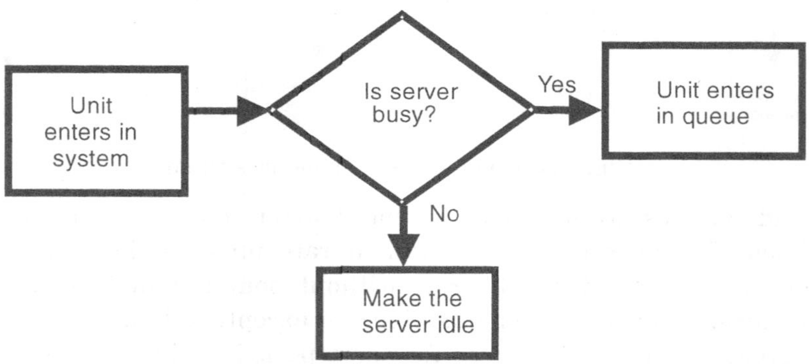

Fig. 4.5 Flow Diagram of Unit Entering in Queueing System

The next event that occurs after service just completed is new unit entering the system. The entered unit may find the server either idle or busy. If the server is busy, the unit enters the queue. If the server is idle and the queue is empty, the unit enters the server. It is impossible for the server to be idle and the queue to be not empty. The figure 4.5 shows the course of action taken when a unit enters the system. From the flow diagram (figure 4.5), a table 4.3 (below) can be drawn with columns as queue status and rows as server status.

Table 4.3 Action taken on unit arrival event

Queue Status / *Server Status*	*Non-Empty*	*Empty*
Server Busy	Enter into Queue	Enter into Queue
Server Idle	Impossible	Enter service

After the competition of a service the server may become idle or remain busy with the next unit. The course of action as described in points below:

(*a*) If the queue is not empty, another unit will enter the server and it will be busy.

(*b*) If the queue is empty, when all the services are complete including the servicing unit then the server will be idle.

(*c*) It is impossible for the server to become busy, if the queue is empty, when all the services are complete.

(*d*) It is impossible for the server to be idle after a service is completed, when the queue is not empty.

Above stated point can be shown in tabular from as in table 4.4

Table 4.4 Server outcomes after unit service completion.

Queue Status / *Server Outcomes*	*Non-Empty*	*Empty*
Server Busy	Enter into Queue	Impossible
Server Idle	Impossible	No unit

Simulations of queueing system generally require the maintenance of an event list for determining what happens next. The even list indicates the times at which the different types of event occur for each unit in the queueing system. The times are "clock" that marks the occurrence of events in time. In simulation, the events usually occur at random. For example, it is not known how long the bank teller will take to complete a transaction or when the next customer will arrive at a grocery checkout counter.

Random numbers are distributed uniformly and independently on the interval [0, 1]. Random digits can be used to form random number by selecting the proper number of digits for each random number and placing decimal point to the left of the value selected. Random numbers can also be generated. When numbers are generated using a set procedure they are often called as *pseudo-random numbers.* As the method is known, it is always possible to know what the sequence of numbers will be prior to the simulation. In a single-server queueing system inter-arrival times and service times are determined from the distributions of these random variables.

Let us simulate the arrival and servicing of N customers by a single server. Let the inter-arrival time of ith customer be AT_i, which denotes the time gap between the arrivals of the $(i - 1)^{st}$ customer and the ith customer into the system.

Let the service time of ith customer is ST_i where $i = 1, 2, ..., N$.

Let cumulative arrival time of ith customer is CAT_i.

Service times (ST_i) and inter-arrival times (AT_i) are generated as samples from some specified probability distribution.

Assuming, initially there is no queue and the server is free. When the first customer arrives, at time zero, directly goes to the service counter. After ST_1 time, the first customer departs from the service counter.

Second customer arrives at $CAT_2 = AT_2$ ...(4.1)

If $ST_1 > CAT_2$ *i.e.*, service time of first customer is greater than arrival time of second customer than the second customer has to wait in the queue.

Let WT_i is the waiting time of ith customer

$$WT_2 = ST_1 - CAT_2 \quad ...(4.2)$$

If $ST_1 < CAT_2$ *i.e.*, service time of first customer is less than arrival time of second customer. This, means, departure of first customer takes place before the arrival of second customer. Thus the service counter is free waiting for the second customer to arrive. The idle time is given by

$$IDT_2 = CAT_2 - ST_1 \quad ...(4.3)$$

Let us consider that $(j - 1)$ customers have arrived and $(k - 1)$ customers have left the system. The next customer to arrive is j^{th} and the next customer to depart is k^{th}.

$$1 \le j \le k \le N \quad ...(4.4)$$

$\therefore$ The queue length is given by

$$k - j - 1 \quad \text{if } k > j \quad ...(4.5)$$

The next arrival time is

$$NAT = CAT_j \quad ...(4.6)$$

The next departure time is

$NDT = CDT_k$ = Cumulative arrival time of k + waiting time of k = service time of k.

$$NDT = CDT_k = CAT_k + WT_k + ST_k \quad ...(4.7)$$

Whether j would arrive first of k would depart first depends on difference between them.

$$DIF = NAT - NDT \quad ...(4.8)$$

If difference DIF is positive than

(*a*) queue length is $k - j - 1$

(*b*) departure would take place first.

(*c*) Reduce the length of queue by 1 as departure takes place first.

(*d*) If the length of queue is zero than the service counter will remain free waiting for a customer to arrive.

If difference *DIF* is negative than

(*a*) arrival takes place first.

(*b*) length of the queue is increased by one.

If difference *DIF* is zero than

(*a*) the next arrival and departure takes place simultaneously.

(*b*) the length of the queue remains same.

Some of the finding for short-term simulations are as follows :

(*i*) The Average Waiting Time (AWT) of the customer is calculated as follows :

Average Waiting Time (in minutes)

$$= \frac{\text{Total time customer wait in queue (in minutes)}}{\text{Total number of customers}} \quad \text{...(4.9)}$$

(*ii*) The probability that a customer has to wait in a queue is calculated as :

$$\text{Probability (wait)} = \frac{\text{Number of customers who wait}}{\text{Total number of customers.}} \quad \text{...(4.10)}$$

(*iii*) The probability that a server is idle can be calculated as :

$$\text{Probability of idle Server} = \frac{\text{Total run time of server (minutes)}}{\text{Total run time of simulation (minutes)}} \quad \text{...(4.11)}$$

(*iv*) The probability of server being busy is calculated as :

Probability of Busy Server = 1 – Probability of idle server

$$= 1 - \frac{\text{Total run time of server (minutes)}}{\text{Total run time of simulation (minutes) (AST)}} \quad \text{...(4.12)}$$

(*v*) The average service time (AST) is calculated as :

$$\text{Average service time (minutes)} = \frac{\text{Total service time (minutes)}}{\text{Total number of customers}} \quad \text{...(4.13)}$$

(*vi*) Average time between arrival (minutes)

$$= \frac{\text{Sum of all time betwen arrivals (in minutes)}}{\text{Number of arrivals} - 1} \quad \text{...(4.14)}$$

One is subtracted from the denominator because the first arrival is assumed to occur at time 0.

(*vii*) The average waiting time of those who wait is calculated as :

$$\text{Average waiting time (minutes)} = \frac{\text{Total time customers wait in queue (in minutes)}}{\text{Total number of customers}} \qquad \text{...(4.15)}$$

(*viii*) The average time a customer spends in the system is calculated in two ways.

$$(a)\ \text{Average time customer spends} = \frac{\text{Total time customers spend in the system (minutes)}}{\text{Total number of customers}} \qquad \text{...(4.16)}$$

$$(b)\ \begin{array}{l}\text{Average time}\\ \text{customer spends}\\ \text{in the system}\end{array} = \begin{array}{l}\text{an Average time}\\ \text{customers spends}\\ \text{waiting in the}\\ \text{queue}\end{array} + \begin{array}{l}\text{Average time}\\ \text{customer spends}\\ \text{in service}\end{array} \qquad \text{....(4.17)}$$

Example 4.1 Single–Server Queue

A small grocery store has only one checkout counter. Assume that the time between customer arrivals is recorded as in table 4.5. Table 4.5 has five inter-arrival times are used to compute the arrival times of sing customers at the queueing system.

Table 4.5 Inter-arrival and Clock Times

Customer	*Inter-arrival time*	*Arrival time on clock*
1	–	0
2	2	2
3	4	6
4	1	7
5	2	9
6	6	15

Table 4.6 contains service times generated at random from a distribution of serving times. Only one, two, three, and four units are possible service times.

Table 4.6 Service Time

Customer	*Service time*
1	2
2	1
3	3
4	2
5	1
6	4

Solution:

From Tables 4.5. The first customer is assumed to arrive at clock time 0. This starts the clock operation. The second customer arrives two time units later, at a clock time of 2. The third customer arrive four time units later at a clock time of 6; and so on.

From Table 4.6. The first customer arrives at clock time 0, and immediately begins service, which requires two minutes. Service is completed at clock time 2. The second customer arrives at clock time 2 and is finished at clock time 3. The fourth customer arrived at clock time 7, but service could not begin until clock time 9. This happens as customer 3 did not finish service until clock time 9.

Table 4.7 is specifically designed for a single-server queue which server customers on a first-in-first-out (FIFO) basis. It keeps track of clock time at which each event occurs. The second column records the clock time of each arrival event, while the last column records the clock time of each departure event.

Figure 4.6 shows the number of customers in the system at the various number of clock times. Table 4.8 is ordered by clock time, in which cash the events may or may not be ordered by customer number.

Table 4.7 Simulation Table

Customer (1)	*Arrival time (clock)* (2)	*Time service begin (clock)* (3)	*Service time (duration)* (4)	*Time service ends (clock)* (5)
1	0	0	2	2
2	2	2	1	3
3	6	6	3	9
4	7	9	2	11
5	9	11	1	12
6	15	15	4	19

Column (5) is calculated as follows:

$$\text{Column 5} = \text{Column 3} + \text{Column 4}.$$

Column (3) is calculated verifying that if the service time is greater than the arrival time than the customer enters the queue and the time service begins is after the completion of the previous customers. Event type can be arrival and departure of the customer regarding the clock time:

1. Customer 1 is in the system from clock time 0 to clock time 2.
2. Customer 2 arrives at clock time 2 and departures at clock time 3.
3. There is no customer in the system from clock time 3 to clock time 6. Customer 3 arriver at clock time 6 and at clock time 7 customer 4 arrives and so from 7 to 9, there are two customers (customer 3 and customer 4) in the system.

4. At clock time 9, two events are occurring simultaneously *i.e.,* departure of customer 3 and arrival of customer 5. Similarly at clock time 2, customer 1 departs and customer 2 arrives.
5. Till clock period 11, there are two customers *i.e.,* customer 4 and customer 5.
6. At clock period 11, customer 4 departs and at clock period 12 customer 5 departs. From clock period 12 to clock period 15 there is no customer in the system. Customer 6 arrives at clock period 15 and departs at clock period 19 *i.e.,* only one customer in the system during this clock duration.

Table 4.8 Chronological Order of Events in Single-Server Queueing System

Event type number	*Clock time*
Arrival 1	0
Departure1	2
Arrival 2	2
Departure 2	3
Arrival 3	6
Departure 4	7
Arrival 3	9
Departure 5	9
Arrival 4	11
Departure 5	12
Arrival 6	15
Departure 6	19

Table 4.9 Simulation Table for Queueing Problem

Customer	*Time since last arrival (in minutes)*	*Arrival time (in minutes)*	*Service time (in minutes)*	*Time of service begin*	*Time customer wait in queue (in minute)*	*Time service ends*	*Time customer spends in system (in minute)*	*Idle time of service*
1	–	0	2	0	0–0=0	0+2=2	2–0=2	0–0=0
2	2–0=2	2	1	2	2–2=0	2+1=3	3–2=1	2–2=0
3	6–2=4	6	3	6	6–6=0	6+3=9	9–6=3	6–3=3
4	7–6=1	7	2	9	9–7=2	9+2=11	(11–9)+2=4	9–9=0
5	9–7=2	9	1	11	11–9=2	11+2=13	(12–11)+ 2=3	11–11=0
6	15–9=6	15	4	15	15–15=0	15+4=19	(19–15)+ 0=4	15–12=3
Total			**13**		**4**		**17**	

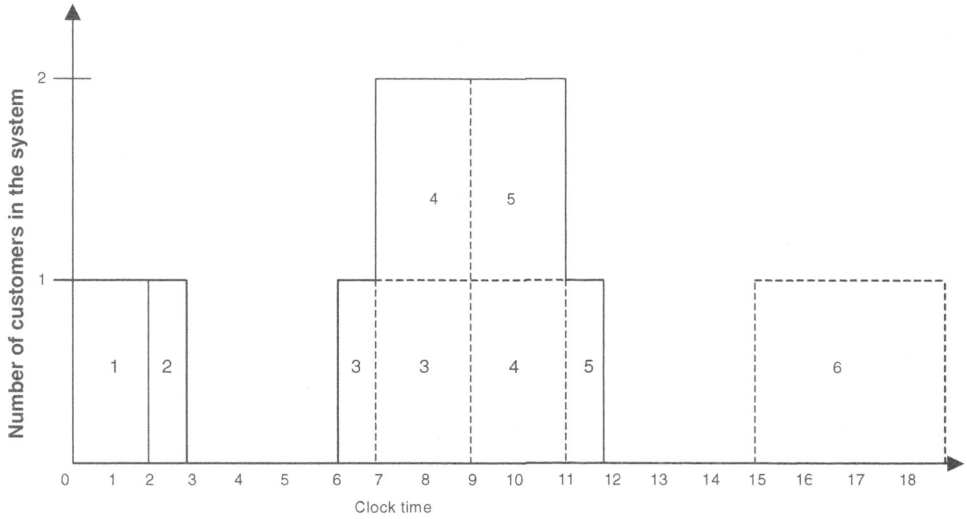

Fig. 4.6 Number of customer in the system at various clock time.

(*i*) Let us now calculate the parameters for short time simulation for this example

$$\text{Average waiting time (minutes)} = \frac{\text{Total time customer wait in queue (minute)}}{\text{Total number of customers}}$$

$$= \frac{4}{6}.$$

Average waiting time = 0.667 minutes.

(*ii*) Probability that a customer has to wait in the queue is

$$\text{Probability (wait)} = \frac{\text{Number of customers who wait}}{\text{Total number of customers}}$$

$$= \frac{2}{6} = 0.33$$

There are only two customers *i.e.,* customer 4 and customer 5 who have to wait for their service to begin.

(*iii*) $$\text{Probability of idle server} = \frac{\text{Total run time of server (minutes)}}{\text{Total run time of simulation (minutes)}}$$

$$= \frac{6}{19}$$

$$= 0.316.$$

(*iv*) $$\text{Probability of Busy Server} = 1 - \text{Probability of Idle Server.}$$

$$= 1 - 0.316$$

$$= 0.684.$$

(*v*) Average service time (minutes) $= \dfrac{\text{Total service time (minutes)}}{\text{Total number of customers}}$

$$= \frac{13}{6}$$

$$= 2.167$$

(*vi*) Average time between arrivals (minutes)

$$\approx \frac{\text{Sum of all times between arrival (minutes)}}{\text{number of arrivals } - 1}$$

$$= \frac{15}{(6-1)}$$

$$= 3 \text{ minutes.}$$

(*vii*) Average waiting time of those who wait (minutes)

$$\text{Total time of a customer} = \frac{\text{Wait in queue (minutes)}}{\text{Total number of customers}}$$

$$= \frac{4}{2}\text{(minutes)}$$

$$= 2 \text{ minutes.}$$

(*a*) Average time customer spends in the system (minutes)

$$\text{Total time of customer} = \frac{\text{Spend in the system (minutes)}}{\text{Total number of customers}}$$

$$= \frac{17}{6}\text{minutes}$$

$$\approx 2.833 \text{ minutes}$$

(*b*) Average time customer spends in the system (minutes) = Average time customer spends waiting in the queue + Average time customer spends in service

Substituting values from (*i*) and (*v*) and *vii* (*b*) = 0.667 minutes + 2.167 minutes.

A decision-maker would be interested in results of this type, but a longer simulation would increase the accuracy of the findings.

Some subjective inferences can be drawn from the above calculations :

(*a*) Less customer has to wait.

(*b*) Average waiting time is not excessive.

(*c*) Server remains idle for almost one-third of the system cycle.

(*d*) Probability of waiting of a customer so that server is free is also less.

(*e*) Cost estimation of waiting in the system can be done.

The event scheduling world view

In the *Event Scheduling* world view, a model describes, for each of the events, the event's effect:

- on the state,
- on the future behavior of the system. This is achieved by *scheduling* new events into the future.

An event scheduling model for the single queue, single server example is given below:

```
declare variables:
t : Time
queue_length : PosInt
cashier_state : {Idle, Busy}
declare events:
start, arrival, departure, end
define events:
start event:
/* scheduled first automatically by simulator */
/* initializations */
queue_length = 0
cashier_state = Idle
/* schedule end of simulation */
schedule end absolute end_time
/* schedule first arrival */
schedule arrival relative 0
arrival event:
schedule arrival relative Random(IATmean, IATspread)
if (queue_length == 0)
if (cashier_state == Idle)
cashier_state = Busy
schedule departure relative Random(SERVmean, SERVspread)
else
queue_length++
else /* for queue_length != 0 */
queue_length++
departure event:
if (queue_length == 0)
```

```
cashier_state = Idle
else /* for queue_length != 0 */
queue_length--
schedule departure relative Random(SERVmean, SERVspread)
end event:
/* terminates simulation */
/* process/output performance metrics */
print time, queue_length /* current */
print average_queue_length
```

The activity scanning worldview

In the *Activity Scanning* worldview, a model describes *conditions* which will activate *activities*. This representation (and its semantics described below) resembles that used in declarative AI (Artificial Intelligence) languages such as Prolog. An activity scanning model for the single queue, single server example is given below.

```
/*declare (and initialize) variables: */
t : Time
queue_length : PosInt = 0
cashier_state : {Idle, Busy} = Idle
t_arrival : Time = 0
t_depart : Time = plusInf
declare activities:
queue_pay, depart, end
queue_pay activity
condition: t >= t_arrival
actions:
if (queue_length == 0)
if (cashier_state == Idle)
keep queue_length == 0
cashier_state = Busy
t_depart = t + Random(SERVmean, SERVspread) /* service time */
else
queue_length++
else /* queue_length != 0 */
queue_length++, keep cashier_state == Busy
t_arrival = t + Random(IATmean, IATspread) /* inter arrival time */
depart activity
```

```
condition: t >= t_departure
actions:
if (queue_length == 0)
cashier_state = Idle
else /* queue_length != 0 */
queue_length--, keep cashier_state == Busy
t_depart = t + Random(SERVmean, SERVspread) /* service time */
end activity
condition: t >= t_end
actions:
print t, queue_length /* current */
print avg_queue_length /* performance metric */
```

4.6 GENERAL QUEUEING SYSTEM

Multiple (identical) servers queue situations are frequently encountered in telecommunications or a customer service environment. When modeling these situations care is needed to ensure that it is a multiple servers queue, not a network of single server queues, because results may differ depending on how the queueing model behaves. One observational insight provided by comparing queueing models is that a single queue with multiple servers performs better than each server having their own queue and that a single large pool of servers performs better than two or more smaller pools, even though there are the same total number of servers in the system.

One simple example to prove the above fact is as follows: Consider a system having 8 input lines, single queue and 8 servers. The output line has a capacity of 64Kbps, considering the arrival rate at each input as 2 packets/sec. So, the total arrival rate is 16 packets/sec. With an average of 2000 bits per packet, the service rate is 64Kbps/2000b = 32 packets/sec. Hence, the average response time of the system is $1/(\mu-\lambda) = 1/(32\text{-}16) = 0.0667$ sec. Now, consider a second system with 8 queues, one for each server. Each of the 8 output lines has a capacity of 8Kbps. The calculation yields the response time as $1/(\mu-\lambda) = 1/(4\text{-}2) = 0.5$ sec. And the average waiting time in the queue in the first case is $\rho/(1-\rho)\mu = 0.25$, while in the second case is 0.03125.

4.6.1 Infinite Servers

While never exactly encountered in reality, an *Infinite Servers* (*e.g.,* M/M/∞) model is a convenient theoretical model for situations that involve storage or delay, such as parking lots, warehouses and even atomic transitions. In these models there is no queue as such; instead each arriving *customer* receives service. When viewed from the outside, the model appears to delay or store each *customer* for sometime.

4.6.2 Many Operators, Infinite Number of Lines

Suppose now that, while keeping everything else in the emergency call center exactly the same as before, the number of telephone operators is increased to m (> 1). The service time associated with each operator is identical and negative exponential. When all operators are busy, the next call in line is assigned to the first operator to become free, while when two or more operators are free, the next incoming call is assigned to an operator in some arbitrary way. The state-transition diagram for this case is shown in figure 4.7. In terms of the queueing system code, this is a $M/M/m$ system with infinite queue capacity and FCFS service. With respect to our fundamental model:

$$\lambda_n = \lambda \quad \text{for } n = 0, 1, 2, 3, \ldots.$$
$$\mu_n = n\mu \quad \text{for } n = 0, 1, 2, 3, \ldots., m-1$$
$$\mu_n = m\mu \quad \text{for } n = m, m+1, m+2, \ldots.$$

Then

$$P_n = \left(\frac{(\lambda/\mu)^n}{n!}\right) P_0 \quad \text{for } n = 0, 1, 2, \ldots., m-1 \qquad \ldots(4.18)$$

$$= \frac{(\lambda/\mu)^n}{m^{n-m}.m!} P_0 \quad \text{for } n = m, m+1, m+2, \ldots\ldots$$

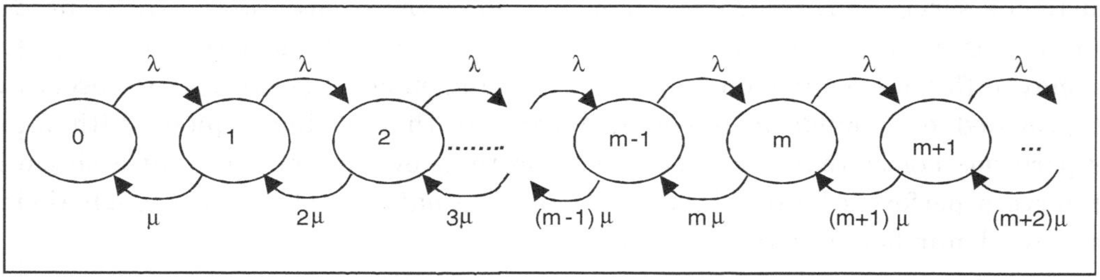

Fig. 4.7 State transition diagram for a M/M/m queueing system with infinite system capacity

and, substituting in $1 = \sum_{n=0}^{\infty} P_n$, we get

$$1 = \sum_{n=0}^{\infty} P_n = \left[\sum_{n=0}^{m-1} \frac{(\lambda/\mu)^n}{n!} + \sum_{n=m}^{\infty} \frac{(\lambda/\mu)^n}{m^{n-m}.m!}\right] P_0$$

$$= \left[\sum_{n=0}^{m-1} \frac{(\lambda/\mu)^n}{n!} + \frac{(\lambda/\mu)^m}{m!} \sum_{n=0}^{\infty} \left(\frac{\lambda}{m\mu}\right)^n\right] P_0 \qquad \ldots(4.19)$$

Using the geometric series expression for the last in the brackets (assuming that $\lambda/m\mu < 1$), we finally have,

$$P_0 = \left[\sum_{n=0}^{m-1} \frac{(\lambda/\mu)^n}{n!} + \frac{(\lambda/\mu)^m}{m!} \frac{1}{1-(\lambda/m\mu)}\right]^{-1} \qquad \text{...(4.20)}$$

With the condition for steady state being

$$\lambda(m\mu) < 1 \qquad \text{...(4.21)}$$

Expressions for other quantities of interest can now be derived using the steady-state probabilities, P_n.

Limiting case: Infinite number of servers. The limiting extension is when the number of servers m, is (countable) finite. In such a situation no user of the queueing system will ever have to wait in line. Since in this case we have

$$\lambda_n = \lambda \quad \text{for } n = 0, 1, 2, 3, 4, \qquad \text{...(4.22)}$$

$$\mu_n = n\mu \quad \text{for } n = 1, 2, 3, 4, 5, \qquad \text{...(4.23)}$$

it follows that

$$P_n = \frac{(\lambda/\mu)^n}{n!} P_0 \quad \text{for } n = 1, 2, 3, 4, 5, \qquad \text{...(4.24)}$$

and

$$1 = \sum_{n=0}^{\infty} P_n = P_0 \sum_{n=0}^{\infty} \frac{(\lambda/\mu)^n}{n!} = P_0 e^{\lambda/\mu} \qquad \text{...(4.25)}$$

thus we can conclude that

$$P_n = \frac{(\lambda/\mu)^n}{n!} e^{-\lambda/\mu} \quad \text{for } n = 0, 1, 2, 3, 4, 5, \ldots\ldots \qquad \text{...(4.26)}$$

This is a remarkable result, stating that the steady-state probability distribution for the number of users present (and, consequently, for the number of busy servers as well) in a M/M/∞ system is Poisson with parameter λ/μ. Note also that steady-state is inevitably reached in this case, since there are always sufficiently many servers to assure that the service rate will eventually exceed the rate of arrivals.

Although one may argue that there are not many systems around with an infinite number of servers, the model of this section is still very useful in numerous applications in which there is only a very low probability that all the servers in a system with many parallel, identical servers will be busy simultaneously. The Poisson distribution result for the steady-state probabilities that we derived can then be used to obtain good approximations of occupancy-related statistics for the system in question. We shall return to this type of approximation in our subsequent discussion of the M/G/∞ queueing system.

Example 4.2 Consider a tool crib where machines arrive in the morning to draw the tools. The number of mechanics arrives at a rate 1 per minute first half an hour of the shift (08 hours) and average number of mechanics served by tool crib operator is 1.2 per minute. Determine whether it is advisable to increase number of tool crib operator. The tool crib operators are paid Rs. 160 per shift and mechanics Rs. 320 per shift.

Solution:

Given λ = 1 per minute = 60 per hour

μ = 1.2 per minute = 72 per hour

Average number of mechanics waiting

$$L_q = \frac{\lambda^2}{\mu(\mu - \lambda)}$$

$= 60^2/(72*(72 - 60))$

$= 4.17$

Number of mechanics in the system

$$L_s = \frac{\lambda}{(\mu - \lambda)} = 60/(72 - 60) = 5$$

Mean waiting time per mechanic

$W_q = L_q/\lambda$

$= 4.17/60$

= 4.17 per minute

= 0.0695 per hour

Mean waiting time in the system per mechanic

$W_s = L_s/\lambda$

$= 5$

Probability to be in idle condition

$= 1 - P$

$= 1 - \lambda/\mu$

$= 1 - 1/1.2$

$= 0.1667$

Loss due to being idle per shift = 8 * 0.1667 * 2 = Rs. 2.67

Number of mechanics arrived per day at the rate = 1 per minute for half an hour

= 30

Total waiting time of mechanics = 30* W_q

= 30*4.17

= 12 minutes

Loss in terms of money per day at the rate Rs. 40 per hour = 125*40/60

= Rs. 83

Since loss in money on mechanic is much more than that lost on idling facility, additional crib operators are required.

4.6.3 MATLAB Implementation of Queueing Systems

Transaction modules

Structure :[block_entry_time start_of_transaction row_of_next_block]

block_entry_time	Time when the transaction enters the block. Usually it will be updated by the blocks the transaction passes.
start_of_transaction	Time at which the transaction has been generated (Simulation clock).
row_of_next_block	Row number (in the source code) of next block, which the transaction has to move to.

Server modules

Structure :[busy_until transaction_counter sum_serve_time idle_time]

busy_until	The time until the server is busy. Is this value less than the simulation clock, the server can be seized by a transaction.
transaction_counter	For statistical reasons each served transaction is counted.
sum_serve_time	Sum of the times, the transactions seized the server.
idle_time	Sum of times, the server has been free.

Queue modules

Structure :[entry_time transaction_counter wait_time_counter]

entry_time	The time, at which the last transaction has entered the queue.
transaction_counter	For statistical reasons each queue transaction is counted.
wait_time_counter	Sum of the times, the transactions have to be waited in the queue.

Files involved in simulation are:

mainsimu.m

The main simulator is implemented in the file mainsimu.m. Before it can be launched, a file name must be supplied via the global variable datei. The choice, not to pass the name as parameter to the MATLAB file may be apologized by the fact, that functions in MATLAB 4 cannot create global variables which survive the run time of the function. That is the reason for running the simulator in a Matlab Script.

simulate.m

Syntax: **The function number = simulate(transactions)**

represents the GPSS- function to simulate. It returns (to simulator) the numbers of transactions which have to be generated from the source file.

generate.m

The Syntax: **function transaction = generate(expected_value, variance)**

generates a transaction in unique distributed time distances. expected_value is the expected value and variance the deviation from this value. The return value is an instance of the transaction vector, which can move through the following blocks.

queue.m

By Syntax: **function output = queue(q, transaction)**

The incoming transaction will be registered in queue *q*. The parameter *q* is a string. It denotes the queue, thus it is possible to hide the internal data structures (no need to initialize) the user has not to deal with anyway (declarative feature of GPSS). Output is the leaving transaction.

seize.m

The Syntax: **function output = seize(sv, transaction)**

seizes the block. The incoming transaction seizes server *sv* immediately if this server is idle, or at the next time the server will be free. The parameter *sv* is a string. The transaction will be updated (block entry time, if the transaction had to wait) and returned as output.

depart.m

Syntax: **function output = depart(ws, transaction)**

The incoming transaction leaves the queue *ws*. The waiting time of the transaction in the queue can be calculated for updating the queue statistics. The transactions will be returned as output.

advance.m

By Syntax: **function output=advance(expected_value, variance, transaction)**

The incoming transaction advances. It spends a randomly determined time value (unique distribution) at this block. The first parameters are as the same as for generate. The transactions will be returned as output.

release.m

By Syntax: **function function output=release(sv, transaction)**

The incoming transaction leaves the server. The server statistics will be updated. The transaction returns as output.

terminate.m

By Syntax: **function output = terminate(number)**

The number of transactions are removed from the system. The global transaction counter are decreased. Output is a dummy transaction which shows the simulator that the program flow for this transaction has stopped. The simulator continues with the next transaction.

transfer.m

By Syntax: **function output = transfer(r_nr, probability, transaction)**

the incoming transaction moves with the probability to the block with the row number r_nr (jumps to labels are not implemented yet).

queustat.m

The Syntax: **function a= queustat(queue)**

calculates and returns (as string) the medium waiting time of transactions in this queue (vector).

servstat.m

The Syntax: **function a= servstat(server)**

calculates and returns (as string) the average utilization time of the server and the average time a transaction has spent on this server.

plotqueu.m

The Syntax: **function plotqueu(queustatus)**

plots the graphics of the statistics of a queue. The interpreter generates for every queue used in a program automatically a structure which contains the waiting time of a transaction in the queue during the simulation.

Simulation examples : Three different examples are presented :

simex1.m This example models a simple single server:

```
simulate(20)
generate(3,1)
queue('warte1',ans)
seize('server1',ans)
depart('warte1',ans)
advance(4,3,ans)
release('server1',ans)
terminat(1)
```

The simulation runs for 20 Transactions. There is one queue warte1 and one server, server1. Every three time units a transaction will be generated. The server name and the queue name is passed as string parameters to the different blocks. The return value of a block is a transaction. The movement of the transaction is solved by passing the return value of the previous block

simex2.m The second example is a demonstration of two parallel but independent (2 generate blocks) servers:

```
simulate(100)
generate(3,1)
```

```
queue('warte1',ans)
seize('server1',ans)
depart('warte1',ans)
advance(3,1,ans)
release('server1',ans)
terminat(1)
generate(3,1)
queue('warte2',ans)
seize('server2',ans)
depart('warte2',ans)
advance(4,3,ans)
release('server2',ans)
terminat(1)
```

simex3.m Third example models one transaction flow which is differently split (parameter transfer block) to be distributed on two servers (*server1*, *server2*). The first transfer-block means, that the transaction is transferred to line number 7 with the probability 0.3 (queuewarte1). If it has not been redirected it is transferred to line number 14 (queuewarte2). After being served the both transactions flows is gathered to utilize server3.

```
simulate(200)
generate(3,1)
transfer(7,0.3,ans)
transfer(14,1,ans)

queue('warte1',ans)
seize('server1',ans)
depart('warte1',ans)
advance(4,3,ans)
release('server1',ans)
transfer(21,1,ans)

queue('warte2',ans)
seize('server2',ans)
depart('warte2',ans)
advance(4,3,ans)
release('server2',ans)
transfer(21,1,ans)
```

```
queue('warte3',ans)
seize('server3',ans)
depart('warte3',ans)
advance(4,3,ans)
release('server3',ans)
terminat(1)
```

The following images of the queue utilizations have been captured after simulating that system:

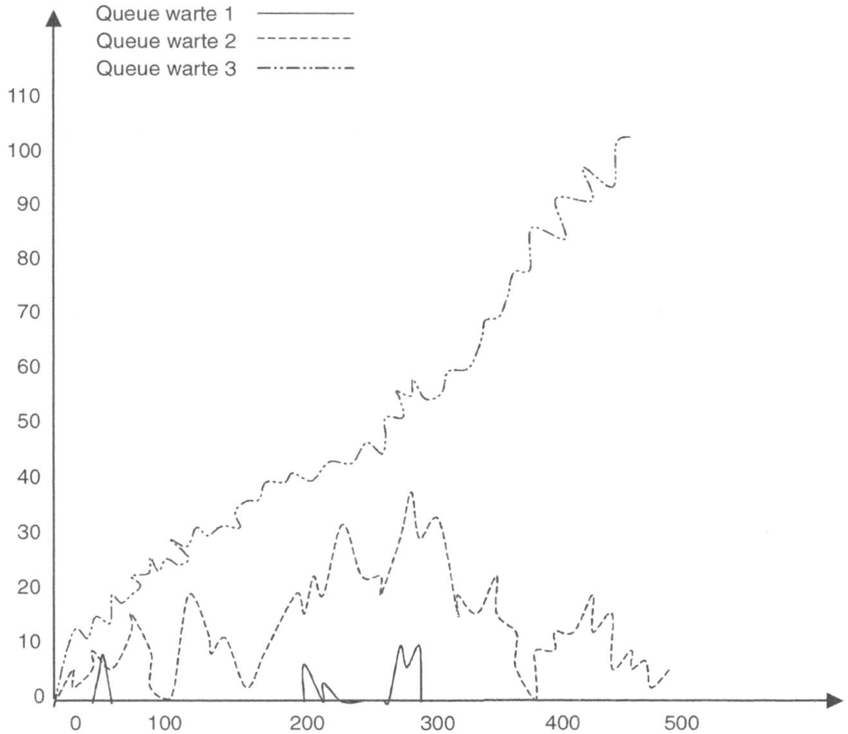

Fig. 4.8 Queueing simulation

Each queue statistic considers all transactions moved through the respective queue. Note that the relevant values for the plots are the queue entry time (x-axis) and the waiting time (y-axis) of a transaction within the queue.

Evaluation

After finishing a simulation all kernel structures remain in memory and can be inspected. Additionally the kernel creates structures for visualization the queue utilization. The name of the structure is a concatenation of the respective queue name and the string stat. To simulate the program simex1 the following commands have to be entered at the MATLAB prompt:

datei='simex1.m'

mainsimu

To show the server statistics for server1, enter servstat(server1). To view the statistics of queue warte1, enter queustat(warte1). To plot the queue utilization of the queue warte1 enter plot(warte1stat(:,1),warte1stat(:,2)), because warte1stat is a two-dimensional array, which contains tupel of the waiting time in a queue during the current simulation time. Alternatively the function plotqueu(warte1stat) can be used as a shortcut.

4.6.4 Poisson Distribution

The Poisson distribution of a discrete random variable x with range R = {0, 1, 2, 3, 4...}, that follows the Poisson probability law

$$P_x = \frac{\lambda^x}{x!} e^{-\lambda} \text{ for all } x \text{ from } R, \lambda > 0$$

is called Poisson distribution with parameter λ. The distribution is positively twisted in figure 4.9.

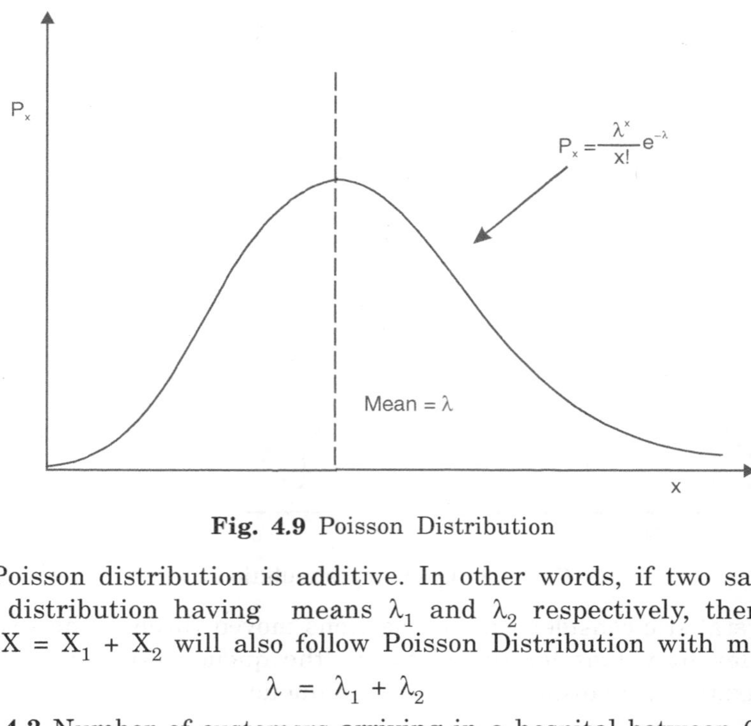

Fig. 4.9 Poisson Distribution

Mean of Poisson distribution is additive. In other words, if two sample X_1 and X_2 under Poisson distribution having means λ_1 and λ_2 respectively, then the sample X constituted by $X = X_1 + X_2$ will also follow Poisson Distribution with mean such that,

$$\lambda = \lambda_1 + \lambda_2$$

Example 4.3 Number of customers arriving in a hospital between 08 AM to 09 AM follow random pattern in the form of Poisson Distribution curve with mean 3. By random survey it is found that mean value is 5 between 09 AM to 10 AM. Determine the probability that not more than 5 patients will call on the hospital between 08 AM to 10 AM daily.

Solution.

Given $\lambda_1 = 3$, and $\lambda_2 = 5$,

therefore

$$\lambda = \lambda_1 + \lambda_2 = 8$$

Now,

$$P_x = \frac{\lambda^x}{x!}e^{-\lambda} = (8^x) * (e^{-8})/(x!)$$

Required probability $$P = P_0 + P_1 + P_2 + P_3 + P_4 + P_5$$

$$= \sum_{x=0}^{x=5} P_x = \sum_{x=0}^{x=5} \frac{8^x}{x!}e^{-8} = 0.19$$

Probability of being more than 5 patients at hospital between 08 AM to 10 AM daily = 0.19

4.7 TWO SERVER QUEUEING SYSTEM

The queueing system describe in previous section, behaves as two server queueing system for M=2. For a two server queueing system, we can prove logarithmic asymptotics for the likelihood that a message from a source that divides its messages between the two servers in a way that minimizes the message's waiting time experiences a large waiting time. The $M/M/2$ a two server queueing system can demonstrate the merit of this asymptotic by comparing its predictions with experimental data. The $M/M/2$ model consists of two queues with limited waiting rooms under fixed order of visits. By treating the method of differential-difference equations we find the equilibrium state equations for the probabilities and a functional equation for the probability generating function. We derive marginal distributions and we indicate how to obtain the general solution of the system of simultaneous equations. We also consider the case in which the travelling time from one queue to the other is a constant.

Following is a FORTRAN program to simulate two-server queue. The arrays have dimensions to handle up to 1000 customers.

```
      INTEGER AT(1000), ST(1000), CAT(1000), CDT(1000, 2), QL(1000)
      INTEGER NDT(2), ISER(1000), SERV(2), IDT(1000,2), QLT
C     2 IN SERV(2) REPRESENTS NUMBER OF SERVERS
C     DATA GENERATION AND INITIALIZATION
      CALL GENRAT(AT, ST)
      CALL INIT(CAT, AT, QL, QLT, IDT, NAT, NDT, SERV, ISER)
      I = 1
      READ, N
100   M = 1
      MNDT = NDT(1)
      IF(NDT(1) .LT. NDT(2)) GO TO 200
```

```
      M = 2
      MNDT = NDT(2)
  200 IF (I .GT. N) GO TO 600
      DIF = NAT - MNDT
      IF (DIF) 30, 40, 50
C     ARRIVAL OF A CUSTOMER TAKES PLACE
  300 CLOCK = NAT
      QLT = QLT +1
      QL(I) = QLT
      I = I+1
      NAT = CAT(I)
      GO TO 700
C     SIMULTANEOUS ARRIVAL AND DEPARTURE OF CUSTOMERS
  400 CLOCK = NAT
      SERV(M) = SERV(1) + 1
      IF (SERV(2) .GT. SERV(1)) SERV(M) = SERV(2) + 1
      IJ = SERV(M)
      ISER(IJ) = M
      NDT(M) = NAT + NDT(M)
      I = I + 1
      NAT = CAT(I)
      GO TO 700
C     DEPARTURE TAKES PLACE AFTER SERVICE
  500 IF(QLT .GT. 0) GO TO 600
C     FACILITY IDLES TILL NEXT ARRIVAL OF CUSTOMER
      IDT(I, M) = DIF
      CLOCK = NAT
      SERV(M) = I
      ISER(I) = M
      NDT(M) = NAT + ST(I)
      CDT(I, M) = NDT(M)
      I = I + 1
      NAT = CAT(I)
      GO TO 700
C     HEAD OF THE QUEUE IS SERVED
  600 CLOCK = MMNDT
```

```
      QLT = QLT - 1
      SERV(M) = SERV(1) + 1
      IF(SERV(2) .GT. SERV(1)) SERV(M) = SERV(2) + 1
      II =SERV(M)
      ISER(II) = M
      NDT(M) = NDT(M) + ST(II)
      CDT(II, M) = NDT(M)
C     END OF THE SIMULATION RUN
700   IF(SERV(M) .LT. N) GO TO 100
      CALL STAT(CAT, CDT, IDT, QL)
      STOP
      END
```

4.8 PREEMPTIVE AND NON-PREEMPTIVE PRIORITIES

Priorities in queueing systems that differentiate among classes of users are generally classified as preemptive or non-preemptive. In either case, as soon as service to any particular user has been completed, the system chooses as the next user a representative of the highest-priority class present. Priorities within classes are determined according to *FCFS, LCFS, SIRO,* or some other discipline. The difference, however, lies in the fact that in systems using preemptive priorities, high-priority users are never kept waiting in favor of lower-priority ones. That is, the system stands ready to interrupt service to any present occupant of the service facility, immediately upon arrival of a user belonging to a class with higher priority than that of the present facility occupant. By contrast, non-preemptive systems never interrupt a service to a user once that service has begun-even if a higher-priority user arrives at the system while this service is going on.

For preemptive systems, what happens to users who get ejected from the service facility is in itself a matter to be specified. In some systems, service to the ejected user-once that user eventually regains hold of the service facility-continues right from the point where it was interrupted. In other systems, service may have to be restarted from scratch. It is also conceivable that an ejected user may be assigned to a priority class higher than his former one, in compensation for being ejected.

It should also be noted that many queueing systems especially in the urban environment operate with different priority rules for different user classes. For instance, it is possible that users in a class with very high-priority status may obtain preemptive service, whereas users of medium importance may enjoy only non-preemptive priority over users in the low-priority classes. Finally, it is also possible that different queue disciplines (for example, FCFS, SIRO, etc.) may be used within different classes of users at the same queueing system. Thus, users who belong to, say, class *A* may queue up according to a FCFS order, whereas users in another class, *B*, may be served in random order.

If nothing else, it should be clear from the above that there exist a confusing number of variations of queueing systems with class priorities. Of those variations, queueing theorists have studied with some success a few and have derived an interesting (but hardly exhaustive) set of results. We shall review now some of the most important and useful of those results, always with reference to the type of queueing model. Facility users in this model are separated into a number, say r, of distinct user classes. Each class is assigned a priority number k, for $k = 1, 2, \ldots, r$, for use of the service facility. By convention, the smaller the priority number, the *higher* the priority of the class.

4.9 WORKING WITH QUEUEING THEORY

This section covers the whole field of queueing theory, ranging from (*i*) stability issues, (*ii*) the characterization of traffic processes in key application areas, (*iii*) methods to analyze queueing models, and (*iv*) Scheduling, optimization and control of queues.

(*i*) **Stability issues.** Obviously, a necessary condition for the stability of a queueing network is that the traffic intensity is smaller than the maximal service capacity in each of its nodes. However, this is not always a sufficient condition. There exist simple two-station networks with one server at each station and with so-called re-entrant lines with priorities that are unstable for a given parameter set for which the traffic intensity at each station is smaller than one. Already for such networks, the stability region does not have a simple structure. The characterization of the stability region for large, complicated, networks is an important open problem. Fluid limits play a crucial role here. Another interesting issue is the speed of convergence to a limiting distribution. In many networks, stability is attained at exponential speed, but this exponent is very sensitive to perturbations of the transition probabilities.

(*ii*) **Characterization of traffic processes.** Traditionally, arrival processes of customers at queues have often been represented by Poisson processes. Important extensions that have received much attention in recent years are Markov-modulated Poisson processes and BMAP (Batch Markovian Arrival Processes). In some manufacturing applications, and at the flow level also in telecom applications, it may be more natural to consider fluid input. Furthermore, analysis of traffic data from various computer-communication systems, like from Ethernet local area networks and the Internet, convincingly demonstrates the presence of features like burst, fractal behavior over a wide range of time scales, and self-similarity. That has led to several exciting new models for traffic processes, including queues with Fractional Brownian Motion as input, and queues fed by on/off sources with heavy-tailed on- and/or off-periods.

(*iii*) **Methods of analysis—Probabilistic/analytic methods.** New traffic processes require new methods for their performance analysis. Accordingly, the study of queueing models with as input a Markovian arrival process, or a fluid input, or a long-range dependent input process, has received much attention in recent years. Another topic that gets much attention at EURANDOM is analytical methods in queueing theory (including boundary value techniques):

- **Approximations and asymptotics.** Very few network models can be analyzed completely. Hence, there is a need for approximation techniques and asymptotic methods. For the case of heavy-tailed distributions, recently obtained limit theorems and asymptotic expansions for heavy-tailed queues and random walks may be useful. In many applications, there is a need for estimating the very small probabilities of 'rare events'. Large-deviation asymptotics form an important topic. In addition, there is growing interest in the simulation of rare events.
- **Computational methods.** In the mathematical theory of queues, powerful analytic methods have been developed leading to results that are often in the form of transforms. For a long time it was assumed that these results were computationally intractable. In the last 10 years it has become clear that, for broad classes of models, efficient and stable numerical methods can be developed yielding accurate numerical solutions. In particular, numerical inversion techniques turn out to be successful. Other numerical methods, like the power series algorithm and the compensation method are based on a more probabilistic approach, which makes computations more transparent and natural. Asymptotic methods are used to obtain accurate approximations. The further development of these and other methods is essential for the solution of practical problems.

(*iv*) **Scheduling, optimization and control of queues.** One of the key problems in scheduling is the assignment of jobs to machines or processors. A broad variety of applications, ranging from call centers via flexible manufacturing systems to web servers, gives rise to fascinating novel stochastic scheduling problems, which deserve attention in the project. The ultimate goal of queueing analysis is the optimal design and operation of a service system. Hence optimization and control of queues are important items in the project. In recent studies, optimal static allocation of capacity to users has been studied, among others, in the framework of a joint project with Philips Research on cable access networks. In the near future, we plan to combine queueing theory and stochastic control theory in the dynamic control of traffic lights at road intersections, and in studying variants of the TCP protocol in the Internet.

4.10 QUEUEING NETWORKS

We have now completed our review of queueing systems. In this section we turn our attention to queueing networks. Interconnected in this case implies any combination of in series and in parallel arrangements. It has already been indicated or implied several times in this chapter that many urban service systems can be viewed as queueing networks. So far, we have seen many results which are useful in analyzing individual components of these networks. The art of queueing network analysis consists of combining the results that apply to individual components and drawing conclusions that describe the properties of the complete urban service system under consideration.

A network of queues is a collection of service centers, which represent system resources, and customers, which represent users or transactions. Analytic evaluation involves using software to solve efficiently a set of equations induced by the network of queues and its parameters. Defining a queueing network model of a particular system is made relatively straightforward by the close correspondence between the attributes of queueing network models and the attributes of computer systems. For example, service centers in queueing network models naturally correspond to hardware resources and their software queues in computer systems, and customers in queueing network models naturally correspond to users or transactions in computer systems. Queueing network models have a richer set of attributes than we have illustrated thus far, extending the correspondence with computer systems. As an example of this richness, specifying the rate at which customers arrive is only one of three available means to describe workload intensity. A second approach is to state the number of customers in the model. This alternative is well suited to representing batch workloads. A third approach is to specify the number of customers and the average time that each customer spends thinking between interactions.

Queueing network models in particular, have become important tools in the design and analysis of computer systems. This is due to the fact that, for many applications, queueing network models achieve a favorable balance between accuracy and efficiency. In terms of accuracy, a large body of experience indicates that queueing network models can be expected to be accurate to within 5 to 10% for utilizations and throughputs and to within 10 to 30% for response times. This level of accuracy is consistent with the requirements of a wide variety of design and analysis applications. Of equal importance, it is consistent with the accuracy achievable in other components of the computer system analysis process, such as workload characterization. In terms of efficiency, we have indicated in the previous section that queueing network models can be defined, parameterized, and evaluated at relatively low cost. Definition is eased by the close correspondence between the attributes of queueing network models and the attributes of computer systems. Parameterization is eased by the relatively small number of relatively high-level parameters. Evaluation is eased by the recent development of algorithms whose running time grows as the product of the number of service centers with the number of customer classes. Queueing network models achieve relatively high accuracy at relatively low cost.

The word "art" has been used intentionally for one should keep in mind that queueing theory offers very few general results that apply expressly to queueing networks. Therefore, in solving problems that involve such networks, much depends on the ingenuity of the analyst in choosing the right simplifying assumptions that preserve the essence of the problem while making the calculation of an approximate solution possible.

4.11 APPLICATIONS

Application of queueing theory to telephony. The Public Switched Telephone Networks (PSTNs) are designed to accommodate the offered traffic intensity with only a small loss. The performance of loss systems is quantified by their grade of service driven by the assumption that if insufficient capacity is available, the call is refused and lost. Alternatively, overflow systems make use of alternative routes to divert calls via different paths; even these systems have a finite or maximum traffic carrying capacity.

However, the use of queueing in telephone network allows the systems to queue their customer's requests until free resources become available. This means that if traffic intensity levels exceed available capacity, customer's calls are here no longer lost; they instead wait until they can be served. This method is used in queueing customers for the next available operator.

A queueing discipline determines the manner in which the exchange handles calls from customers. It defines the way they will be served, the order in which they are served, and the way in which resources are divided between the customers. Here are details of three queueing disciplines:

- **First In First Out**—This principle states that customers are served one at a time and that the customer that has been waiting the longest is served first.
- **Last In First Out**—This principle also serves customers one at a time; however the customer with the shortest waiting time will be served first.
- **Processor Sharing**—Customers are served equally. Network capacity is shared between customers and they all effectively experience the same delay.

Queueing is handled by control processes within exchanges, which can be modeled using state equations. Queueing systems use a particular form of state equations known as Markov chains which model the system in each state. Incoming traffic to these systems is modeled via a Poisson distribution and is subject to Erlang's queueing theory assumptions:

- **Pure-Chance Traffic**—Call arrivals and departures are random and independent events.
- **Statistical Equilibrium**—Probabilities within the system do not change.
- **Full Availability**—All incoming traffic can be routed to any other customer within the network. Congestion is cleared as soon as servers are free.

Classic queueing theory involves complex calculations to determine call waiting time, service time, server utilization and many other metrics which are used to measure queueing performance.

Call centers. The flow of calls begins with K trunk lines that connect to the call center. There are $w \leq k$ work stations, or seats, at which $N \leq w$ agents serve incoming calls. An arriving call that finds all k trunk lines occupied (let's assume there are 8 trunk lines), receives a busy signal and is blocked from entering the system. Else, it is connected to the call center and occupies one of the free lines. If fewer than N agents are busy, then the call is routed directly to an agent and is served. But, if there are more calls in the system and all agents are occupied, then the call waits in the queue until an agent serves a call and that call exits the system. Once the call is served, the resources are released *e.g.*, trunk line, agent, work station.

Some calls are considered retrials, because they are not served and attempt to re-enter the system. For some calls, the customer voluntarily abandons the call and does not call back. Also, customers that are served may attempt to re-enter the system; this happens sometimes if there was no first call resolution (for customer service centers) and/or if the customer needed to order something else (for inbound order centers).

The number of trunk lines acts as an upper bound (k). The number of agents act as an upper bound on how many simultaneous calls can be in service simultaneously. A call center manager dynamically changes the number of agents on and off the floor based on expected demand and staffing availability. Call centers and other operation centers like it are highly complex and dynamic. The model above is a very simple system. But, it is easy to see how Call Centers are Queues and all the tools that Queueing Theory makes available to us can be applied to Call Centers.

SUMMARY

Information and communication technology is a vital sector in today's world economy. The future development of this field strongly depends on contributions from mathematics. In the early stages of this development in the design of computer-communication systems, the emphasis was on functionality. In recent years quality of service has become the most important criterion, which is expressed in terms of performance and reliability of the systems in relation to telematics applications. Queueing networks also provide the models for the description of manufacturing systems and for the analysis of their performance and reliability aspects. These economically vital applications of queueing networks make them into objects that are of prime interest.

Queueing phenomena occur in several real-life situations when resources (machines in a factory, elevators, telephone lines, traffic lights) cannot immediately render the amount or the kind of service required by their users. Similar congestion phenomena also arise at the byte level, in modern data-handling technologies (for example, communication systems, computer networks, etc.); they are typically less visible but their effects at user level are usually very important. Such congestion phenomena are often very effectively studied by mathematical methods from queueing theory. Adopting the abstract terminology from queueing theory, the object of study is formulated as a network of service units with customers requiring services at those units. The nature of the arrival and service processes is usually such that they have to be represented by stochastic processes. Accordingly, queueing theory is an area of applied probability theory and of stochastic operations research.

We have seen that queueing theory is an extremely active area of research. One of the key reasons for its strong viability is that, time and again, interesting new questions from, mainly, computer-communications and manufacturing give rise to new and challenging queueing problems. Much research is being triggered by the need to understand and control the behavior of modern computer system, communication and manufacturing systems, and thus to improve their design and performance.

In working with queueing theory one must, first of all, take the particular real-world system of interest, study this system, and create (or simply choose from the list of models in queueing theory) a mathematical model to represent it. Through the analysis of this mathematical model, one then obtains the answers, which supposedly apply to the original system as well.

Most of the exact results of queueing theory apply to queueing systems in which the inter-arrival times or the service times or (ideally) both are negative exponential. Fortunately, there are many real-world systems for which at least the inter-arrival times are negative exponential. The main reason is that many arrival processes observable in practice can be modeled as Poisson processes (which in turn imply negative exponential inter-arrival times). This is especially true when one refers to *urban* service systems, where Poisson (or nearly Poisson) arrival processes are abundant.

Queueing theory is very good at estimating the low moments and central moments of such important quantities as the waiting times or the number of users present in queueing systems but not nearly as good at computing the probability distributions for these quantities. Indeed, in all but a handful of cases, the only approach available for obtaining probability distributions for most of the quantities of interest in queueing theory is through the use of a combination of transform analysis and numerical analysis techniques.

EXERCISE QUESTIONS

1. Explain the Working difference of Queueing System with other systems.
2. Explain the basics components of a Queueing system.
3. Explain the basic facts about Queueing system.
4. What do you understand by Queueing Model?
5. What do you mean by number of servers in a queueing system?
6. Explain the difference between single Server Queueing system and general queueing system.
7. Explain the Working difference of multi-server queueing system and single queueing system.
8. Explain the preemptive and non-preemptive priorities in a queueing system.
9. Explain the real-life applications queueing system.
10. What do you understand by queueing Networks? Explain its advantages.
11. Explain the how general queueing system can be used as two server queueing system?
12. Explain the use of queueing systems in call centers and telephone networks.
13. A manufacturing plant has a tool crib operated by one person. There are 10 mechanics who use the tool crib, causing waiting appears more. The problem is to decide optimum number of tool crib operators so that the total cost can be minimized. Assume wage rate for tool crib operator is Rs. 80 and for mechanics is Rs. 100 per 5 hours.
14. Consider self-service store with one cashier. Assume Poisson arrival and exponential service times. Suppose 9 customers arrive at an average time of every 5 minutes and cashier can serve 2 in 1 minute find out the following:

    (*a*) Average number in queue.

    (*b*) Probability of having more than 15 customers in the system.

    (*c*) The probability that a customer has to be in waiting line for more than 2 minutes.
15. Consider question 14. If the service time can be speeded up to 3 in 1 minute, by using different cash counter. Determine the effect on the quantities.
16. A telephone exchange has two long distance operators. The company finds that during the peak load, long distance calls arrive in Poisson fashion at an average rate of 15 per hour. The length of service on these calls is approximately exponentially distributed with mean of 5 minutes. Find the following:

    (*a*) What is the probability that the subscriber will have to wait for his long distance call during peak hours of the day?

    (*b*) If the subscriber will wait and are serviced in turns, what is the expected waiting time?
17. Consider a queuing system, the arrival rate, λ = per hour and service rate, μ = 8 per hour. Assume the conditions for use of the single channel queuing system , find out the following:

    (*i*) The probability that the server is idle.

    (*ii*) The probability that there are at least two customers in the system.

    (*iii*) Expected time that a customer is in the queue.
18. The problems arrive at a computer center in Poisson fashion with a mean arrival rate of 20 per hour. The average computer job requires 10 minutes of the terminal time. Calculate the following:

    (*i*) Average number of problems waiting for the computer use.

    (*ii*) The percent of time an arrival can walk right in without having to wait.

Chapter 5

INVENTORY SYSTEM

5.1 INTRODUCTION

Inventory Control is a major activity of any organization. More than 90% of current asset consists of material in the form of Inventory. Inventory Control is designed to support the requisition processing, inventory management, purchasing, and physical inventory reconciliation functions of inventory management through a set of highly interactive capabilities. Lack of Inventory causes stock outs causing loss to an organization. Stock out for a retailer, results loss of goodwill and opportunity cost. The stock out for a manufacturer, results production holdup, idling of manpower and facilities, loss of production which causes delayed deliveries which in turn results losses due to penalty clauses, results opportunity cost and loss of goodwill.

The design of Inventory Control is based on the following key objectives:

- To provide information on the availability of stocked items and the status of stocked requisitions.
- To facilitate timely requisition processing.
- To automatically record and service backorders.
- To help minimize inventory investments consistent with service objectives by basing purchasing decisions on usage history.
- To provide automated tools to assist servicing, purchasing, and management of the inventory.
- To improve financial control of the inventory by charge backs to the user organizations.
- To improve financial control of the inventory by periodic reconciliation of the inventory balances with the physical counts.

Inventory Control utilizes a set of user-maintained master tables, a set of system-maintained master tables, transaction document types, and offline programs to meet these objectives. It also creates inventory control management reports.

Inventory management refers to short-term decisions regarding supplies, inventories, production levels, and operations infrastructure. It is an important activity towards ensuring smooth production process in organizations. An efficient inventory management system facilitates in optimum utilization of resources.

Most small businesses underestimate the importance of their inventory or of inventory management software. They do not realize that many of the headaches are caused by a lack of control and knowledge of their inventory. Whether it is a lack of knowledge of the quantity of a certain product, businesses continue to use outdated systems that do not allow them to get the most out of their inventory. Inventory management systems when used properly; allow a business to make established analysis of products and markets that help them make better business decisions. That is why we need to simulate such systems. They keep a tight customer control to allow business owners to better serve their customers, and keep a detailed and accurate record of their customers purchase history as well as a way to properly reorder inventory. With a tight control of inventory, owners know when products are been stolen, when products are not rotating properly, or when products need to be reordered. By default, the business begins to develop an organization and by a control of inventory, profits begin to increase. Inventory Management Systems allow programmed owners to make decisions about promotions and specials and let owners know when a product is no longer being profitable.

5.2 INVENTORY SYSTEM

In an inventory control method and system, changes of sales for individual goods are forecasted and the excess or deficiency of a stock of each of the goods at the present point of time is estimated from the results of forecast. In order to facilitate an inventory control, merchandise information is sorted and displayed in accordance with the degree of urgency, the degree of importance or the like of inventory adjustment on the basis of the results of estimation.

In inventory system what is claimed is:

1. An inventory control method comprising computer aided steps of:
    - forecasting a cumulative total of sales for goods by using a result of sales from other goods which are selected and inputted with the use of an interactive graphics system, which may exhibit a similar sales change pattern to the goods;
    - obtaining a sum of an actual result of sales and an actual stock for the goods;
    - comparing the sum with the forecasted cumulative total of sales for the goods by displaying the forecasted information on a graph as reference information and comparing the reference information to actual inventory information;
    - determining an excess or deficiency of the actual stock for the goods on the basis of the graphic comparing;
    - outputting information of the goods corresponding to the determined excess or deficiency of the actual stock inventory for the goods, wherein said outputted

information is in the form of a percent ratio and is labeled, the stock warning index, to provide the necessary level of priority and degree of urgency corresponding to the goods; and,

- adjusting the actual stock inventory in accordance with the outputted information.

2. The inventory control method according to claim 1, wherein the result of sales from the other goods is used as a sales change model pattern, and further including creating a whole model pattern by using an interactive graphics system.
3. An inventory control system comprising:
    - a means for forecasting a cumulative total of sales for goods by using a result of sales stored in a database for other goods which may exhibit a similar sales change pattern to the goods;
    - a means for obtaining a sum of an actual result of sales and an actual stock for the goods stored in a sales/stock results file;
    - a means for interactively and graphically comparing the obtained sum with the forecasted cumulative total of sales for the goods;
    - a means for determining an excess or deficiency of the actual stock inventory for the goods on the basis of a result from the comparing means;
    - a means for outputting information comprising a stock warning index, which prioritizes an urgency of adjusting the actual stock inventory resulting from the determined excess or deficiency of the actual stock inventory for the goods; and,
    - a means for adjusting the actual stock inventory in accordance with the stock warning index.
4. The inventory control system according to claim 3 above, wherein in the means for forecasting the result of sales for the other goods stored in the sales/stock results file, is used as a sales change model pattern.
5. An inventory control system comprising:
    - a means for forecasting a change in sales for goods that are subject to inventory control, by using a model pattern of a predetermined change of sales for the goods stored in a time-to-sales-correspondence file;
    - a means for monitoring a difference between the forecasted change in sales for the goods and an actual change in sales for the goods stored in a sales/stock results including means for daily monitoring by calculation of a stock warning index;
    - a means for outputting the stock warning index for allowing modification of the model pattern if the monitored difference is larger than a predetermined level; and,
    - a means for adjusting actual stock inventory in accordance with said outputted stock warning index.
6. The inventory control system according to claim 5 above, wherein the forecasting means is operated before the goods are on sale.

5.3 BACKGROUND OF THE INVENTION

The present invention relates to an inventory (or stock) control method and system in a merchandise information processing system used in a retail industry such as a departmental store, and more particularly to a stock-warning method and system suitable for support of inventory control operations (or works) for goods or merchandises such as fashion goods which have a large change of sales.

The conventional inventory control operation supporting methods are described here in below:

(1) Ordering Point Method. The ordering point method is a method in which a stock of goods is always (or continuously) monitored and a fixed quantity Q of goods is ordered when a stock level falls below a fixed value *K*. *K* is called an ordering point (or reorder level) In this method, the ordering quantity is always constant though the order is made irregularly. A great problem is that the stock level must be continuously monitored.

(2) Periodic Ordering Method. The periodic ordering method is a method in which the optimum ordering quantity Q is estimated at every fixed interval *n* and the estimated quantity of goods are ordered. The interval *n* is selected to be an economic ordering interval. This method is mainly employed for the following reasons:

(*a*) It is difficult to continuously monitor the stock level.

(*b*) A stable stock level required in a target period for a sale plan is not attainable.

(*c*) It is not possible in view of practical affairs to give an order at an arbitrary day.

(*d*) Goods may have a change of the specification thereof and hence the settlement cannot be made with only a predetermined ordering procedure.

A task in the ordering point method is to determine a proper ordering point. A task in the periodic ordering method is to accurately estimate the ordering quantity. Generally, the ordering point method handles goods for which a stock level required is stable, the quantity of a stock can be grasped at a look and only the order of the same quantity is required every time. The periodic ordering method is mainly used for large-sized goods which are of high cost and have a relatively longer lead time (or time for execution of order).

5.4 BASIC FUNCTION OF INVENTORY

The basic function of stock (inventory) is to insulate the production process from changes in the environment as shown in figure 5.1 below. One point to note from this diagram is that most of the activities are a cost—it is only at the final point (sales of finished goods) that we get revenue to set against our costs and hopefully make a profit (= revenue - cost). Hence if we have cost associated with stock we need to deal with that stock in an *Effective*, *Efficient* and *Economic* manner.

We shall consider the problem of ordering raw material stock but the same basic theory can be applied to the problem of deciding the finished goods stock; and deciding the size of a batch in a batch production process. The costs that we need to consider so that we can decide the amount of stock to have can be divided into stock holding costs and stock ordering (and receiving) costs as below. Here conventionally, management costs are ignored.

Inventory—Inventory is the list of movable items which are required to manufacture a product or maintain equipment. It is a unique item having unique identification number and specification. Following constitute an inventory:

- Components and raw material
- Finished goods
- Work–in–progress.

Holding costs—associated with keeping stock overtime

- storage costs
- rent/depreciation
- labor
- overheads (*e.g.*, heating, lighting, security)
- money tied up (loss of interest, opportunity cost)
- obsolescence costs (if left with stock at end of product life)
- stock deterioration (lose money if product deteriorates at the same time as held)
- theft/insurance.

Ordering costs—associated with ordering and receiving an order

- clerical/labor costs of processing orders
- inspection and return of poor quality products
- transport costs
- handling costs.

Carrying cost—This is the cost of holding an item in the store that is issued or sold to someone. This costs includes:

- Interest on capital cost
- Rent, depreciation, taxes, etc.
- Cost of wastages, obsolescence, damages, etc.
- Maintenance cost
- Operating costs of stores like direct labor and overhead like electricity, etc.

Shortage cost—These are the costs incurred due to shortage of goods. It consists of following:

- Loss of goodwill
- Back order costs
- Opportunity costs.

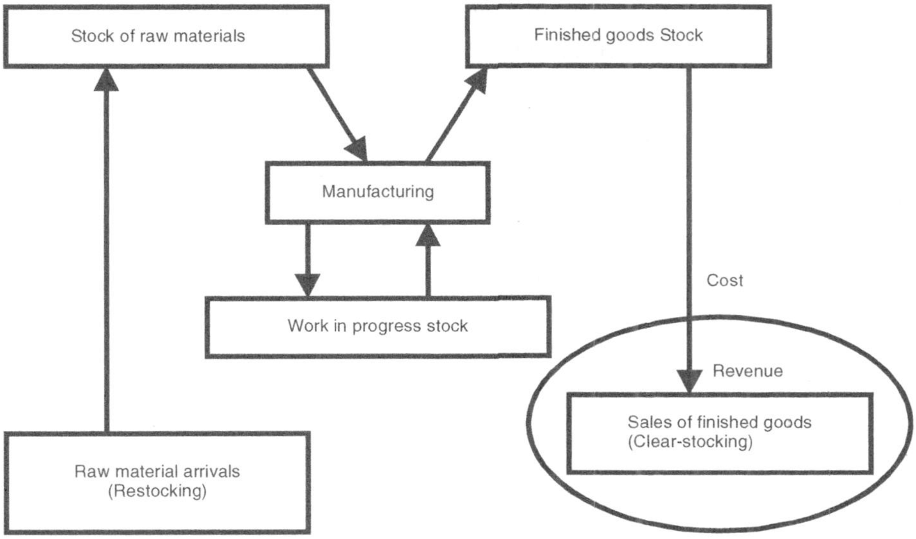

Fig. 5.1 Basic function of inventory

Constant usages rate—When a firm buys requirement at the beginning of each year and consumption is constant then average inventory is obtained by the following formula:

Average inventory = (Opening Stock + Closing stock)/2

Variable usages rate—When usage consumption rate is varying from month to month following methods are used:

(*a*) Simple average method

Average inventory = (Opening Stock + Closing stock)/2

(*b*) Six months average method

Average inventory = (Opening Stock + after six months stock + Closing stock)/3

(*c*) Quarterly average method

Average inventory = (Quarterly Stock + Closing stock)/5

(*d*) Monthly average method

Average inventory = (Sum of 12 months Stock + Closing stock)/13

A stock out occurs when we have insufficient stock to supply customers. Usually stock outs occur in the order lead time, the time between placing an order and the arrival of that order. Given a stock out the order may be lost completely or the customer may choose to backorder, *i.e.*, to be prepared to wait until we have sufficient stock to supply their order.

In this basic model we have the situation where company orders from an outside supplier that outside supplier delivers to us precisely the quantity we ask for; and we pass that stock onto customers either external customers, or an internal customer within the same company (*e.g.*, if ordering raw materials for use in the production process).

Let us assume:

- R = Stock used up at a constant rate (units per year)
- c_o = Fixed set-up cost for each order—often called the order cost
- c_h = Variable stock holding cost per unit per year.

Let us assume that no lead time between placing an order and arrival of the order, and the amount to order each time, often called the *batch* (or *lot*) size. With these assumptions the graph of stock level overtime takes the form shown below.

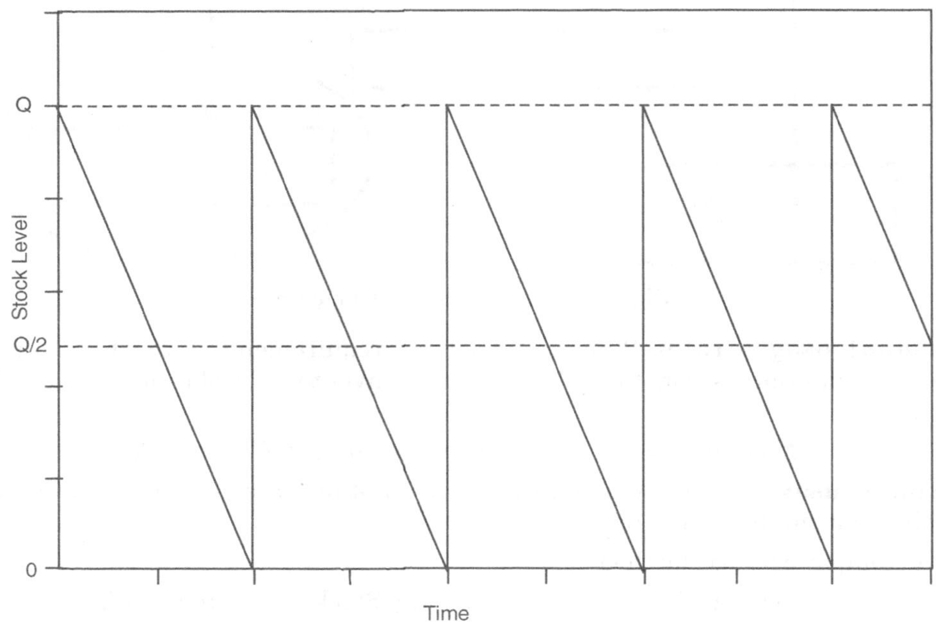

Fig. 5.2 Stock level overtime

Consider drawing a horizontal line at $Q/2$ in the above diagram. If we were to draw this line then it is clear that the times when stock exceeds $Q/2$ are exactly balanced by the times when stock falls below $Q/2$. In other words we could equivalently regard the above diagram as representing a *constant* stock level of $Q/2$ overtime. Hence we have:

$$\text{Annual holding cost} = c_h(Q/2) \qquad ...(5.1)$$

where $Q/2$ is the average (constant) inventory level.

$$\text{Annual order cost} = c_o(R/Q) \qquad ...(5.2)$$

where (R/Q) is the number of orders per year (R used, Q each order)

$$\text{So total annual cost} = c_h(Q/2) + c_o(R/Q) \qquad ...(5.3)$$

Total annual cost is the function that we want to minimize by choosing an appropriate value of Q. Obviously, there is a purchase cost associated with the R units per year. However, this is just a constant as R is fixed so we can ignore it here. The diagram below illustrates how these two components (annual holding cost and annual order cost) change as Q, the quantity ordered, changes. As Q increases holding cost increases but order cost decreases. Hence the total annual cost curve is as shown below somewhere on that curve lies a value of Q that corresponds to the minimum total cost.

We can calculate exactly which value of Q corresponds to the minimum total cost by differentiating total cost with respect to Q and equating to zero.

$$\partial(\text{total cost})/\partial Q = c_h/2 - c_o R/Q^2 = 0 \text{ for minimization} \quad ...(5.4)$$

which gives

$$Q^2 = 2c_o R/c_h \quad ...(5.5)$$

Hence the best value of Q (the amount to order = amount stocked) is given by $Q = (2Rc_o/c_h)^{0.5}$ and this is known as the *Economic Order Quantity (EOQ)*.

To get the total annual cost associated with the EOQ we have from before that total annual cost = $c_h(Q/2) + c_o(R/Q)$, so putting $Q = (2Rc_o/c_h)^{0.5}$ into this we get that the total annual cost is given by

$$c_h((2Rc_o/c_h)^{0.5}/2) + c_o(R/(2Rc_o/c_h)^{0.5}) = (Rc_o c_h/2)^{0.5} + (Rc_o c_h/2)^{0.5} = (2Rc_o c_h)^{0.5} \quad ...(5.6)$$

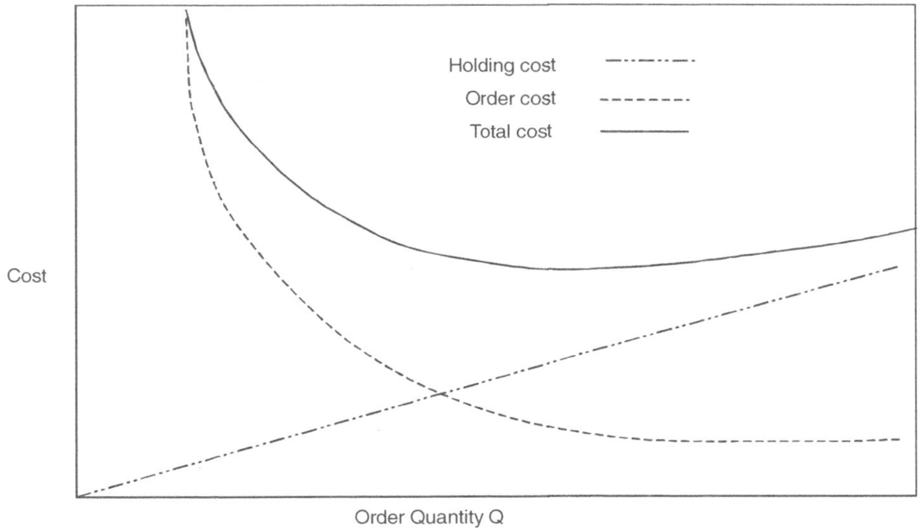

Fig. 5.3 Holding cost, order cost, and total cost in an inventory system

Hence total annual cost is $(2Rc_o c_h)^{0.5}$ which means that when ordering the optimal (EOQ) quantity we have that total cost is proportional to the square root of any of the factors (R, c_o and c_h) involved. For example, if we were to reduce c_o by a factor of 4 we would reduce total cost by a factor of 2 (note the EOQ would change as well). This, in fact, is the basis of Just-in-Time (JIT), to reduce (continuously) c_o and c_h so as to drive down total cost.

Example 5.1

A retailer expects to sell about 200 units of a product per year. The storage space taken up in his premises by one unit of this product is costed at \$20 per year. If the cost associated with ordering is \$35 per order what is the economic order quantity given that interest rates are expected to remain close to 10% per year and the total cost of one unit is \$100.

We use the *EOQ* formula,

$$EOQ = (2Rc_o/c_h)^{0.5} \qquad ...(5.7)$$

Here, $R = 200,$

$$c_o = 35$$

and the holding cost c_h is given by

$$c_h = \$20 \text{ (direct storage cost per unit per year)} + \$100 \times 0.10$$

This term the money interest lost if one unit sits in stock for one year, *i.e.*,

$$c_h = \$30 \text{ per unit per year}$$

Hence,

$$EOQ = (2Rc_o/c_h)^{0.5} = (2 \times 200 \times 35/30)^{0.5} = 21.602$$

But as we must order a whole number of units we have that:

$$EOQ = 22$$

We can illustrate this calculation by reference to the diagram below which shows order cost, holding cost and total cost.

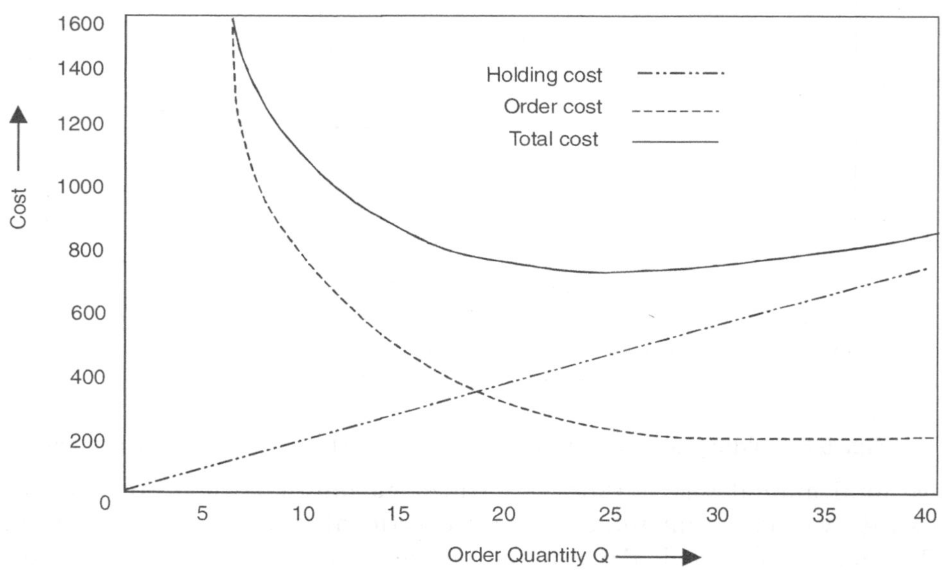

Fig. 5.4 Reference diagram showing order cost, holding cost and total cost

With this *EOQ* we can calculate our total annual cost from the equation

$$\text{Total annual cost} = c_h(Q/2) + c_o(R/Q) \qquad ...(5.8)$$

Hence for this example we have that

Total annual cost = (30 × 22/2) + (35 × 200/22) = 330 + 318.2 = \$648.2

If we had used the exact Q value given by the EOQ formula (*i.e.*, $Q = 21.602$) we would have had that the two terms relating to annual holding cost and annual order cost would have been exactly equal to each other *i.e.*,

$$\text{holding cost} = \text{order cost at } EOQ \text{ point}$$

or $$(c_h Q/2) = (c_o R/Q) \text{ so that } Q = (2Rc_o/c_h)^{0.5} \quad ...(5.9)$$

In other words, as in fact might seem natural from the shape of the Holding Cost and Order Cost curves, the optimal order quantity coincides with the order quantity that exactly balances Holding Cost and Ordering Cost. Note however that this result only applies to certain simple situations. It is not true (in general) that the best order quantity corresponds to the quantity where holding cost and ordering cost are in balance.

Example 5.2

Suppose, for administrative convenience, we ordered 20 and not 22 at each order—what would be cost penalty for deviating from the EOQ value?

Solution:

With a Q of 20 we look at the total annual cost $= (c_h Q/2) + (c_o R/Q)$

$$= (30 \times 20)/2 + (35 \times 200/20)$$

$$= 300 + 350 = \$650$$

Hence the cost penalty for deviating from the EOQ derived value of 22 and ordering 20 at each order is \$650 – \$648.2 = \$1.8

Extensions

In order to illustrate extensions to the basic EOQ calculation we will consider the following example:

A company uses 12,000 components a year at a cost of 5 cents each. Order costs have been estimated to be \$5 per order and inventory holding cost is estimated at 20% of the cost of a component per year. What is the EOQ?

Here R = 12000, $c_o = 5$ and as the inventory holding cost is 20% per year the annual holding cost per unit

$$c_h = \text{cost per unit} \times 20\%$$

$$= \$0.05 \times 0.2 \text{ per unit per year}$$

$$= 0.01.$$

Hence $$EOQ = (2Rc_o/c_h)^{0.5}$$

$$= (2 \times 12000 \times 5/0.01)^{0.5}$$

$$= 3464$$

5.5 WORKING WITH AN INVENTORY SYSTEM

An important class of simulation problems involves inventory systems. Let us consider a company that sells a single product. Suppose it would like to be familiar with how many items it should have in inventory for each of the next n months, where n is the fixed input parameter. The times between demands are independent and identically distributed (IID) exponential random variables with a mean of 0.1 month. Identically distributed means the inter-arrival time has the same probability distribution. The demand-size random variate D must be discrete and can be generated as follows:

First divide the unit interval into the continuous subintervals as

$$\left.\begin{aligned} C_1 &= \left[0\ ,\ \frac{1}{6}\right], \\ C_2 &= \left[\frac{1}{6},\ \frac{1}{2}\right], \\ C_3 &= \left[\frac{1}{2}\ ,\ \frac{5}{6}\right],\ \text{and} \\ C_4 &= \left[\frac{5}{6}\ ,\ 1\right] \end{aligned}\right] \qquad \text{...(5.10)}$$

The width of C_1 is $\frac{1}{6} - 0 = \frac{1}{6}$,

C_2 is $\frac{1}{2} - \frac{1}{6} = \frac{1}{3}$,

C_3 is $\frac{5}{6} - \frac{1}{2} = \frac{1}{3}$, and

C_4 is $1 - \frac{5}{6} = \frac{1}{6}$.

So, the sizes of demands D, are IID random variable with

$$D = \begin{cases} 1 \textit{ with probability } 1/6 \\ 2 \textit{ with probability } 1/3 \\ 3 \textit{ with probability } 1/3 \\ 4 \textit{ with probability } 1/6 \end{cases} \qquad \text{...(5.11)}$$

At the beginning of each month the company reviews the inventory level and divides how many items to order from its supplier.

When an order is placed, the time required for it to arrive is a random variable that is distributed uniformly over a period and is called delivery lag or lead time.

When a demand occurs, if the inventory level is at least as the demand, it is satisfied immediately.

If the demand exceeds the inventory level, the excess of the demand over supply is backlogged indicating shortage and these units of goods are back ordered. In this case, the new inventory level is equal to the old inventory level minus the demand size, resulting in negative inventory level. When an order arrives, it is first used to eliminate as much of the backlog (if any) as possible. The remainder of the order (if any) is added to the inventory. Shortage results in lost sale and loss of goodwill. To avoid shortages, a buffer, or safety, stock should be carried out.

Carrying stock in inventory has an associated cost known as opportunity cost *i.e.*, it is having capital tied up in inventory rather than invested elsewhere and not having the funds available for other investment purpose. Another cost is the holding or carrying cost. This includes cost like renting of warehouse, maintenance, insurance, taxes, interest, deterioration, etc. An alternative to carrying high inventory is to make more frequent reviews, and consequently, more frequent purchases; Reordering cost is associated with this.

When a backlog occurs in the company then, backlog cost includes cost of extra record keeping when a backlog exists as well as loss of customer goodwill. Larger inventories decrease the possibilities of shortage. These costs can be traded off in order to minimize the total cost of an inventory system.

If a company order X items then the cost incurred is calculated by considering a setup cost k and investment cost per item ordered i.

$$\text{Cost } (C) = k + iX \quad \text{...(5.12)}$$

The lead time or delivery lag is between 0.5 and 1 month. If the company uses a stationary (s, S) policy to decide how much to order, *i.e.*,

$$X = \begin{cases} S - I & \text{if } I < s \\ 0 & \text{if } I \geq s \end{cases} \quad \text{...(5.13)}$$

where, I is the inventory level at the beginning of the month.

Let $I(t)$ be the inventory level at time t, can be positive, negative, or zero.

$I^+(t) = \max(I(t), 0)$. Inventory at time t, always positive values as it denotes physical quantities on hand.

$I^-(t) = \max(-I(t), 0)$. When backing log at time t.

The points of time at which $I(t)$ decreases are the ones at which demands occur.

Holding costs are still increased when $I^+(t) = 0$. Our aim is to compare ordering policies and so opportunity cost and holding cost are ignored.

The time-average (per month) is the number of items hold in inventory for the n-month period.

$$\bar{I}^+ = \frac{\int_n^0 I^+(t)dt}{n} \quad \text{...(5.14)}$$

where $I^+(t)$ is number items held in inventory at time t.

Thus,

$$\text{average holding cost per months} = h\,\bar{I}^+ \quad \text{...(5.15)}$$

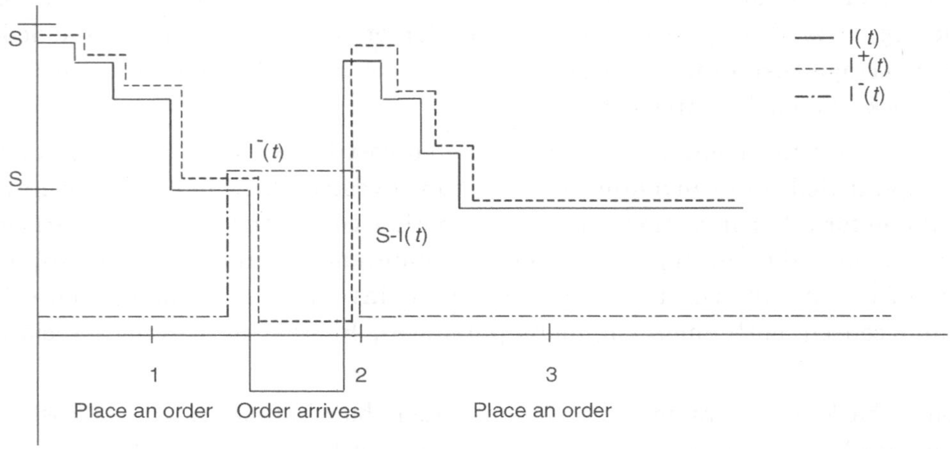

Fig. 5.5 Realization of I(t), $I^+(t)$, and $I^-(t)$

where h is holding cost of per item per month in inventory. Suppose the company had a backlog then the time-average number of items in backlog is

$$\bar{I}^- = \frac{\int_n^0 I^-(t)dt}{n} \qquad ...(5.16)$$

Thus, the average backlog cost per month is $\pi \bar{I}^-$

...(5.17)

where π is the backlog cost per item per month in backlog.

Obtain a U (0,1) random Variate, U from the random-number generator. If U falls in C_1, return D = 1, if U falls in C_2, return D = 2; and so on.

Since U is uniformly distributed over (0, 1) the probability that U falls in C_1 $\frac{1}{6}$ is, this agrees with desired probability that D = 1.

The delivery lags are uniformly distributed, but not over the unit interval [0, 1]. In general we can generate a random variate distributed uniformly over any interval (a, b) by generating a U (0, 1) random number U, and then returning a + U [b − a].

Our model of inventory system uses *four* types of events (as shown in table 5.1):

Table 5.1 Event Description

Event Type	*Event Description*
1	Arrival of an order to the company from the supplier.
2	Demand for the product from a customer.
3	End of simulation after n month.
4	Inventory evaluation at the beginning of a month.

End simulation even being exception, all other three events involves state change. For these three events flow chart can be drawn. Assuming initial inventory level as $I(0) = 60$ and no order in outstanding. We simulate the inventory system for $n = 120$ months. Average Total cost per month of following policies is compared.

s	20	40	20	20	40	40	40	60	60
S	40	60	80	100	60	80	100	80	100

The order-arrival event is shown in flow chart (figure 5.6). When a previous placed order has been arrived from the customer, the following tasks must be carried out:

(*a*) Increase the inventory level by the amount of order.

(*b*) Remove the order arrival from the consideration.

The demand-event is shown in flow chart (figure 5.7). In this even following *there* tasks must be carried out to process the changes necessary to represent the demand's occurrence:

(*a*) Demand size is generated.

(*b*) Inventory is reduced by its demand size.

(*c*) Time of the next demand is scheduled into the event list.

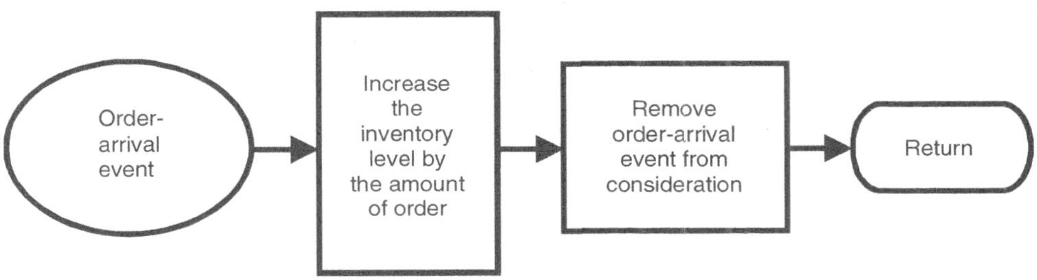

Fig. 5.6 Flow chart of order-arrival event, inventory model

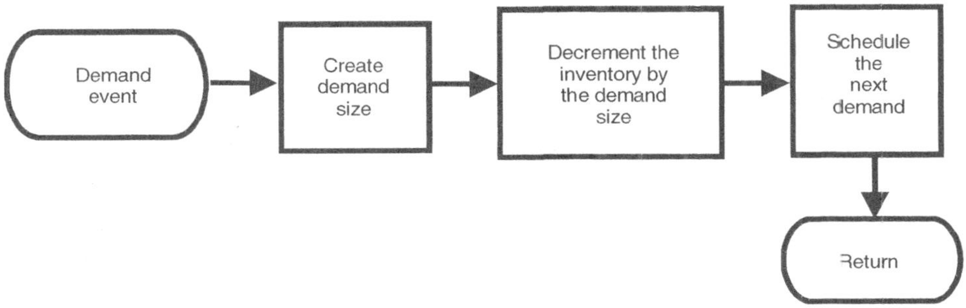

Fig. 5.7 Flow chart of order-arrival event, inventory model

Demand event is the place where a backlog can occur *i.e.,* the inventory level might become negative. The inventory-evaluation event takes place at the beginning of each month. In this event the inventory-level at a time t *i.e.,* I(t) is compared with reorder point s as shown in figure 5.8.

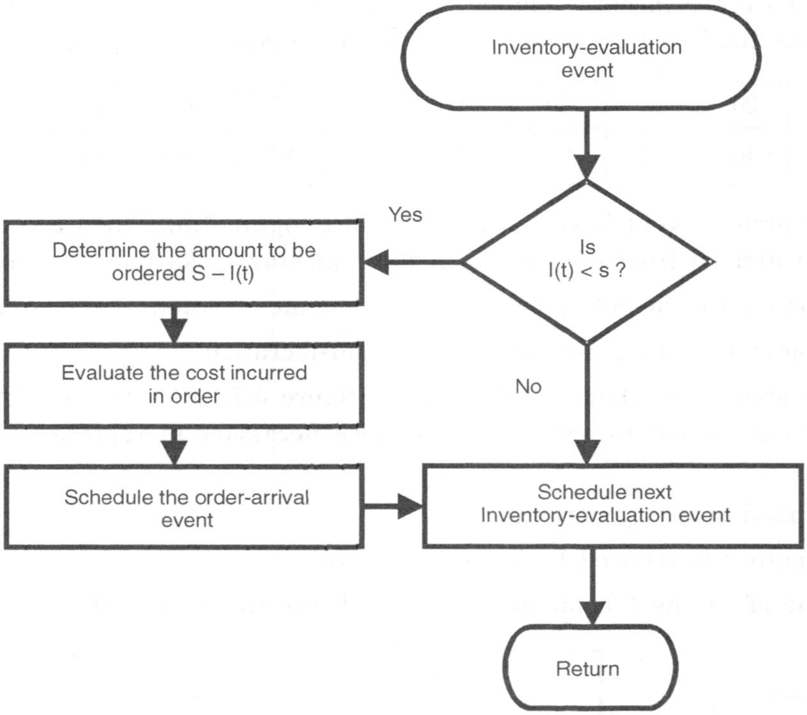

Fig. 5.8 Flow chart for inventory, evaluate on event, inventory model

(*a*) If I(t) is at least s then

(*i*) No order is placed

(*ii*) Schedule the next evaluation into the event list.

(*b*) If I(t) < S, then

(*iii*) Place an order for S – I(t) items

(*iv*) Calculate the cost incurred on the order.

(*v*) Schedule the order arrival.

(*vi*) Schedule the next evaluation into the event list.

A simulation model of this inventory system can be easily constructed by stepping time forward in the fixed investment of a month, starting with month and continuing up to month 120. On a typical month, Month I, first we check to see if merchandise is due to arrive. If yes, then the existing stock S is increased by the quantity that was ordered. If D is the demand of month, and if $D \leq S$, stock at the beginning of the month will be $(S - D)$. If $D > S$, then our stock will be zero, and there will be backlog. In either case we calculate the total cost resulting from current month and add it to the total cost c incurred till last month. Then we determine the inventory on hand plus units on order are greater than reorder point. If not place an order and calculate the amount ordered and the schedule of order arrival. Repeat this procedure for 120 months.

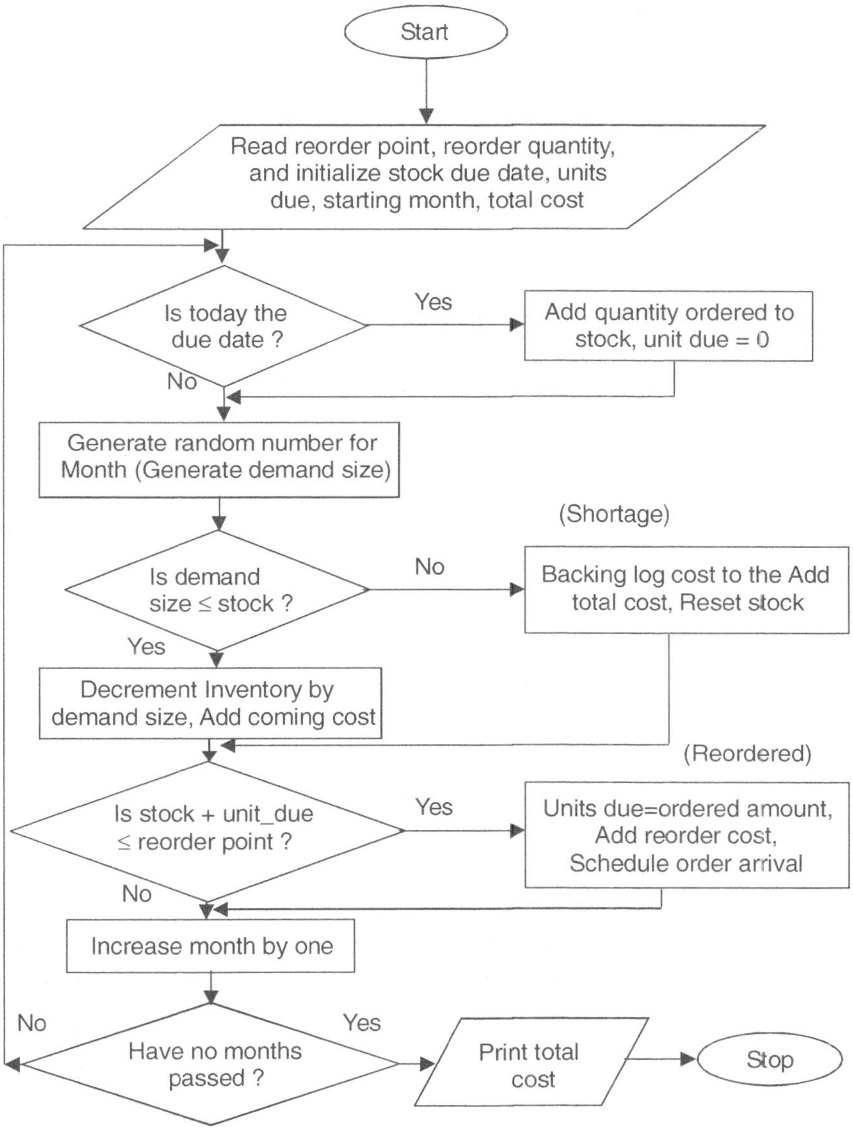

Fig. 5.9 Cost of Inventory Policy (s, S)

If the value of I(t) is negative, update area under I(t), if positive update area under $I^+(t)$, if zero, than no update takes place. When this flow chart is executed with following data the result is obtained:

Single Product Inventory System

Initial inventory level	60 months			
Number of demand sizes	4			
Distribution function of demand sizes 0	0.167	0.500	0.833	1.000
Mean inter-demand time	0.10 months			
Delivery lag range	0.50 to 1.00 month			
Length of the Simulation	120 months			
	K = 32.0	i = 3.0,	h = 1.0	pi = 5.0
Number of policies	9			

On combining all the these event flow chart into figure 5.9 we have,

Table 5.2 Cost of Inventory Policy (*s*, *S*)

Policy (s, S)	*Average total cost*	*Average ordering cost*	*Average holding cost*	*Average shortage* cost
(20, 40)	126.61	99.26	9.25	18.10
(20, 60)	122.74	91.42	17.39	14.83
(20, 80)	123.86	87.36	26.24	10.26
(20, 100)	125.32	81.37	36.00	7.95
(40, 60)	126.37	91.43	25.99	1.95
(40, 80)	125.46	88.40	35.92	1.14
(40, 100)	132.34	85.62	46.42	1.30
(60, 80)	150.02	103.69	44.02	0.31
(60, 100)	143.20	89.15	53.91	0.24

The three separate components of the average total cost per month are reported to see how they respond individually to changes in s and S, as a possible check on the model and the code. For the example, fixing s = 20 and increasing S from 40 to 100.

(*a*) increases holding cost.

(*b*) decreases ordering cost.

(*c*) decreases shortage cost.

Since ordering up to larger values of S implies that these larger order will be placed less frequently, thereby avoiding the fixed ordering cost most often. Fixing S = 100 and increasing s from 40 to 80 leads to

(*a*) decrease in shortage cost.

(*b*) increase in holding cost.

(*c*) increase in ordering cost.

Since increment in s translates into less willingness to let the inventory level fall to low values. Since the overall criterion of total cost per month is the sum of three components that move in sometimes different directions in reactions to changes in s and S, we cannot predict even the direction of movement of this criterion without the simulation. Thus we simply look at the values of this criterion, and it would appear that the (60, 80) policy the best, having an average total cost of Rs. 150.02 per month.

In the present context where the length of the simulation is fixed, what we really want to estimate for each policy is the expected average total cost per month for the first 120 months. The numbers are estimates of these expected values, each estimate based on a sample of size I. Since these estimates have large variances, the ordering of them may differ considerably from the ordering of the expected values, which is the desired information. The ordering of the new estimates might also be different. If we re-run the nine simulations using different U(0, 1) random variates, the estimates obtained might differ greatly from those in table 5.2. The ordering of the new estimates might also be different.

5.6 WHO NEED INVENTORY CONTROL

Devising an efficient system of counting and maintaining a stock of inventory items has long been an laborious task for many shop owners. But the old methods of cataloging by part or item numbers have all but disappeared since the creation of electronic catalogs and the use of computer software programs to track stock-keeping units (SKUs). Inventory management is necessary for owners who want to maintain a stocking service for quick turnaround to help ensure total customer satisfaction. The "fill rate" of an item on a managed inventory list must be maintained to avoid shortages of frequently used items. Even when utilizing an inventory management system, occasional shortages will still occur.

To be successful in today's fast-paced, highly-competitive environment, shops need to have the necessary parts in stock or have reliable suppliers to meet customer demands at a moment's notice. Either way, shops must have a practical, efficient method for managing inventory in order to stay in business and satisfy their customers. Shops in larger cities tend to have more options for inventory stocking. Since there are often numerous parts suppliers nearby, there is less of a need to stock certain parts. Shops that stock belts, hoses or other hard part items sometimes do so only to find a marketing position in their area. Stocking inventory can sometimes yield the benefit of bulk discounts.

However, some shops refuse to stock any items at all. Frequently, the philosophy here is that the shop does not want to "tie up" money in unused inventory that often depreciates while sitting on the shelf. The advantage of this philosophy is that the shop does not spend much time or money on an inventory system since it depends solely on its parts suppliers to stock the items the shop moves frequently.

5.7 BENEFITS OF INVENTORY CONTROL

An inventory control system is an integrated package of software and hardware used in warehouse operations, and elsewhere, to monitor the quantity, location and status of inventory as well as the related shipping, receiving, picking and put away processes. In common usage, the term may also refer to just the software components.

Modern inventory control systems rely upon barcodes. Inventory objects could include any kind of physical asset: merchandise, consumables, circulating tools, fixed assets, library books, or capital equipment. To record an inventory transaction, the system uses a barcode scanner to automatically identify the inventory object, and then collects additional information from the operators via fixed terminals (workstations), or mobile computers.

Accessibility. Profit drain, with regard to lost sales, is always one risk a shop takes when it depends upon a parts network outside of its in-house forum to supply inventory management needs. Shops that are outside of the network of a warehouse supply area, as well as those which depend upon niche markets for their success can use automotive computer software programs to list, count and order parts automatically.

Stock Status. The benefits of keeping significant quantities of parts in stock are not always clear. The financial benefit must be high enough to justify not only the cash expenditures for the stocked items, but also the time and money spent managing the inventory, whether it is for employee time or for computer hardware and software.

Pace in Business. Tire stores tend to use some of the best inventory systems on the market. The reason is not surprising considering the fluid nature of the tire business and the importance of having the right tires in stock. Custom-designed software systems are the most often used programs for these businesses. Many tire dealers also depend on corporate designed systems for total shop management as well as inventory control when they are associated with a franchise. The biggest plus of having one of these systems, according to several shop owners, is having a comprehensive, proven inventory management system that tracks problem areas and automatically makes corrections when needed.

Convenient. Body shops use integrated management systems to track inventory, in addition to performing tasks such as payroll and estimating. Parts are stored in a separate building until they are needed for the repair. Inventory of paint in body shops is usually kept in stock and managed with customized inventory systems integrated as part of the shop's master management program. Shops that have been using computers for estimating and for technical programs should look to expand those efforts toward a good inventory software program. The most important part of any inventory programming effort is finding the time to set it up properly.

5.8 INVENTORY SOFTWARE FEATURES

Following are some standard features that adequate shop inventory management software programs should include:

- **Encryption:** Represents a dealer code for any particular item to be followed on inventory roles.
- **Tax digest information:** Answers whether the item taxed at the time of sale (retail) or by the purchaser (resale).

- **Inventory tracked:** Represents the majority of items found as SKUs in typical automotive inventory. In some cases, software will track operations and automatically reorder parts or supplies when needed. A typical example is a case of grease cartridges for chassis lubrication. If 12 typical lube jobs deplete a cartridge, and there are 12 cartridges to a case, then after 144 lube jobs have been tracked by the inventory block, automatic reorder will take place.
- **Sales price:** Items may be bumped up or down individually or as part of a trend across the inventory block. Criteria for pricing up or down may be initiated by a single vendor code on the last reorder.
- **Last sale date:** This is important data used to measure the amount of time an item sits on a shelf, or the movement rate of that particular item.
- **Costs:** This refers to the standard buying prices of items stocked. This area may also track trends in price increases on items.
- **Sales traffic:** Must show the total activity of a product or group of products as they move in or out of inventory. This function is used by programs to identify trends through a graphing format, or to alert inventory managers of changing factors that may affect gross profits or result in bottlenecks in operations.
- **Quantity price structuring:** Must be used by inventory programs to track and maintain quantity levels, and ensure adequate buying levels set in the program's directory. In any given program, the upgrade of an item because of increased upward traffic will cause the program to automatically seek out the next buying level during the automated reorder.
- **Alternative vending:** Must be used to store a second or third choice of a stocked item from an on-site or off-site source. This data may be manipulated by off-site vendors with regard to each individual shop's buying venue.
- **Register, total records:** Must include the on-hand dollars, purchase units, purchase dollars, unit sales total, etc. Shipping dates may be projected, and order confirmations will be accumulative if more than one order date has been set.
- **Just-in-time approach:** In today's competitive world shorter product life cycles, customers rapid demands and quickly changing business environment is putting lot of pressures on manufacturers for quicker response and shorter cycle times. Now the manufacturers put pressures on their suppliers. One way to ensure quick turnaround is by holding inventory, but inventory costs can easily become prohibitive. A wiser approach is to make your production agile, able to adapt to changing customer demands. This can only be done by JUST IN TIME (JIT) philosophy.

5.9 JIT IN INVENTORY CONTROL

Just-In-Time (JIT) is a term used widely recognized today as the one of the most efficient manufacturing system in the world. In simple words we can explain JIT only required necessary units are provided in necessary quantities at necessary times. Producing one unit extra is as bad is being one unit short. Completing one day early is as bad as finishing one day late. Items are supplied "just-in-time".

The concept is very simple, if you produce only what you need when you need it, then there is no room of error. JIT has truly changed the face of manufacturing and transformed the global economy. JIT is both a philosophy and collection of management methods and techniques used to eliminate waste (particularly inventory). In JIT workers are multifunctional and are required to perform different tasks. Machines are also multifunction and are arranged in small U-shaped work cells that enable parts to processed in a continuous flow through the cell. Workers produce pars one at a time within cells and transport those parts between cells in small lots. Environment is kept clean and free of waste so that any unusual occurrence are visible. Schedules are prepared only for the final assembly line, in which several different models are assembled at the same line. Requirements for the component parts and subassemblies are then pulled through the system. The pull elements of JIT do not work unless production is uniform and lot sizes are low. Pull system is also used to order material from suppliers. They make be requested to make multiple deliveries of the same item in the same day, so the manufacturing system must be flexible.

Just-in-time inventory is viewed as the waste of resources and considered as obstacle in improvement. As there is little buffer inventory between the workstations, so the quality must be high and efforts are made to prevent machine breakdowns. When all these things are taken into consideration, system produces high-quality goods, quickly and at low cost. This system is also being able to respond to changes in customer demands. These elements of JIT can also be applied to the almost any operation, including service operations.

5.10 GENERATION OF POISSON AND ERLANG VARIATES

If the interval time of customers is exponentially distributed then the number of customers arriving in a particular period is generated by a Poisson distribution. The Poisson distribution is a discrete probability distribution. It expresses the probability of a number of events occurring in a fixed period of time if these events occur with a known average rate, and are independent of the time since the last event.

The distribution was discovered by Simeon-Denis Poisson, together with his probability theory. The work focused on certain random variables N that count, among other things, a number of discrete occurrences (say "arrivals") that take place during a time-interval of given length. The probability that there are exactly k occurrences (k being a non-negative integer, k = 0, 1, 2, ...) is:

$$f(k,\lambda) = \frac{e^{-\lambda}}{k!}\lambda^k \qquad ...(5.18)$$

where

- e = the base of the natural logarithm (e = 2.71828...),
- k = the number of occurrences of an event—the probability of which is given by the function,
- $k!$ = the factorial of k,
- λ = a positive real number, equal to the expected number of occurrences that occur during the given interval. For instance, if the events occur on average

every 4 minutes, and you are interested in the number of events occurring in a 10 minute interval, you would use as model a Poisson distribution with $\lambda = 10/4 = 2.5$.

As a function of k, this is the probability mass function. The Poisson distribution can be derived as a limiting case of the binomial distribution. The Poisson distribution is sometimes called a Poissonian, analogous to the term Gaussian for a Gauss or normal distribution.

Generation of Poisson Variates. Our goal is to find random values of k. To generate this we can use the relationship between the exponential and Poisson distribution. Suppose we generate exponentially distributed intervals $t_1, t_2, t_3, t_4, t_5, \ldots\ldots$ with expected values equal to $1/\lambda$, and then add these intervals

$$t = t_1 + t_2 + t_3 + t_4 + \ldots\ldots \quad \ldots(5.19)$$

till their sum exceeds 1. Now we count how many t_i's were added. This count k then we have

$$t_1 + t_2 + t_3 + t_4 + \ldots\ldots + t_k \leq t_1 + t_2 + t_3 + t_4 + \ldots\ldots + t_{k+1} \quad \ldots(5.20)$$

Now these exponentially distributed variates $t_1, t_2, t_3, t_4, t_5, \ldots\ldots$ with average value $1/\lambda$, can themselves be generated by means of relationship

$$t_i = -(1/\lambda)\log u_i \quad \ldots(5.21)$$

where u_i's are uniformly distributed random numbers in range [0, 1].

By generating t_i's and counting how many of them occurred within one unit, we get random values of k.

Now,

$$-(1/\lambda)(\log u_1 + \log u_2 + \log u_3 + \log u_4 \ldots\ldots + \log u_k) \leq 1 < -(1/\lambda)(\log u_1 + \log u_2 + \log u_3 + \log u_4 \ldots\ldots + \log u_{k+1}) \quad \ldots(5.22)$$

Which gives $u_1, u_2, u_3, u_3, u_4, \ldots\ldots, u_k \geq e^{-\lambda} > u_1, u_2, u_3, u_3, u_4, \ldots\ldots, u_{k+1}$

Now we can generate uniformly distributed random numbers and continue to take their products till it becomes less then $e^{-\lambda}$; $(n - 1)$ gives the random variable k, where n, is the number of terms.

Generation of Erlang Variates. An Erlang-m distributed random variable is the sum of m independent and identically distributed exponential distributions. Its density function is

$$-h_m(t) = \frac{1}{(m-1)!} \times \left(\frac{1}{\beta}\right)^m \times t^{m-1} \times e^{-1/\beta} \quad \ldots(5.23)$$

where β is the average value of each of the m constituent exponential distributions, and $m\beta$ is the average value of the Erlang distribution.

For $m = 1$, we have

$$h_1(t) = \frac{1}{\beta} e^{-t/\beta} \quad ..(5.24)$$

To generate a sample form an Erlang-m distribution with mean time $m\beta$ units, we have to generate β, and add them.

5.11 FORECASTING AND REGRESSION ANALYSIS

Regression is the study of relationships among variables, a principal purpose of which is to predict, or estimate the value of one variable from known or assumed values of other variables related to it. Regression analysis is a statistical technique for quantifying the relationship between variables. In simple regression analysis, there is one dependent variable for example, sale to be forecast and one independent variable. The values of the independent variable are typically those assumed to cause or determine the values of the dependent variable. Thus, if we assume that the amount of advertising spent on a product determines the amount of its sales, we could use regression analysis to quantify the precise nature of the relationship between advertising and sales. For forecasting purposes, knowing the quantified relationship between the variables allows us to provide forecasting estimates. The Multiple Regression Analysis and Forecasting model provides a solid basis for identifying value drivers and forecasting business plan data. While it utilizes a range of commonly employed statistical measures to test the validity of the analysis, results are summarized in text for ease of use. Once relationships have been identified, forecasting can be accomplished based on a range of available methodologies.

Variables of Interest: To make predictions or estimates, we must identify the effective predictors of the variable of interest: which variables are important indicators? Can they be measured at the least cost? Which carry only a little information? Which are redundant?

Predicting the Future: Predicting a change overtime or extrapolating from present conditions to future conditions, is not the function of regression analysis. To make estimates of the future, use time series analysis.

Experiment: Begin with a hypothesis about how several variables might be related to another variable and the form of the relationship.

Simple Linear Regression: A regression using only one predictor is called a simple regression.

Multiple Regressions: Where there are two or more predictors, multiple regressions analysis is employed.

Data: Since it is usually unrealistic to obtain information on an entire population, a sample which is a subset of the population is usually selected. For example, a sample may be either randomly selected or a researcher may choose the x-values based on the capability of the equipment utilized in the experiment or the experiment design. Where the x-values are pre-selected, usually only limited inferences can be drawn depending upon the particular values chosen. When both x and y are randomly drawn, inferences can generally be drawn over the range of values in the sample.

Scatter Diagram: A graphical representation of the pairs of data called a scatter diagram can be drawn to gain an overall view of the problem. Is there an apparent relationship? If the points lie within a band described by parallel lines, we can say there is a linear relationship between the pair of x and y values. If the rate of change is generally not constant, then the relationship is curvilinear.

The Model: If we have determined that there is a linear relationship between t and

y we want a linear equation stating y as a function of x in the form $y = a + bx + e$ where a is the intercept, b is the slope and e is the error term accounting for variables that affect y but are not included as predictors, and/or otherwise unpredictable and uncontrollable factors.

Least-Squares Method: To predict the mean y-value for a given x-value, we need a line which passes through the mean value of both x and y and which minimizes the sum of the distance between each of the points and the predictive line. Such an approach should result in a line which we can call a "best fit" to the sample data. The least-squares method achieves this result by calculating the minimum average squared deviations between the sample y points and the estimated line. A procedure is used for finding the values of a and b which reduces to the solution of simultaneous linear equations. Shortcut formulas have been developed as an alternative to the solution of simultaneous equations.

Solution Methods: Techniques of Matrix Algebra can be manually employed to solve simultaneous linear equations. When performing manual computations, this technique is especially useful when there are more than two equations and two unknowns.

Use and Interpretation of the Regression Equation: The equation developed can be used to predict an average value over the range of the sample data. The forecast is good for short to medium ranges.

Measuring Error in Estimation: The scatter or variability about the mean value can be measured by calculating the variance, the average squared deviation of the values around the mean. The standard error of estimate is derived from this value by taking the square root. This value is interpreted as the average amount that actual values differ from the estimated mean.

Confidence Interval: Interval estimates can be calculated to obtain a measure of the confidence we have in our estimates that a relationship exists. These calculations are made using t-distribution tables. From these calculations we can derive confidence bands, a pair of non-parallel lines narrowest at the mean values which express our confidence in varying degrees of the band of values surrounding the regression equation.

Assessment: How confident can we be that a relationship actually exists? The strength of that relationship can be assessed by statistical tests of that hypothesis, such as the null hypothesis, which are established using t-distribution, R-squared, and F-distribution tables. These calculations give rise to the standard error of the regression coefficient, an estimate of the amount that the regression coefficient b will vary from sample to sample of the same size from the same population. An Analysis of Variance (ANOVA) table can be generated which summarizes the different components of variation.

5.11.1 The Simplest Regression Analysis Models

The simplest regression analysis models the relationship between two variables using the following equation:

$$Y = a + bX,$$

where Y is the dependent variable and X is the independent variable. Note that this simple equation denotes a "linear" relationship between X and Y. So this form would be appropriate if, when we plotted a graph of Y and X, we tended to see the points roughly form along a straight line (as compared to having a curvilinear relationship). When we have several past concurrent observations of Y and X, regression analysis provides a means to calculate the values of a and b, which are assumed to be constant. Since you will then know a and b, if we can provide an estimate of X in some future period, we can calculate a future value of Y from the above equation.

Example 5.3

We can illustrate regression analysis using data from 1976–1989 for both the annual value of sales of semiconductors (in \$M) and a likely leading indicator of these sales, namely Producers' durable equipment investment (in \$B). First, a graph of the relationship between these two variables suggests that they might be related in a linear fashion:

We can run a regression of sales on durable equipment investment, which has an equation that looks like this:

$$\text{Sales} = a + b\ (\text{Investment})$$

Using this data, we get the following results:

$$\text{Sales} = -5513.7 + 52.3\ (\text{Investment})$$

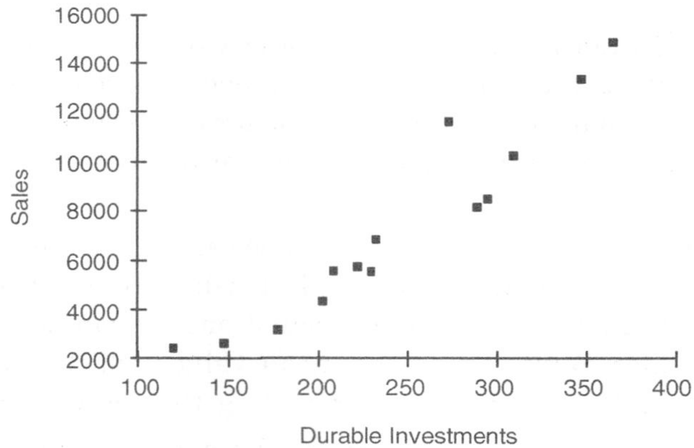

Fig. 5.10 Sales vs. Investments

The last line are the "t-statistics" for the estimate of a (a = –5513.7) and b (b = 52.3). These t-statistics allow us to test whether the estimates are significantly different from 0. If the estimate is not different from 0, then it should be considered 0 when using the regression equation for a forecast. This is a distinct advantage of regression analysis because it allows to assess whether the linear relationship might have occurred by chance.

As a quick rule of thumb, if the number of observations is between 5 and 20, at greater than 3 assures that our estimate is significantly greater than 0 with a confidence of 95%. If the number of observations is greater than 20, at greater than 2 is good enough. In the above example, our estimates of a and b are both significantly greater than 0.

To make a forecast, let us assume that the leading indicator estimate for Producers' durable equipment investment for next year is 370. Plugging this into the above equation, our forecast would be:

$$\text{Sales} = -5513.7 + 52.3 \times (370) = 13837$$

Note that if our estimate of "a" was not statistically significant (*i.e.*, $t < 3$), then we would calculate next period's forecast of Sales as:

$$\text{Sales} = 0 + 52.3 \times (370) = 19351$$

When we want to compare models of different size (different numbers of independent variables and/or different sample sizes) we must use the Adjusted R-Squared, because the usual R-Squared tends to grow with the number of independent variables. The Standard Error of Estimate, *i.e.*, square root of error mean square, is a good indicator of the "quality" of a prediction model since it "adjusts" the Mean Error Sum of Squares (MESS) for the number of predictors in the model as follow:

MESS = Error Sum of Squares/(N – Number of Linearly Independent Predictors)

If one keeps adding useless predictors to a model, the MESS will become less and less stable. R-squared is also influenced by the range of dependent value; so, if two models have the same residual mean square but one model has a much narrower range of values for the dependent variable that model will have a higher R-squared. This explains the fact that both models will do as well for prediction purposes.

Predictions by Regression. The regression analysis has three goals: predicting, modeling, and characterization. What would be the logical order in which to tackle these three goals such that one task leads to and/or and justifies the other tasks? Clearly, it depends on what the prime objective is. Sometimes you wish to model in order to get better prediction. Then the order is obvious. Sometimes, we just want to understand and explain what is going on. Then modeling is again the key, throughout of sample predicting may be used to test any model. Often modeling and predicting proceed in an iterative way and there is no 'logical order' in the broadest sense. We may design model to get predictions, which enable better control, but iteration is again likely to be present and there are sometimes special approaches to control problems. The following contains the main essential steps during modeling and analysis of regression model building, presented in the context of an applied numerical example.

$$\bar{x} = \Sigma x/n \quad \text{This is just the mean of the } x \text{ values.}$$

$$\bar{y} = \Sigma y/n \quad \text{This is just the mean of the } y \text{ values.}$$

$$S_{xx} = SS_{xx} = \Sigma(x(i) - \bar{x})^2 = \Sigma x^2 - (\Sigma x)^2/n$$

$$S_{yy} = SS_{yy} = \Sigma(y(i) - \bar{y})^2 = \Sigma y^2 - (\Sigma y)^2/n$$

$$S_{xy} = SS_{xy} = \Sigma(x(i) - \bar{x})\,(y(i) - \bar{y}) = \Sigma x \,.\, y - (\Sigma x)\,.\,(\Sigma y)/n$$

$$\text{Slope } m = SS_{xy}/SS_{xx}$$

$$\text{Intercept, } b = \bar{y} - m.\bar{x}$$

$$y\text{-predicted} = \text{yhat}(i) = m \,.\, x(i) + b.$$

$$\text{Residual}(i) = \text{Error}(i) = y - \text{yhat }(i).$$

$$\text{SSE} = S_{res} = SS_{res} = SS_{errors} = \Sigma[y(i) - \text{yhat}(i)]^2.$$

Standard deviation of residuals = s = S_{res} = S_{errors} = $[SS_{res}/(n-2)]^{1/2}$.

Standard error of the slope (m) = S_{res} / $SS_{xx}^{1/2}$.

Standard error of the intercept (b) = $S_{res}[(SS_{xx} + n.\ \bar{x}^2)/(n\ .\ SS_{xx})]^{1/2}$.

An Application: A taxicab company manager believes that the monthly repair costs Y of cabs are related to age X of the cabs. Five cabs are selected randomly and from their records we obtained the following data: (x, y) = {(2, 2), (3, 5), (4, 7), (5, 10), (6, 11)}. Based on our practical knowledge and the scattered diagram of the data, we hypothesize a linear relationship between predictor X, and the cost Y.

Now the question is how we can best (*i.e.*, least square) use the sample information to estimate the unknown slope m and the intercept b? The first step in finding the least square line is to construct a sum of squares table to find the sums of x values Σx, y values Σy, the squares of the x values Σx^2, the squares of the x values Σy^2, and the cross-product of the corresponding x and y values Σxy, as shown in the following table:

Table 5.3 values of Σx, Σy, Σx^2, Σxy, and Σy^2

	x	y	x^2	xy	y^2
	2	2	4	4	4
	3	5	9	15	25
	4	7	16	28	49
	5	10	25	50	100
	6	11	36	66	121
SUM	**20**	**35**	**90**	**163**	**299**

The second step is to substitute the values of Σx, Σy, Σx^2, Σxy, and Σy^2 into the following formulas:

$$SS_{xy} = \Sigma xy - (\Sigma x)(\Sigma y)/n = 163 - (20)(35)/5 = 163 - 140 = 23$$
$$SS_{xx} = \Sigma x^2 - (\Sigma x)^2/n = 90 - (20)^2/5 = 90 - 80 = 10$$
$$SS_{yy} = \Sigma y^2 - (\Sigma y)^2/n = 299 - 245 = 54$$

Use the first two values to compute the estimated slope:

$$\text{Slope} = m = SS_{xy}/SS_{xx} = 23/10 = 2.3$$

To estimate the intercept of the least square line, use the fact that the graph of the least square line always pass through ($\bar{x}, \bar{y}$) point, therefore,

$$\text{The intercept} = b = \bar{y} - (m) \times (\bar{x}) = (\Sigma y)/5 - (2.3)\times(\Sigma x/5)$$
$$= 35/5 - (2.3) \times (20/5) = -2.2$$

Therefore the least square line is:

$$y\text{-predicted} = \text{yhat} = mx + b = -2.2 + 2.3x.$$

After estimating the slope and the intercept the question is how we determine statistically if the model is good enough, say for prediction. The standard error of slope is:

Standard error of the slope $(m) = S_m = S_{res}/S_{xx}{}^{1/2}$,

and its relative precision is measured by statistic

$$t_{slope} = m/S_m.$$

For our numerical example, it is:

$$t_{slope} = 2.3 / [(0.6055)/ (10^{1/2})] = 12.01$$

which is large enough, indication that the fitted model is a good one.

You may ask, in what sense is the least squares line the "best-fitting" straight line to 5 data points. The least squares criterion chooses the line that minimizes the sum of square vertical deviations, *i.e.*,

$$\text{residual} = \text{error} = y - y\text{hat}:$$

$$\text{SSE} = \Sigma(y - y\text{hat})^2 = \Sigma(\text{error})^2 = 1.1$$

The numerical value of SSE is obtained from the following computational table for our numerical example.

Table 5.4 Numerical value of SSE

x Predictor	*–2.2+2.3x y-predicted*	*y observed*	*error y*	*squared errors*
2	2.4	2	–0.4	0.16
3	4.7	5	0.3	0.09
4	7	7	0	0
5	9.3	10	0.7	0.49
6	11.6	11	–0.6	0.36
			Sum=0	**Sum=1.1**

Alternately, one may compute SSE by:

$$\text{SSE} = SS_{yy} - m\ SS_{xy} = 54 - (2.3) \times (23) = 54 - 52.9 = 1.1$$

as expected. Notice that this value of SSE agrees with the value directly computed from the above table. The numerical value of SSE gives the estimate of variation of the errors s^2:

$$s^2 = \text{SSE}/(n - 2) = 1.1/(5 - 2) = 0.36667$$

The estimate the value of the error variance is a measure of variability of the y values about the estimated line. Clearly, we could also compute the estimated standard deviation s of the residuals by taking the square roots of the variance s^2. As the last step in the model building, the following Analysis of Variance (ANOVA) table is then constructed to assess the overall goodness-of-fit using the F-statistics:

Table 5.5 Analysis of Variance Components

Analysis of Variance Components					
Source	*DF*	*Sum of Squares*	*Mean Square*	*F Value*	*Prob > F*
Model	1	52.90000	52.90000	144.273	0.0012
Error	3	SSE = 1.1	0.36667		
Total	4	SS_{yy} = 54			

For practical proposes, the fit is considered acceptable if the F-statistic is more than five-times the F-value from the F distribution tables at the back of your textbook. Note that, the criterion that the F-statistic must be more than five-times the F-value from the F distribution tables is independent of the sample size.

Notice also that there is a relationship between the two statistics that assess the quality of the fitted line, namely the T-statistics of the slope and the F-statistics in the ANOVA table. The relationship is:

$$t^2_{\text{slope}} = F$$

This relationship can be verified for our computational example.

Predictions by Regression: After we have statistically checked the goodness of-fit of the model and the residuals conditions are satisfied, we are ready to use the model for prediction with confidence. Confidence interval provides a useful way of assessing the quality of prediction. In prediction by regression often one or more of the following constructions are of interest:

1. A confidence interval for a single future value of Y corresponding to a chosen value of X.
2. A confidence interval for a single pint on the line.
3. A confidence region for the line as a whole.

5.12 APPLICATIONS

An inventory control system may be used to automate a sales order fulfillment process. Such a system contains a list of order to be filled, and then prompts workers to pick the necessary items, and provides them with packaging and shipping information. Real time inventory control systems use wireless, mobile terminals to record inventory transactions at the moment they occur. A wireless LAN transmits the transaction information to a central database. Physical inventory counting and cycle counting are features of many inventory control systems which can enhance the organization.

The Inventory Control application also provides the ability to monitor inventory transactions, analyze inventory levels, classify inventory for positive control and maintain a history of inventory use as a guide for better planning. Specific features of the Inventory Control application include Inventory gross usage maintenance; Two-step cycle counting; Inventory reorder quantity maintenance including reorder quantities, reorder; Points, and safety stock; Material analysis; Economic order quantity processing; Inventory display (by part number); Inventory analysis; Inventory history display and report; Part number cross reference capability; Inventory history display by part number or transaction types; Stock status report.

SUMMARY

With the rapid pace of change in today's retail industry, it is often easy to forget about the importance of getting the basics right. Inventory and how it is managed is a fact of every retailer's life and the common denominator of all retail businesses. The right inventory tracking system makes our life easier and our business more profitable. A good inventory tracking system tells what merchandise is in stock, what is on order, when it will arrive and what we have sold. With such a system, we can plan purchases intelligently and quickly. Researches indicate that stockless inventory has been shown to dramatically reduce hospitals' operating costs while posting annual savings. Despite the savings, and despite the need for hospitals to focus on their bottom line, stockless inventory seems to have lost its momentum.

Inventory management is an important activity towards ensuring smooth production process. Accounting information plays a key role in inventory management. Just-in-Time (JIT) manufacturing involves purchasing the raw materials and going ahead with the production process as and when the demand arises. JIT is an approach towards minimizing waste and maximizing productivity.

EXERCISE QUESTIONS

1. What do you understand by Simulation of an Inventory System ?
2. How Inventory System simulation is different from other system simulations ?
3. Explain the area where Inventory systems are used.
4. Explain the elements of an Inventory model.
5. Explain the benefits of Inventory Control in organizations?
6. Explain the features of a good inventory software.
7. What is JIT approach in inventory control?
8. Explain major points to be included in an inventory system.
9. Explain Poisson and Erlang distributions. How Poisson and Erlang distribution can be used to generate Poisson and Erlang variates?
10. Explain the role of random numbers in generation of Poisson and Erlang variates.
11. What do you understand by forecasting? Explain its importance in regression analysis.
12. Explain inventory predictions by regression analysis.
13. Explain the applications of inventory systems.

14. A firm procures the requirement of material at the beginning of the financial year. Let annual consumption is 12000. Determine the average inventory for the following consumption pattern:

(*a*) Constant usages rate of 1000 per month.

(*b*) Variable usages rate as given below.

Usages	***Month***
2000	April
1800	May
1700	June
1600	July
1200	August
1000	September
800	October
7000	November
500	December
350	January
250	February
100	March

15. Assuming that the annual quantity of an item required cost \$2,400 the cost f placing a purchase order is \$ 20 per year and the inventory carrying cost is 15% per year, what will be the inventory carrying cost variation inversely with the number of orders and the cost of buying?

16. An organization required 10,000 units of an item per year. The cost of ordering is \$100 per order. The inventory carrying cost is 20%. The unit price of an item is \$10. Determine EOQ.

17. A company requires 1500 units per month of an item. Order cost is \$50 per order. The carrying cost is 15% per year while unit cost of an item is \$10. Determine the economic lot size and maximum total variable cost.

18. Demand for a certain part ordered by a company tends to be constant, at a monthly rate of 1000 units. The per-unit holding cost of this item is \$5 per year, and the cost of placing an order is \$25.

(*i*) Determine optimal order size. How often an order should be placed, to the nearest day.

(*ii*) Show that the annual holding cost and ordering cost are equal when the optimal order size is used. What is the total relevant cost?

(*iii*) The company wishes to order only once other week. By what percentage will it increase the total relevant cost?

(*iv*) Assume this part can be ordered only in multiples of 100 units. What is the total relevant cost?

19. A manufacturer has to supply 6000 units of his product to his customers per year. Shortages are not allowed and storage cost amount to \$6 per unit per year. The setup cost per run is \$800. Determine –

(*i*) the economic order quantity

(*ii*) the minimal average yearly cost

(*iii*) the optimal number of orders per year

(*iv*) the optimal period of supply per optimal order

(*v*) the increase in the total cost associated with ordering 30% more than EOQ.

20. Find the optimal order quantity of a product for which price-breaks are as follows:

Quantity (Units)	***Unit Cost (\$)***
Below 100	200
101 to 200	180
Above 200	150

The monthly demand to the product is 400 units. The storage cost is 20% per year of the price of the product per unit. The ordering cost is 50% per order.

Chapter 6

Design and Evaluation of Simulation Experiments

6.1 INTRODUCTION

The fact that a model compiles, executes, and produces numbers does not guarantee that it is correct or that the numbers being generated are representative of the system being modeled. After the development, the model is functionally complete, we should ask, Does it work correctly? There are two aspects to this question. First, does it operate the way the analyst intended? Second, does it behave the way the real-world system does or will? We find the answers to these questions through model verification and model validation. Verification seeks to show that the computer program performs as expected and intended. Validation on the other hand, questions whether the model behavior validly represents that of the real-world system being simulated. Verification is a vigorous debugging aimed at showing that the parts of the model work independently and together using the right data at the right time. Even though the analyst thinks he or she knows what the model does and how it does it, anyone who has done any programming knows how easy it is to make errors. Throughout the verification process, we try to find and remove unintentional errors in the logic of the model. Validation on the other hand, is the process of reaching an acceptable level of confidence that the inferences drawn are correct and applicable to the real-world system being represented. We are basically trying to answer the questions: Does the model adequately represent the real-world system? Is the model generated behavioral data characteristic of the real-world system's behavioral data? Does the simulation model user have confidence in the model's results?

Through validation, we try to determine whether the simplifications and omissions of detail that we have knowingly and deliberately made in our model, have introduced unacceptably large errors in the results. Validation is the process of determining that we have built the right model, whereas verification is designed to see if we have built the model right. Model verification and validation are often difficult and time consuming but are extremely important to success. If the model and results are not accepted by the decision makers, then the effort has been wasted. It is absolutely mandatory that we be able to transfer our confidence in the model to the people who must use the results.

With the steadily increasing power of computers, computer simulation has become a relatively rapid process. After doing one simulation, we can quickly revise it and conduct others. Therefore, it is almost always best to think of simulation as an iterative process: We conduct a simulation experiment, look at the results and find as many new questions as answers to our original questions. Each simulation experiment suggests subsequent simulation experiments. Through a succession of these experiments, we gradually gain the better understanding we originally sought. To a large extent, it is fruitful to approach simulation in the spirit of exploratory data analysis.

A major purpose of simulation experiments, often as a means to other ends, is to estimate unknown quantities of interest. When we plan to conduct a simulation experiment, in addition to knowing what quantities we want to estimate, it is also good to have a rough idea how long it will take to obtain a reliable estimate: Should the experiment take two seconds, two hours or two years? In this chapter we discuss techniques that can be used, before a simulation is conducted, to estimate the computational effort required to obtain desired statistical precision for contemplated simulation estimators. Given information about the required computational effort, we can decide what cases to consider and how much computational effort to devote to each. We can even decide whether to conduct the experiment at all. We can also decide if we need to exploit variance reduction techniques or efficiency improvement techniques.

The theoretical analysis complements the experience we gain from conducting many simulation experiments. Through experience, we can learn about the amount of computational effort required to obtain desired statistical precision for simulation estimators, in various settings. The analysis and computational experience should reinforce each other, giving us better judgment. The methods in this chapter are intended to help develop more reliable expectations about statistical precision. We can use this knowledge, not only to design better simulation experiments, but also to evaluate simulation output analysis, done by others or ourselves. At first glance, the experimental design problem may not seem very difficult. First, we might think, given the amazing growth in computer power, that the computational effort rarely needs to be that great, but that is not the case: Many simulation estimation goals remain out of reach, just like many other computational goals; Second, we might think that we can always get a rough idea about how long the runs should be by doing one *pilot run* to estimate the required simulation run lengths. However, there are serious difficulties with that approach. First, such a preliminary experiment requires that we set up the entire simulation before we decide whether or not to conduct the experiment. Nevertheless, if such a sampling procedure could be employed consistently with confidence, then the experimental design problem would indeed not be especially difficult. In typical simulation experiments, we want to estimate steady-state means for several different input parameters. Unfortunately, doing a pilot run for one set of parameters may be very misleading, because the required run length may change dramatically when the input parameters are changed.

Some computational experience or additional experiments on the selected computer are needed to convert simulation time into computational effort. Since there is a degree of freedom in choosing the measuring units for time, it is important to normalize these time units. On the positive side, focusing on required simulation time has the advantage that it yields characterizations of computational effort that are independent of the specific computer used to conduct the simulation. It seems best to try to account for that important factor separately.

This chapter gives a survey on the use of statistical designs for what-if analysis in simulation, including sensitivity analysis, optimization, and validation/verification. Sensitivity analysis is divided into two phases. The first phase is a pilot stage, which consists of screening or searching for the important factors among hundreds of potentially important factors. The second phase uses regression analysis to approximate the input/output transformation that is implied by the simulation model; the resulting regression model is also known as a meta-model or a response surface. Regression analysis gives better results when the simulation experiment is well-designed, using either classical statistical designs (such as fractional factorials) or optimal designs. To optimize the simulated system, the analysts may apply Response Surface Methodology (RSM); RSM combines regression analysis, statistical designs, and steepest-ascent hill-climbing. To validate a simulation model, again regression analysis and statistical designs may be applied.

6.2 DEVELOPMENT OF SIMULATION EXPERIMENTS

6.2.1 Optimal Solution for Development of Simulation Experiment

For development of simulation experiment, the objective is to minimize the material handling cost of the simulation system. While it is important to reduce the amount of material handling, the traditional methods do not address the actual time at which the material is transported. In today's short cycle time production environments, the timing of material movement may have a bigger impact on the productivity of the system than its cost. A facility layout optimization technique can be used to take into consideration the dynamic characteristics and operational constraints of the system as a whole, and can be able to solve the facility layout design problem based on a system's performance measures, such as the cycle time and productivity. Each layout solution can be presented in the form of a string that is suitable for analysis by a genetic algorithm technique. These solutions are then translated into simulation models by a specially designed automated simulation model generator. Genetic algorithms are used to optimize the layout for manufacturing effectiveness while simulation serves as a system performance evaluation tool. Combined with a statistical comparison technique to reduce the simulation burden, the test results demonstrate that the proposed approach overcomes the limitations of traditional layout optimization methods and is capable of finding optimal or near optimal solutions.

6.2.2 Final Experimental Design

Now that we have developed the model, verified its correctness, and validated its adequacy, we again need to consider the final strategic and tactical plans for the execution of the experiment(s). We must update project constraints on time (schedule) and costs to reflect current conditions. Even though we have exercised careful planning and budget control from the beginning of the project, we must now take a hard, realistic look at what resources remain and how best to use them. We will also have learned more about the system in the process of designing, building, verifying and validating the model which we will want to incorporate into the final plans. The design of a computer simulation experiment is essentially a plan for purchasing a quantity of information that costs more or less depending upon how it was acquired. Design profoundly affects the effective use of experimental resources because:

- The design of the experiments largely determines the form of statistical analysis that can be applied to the data.
- The success of the experiments in answering the desired questions is largely a function of choosing the right design.

Simulation experiments are expensive both in terms of the analyst's time and labor and in some cases, in terms of computer time. We must therefore carefully plan and design not only the model but also its use.

6.2.3 Experimentation and Analysis

Next we come to the actual running of the experiments and the analysis of the results. We now have to deal with issues such as how long to run the model, what to do about starting conditions, whether the output data are correlated, and what statistical tests are valid on the data. Before addressing these concerns, we must first ascertain whether the real system is terminating or non-terminating because this characteristic determines the running and analysis methods to be used. In a terminating system, the simulation ends when a critical event occurs. For example, a bank opens in the morning empty and idle. At the end of the day it is once again empty and idle. Another example would be a duel where one or both participants are killed or the weapons are empty. In other words, a system is considered to be terminating if the events driving the system naturally cease at some point in time. In a non-terminating system, no such critical event occurs and the system continues indefinitely (for example, a telephone exchange or a hospital). A second system characteristic of interest is whether the system is stationary or non-stationary. A system is stationary if the distribution of its response variable (and hence it's mean and variance) does not change overtime. With such systems we are generally concerned with finding the steady-state conditions, *i.e.*, the value which is the limit of the response variable if the length of the simulation went to infinity without termination. Whether the system is terminating or non-terminating, we must decide how long to run the simulation model *i.e.*, we must determine sample size. But first we must precisely define what constitutes a single sample. There are several possibilities:

1. Each transaction considered a separate sample. For example, turn-around time for each job or total time in the system for each customer.
2. A complete run of the model. This may involve considering the mean or average value of the response variable for the entire run as being a datum point. Multiple runs are referred to as replication.
3. A fixed time period in terms of simulated time. Thus a simulation may be run for n time periods, where a time period is an hour or a day or a month.

4. Transactions aggregated into groups of fixed size. For example, we might take the time in the system for each 25 jobs flowing through and then use the mean time of the group as a single datum point. This is usually referred to as batching.

If the system is a non-terminating, steady-state system we must be concerned with starting conditions, *i.e.*, the status of the system when we begin to gather statistics or data. If we have an empty and idle system *i.e.*, no customers present, we may not have typical steady-state conditions. Therefore, we must either wait until the system reaches steady-state before we begin to gather data (warm-up period), or we must start with more realistic starting conditions. Both of these approaches require that we should be able to identify when the system has reached steady-state.

Finally, most statistical tests require that the data points in the sample be independent *i.e.*, not correlated. Since many of the systems we model are queueing networks, they do not meet this condition because they are auto-correlated. Therefore, very often we must do something to insure that the data points are independent before we can proceed with the analysis.

Assuring total quality in a modeling and simulation effort involves the measurement and assessment of a variety of quality characteristics such as accuracy, execution efficiency, maintainability, portability, reusability, and usability (human-computer interface). Verification, validation, testing, accreditation, certification and credibility assessment activities primarily deal with the measurement and assessment of *accuracy* of models and simulations.

An activity of accuracy assessment can be labeled as verification or validation based on an answer to the following question: In assessing the accuracy, is the model behavior compared with respect to the corresponding system behavior through mental or computer execution? If the answer is "yes" then model validation is conducted; otherwise, it implies that the transformational accuracy is judged implying model verification.

Model Testing is ascertaining whether inaccuracies or errors exist in the model. In model testing, the model is subjected to test data or test cases to determine if it functions properly. "Test failed" implies the failure of the model, not the test. A test is devised and testing is conducted to perform either validation or verification or both. Some tests are devised to evaluate the behavioral accuracy (*i.e.*, validity) of the model, and some tests are intended to judge the accuracy of model transformation from one form into another (verification). Sometimes, the whole process is called model verification, validation and testing.

Accreditation is "the official certification that a model or simulation experiment is acceptable for use for a specific purpose."

6.3 PRINCIPLES OF VERIFICATION, VALIDATION AND ACCREDITATION

Following are the major principles used in verification, validation and accreditation of simulation experiments:

1. Verification and Validation must be conducted throughout the entire modeling and simulation life cycle.
2. The outcome of Verification, Validation and Accreditation should not be considered as a binary variable where the model or simulation is absolutely correct or absolutely incorrect.
3. A simulation experiment is built with respect to the modeling and simulation objectives and its credibility is judged with respect to those objectives.
4. Verification and Validation requires independence to prevent developer's bias.
5. Verification, Validation and Accreditation is difficult and requires creativity and insight.
6. Credibility can be claimed only for the prescribed conditions for which the model or simulation is verified, validated and accredited.
7. Verification, Validation and Accreditation must be planned and documented.
8. Type I, II and III errors must be prevented.
9. Errors should be detected as early as possible in the modeling and simulation life cycle.
10. Multiple response problems must be recognized and resolved properly.
11. Successfully testing each submodel (module) does not imply overall model credibility.
12. Double validation problem must be recognized and resolved properly.
13. Simulation model validity does not guarantee the credibility and acceptability of simulation results.
14. A well-formulated problem is essential to the acceptability and accreditation of modeling and simulation results.

6.3.1 Verification, Validation and Accreditation in Two Modeling and Simulation Life Cycles

Verification, Validation and Accreditation activities in the modeling and simulation life cycle are depicted in figure 6.1. The fundamental phases of the life cycle are present in figure. Verification and Validation is not a phase or step in the modeling and simulation life cycle, but a continuous activity throughout the entire life cycle. The life cycle should not be interpreted as strictly sequential. The sequential representation of some arrows is intended to show the direction of development throughout the life verification, validation and accreditation activity may necessitate returning to an earlier process and starting all over again. Conducting verification and validation for the first time in the life cycle when the modeling and simulation application is completed, is analogous to the teacher who gives only a final examination. No opportunity is provided throughout the semester to notify the student that he or she has serious deficiencies. Severe problems may go undetected until it is too late to do anything but fail the student. Frequent tests and homework throughout the semester are intended to inform the students about their deficiencies so that they can study more to improve their knowledge as the course progresses. The situation in conducting verification and validation is exactly analogous. The verification, validation and accreditation activities throughout the entire modeling and simulation life cycle, are intended to reveal any quality deficiencies that might be present as the modeling and simulation progresses from the problem definition to the completion of the modeling and simulation application. This allows us to identify and rectify quality deficiencies during the life cycle phase in which they occur.

6.4 SIMULATION EXPERIMENTATION

First let us consider discrete event simulation and examines the different types of experiments that are performed with simulation models. Optimization techniques can be used to introduce, which help to establish the best model choices for a defined goal.

Discrete Event Simulation (DES) is an extremely valuable technique for investigating the behavior of many business processes ranging from manufacturing layouts to the operation of modern contact centers, from the handling of patient arrival at emergency departments to the processing of Internet enquiries on a web site. DES can handle vast complexity whereas algorithmic methods, such as Petri-net analysis for example, run into limitations beyond which they cannot hope to perform. With a simulation model the creator simply sets up the correct real-world rule at each stage where a real-world decision is made. The model then plays the real-world scenario forward taking these decisions in turn. This gives great insight into the performance of the described system in terms of throughput, services levels, resource utilizations, profitability, etc.

How to validate simulation. This gives a survey on how to validate simulation models through the application of *statistical* techniques, such that the type of technique actually applied depends on the availability of data on the real system. Regarding this data availability, we can distinguish three situations:

(*i*) No real-life data are available,

(*ii*) There is only data on the real output (not the corresponding input or scenario),

(*iii*) Besides the output data, the corresponding input or trace is also known, which is used to perform so-called trace driven or correlated inspection simulation.

The validation is plentiful, however, the focus in not on the role of data availability in the choice of statistical tests! This contribution has such a focus. So we concentrate on validation that uses mathematical statistics. After all, simulation means experimentation, and any experimentation calls for statistical analysis, preceded by statistical design. Obviously, such a statistical analysis is only part of the whole validation process (other parts are graphical summaries, animation for 'face validity', *etc.,* many types of validation are used and proposed in practice and theory. However, if mathematical statistics is used, then the correct statistics should be used. Which type of statistical procedure is correct obviously depends on the kind of data that are available for analysis. Briefly, our main conclusions will turn out to be as follows:

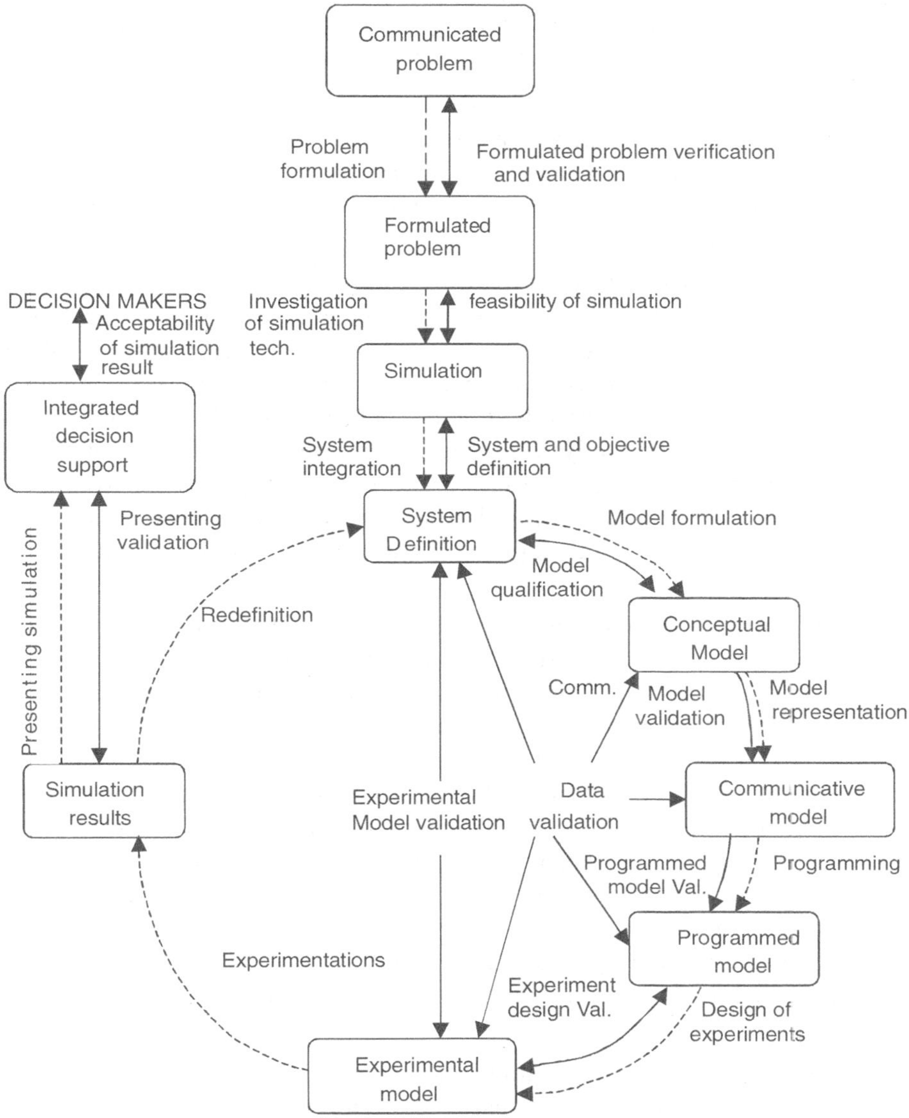

Fig. 6.1 Validation in Modeling and Simulation life cycle

Case (i): Even if real data are missing, there is still *expert knowledge*. For example, we all are experts in waiting atqueue, so we know that if more customers arrive per hour, then waiting times increase—unless more cashiers become active. However, this knowledge is *qualitative*; to obtain quantitative knowledge, a simulation model is developed (*i.e.*, the sign or direction of the effect is known, not its magnitude). If the simulation model's input/output behavior violates this qualitative knowledge, the model should be seriously questioned: are there programming and conceptual errors?

Case (*ii*): If data on the real output are available, then we can apply the classical two-sample Student *t*-statistic provided the data are approximately normally distributed. In case of non-normality we can use distribution-free tests or bootstrapping.

Case (*iii*): In trace-driven simulation we can apply a particular kind of regression analysis (compute the differences and sums of real and simulated outputs; regress these differences on the sums, and test for zero intercept and zero slope). In case of non-normality, however, bootstrapping of the difference between the average simulated and real outputs gives best results.

No Real Data Available. How realistic is it to assume that there is no data on the real system being simulated? Indeed, in some applications, such data are either completely missing or scarce. Examples are data on nuclear war, nuclear accidents, global warming or greenhouse effect. If no data on the real system are available, then strong validation claims are impossible. Yet the analysts should at least perform sensitivity analysis (or what-if analysis). We define sensitivity analysis as the systematic investigation of the reaction of the simulation responses to extreme values of the model's input or to drastic changes in the model's structure. For example, what happens to the customers' mean waiting time when their arrival rate doubles; what happens if the priority rule is changed by introducing 'fast lanes'?

Real Output Data. How realistic is it to assume that there is data on the output not the input of the real system? Let us return to the case study on the search for mines by means of sonar. In this case study it is impossible to measure the environment namely, the temperature and the salinity of the sea water that affect sonar performance at all times and places. To obtain real output data on the detection of mines, the navy has one team deposit mines on the sea bottom; next another team searches for these mines (in general, the military conducts field tests; likewise, private companies build pilot plants to obtain data). In general, if the real-world scenarios are not measured, then only the outputs of the real and the simulated systems can be compared. Note that in some situations the analysts are 'drown by the numbers'; examples are data on supermarket sales and on telecommunication operations. In general, data are abundant if systems are electronically monitored; examples are Point Of Sale Systems (POSS) and Electronic Data Interchange (EDI).

Real I/O Data: Trace-Driven. Comparing data on the real and the simulated systems makes more sense if both systems are observed under similar scenarios; for example, a busy day at the real supermarket should be compared with a busy day at the simulated store. More specifically, in queueing systems such a supermarkets input data consists of customers' arrival times and cashiers' service times, whereas output data concerns customers' waiting times. Trace-driven simulation means that the analysts feed real input data into the simulation program, in historical order. After running the simulation program, the analysts compare the time series of simulated output with the historical time series of real output.

6.4.1 Experimentation

With a discrete event simulation model it is possible to conduct experiments which show the ranges of current and projected outcomes without the need for costly pilot schemes that disrupt the current process. The experimentation is carried out at a number of levels. At one level a user simply wishes to establish the variability of the current process given certain input rates and profiles. Simulation can establish the projected variation using two similar, yet different, methods. However the experimentation options hold true either a short period of experimentation can be repeated many times (with different random number sampling) or a model can be run much longer and the range of random effects can be observed in that way. How many repeats or how long to run a model are questions that can be answered by a combination of input and output data analysis. It is important that when running a model that it experiences all the randomness of the input data and that the output results 'settle down' before conclusions are drawn.

At a second level a user may wish to alter different parameters within a model to observe the different effects. Again with this type of experimentation the range of results might also be important, again accomplished through elongated or repeated experiments. At a third level a user may wish to compare one model with another. For example, in manufacturing there may be two investment options production layout A and production layout B. These may indeed be the only options although often within each solution too there may be parameter choices (*e.g.*, buffer storage level options). In addition there is again the optional value of establishing the range of results. With all these levels of experimentation there are a variety of experimental designs that can be used: different numbers of replications, different types of factorial experimental design ranging from full factorial to half factorial to Latin square type designs where different parameter combinations are chosen. For different models the model itself can simply be considered a different type of parameter.

6.4.2 Formulating the Problem

Sometimes formulation of problem can be a straightforward process. For example, determining optimum buffer capacities between 10 machines in a line simply offer each capacity as a single parameter that can vary. Some optimizations can be more difficult to express in terms of parameters that can vary, for example, a permutation example such as ordering a sequence of operations in the most efficient manner. Here each operation cannot sample independently which position in the sequence it will be as each must end up with a different sequence number. By simply rejecting invalid options and moving on-to another set is inefficient and for many algorithms does not work well where most solutions generated are invalid. A practical solution to this example is to have n parameters for a sequence of n operations and to allow the first to vary between 1 and n, the second between 1 and n-1, the third between 1 and n-2, and so on. Each parameter choice defines the number of the operation in the ordered set of operations and removes the choice from the ordered set. It can be seen that in practice therefore only n-1 parameters are needed as the last choice is always the only operation left in the set.

There are few problems that arise in simulation experiments that cannot be formulated in some way using mathematical procedures. Another interesting type of optimization is where there are a very high number of different options. In this case it is important to structure the problem in the most efficient way for the optimization algorithm. There are often different ways of formulating a problem and the way that is chosen can have a direct effect on the success of the optimization. For example, a model with 200 staff available for work during a 24 hour period to work on a particular office process should be built to determine the optimal work times for the staff. This problem could be formulated as an experiment with 48 parameters representing the number of staff on shift in each half hourly period. Each parameter could vary between 0 and 200. The problem with this is that the overall number of different permutations is 200 to the power of 48. This is an astronomical number and any optimization engine will struggle to learn enough about the solution space in the time available. Alternatively the problem could be formulated differently. There might realistically be 8 different shift patterns that each worker could be assigned to. If each worker chooses a shift pattern then this could result in 200 parameters each varying between 1 and 8. Again, this creates a very large number of options. Alternatively, the problem could be formulated with the number of staff on each shift being the parameter. This results in 8 parameters varying between 1 and 200. With the added constraint that all the 8 parameters must add up to less than 201 then this cuts down the number of options dramatically and the problem becomes much easier for the algorithm to tackle. This is a difficult subject area. Happily there are many simulation optimizations where the options are simply stated but for the more complex more experience is needed to gauge the number of alternatives and how an algorithm might cope with the complexities.

6.4.3 Optimization

Defining an Optimization Experiment. It is common within experimentation that it is desired to find the best solution. Best can mean many different things, highest throughput levels, lowest costs, highest services levels, etc. Usually it means a specific combination of these types of factors. Within optimization it is important to define what the best solution looks like. This is encapsulated in an objective function which can be as simple or as complex as required. Now that the objective of the optimization is established the next step is to define what can vary (often called the optimization parameters). These parameters can be simple numbers such as the number of staff employed on each shift or can be flags indicating different complex control options or behaviors for a model. For example, it may be of interest to investigate flexible labor arrangements in a factory. For this type of example a flag can enact different resource rules in a model one indicating separate defined resources and one indicating the use of any of a number of resource pools. There may be constraints too. For example, in a model looking at an office business process the manning level for the seven different stages of a particular process may be between 20 and 30 people. However, the overall staff requirement must be below 190 due to space considerations. Other input data items which need to be set for a simulation experiment also need to be established for optimization too. For example, how long should a model run be, should there be a warm-up period for a model to allow it to reach equilibrium and how many replications of each set of parameters should be allowed, there are any textbooks on simulation that offer guidance on these matters. Once the objective is defined and all the parameters and constraints have been set, then the model optimization is ready to run. An optimization is a series of experiments where the next experiment is determined based on the results found so far. The sequence can be determined and affected manually or automatically using an optimization algorithm. Optimization can be thought of as intelligent experimentation. Optimization algorithms attempt to improve the results being achieved through learning the effects of adjusting each parameter in combination with other parameter settings.

Optimization Algorithm Methodology. Within a simulation model, an optimization algorithm typically works in the following way:

(*i*) An initial set of parameter values is chosen and one or more replication experiments is carried out with these values.

(*ii*) The results are obtained from the simulation runs and the optimization algorithm then chooses another parameter set to try.

(*iii*) The new values are set and the next experiment set is run.

(*iv*) Steps (*ii*) and (*iii*) are repeated until either the algorithm is stopped manually or a set of defined finishing conditions are met.

Optimization Guarantee. With this type of heuristic algorithm it is impossible to guarantee to always find an optimal solution using a reduced experiment set. The reason for this can be seen with the following example model. Suppose a model is constructed that returns a random number as the objective function value. With this model it can be seen that logically the only way to find the optimal value returned is to try all permutations. It is not possible to infer any information about one result/parameter set from another (in fact in this model the parameters have no effect). There is no way for any algorithm to learn any useful information to guide it towards the best solution. Hence it can be seen that no algorithm can be guaranteed to find the best or optimal solution. Only trying all combinations can guarantee this.

Solution Space. The solution space of an experiment is often described as the multi-dimension plot of the objective function value against the parameter values. Considering it in simplistic terms with two parameters it can be visualized as a terrain map with the x and y coordinates being parameter values and the best result being represented by the highest mountain or the deepest sea. The most difficult type of solution space for any algorithm to search is one where the terrain is especially rough with many cliffs, chasms, crevasses and all manner of quickly changing slopes and gradients. This type of solution space is often set as a theoretical test for an optimization engine and indeed these are the hardest tests. Fortunately the majority of simulation models do not experience such wild variability. This is not to say that the landscape of a simulation solution space is bland but there is usually much method, rather than total madness. A typical solution space will have some cliff faces and a number of different peak areas but typically there will a fair degree of rolling hillsides too. Typically optimization algorithms can learn quickly from the different sloping regions and can also learn about a relatively small number of complicated areas too. Therefore, optimization algorithms can work well for typical simulation experiments and indeed quickly. The success of an optimization algorithm is often measured as the speed at which it can find an optimal or near optimal solution. Speed is important because a simulation experiment is not an instantaneous calculation, simulation experiments take time. Usually it is not possible to conduct millions of experiments and therefore a good algorithm must learn quickly in order to find good results in a reasonable timeframe.

Non-simplistic Algorithms. When optimization algorithms are trying to find a better solution they will change a parameter or parameters and rerun the model. A measure of the success of this will be if the answer obtained is better than the previous one. However, if the algorithms always only choose a better solution answer as the next base to select the next change then this is too simplistic. The reason for this is that by always climbing, the summit of a hill is reached and the climber can go no further despite higher peaks in the distance. In optimization terms this is called finding a local optimum. However an algorithm needs to find good global solutions, not good local ones. Therefore the algorithm needs to be able to descend in order to ascend again. There are many different types, Genetic Algorithms, Simulated Annealing, Tabu Search; these are all improvements on a simple hill climb algorithm although none will climb up a single hump hill so fast. Other techniques can be included in the algorithm, for example, learning techniques to adapt the behaviors of the algorithms based on the data found and neural networks to mimic brain learning. These techniques are making the optimization algorithms of today extremely sophisticated at identifying good solutions.

Optimizer Control. Optimizer control offers the easy selection of parameters to change, constraints, run/warm-up duration, and is also the place to choose whether the objective function should be maximized or minimized. Other useful and time-saving devices include:

- Simple analyze experiments to determine the variability of typical runs helps to determine the number of replications required.
- An answer pool saving data as the algorithm runs enabling lightning fast re-runs and the re-uses of results in other algorithmic runs.
- A tolerance setting to abort multiple runs if the first replication is so far removed from the optimal found as to make further replications a waste of time and unnecessary.
- Optional tracking for any other parameters that may be of interest in the results set from the simulation.

Algorithm Choice. The optimizer offers a wide choice of options for experimentation. These include:

- Random solutions—to enable an appreciation of the shape of the solution space.
- All combinations—this option should indeed be chosen if time allows as it covers all possibilities.
- Min/Mid/Max—tests the extremes and mid-points of all parameter settings. It covers all options for non-range parameters.
- Hill Climb—a simple algorithm. Fast but prone to get stuck in local optima.
- Adaptive Thermo statistical SA—The main algorithm, a variant of simulated annealing with extra adaptive nature. It includes some elements of tabu search developed by Lanner in conjunction with optimization experts specifically to tackle simulation experimentation.

- Six Sigma Algorithms—An adaptation of the SA algorithm to ensure that the amount of change from a defined ASIS situation is limited. Useful for determining the best improvements that can be made without wholesale redesign of a process.

Results Charts and Tables. Optimizer presents its reports as the algorithm is running. The main tables and charts can be interacted with during the run to view, sort, copy, paste and analyze. The results report on the value of the objective function, parameter settings, tracked function values, variations between replications, confidence intervals and other analyses such as parameter effects.

Different Optimization Types. There are many different types of simulation experiments that can be carried out. Typically optimization is useful where there are ranges and sets of parameters and models that can be expressed as options and where the best solution can be expressed clearly. Model examples where optimization is used:

- Organizational control and process flows can be changed to improve performance.
- Determining resource numbers.
- Determining Storage Requirements.
- Determining Control and Priorities.
- Determining layout of the model. For example, what order should we place our chemical tanks for this production process to maximize the effectiveness of the shuttle transfer mechanism.
- Determining Options for Improvement.

6.4.4 Analysis of Simulation Experiments

By analysis we mean, not the traditional methods to design statistical experiments, but rather techniques that can be used, before a simulation is conducted, to estimate the computational effort required to obtain desired statistical precision for contemplated simulation estimators. In doing so, computational effort are represented by simulation time, and that in turn by either the number of replications or the run length within a single simulation run. The quantities of interest will be estimated by sample means. In great generality, the required length of a single simulation run can be determined by computing the asymptotic variance and the asymptotic bias of the sample means. Existing theory supports this step for a sample mean of a function of a Markov process. We would prefer to do the calculations directly for the intended simulation model, but that usually is prevented by model complexity. Thus, as a first step, we usually approximate the original model by a related Markovian model that is easier to analyze. For example, relatively simple diffusion-process approximations to estimate required simulation run lengths for queueing models can often be obtained by heavy-traffic stochastic-process limits.

Simulations are controlled experiments. Before we run a simulation program and analyze the output, we need to choose a simulation model and decide what output to collect; we need to design the simulation experiment. Since stochastic simulations require statistical analysis of the output, it is often appropriate to consider the perspective of experimental design. Simulations are also explorations. We usually conduct simulations because we want to learn more about a complex system we inadequately understand. To head in the right direction, we should have some well-defined goals and questions when we start, but we should expect to develop new goals and questions as we go along. When we think about experimental design, we observe that the time scale for computer simulation experiments tends to be much shorter than the time scale for the agricultural and medical experiments that led to the theory of experimental design.

6.4.5 Experimental Design for Simulation

Here we introduce some of the ideas, issues, challenges, solutions, and opportunities in deciding how to experiment with a simulation model to learn about its behavior. Careful planning, or designing, of simulation experiments is generally a great help, saving time and effort by providing efficient ways to estimate the effects of changes in the models inputs on its outputs. Traditional experimental-design methods are discussed in the context of simulation experiments, as are the broader questions pertaining to planning computer-simulation experiments.

The real meat of a simulation project is running a model and trying to understand the results. To do so effectively, we need to plan ahead before doing the runs, since just trying different things to see what happens can be a very inefficient way of attempting to learn about our models (and hopefully the systems.) behaviors. Careful planning of how we are going to experiment with our models will generally repay big dividends in terms of how effectively we learn about the systems and how we can exercise our models further. This looks at such *experimental design* issues in the broad context of a simulation project. The term experimental design has specific connotations in its traditional interpretation; later sections cover the issues of planning our simulations in a broader context, which consider the special challenges and opportunities when conducting a computer-based simulation experiment rather than a physical experiment. These include questions of the overall purpose of the project, what the output performance measures should be, how we use the underlying random numbers, measuring how changes in the inputs might affect the outputs, and searching for some kind of optimal system configuration. Specific questions of this type might include:

- What model configurations should be run?
- How long should the runs be?
- How many runs should make?
- How should interpret and analyze the output?
- What is the most efficient way to make the runs?

6.4.6 Sensitivity of Outputs on Changing of Inputs

As part of building a simulation model, developer has to specify a variety of input factors. These include quantitative factors like the mean inter-arrival time, the number of servers, and the probabilities of different job types. Other input factors are more logical or structural in nature, like whether failure/feedback loops are present, and whether a queue is processed first-in-first-out or shortest-job-first. There can also be factors that are somewhere between being purely quantitative and purely logical/structural, like whether the service-time distribution is exponential or uniform. Another classification dimension of input factors is whether they are (in reality) controllable or not. However, when exercising a simulation model, all input factors are controllable, whether or not they can in reality be set or changed at will. For instance, developer cannot just cause the arrival rate to a call center to double, but he/she has no problem doing so in his/her simulation model of that call center. In any case, exactly how he/she specify each input factor will presumably have some effect on the output performance measures. Accordingly, it is sometimes helpful to think of the simulation as a function that transforms inputs into outputs:

$$\text{Output1} = f_1(\text{Input1, Input2, ...})$$

$$\text{Output2} = f_2(\text{Input1, Input2, ...})$$

...

where the functions f_1, f_2, f_3 ... represent the simulation model itself. It is often of interest to estimate how a change in an input factor affects an output performance measure, *i.e.*, how sensitive an output is to a change in an input. If developer knew the form of the simulation functions f_1, f_2, f_3 ..., this would essentially be a question of finding the partial derivative of the output of interest with respect to the input of interest. But of course developer does not know the form of the simulation functions otherwise developer would not be simulating. Accordingly, there are several different strategies for estimating the sensitivities of outputs to changes in inputs. These strategies have their own advantages, disadvantages, realms of appropriate application, and extra information they might provide the developer.

Which Inputs are Important? If the number of factors is even moderately large, the number of possible factor level combinations simply explodes far beyond anything remotely practical. It is unlikely, though, that all input factors are really important in terms of having a major impact on the outputs. At the very least, there will be big differences among the factors in terms of their impact on the responses. Since it is the number of factors that causes the explosion in the number of combinations, it would be most helpful to identify early in the course of experimentation which factors are important and which are not. The unimportant factors can then be fixed at some reasonable value and dropped from consideration, and further investigation can be done on the important factors, which will be fewer in number. There are several such factor screening designs in the literature, and they can be extremely helpful in transforming a rather hopelessly large number of runs into something that is eminently manageable.

What is the Best Combination of Inputs? Sometimes we have a single output performance measure that is of overriding importance in comparison with the other outputs (different outputs can conflict with each other, like the desirability of both high machine utilization and short queues). This might be a measure of direct economic importance, like profit or cost. If we have such a measure, we would probably like to look for an input factor combination that optimizes this measure. Mathematically, this can take the form of some kind of search through the space of possible factor combinations. If there are a lot of input factors, the dimension of the search space is high, requiring a lot of simulations at a lot of different points. And in stochastic simulation, the responses are subject to uncertainty, which must be taken into account when deciding how best to proceed with our search. Fortunately, several heuristic search methods have been developed that moves us from one point to a more promising one, and make these decisions based on a host of information that is available. And we are now beginning to see some of these methods coded into commercial-grade software and even integrated in with some simulation software products.

6.5 CLASSICAL EXPERIMENTAL DESIGN

A wide variety of approaches, methods, and analysis techniques, known collectively as *experimental design*, has been around for many decades. One of the principal goals of experimental design is to estimate how changes in input factors affect the results, or responses, of the experiment. While these methods were developed with physical experiments in mind (like industrial or agricultural applications), they can fairly easily be used in computer simulation experiments as well. In fact, using them in simulation presents several opportunities for improvement that are difficult or impossible to use in physical experiments. As a basic example of such techniques, suppose it identify just two values, or *levels*, of each of input factors. There is no general prescription on how to set these levels, but you should set them to be opposite in nature but not so extreme that they are unrealistic. If you have k input factors, there are thus $2k$ different combinations of the input factors, each defining a different configuration of the model; this is called a *2k factorial design*. Referring to the two levels of each factor, you can form what is called a *design matrix* describing exactly what each of the $2k$ different model configurations are in terms of their input factor levels. If an interaction is present between two factors, then the main effect of those factors cannot be interpreted in isolation, which brings up the issue of limitations of these kinds of designs.

There is a regression model underlying designs like these, which have present an independent-variable term involving each factor on its own (linearly), and then possible cross-products between the factor levels, representing interactions. As suggested, significant interactions cloud the interpretation of main effects, since presence of the cross product causes the main effect no longer to be an accurate measure of the effect of moving this factor. One way around this limitation is to specify a more elaborate and more general underlying regression model, and allow for more than just two levels for each input factor. This gives rise to more complex designs, which must be set up and analyzed in more sophisticated ways. Another difficulty with full-factorial designs is that if the number of factors becomes even moderately large, the number of runs explodes (it is, after all, literally exponential in the number of factors). A way around this is to use what are known as *fractional-factorial* designs in which only a fraction (sometimes just a small fraction) of all the possible factor-combinations are run. You must take care, however, to pick the subset of the runs very carefully, and there are specific prescriptions on how to do this in the references cited earlier. The downside of doing only a fraction of the runs is that you have to give up the ability to estimate at least some of the potential interactions, and the smaller the number of runs the fewer the number of interactions you can estimate. A final limitation of these kinds of designs is that the responses are random variables, as are all outputs from stochastic simulations. Thus, your estimates of things like main effects and interactions are subject to possibly considerable variance. Unlike physical experiments, though, you have the luxury in simulation of *replicating* (independently repeating) the runs many times to reduce this variance, or perhaps replicating the whole design many times to get many estimates of main effects and interactions, which could then be combined to form, say, a confidence interval on the expected main effects and interactions in the usual way. This is a good approach for determining whether a main effect or interaction is really present if the confidence interval for it does not contain zero, then it appears that it is really present.

Experimental Design for Simulation. One of the principal goals of experimental design is to estimate how changes in input factors affect the results, or responses, of the experiment. Design of experiments is an area known for a long time. Several aspects of design of experiments are still investigated. Experimental design for simulation is a well-developed area of knowledge but not very straightforward for the novice simulationist. A field related to experimental design for simulation is simulation-based optimization which is a very important topic in discrete event simulation. In simulation-based optimization, heuristic optimization techniques such as genetic algorithms, simulated annealing, and tabu search are used to have simulation as a basis for optimization.

Simulation Environments to Support Experimental Design. Experimental design facilities are not yet fully explored in simulation environments. Opportunities still exist for academic research and industrial development. Recently, two optimization packages are reported for simulation-based optimization. It was also asserted that, "Simulation-based optimization is just in its infancy. However, it appears that it will have a considerable impact on the practice of simulation in the future, particularly when computers become significantly faster." It appears that currently the time is ripe especially for teams of researchers/implementers with strong background in advanced software environments, software agents, and statistics to implement advanced features in simulation environments.

Software Agents. Software agents are software modules that can work as assistants to users or to other agents. They have cognitive abilities such as autonomy (usually limited for the purpose of not creating havoc in software environments), perception, goal processing and goal-directed knowledge processing; and they can affect their knowledge environment directly if their environment is purely software, or indirectly through actuators. Agent-supported simulation experiment is use of agent technology to support simulation activities which comprise front-end and back-end activities of a modeling and simulation environment, agent-supported validation and verification, as well as agent-supported program generation, program integration, and program understanding for documentation and/or maintenance purposes. Agent-supported simulation is one of the aspects of agent-directed simulation. Two other aspects are agent simulation and agent-based simulation.

In considering use of software agents (in any aspect of agent-directed simulation), one should take into account an important characteristic of them that is the ability to accept a variety of inputs (some of these characteristics are not yet fully explored). As seen in table 6.1, input to a software module, here to a software agent, can be generated externally or internally. Externally generated inputs are of two types: passively accepted and actively perceived inputs. Passively accepted inputs consist of mostly conventional inputs which can be accepted via coupling, argument passing, message passing, or accessing knowledge in a common area. Their nature can be data, facts, forced events, sensations (*i.e.*, input coming from sensors, usually in analog form), and goals imposed to the agents. Active perception of exogenous inputs includes perception, *i.e.*, interpreted sensory data (which require decoding, selection (filtering), recognition, and regulation). Second type of active perception of exogenous inputs consists of perceived goals. A third possibility is evaluated input where either inputs and/or their sources can be scrutinized for their acceptability, reliability, and credibility. Endogenous inputs or internally generated inputs are also of two types: Actively perceived endogenous inputs are based on introspection. They consist of (observed or monitored) perceived internal facts and events as well as lack of them. The second category of endogenous inputs is the generated endogenous inputs. They consist of anticipated future data and events in anticipatory systems as well as internally generated questions, hypotheses, and goals.

Table 6.1.Types of Inputs for Software Modules (including Agents)

Source of input	*Mode of input*	*Type of input*
Exogenous input (externally generated input)	**Passive acceptance** of exogenous input (imposed or forced input)	**Type of access to input:** coupling, argument passing, knowledge in a common area, message passing. - **Data** (facts) - Forced **Events** - **Sensation** (converted sensory data: from analog to digital; single or multi sensor: sensor fusion) - **External goals** (imposed goals)
	Active perception of exogenous input (perceived input)	- **Perception** (interpreted, sensory data and detected events) includes: decoding, selection (filtering), recognition, regulation. - **Perceived goals** - **Evaluated inputs** - evaluation of inputs (acceptability) - evaluation of source of inputs (reliability, credibility)
Endogenous input (internally generated input)	**Active perception** of endogenous input	- **Introspection** (perceived internal facts, events; or realization of lack of them)

	Generation of endogenous input	- **Anticipated facts** and/or **events** (anticipatory systems) - **Internally generated questions** - **Internally generated hypotheses** by: - Expectation-driven reasoning (Forward reasoning, Bottom-up reasoning, Data-driven reasoning) - Model-driven reasoning - **Internal goals** (internally generated goals).

6.6 VALIDATION OF SIMULATION EXPERIMENT

In most cases, the meaning of computer simulation is strongly connected to the idea numerical calculations. A computer simulation is a numerical solution of a complex mathematical problem. Therefore, the problem of validation of its results should be only a problem of judging the underlying computational methods. However, it will be argued, that this is not the case. Validation constitutes one of the central epistemological problems of computer simulation methods. Here we attempt to show how the characteristics of simulation, *i.e.*, the imitation of a dynamic, constitute the problem of validation even in the case of the natural sciences and what consequences arise.

Here we illustrate some of the problems which arise when the validity of computer simulations has to be judged. It is the performance of the symptoms which decide about the quality of a simulation. This might be different in the case of computer simulations, which are going to become an important tool of knowledge production, especially in cases, where theoretical or experimental strategies fail because of complexity. To get an answer in this case one has to determine the epistemic status of the knowledge produced by a computer simulation. If it is a numerical solution of an underlying mathematical model, *i.e.*, the calculation of the variables defined by it, the quality of a computer simulation depends on the quality of calculation, especially on the ability to handle unavoidable calculation errors. But if a computer simulation is not merely a calculation of variables but rather an imitation of a model's behavior in space and time, its quality is an open question which has to be answered if one wants to rely on its results.

If one believes that simulations are numerical calculations, there seems to be a difference between simulation models based on a mathematical model which, *e.g.*, represents the physical laws of hydrodynamics as it is the case in climate research, and simulation models based on a few qualitative assumptions about the leading mechanisms as for instance in so-called agent based simulation models in the social sciences. There should be no doubt about the validity of the model and the results of the simulation. The only open question will be whether the physical model is complex enough to produce the dynamics in which one is interested in. In other words: The reliability of the knowledge produced by computer simulation is taken for granted if the physical model is correct. In the second case of social simulations in general there is no theoretical model on which one could rely. The knowledge produced in this case seems to be valid if some of the characteristics of the social dynamics known from experience with the social world are reproduced by the simulation. In this case the simulation might be seen as a proof for the basic assumptions of the underlying phenomenological model.

It is consensus that validation constitutes one of the central problems of computer simulation methods. There is a wide variety of accounts of different strategies for validating simulations in social sciences. Nevertheless, there can be distinguished a common starting point. In the following, it is called the common view on validation. It is based on the assumption of a double correspondence, or analogy:

(*i*) First, the social sciences are structurally equivalent to the natural sciences. Hence, considerations about validity in the social sciences can draw directly on knowledge and practices of validation in the natural sciences.

(*ii*) Computer simulations are analogous to theories in general.

Combining these two components, the common view holds that the discussion on validating simulation experiments in the social sciences has to follow the lines of the discussion about confirmation of scientific theories, referring mainly to theories in physics. The common view treats simulations as analogous to scientific theories in general. Consequently, the problem of validation is debated in close connection to the classical standpoints of philosophy of science regarding confirmation of theories. By and large, the discussion about validation of simulation is reflecting the development of the now "classical" positions in philosophy from logical empiricism over hook.

Our aim is to show that the validation problem of computer simulation is the same in both cases. However, contrary to the common view on the validation problem, this is by no means an argument that the social sciences can participate on the success story of the natural sciences. Our argument will be that simulation experiments are even in the case of exact mathematical models imitations of a complex social or natural dynamics by the means of an adequate generative mechanism. Thus, even in strongly theory-driven sciences, simulations are not numerical solutions of a theoretical, even if complex, model. For this reason neither in the natural sciences nor in the social sciences computer simulations can be validated by theoretical arguments.

Experiment Validation. Many different types of modeling and simulation applications are used in dozens of disciplines under diverse objectives including acquisition, analysis, education, entertainment, research, and training. Modeling and simulation application verification and validation are conducted to assess mainly the *accuracy*, which is one of many indicators affecting the modeling and simulation application quality. Much higher confidence can be achieved in accuracy if a quality-centered approach is used. Here we discuss a quality model for assessing the quality of large-scale complex modeling and simulation applications as integrated with verification and validation. The guidelines provided herein should be useful for assessing the overall quality of modeling and simulation application.

Quality is a critically important issue in almost every discipline. Whether we manufacture a product, employ processes or provide services, quality often becomes a major goal. The U.S. Department of Defense (DoD) is the largest sponsor and user of Modeling and Simulation applications in the world. DoD uses many types of modeling and simulation applications (such as continuous, discrete-event, distributed, hardware-in-the-loop, software-in-the-loop, humanin-the-loop, Monte Carlo, parallel, and synthetic environments bringing together simulations and real-world systems) for the purpose of acquisition, analysis or training. DoD modeling and simulation applications typically are large-scale and complex and cost millions of dollars to develop over many years. Assuring the quality of diverse types of large-scale and complex modeling and simulation applications poses significant technical and managerial challenges. Modeling and simulation applications are mostly made up of software or are software based. Software is inherently complex and very difficult to engineer. Under the current technology, we are incapable of developing a reasonably large and complex software product and guaranteeing its 100% accuracy. Accuracy is considered just one of many quality characteristics of modeling and simulation application and is judged by conducting Verification and Validation.

Modeling and simulation application quality is the degree to which the application possesses a desired set of characteristics. Quality assessment is situation dependent since the desired set of characteristics changes from one modeling and simulation application to another. Modeling and simulation application quality is typically assessed by considering the modeling and simulation application requirements, intended uses, and project objectives. Three major indicators influence the modeling and simulation application quality. Assessments such as quality assessment, accuracy assessment, credibility assessment, and certification assessment are all confidence building activities. We can achieve much better confidence in modeling and simulation application quality if we perform the assessment from the perspectives (indicators) of product, process, and project.

6.6.1 Modeling and Simulation Product Quality Assessment

The term modeling and simulation product implies either the overall completed modeling and simulation application, or a work product created during the modeling and simulation development life cycle such as conceptual model, modeling and simulation requirements specification, modeling and simulation design specification, and an executable modeling and simulation module. The quality model can be applied by geographically dispersed subject-matter experts in a collaborative manner by using the Evaluation Environment (EE) software system. The quality of a particular modeling and simulation work product can also be assessed by using the EE methodology and software. For each modeling and simulation work product, a hierarchy of indicators should be created for assessing the quality of that work product. Each quality indicator is defined below, which says that modeling and simulation:

- Requirements quality is the degree to which the requirements possess a desired set of characteristics.
- Requirements accuracy is the degree to which the requirements possess sufficient transformational and representational accuracy.

- Requirements verity is assessed by conducting modeling and simulation requirements verification.
- Requirements verification is substantiating that the modeling and simulation requirements are transformed from higher levels of abstraction into their current form with sufficient accuracy judged with respect to the modeling and simulation intended uses.
- Requirements verification addresses the question of "Are we creating the modeling and simulation requirements right?"
- Requirements validity is assessed by conducting modeling and simulation requirements validation.
- Requirements validation is substantiating that the modeling and simulation requirements represent the real needs of the application sponsor with sufficient accuracy.
- Requirements validation addresses the question of "Are we creating the right modeling and simulation requirements?"
- Requirements clarity is the degree to which the requirements are unambiguous and understandable.
- Requirements unambiguity is the degree to which each statement of the requirements can only be interpreted one way.
- Requirements understandability is the degree to which the meaning of each statement of the requirements is easily comprehended by all of its readers.
- Requirements completeness is the degree to which all parts of a requirement are specified with no missing information, *i.e.*, each requirement is self-contained. For example, "radar search pulse rate must be 10" is an incomplete requirement because it is missing the "per second" part. The requirement "missile kill assessment delay must follow the Uniform probability distribution" is incomplete because it is missing the range parameter values. Also use of the place holder "TBD" (To be determined or to be defined), "TBR" (To be resolved), "TBP" (To be provided), and use of the phrases such as "as a minimum", "as a maximum", and "not limited to" are indications of incomplete requirements specification.
- Requirements consistency is the degree to which (*a*) the requirements are specified using uniform notation, terminology, and symbol, and (*b*) anyone requirement does not conflict with any other.
- Requirements feasibility is the degree of difficulty of implementing a single requirement, and simultaneously meeting conflicting requirements. Sometimes requirements conflict with each other. It may be possible to achieve a requirement by itself, but it may not be possible to achieve a number of them simultaneously.
- Requirements modifiability is the degree to which the requirements can easily be changed.
- Requirements stability is (*a*) the degree to which the requirements are changing while the modeling and simulation application is under development, and (*b*) the possible effects of the changing requirements on the project schedule, cost,

risk, quality, functionality, design, integration, and testing of the modeling and simulation application.

- Requirements testability is the degree to which the requirements can easily be tested. A testable requirement is the one that is specified in such a way that pass/fail or assessment criteria can be derived from its specification. For example, the following requirement specification is not testable: "The probability of kill should be estimated based on the simulation output data." The following requirement specification is testable: "The probability of kill should be estimated by using a 95% confidence interval based on the simulation output data."
- Requirements traceability is the degree to which the requirements related to a particular requirement can easily be found. Requirements should be specified in such a way that related requirements are cross-referenced. When it is necessary to change a requirement, those requirements affected by the changed requirement should be easily identified by using the cross references.

6.6.2 Modeling and Simulation Process Quality Assessment

The term modeling and simulation process implies a process used to create a work product during the modeling and simulation development life cycle such as conceptual modeling, requirements engineering, design, implementation, integration, experimentation, and presentation. The quality of a particular modeling and simulation life cycle process can be assessed by creating a hierarchy of indicators and using the EE methodology and software. The manner by which a particular modeling and simulation life cycle process is conducted significantly affects the quality of the work product created under that process. Using a structured proven methodology based on industry best practices certainly increases the process quality, which in turn increases the product quality. For example, conducting the modeling and simulation requirements engineering process by employing a use case-based approach based on the UML technology versus an adhoc approach makes a big difference in the modeling and simulation requirements quality. Knowing that the modeling and simulation requirements engineering process is properly conducted by using industry best practices increases our confidence in the quality of the modeling and simulation process and in the quality of the modeling and simulation work product created under that process. Many indicators influence the modeling and simulation process quality including the following:

- *Acceptability*—the degree to which the defined process is acceptable to and usable by the people who are tasked to execute the process.
- *Maintainability*—the degree to which the process can evolve to reflect changing organizational requirements or identified process improvements.
- *Quality* of the methodology used in executing the process.
- *Quality* of the way the methodology is applied in executing the process.
- *Rapidity*—the degree to which the process can be rapidly executed.
- *Reliability*—the degree to which the process is designed in such a way that process errors are avoided or trapped before they result in product errors.

- *Robustness*—the degree to which the process can be continued in spite of unexpected problems.
- *Supportability*—the degree to which the process activities can be supported by computer-aided software engineering (CASE) tools.
- *Understandability*—the degree to which the process is explicitly defined and easy to comprehend.
- *Visibility*—the degree to which the process activities culminate in clear results so that the process progress is externally visible.

6.6.3 Modeling and Simulation Project Quality Assessment

The third major quality indicator is called project, people, or personnel. This indicator can be decomposed into a hierarchy of indicators including:

(*a*) capabilities or maturity of an organization in developing a large-scale and complex modeling and simulation application,

(*b*) quality of application, and

(*c*) quality of the people tasked to develop the M&S application.

The Software Engineering Institute at Carnegie Mellon University has led the development of Capability Maturity Model Integration (CMMI) models to provide guidance for creating institutionalized defined processes. Each CMMI model has two forms of representation: continuous and staged. The continuous representation depicts the *capabilities* of an organization. The staged representation depicts the maturity of an organization. Figure 6.2 shows the staged representation of the CMMI for Systems Engineering and Software Engineering (CMMI-SE/SW), which is the one that can be used for modeling and simulation application development. Certification at maturity level 3 implies that the organization has institutionalized, defined, and documented all of the process areas listed under levels 2 and 3 in figure 6.2 and is ready to execute them for the development of a large-scale and complex modeling and simulation application. In addition to being CMMI certified by a credible authority at a contractually required level, the overall modeling and simulation application quality is affected by how well the CMMI process areas are executed as well as by the quality of the people employed for the development and management of the modeling and simulation application.

6.6.4 A Quality Model for Modeling and Simulation Applications

A quality model is a characterization of a framework under which the quality is assessed. Based on the Hewlett-Packard's FURPS+ software quality model, a modeling and simulation application quality theoretical model with the hierarchy of indicators has been proposed. The hierarchy of quality indicators is given for the higher levels of the quality model. The leaf indicators need to be further decomposed into other indicators until the leaf indicators are directly assessable. The hierarchy forms an acyclic graph where an indicator may influence more than one parent indicator such as the Accuracy indicator influencing Reliability and Functionality.

Some of the quality indicators may not be applicable for some modeling and simulation applications. Many different types of modeling and simulation application exist such as continuous discrete-event, distributed, hardware-in-the-loop, software-in-the-loop, human-in-the-loop, Monte Carlo, parallel, and synthetic environments bringing together simulations and real-world systems. Modeling and simulation application may be used for, many different purposes including acquisition, entertainment, analysis education, research, and training. The modeling and simulation application type and the purpose for which it is constructed should be taken into consideration in modifying and expanding the hierarchy of indicators.

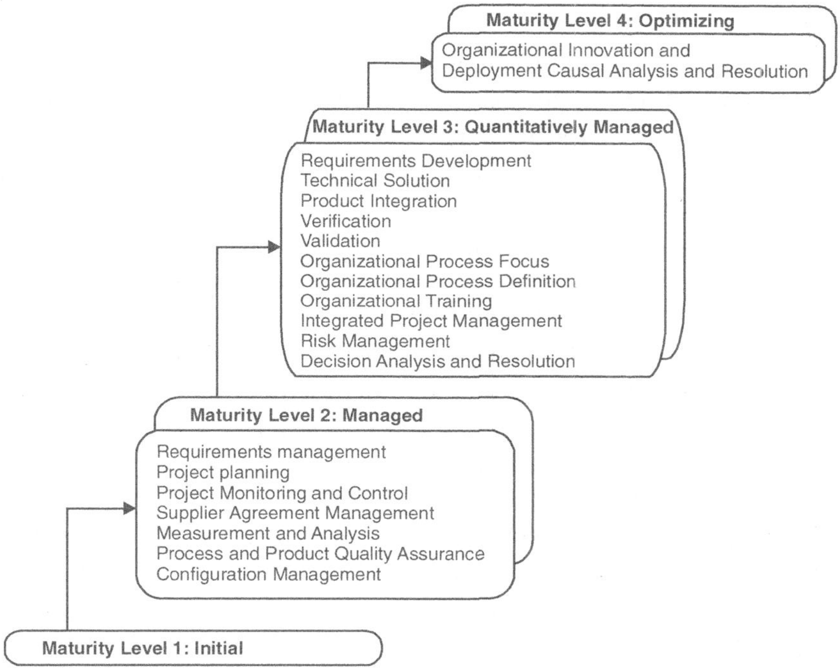

Fig. 6.2 SE/SW-CMMI Stage process simulation experiment

Definitions of the indicators of the quality model are given below.

Modeling and simulation Application Dependability is the degree to which the modeling and simulation application.

(*a*) delivers services when requested,

(*b*) delivers services as specified,

(*c*) operates without catastrophic failure, and

(*d*) protects itself against accidental or deliberate intrusion.

6.6.5 Some Facts about Modeling and Simulation Experiments

Modeling and simulation Application:

- *Availability* is the probability that the modeling and simulation application functions according to its requirements at a given point in time. Availability refers to the ability of the modeling and simulation application to deliver services when requested.

- *Reliability* is the degree to which the modeling and simulation application performs its required functions without failure under prescribed conditions in a specified period of time for a specific purpose.
- *Reliability* refers to the ability of the modeling and simulation application to deliver services as specified.
- *Accuracy* is the degree to which the modeling and simulation application possesses sufficient transformational and representational/behavioral accuracy.
- *Verity* is assessed by conducting modeling and simulation application verification, which is substantiating that the modeling and simulation application is transformed from one form into another with sufficient accuracy.
- *Verification* addresses the question of "Are we building the modeling and simulation application right?"
- *Validity* is assessed by conducting modeling and simulation application validation, which is substantiating that the modeling and simulation application possesses sufficient representational and behavioral accuracy.
- *Validation* addresses the question of "Are we building the right modeling and simulation application?"
- *Application Mean Time to Failure* (MTTF) is the average time between observed modeling and simulation application failures. MTTF = 300 hours means that, on the average, one failure can be expected to occur every 300 hours.
- *Mean Time to Restore* (MTTR) is the average time it takes to restore the modeling and simulation application after failure.
- *Recoverability* is the degree to which the modeling and simulation application provides mechanisms to enable users to recover from errors.
- *Safety* is the ability of the modeling and simulation application to operate, normally or abnormally, without threatening people or the environment. Modeling and simulation safety refers to the ability of the modeling and simulation application to operate without catastrophic failure. The safety may be an issue particularly for training simulations.
- *Application Security* is the degree to which the modeling and simulation application provides protection and authentication of information in transit or stationary, as well as the confidentiality of sensitive information.
- *Functionality* is the degree to which the modeling and simulation application completely captures all of the desired functional modules that need to be present.
- *Capability* is the degree to which the modeling and simulation application is capable of performing its feature set, *e.g.*, capability of simulating a particular combat at the soldier level of granularity.
- *Detailedness* is the degree to which the modeling and simulation application is characterized by abundant use of detail or thoroughness of treatment.

- *Feature Set* is the degree to which the modeling and simulation application provides the set of features that need to be present, *e.g.*, simulating a particular combat.
- *Generality* is the degree to which the modeling and simulation application can be used for a wide range of intended uses.
- *Performance* is the degree to which the modeling and simulation application executes its work in a speedy, efficient, and productive manner.
- *Algorithmic Efficiency* is the degree to which the algorithms used in the modeling and simulation application provide the optimal execution time.
- *Architectural Efficiency* is the degree to which the modeling and simulation application architecture enables the optimal execution time.
- *Communication Efficiency* is the degree to which the modeling and simulation application fulfills its purpose of communicating with its user over a network without waste of resources. Communication efficiency is influenced by the communication protocol (*e.g.*, HTTP or RMI) used by the modeling and simulation application, encryption/decryption of the communication, or the existence of a firewall.
- *Resource Use Efficiency* is the degree to which the modeling and simulation application fulfills its purpose without waste of resources such as CPU, main memory, and hard disk space.
- *Supportability* is the degree to which the modeling and simulation application can be supported.
- *Compatibility* is the degree to which the modeling and simulation application can be integrated into or used with other modeling and simulation applications, products, or systems.
- *Configurability* is the degree to which the modeling and simulation application can easily be set-up or configured for a particular application or intended use.
- *Conformity* is the degree to which the modeling and simulation application adheres to standards and conventions.
- *Installability* is the degree to which the modeling and simulation application can easily be prepared for use.
- *Interoperability* is the degree to which the modeling and simulation application in a distributed environment (*e.g.*, federation of models) can exchange data with one or more other modeling and simulation applications and be able to use the data that has been exchanged.
- *Localizability* is the degree to which the modeling and simulation application can easily be adopted, preferably via preferences or options, (*a*) to satisfy the needs of languages other than English, and (*b*) to local standards such as decimal separator, currency symbol, time zone, calendar, etc.

- *Maintainability* is the degree to which the modeling and simulation application facilitates changes for:
    - ➤ Adaptations required as the modeling and simulation application's external environment evolves (*adaptive maintenance*),
    - ➤ Fixing bugs and making corrections (*corrective maintenance*),
    - ➤ Enhancements brought about by changing customer requirements (*perfective maintenance*), and
    - ➤ Preventing potential problems or for reengineering (*preventive maintenance* or *software reengineering*).
- *Adaptability* is the degree to which the modeling and simulation application can accommodate changes to its external environment.
- *Correctability* is the degree to which the modeling and simulation application facilitates changes for fixing bugs and making corrections.
- *Extensibility* is the degree to which the modeling and simulation application capabilities can be extended by modifying current features or adding new features.
- *Preventability* is the degree to which the modeling and simulation application facilitates changes for preventing potential problems or for reengineering.
- *Portability* is the degree to which the modeling and simulation application can easily be transformed to run on more than one hardware or software environment.
- *Testability* is the degree to which the modeling and simulation application facilitates the creation of test criteria and conducting tests to determine whether those criteria have been met.
- *Usability* is the degree to which the modeling and simulation application can easily be employed for its intended use.
- *Documentation Quality* is the degree to which the modeling and simulation application external documentation (*e.g.*, user manuals, reference guides, and online help) possesses a desired set of characteristics.
- *Ease of Experimentation or Exercise Specification* is the degree to which a simulation experiment (for analysis) or a simulation exercise (for training) can easily be specified.
- *Ease of Input Specification* is the degree to which the input conditions and data of the Modeling and Simulation application are easily specified under a set of prescribed intended uses.
- *Ease of Learning* is the ease with which the modeling and simulation application can be learned.
- *Output Understandability* is the degree to which the meaning of the modeling and simulation application output is easily comprehended by its users under a set of prescribed intended uses.

6.6.6 Modeling and Simulation Verification and Validation

Modeling and simulation verification and validation typically focuses on the assessment of modeling and simulation transformational accuracy (verification) and representational/behavioral accuracy (validation). The quality model has accuracy being evaluated by the modeling and simulation verity and modeling and simulation validity indicators. Modeling and simulation verity is assessed by conducting modeling and simulation verification, and modeling and simulation validity is assessed by conducting modeling and simulation validation. Undoubtedly, accuracy is the most important quality characteristic of modeling and simulation application. Verification and validation is used to assess the accuracy quality characteristic. However, under the current state of the art, we are unable to claim a level of accuracy of a reasonably large and complex modeling and simulation application with 100% confidence due to many reasons including modeling and simulation complexity, reliance on human judgment, qualitative measurements, lack of data, and lack of exhaustive testing. Hence, modeling and simulation validation is viewed as a confidence building activity.

In case of large and complex modeling and simulation application, the confidence building activity must be performed by assessing not only the modeling and simulation accuracy, but also other modeling and simulation quality characteristics such as the ones given in the quality model. Successful assessment of the overall modeling and simulation application quality increases our confidence in modeling and simulation accuracy. The validation activities must be tied to a well-structured modeling and simulation development life cycle. Validation is not a stage but a continuous activity carried out hand in hand with the modeling and simulation development throughout the entire life cycle. The use of a well-structured modeling and simulation development life cycle is critically important for effectively conducting the validation and confidence building activities. More than 100 verification and validation techniques exist. The validation techniques are applicable for use during different stages of the modeling and simulation application development life cycle. Each validation technique provides information from a different perspective so as to increase our confidence in the modeling and simulation accuracy. The more validation techniques are applied the more information is provided and the more confidence is gained in the modeling and simulation accuracy.

6.6.7 Validation of Simulation Based Models

Validation is the most incomprehensible part of developing a simulation experiment. Nevertheless, no experiment can be accepted unless it has passed the tests of validation, since the procedure of validation is vital to ascertain the credibility of the model. Validation procedures are usually framework based and dynamic, but a methodical procedure can be followed by a modeler (or researcher) in order to authenticate the experiment. Reasons for the failure of the model have also been explored. This chapter finally focuses on the widely approved validation schemes (both quantitative and qualitative) and techniques in practice, since no one test can determine the credibility and validity of a simulation experiment. Moreover, as the experiment passes more tests (both quantitative and qualitative) the confidence in the experiment increases correspondingly.

Model Validation Issues. Validation has been one of the unresolved problems of systems modeling. It is true for simulation models in general and system dynamic models in particular. System dynamic modeling makes use of computer simulation (packages like MATLAB) to generate the consequences for studying the dynamic behavior of the system. In contrast, validations of Optimization Models, Decision Theory or Game Theory are often not questioned since the solution procedures are elegant and correct. Reasons for conceptual and simulation models having received more criticism could be the ease with which the models and their overall results being understandable. Another reason being, the simulation model of any system could only be an approximation of the actual system, no matter the amount of time spent on the model building. Hence if the model produced is not a 'close' enough approximation to this actual system, conclusions derived from such model are likely to be divergent and erroneous, leading to possible costly decision mistakes been made. According to Law, validation can be done for all simulation models regardless of whether their corresponding systems exist presently or would be built-in future. The technique applied would depend on the availability of data in the real system. There is no such thing as an absolutely valid model; credibility of a model can be claimed only for the intended use of the model or simulation and for the prescribed conditions under which the model or simulation has been tested. Perfect validation and verification are impossible; the emphasis should be more on model testing *i.e.*, the process to build confidence that a model is appropriate for the purpose. Some models may be better than others; some models, while not completely valid, possess a greater degree of authenticity than others. Furthermore, all models are, in a sense, wrong because there could always be a counter test to which the model did not conform to completely. Nevertheless, the power of a model or modeling technique is a function of validity, credibility, and generality. Hence model validation is not an option but a necessity in a dynamic modeling scenario. Usually the simplest model, which expresses a valid relation, will be the most powerful; however, there is no single test that would allow the modelers to assert that their models have been validated. Rather, the level of confidence in the model can increase gradually as the model passes more tests. The relationships of cost (a similar relationship holds for the amount of time) of performing model validation and the value of a model to the user as a function of model confidence are shown in figure below. As shown in the figure 6.3, the value of the model increases as the level of confidence in the model is increased; correspondingly the cost of model validation also increases.

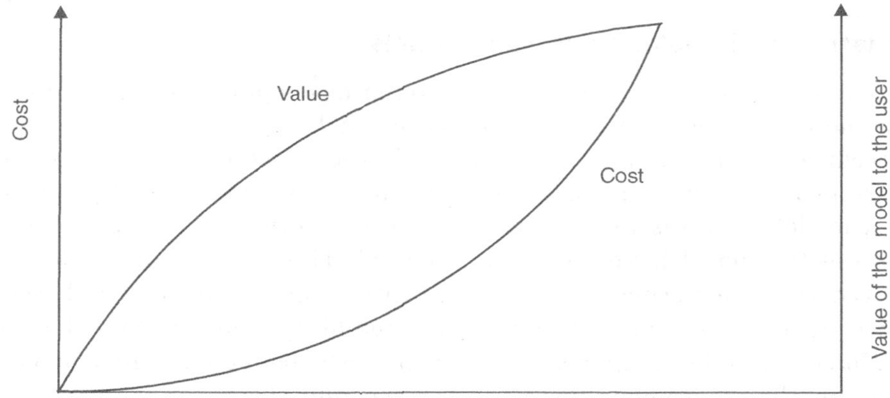

Fig. 6.3 Value, cost vs. model confidence

Validation cannot be carried out by the modeler (or researcher) alone, communication with the client (or user) plays a large role in building a valid model and establishing its credibility. Another relevant issue of concern is that by how much the model output could deviate from system output and still remain valid. Since the model created is an approximation of the actual system, some errors and approximations are unavoidable. Model validation thus resides in decision between the modeler and client; when both groups are satisfied, the model is considered valid.

Methodology for Validation. Validation deals with the assessment of the comparison between 'sufficiently accurate' computational results from the simulation and the actual/hypothetical data from the system. Validation does not specifically address how the simulation model can be changed to improve the agreement between the computational results and the actual data. The fundamental strategy of validation involves identification and quantification of the error and uncertainty in the conceptual/simulation models, quantification of the numerical error in the computational solution, estimation of the simulation uncertainty, and finally, comparison between the computational results and the actual data. Thus, accuracy is measured in relation to actual/hypothetical data, our best measure of reality. This strategy does not assume that the actual/hypothetical data are more accurate than the computational results. The strategy only asserts that simulation results are the most faithful reflections of reality for the purposes of validation.

Model Validation Process. Figure 6.4 below shows the model validation process in a simpler form. The 'problem entity' is the system (real or proposed, for example, dynamics of integrated Knowledge Management and Human Resource Management can be considered as a problem entity) to be modeled; the 'conceptual model' is the mathematical/verbal representation (influence diagram) of the problem entity developed for a particular study; and the computerized model is the conceptual model implemented on a computer (simulation model). The inferences about the problem entity are obtained by conducting simulations on the computerized model in the experimentation phase.

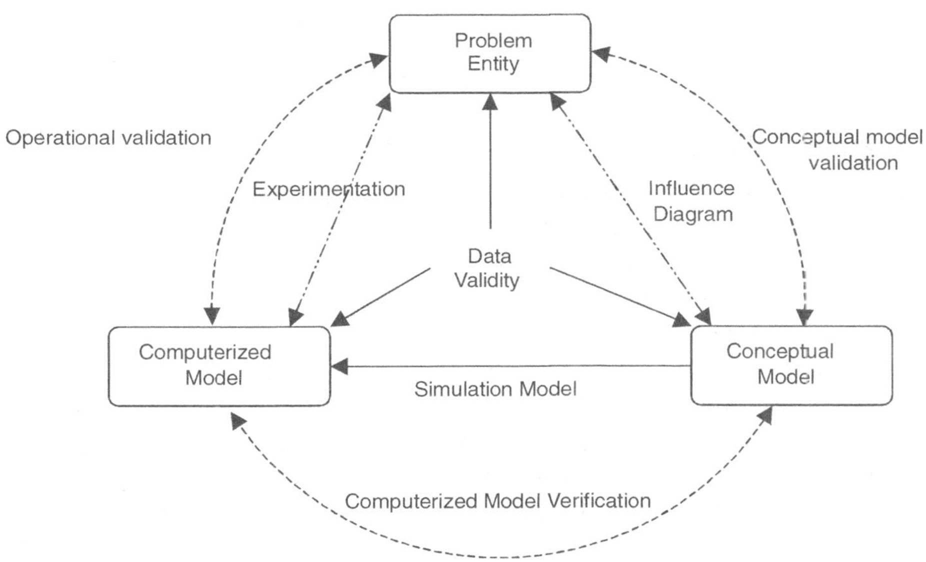

Fig. 6.4 Model validation process

There are three steps in deciding if a simulation is an accurate representation of the actual system considered, namely, verification, validation and credibility. *Conceptual model validation* is the process of determining that the theories and assumptions underlying the conceptual model are correct and that the model representation of the problem entity is reasonable for the intended purpose of the model. *Computerized model verification* is the process of determining that the model implementation accurately represents the developers' conceptual description of the model and the solution to the model. *Operational validation* is defined as determining that the model's output behavior has sufficient accuracy for the model's intended purpose over the domain of the model's intended applicability. Operational validity determines the models credibility. *Data validity* is defined as ensuring that the data necessary for model building, model evaluation and conducting the model experiments to solve the problem are adequate and correct.

Reasons for Failure of Models. Some of the reasons due to which the models fail the validation tests are enumerated as follows:

- *Model-structure*—In both the conceptual model and the simulation model mathematical simplifications might be inadequate for capturing complex dynamics.
- *Numerical solution*—The solution of the simulation model might differ dramatically from the ideal solution.
- *Input values*—Proper numerical values of the inputs that describe the scenario for prediction might be known only approximately.
- *Observation errors*—Inaccurate observations of real system.
- *System noise*—Failure to recognize random changes existent in the system.
- *Project management errors*—These errors revolve around project management and related communication issues.
- *Inappropriate simulation software*—Either too inflexible or too difficult to use.
- Misinterpretation of simulation results.

6.6.8 Validation Schemes

Validation Scheme as Proposed by Forrester and Senge. This validation criterion is used to validate quantitative as well as qualitative models. The validation scheme is mainly divided into four phases; as the model passes more tests under every phase the confidence in the model increases correspondingly. The validation scheme as proposed by Forrester and Senge is enumerated below:

Importance of Model Objective: The validity of a model cannot be greater than the objective set for it. Therefore, the model objective must be a justified representation of the values prevalent in the real system. The method of setting model objectives by the conceptualization of problems in the existent system seems unstructured, unless the problem elicitation is done under the guidance of experts from the various subsystems existent within the system. A model could be proven valid by a series of methods, but the validation may be totally useless if the objectives are wrongly set.

Validating Model Structure: These tests help in establishing confidence in the model structure.

Tests of suitability

Following tests are performed for suitability:

Structure-Verification Test: This test is meant to answer the following question "Is the model structure not in contradiction to the knowledge about the structure of the real system, and have the most relevant structures of the real system been modeled?"

Dimensional-Consistency Test: "Do the dimensions of the variables in every equation balance on each side of the equation?" This test verifies whether all equations are dimensionally constant.

Extreme-Conditions Test: "Does every equation in the model make sense even if subjected to extreme but possible values of variables?" Policy equations are scrutinized for their applicability in extreme conditions.

Boundary-Adequacy Test: This test verifies whether the model structure is appropriate for the model purpose "Is the model aggregation appropriate and includes all relevant structure containing the variables and feedback effects necessary to address the problem and suit the purposes of the study?"

Tests of consistency

Following tests are performed for consistency:

Face Validity Test: "Does the model structure looks like the real system? Is it a recognizable representation of the real system? Does a reasonable fit exist between the feedback structure of the model and the essential characteristics of the real system?"

Parameter-Verification Test: Parameters and their numerical values should have real system equivalents. "Do the parameters correspond conceptually and numerically to real life? Are the parameters recognizable in term of real systems, or are some parameters contrived to balance the equations? If the values selected for the parameters consistent with the test information are available about the real system?"

Test of utility and effectiveness

Following tests are performed for effectiveness:

Appropriateness for Audience: "Is the size of the model, its simplicity or complexity, and its level of aggregation or richness of detail appropriate for the audience for the study?" The more the appropriate a model for the audience the more will be the audience's perception of model validity.

Validating Model Behavior: These tests help in establishing confidence in the model behavior.

Tests of suitability (phase II)

Following tests are performed for suitability:

Parameter Sensitivity Test: "Is the behavior of the model sensitive to reasonable variations in parameter values, *i.e.*, do the modes of the behavior change with parameter variations?" *Structural sensitivity test:* "Is the behavior of the model sensitive to reasonable structural reformulation, *i.e.*, do the modes of the behavior change with structural variations?"

Tests of consistency (after testing suitability phase II)

Behavior-Reproduction Test: Here the generated model behavior is judged with the historical behavior. "How well the model generated behavior matches observed behavior of the real system in terms of symptom generation, frequency generation, relative phasing, multiple mode, and behavior characteristics?"

Behavior-Prediction Test: This test calls for pattern prediction. "Whether or not a model generates qualitatively current patterns of future patterns of future behavior in terms of periods, shape or other characteristics?

Behavior-Anomaly Test: Behavior conflicting with the real system helps in finding obvious flaws in the model. "Does behavior shown by the model is conflicting with the real system behavior and how implausible behavior arises if the assumptions are altered?"

Family Member Test: Whenever possible, attempt should be made to build a general model of the class of system to which a particular member belongs. The general theory is depicted in the structure. Parameter values are chosen to depict a particular situation. By choosing a different set of parameter values the model can be applied to other situation as well.

Surprising Behavior Test: "Does the model under some test circumstances produces dramatically unexpected or surprise behavior, not observed in the real system? Whether such a surprise behavior is due to model structure or some causes in the real system can be assigned to such a behavior?"

Extreme-Policy Test: "Does the model behave in an expected fashion under extreme policies, even ones that have never been observed in the real system?" If the model behaves in an expected fashion under extreme policies, then it boosts confidence in the model.

Boundary Adequacy (Behavior) Test: "Does the model include the structures necessary to address the issues for which it is designed?" If an extra model structure does not change the behavior, then this extra structure is not necessary. Alternatively, if a model structure does not reproduce desired model behavior, it calls for inclusion of additional model structure.

Behavior-Sensitivity Test: "Whether plausible shifts in parameters can cause model to fail behavior tests previously passed?" Here the sensitivity of the model to changes in parameter values is judged.

Statistical tests: "Does the model behavior statistically like data from real system?"

Tests of utility and effectiveness (phase II)

Counter Intuitive Behavior: "In response to some policies, does the model exhibit behavior that at first contradicts intuitions and later, with the aid of the model, is seen as a clear implication of the structure of the system?" "Is the model capable of generating new insights or at least the feeling of new insights, about the nature of the problem addressed and the system within it arises?"

Tests of suitability (phase III)

Policy Sensitivity and Robustness Test: The sensitivity of a policy with respect to change in parameter values is judged during this test. "Whether the model based policy recommendations change with reasonable changes in parameter values or reasonable alteration in equation formulations?"

Tests of consistency (phase II)

Changed Behavior Prediction Test: "Whether the model correctly predicts how behavior of the system will change, if a governing policy is changed?"

Boundary Adequacy (Policy) Test: "Whether modifying the model boundary (*i.e.*, conceptualization of additional structure) would alter policy recommendations arrived by using the model?"

System Improvement Test: "Whether the policies found beneficial after working with a model, when implemented, also improve real system behavior?"

Test of utility and effectiveness:

Implementable Policy Test: "Can those responsible for policy in the real system be convinced of the value of model-based policy recommendations? How is the real system likely to respond to the process of implementation?" The policy recommendations should be such formulated and argued so as to fit in the mental models of those to whom they are addressed.

Validation Scheme as Proposed by Khazanchi. This validation criterion is mainly used to validate qualitative/conceptual models and consists of a set of criteria for validation. The criteria for validation as suggested by Khazanchi are as follows:

1. *Is it believable/reasonable*? This criterion is useful to assess the apparent reasonableness of an idea and could be demonstrated by deduction from past research or theories.
2. *Is it feasible*? A feasible concept would be operational only if it would be open to graphical, mathematical, illustrative characterization.
3. *Is it effective*? An effective conceptual model should have the potential of serving our scientific purposes.
4. *Is it pragmatic*? This criterion emphasizes that concepts and conceptual models should have some degree of logical self-consistency or coherence with other concepts and conceptual models in the discipline.
5. *Is it empirical*? Empirical content implies that a concept or conceptual model must have "empirical testability".
6. *Is it predictive*? A conceptual model that is predictive would, at the least, demonstrate that given certain antecedent conditions, the corresponding phenomenon was somehow expected to occur.
7. *Is it inter-subjectively certifiable*? This criterion states that investigators with differing philosophical stance must be able to verify the imputed truth content of these concepts or conceptual structures through observation, logical evaluation, or experimentation.
8. *Is it inter-methodologically certifiable*? This criterion provides that investigators using different research methodologies must be able to test the veracity of the concept or conceptual model and predict the occurrence of the same phenomenon.

6.6.9 Other Validation Techniques

Combinations of these techniques are generally used for validating a simulation model. These tests can be used in addition to the validation schemes in the preceding section to increase the credibility of the model. These comparison techniques perform following tests:

1. *Comparison with other models*: Different outputs of the simulation model being validated are compared to those of other 'valid' models.
2. *Degenerate test*: This has to do with appropriately selecting values of the input and internal parameters to test the degeneracy of the model's behavior. For instance, test to see if the average number in the queue of a single server continues to increase with respect to time when the arriving rate is larger than the service rate.
3. *Events validity*: The events of occurrences of the simulation model are compared to those of the real system to see if they are similar for example, verify the exit rate of employees.
4. *Face validity*: This has to do with asking knowledgeable people if the system model behavior is reasonable.
5. *Historical data validation:* The experimental data is compared with the historical data; to check whether if the model behaves in the same way the system does.
6. *Predictive validation*: The model is used to predict the system's behavior, and then comparison is made between the real system behavior and the model's forecast to determine if they are the same.
7. *Schellenberger's criteria*: This include technical validation which has to do with identifying all divergences between the model assumptions and perceived reality as well as the validity of the data used, operational validity which addresses the question of how important these divergences are and dynamic validation which ensures that the model will continue being valid during its lifetime.
8. *Scoring model approach*: Scores (or weights) are determined subjectively when conducting various aspects of the validation process and then combined to determine category scores and an overall score for the simulation model. A simulation model is considered valid if its overall and category scores are greater than some passing scores.
9. *Clarity*: Clarity refers to the extent to which the model clearly communicates the implied causality/linkages.
10. *Black-box validation*: This test is concerned with determining whether if the entire model is an adequately accurate representation of the real-world.
11. *Extreme condition test*: The model structure and output should be reasonable for any extreme and unlikely combination of values in the system. For example, if in-process inventories are zero, production output should be zero.

6.6.10 Validation of Simulation Experiments

This section gives a survey on how to validate simulation models through the application of mathematical statistics. The type of statistical test actually applied, depends on the availability of data on the real system: (*i*) no data, (*ii*) only output data, and (*iii*) both input and output data. In case (*i*), the system analysts can still experiment with the simulation model to obtain simulated data. Those experiments should be guided by the statistical theory on design of experiments (DOE); an inferior but popular approach is to change only one factor at a time. In case (*ii*), real and simulated output data may be compared through the well-known student *t*-statistic. In case (*iii*), trace-driven simulation becomes possible. Then validation, however, should not proceed as follows: make a scatter plot with real and simulated outputs, fit a line, and test whether that line has unit slope and passes through the origin. Instead, better tests are presented. Several case studies are summarized, to illustrate the three types of situations.

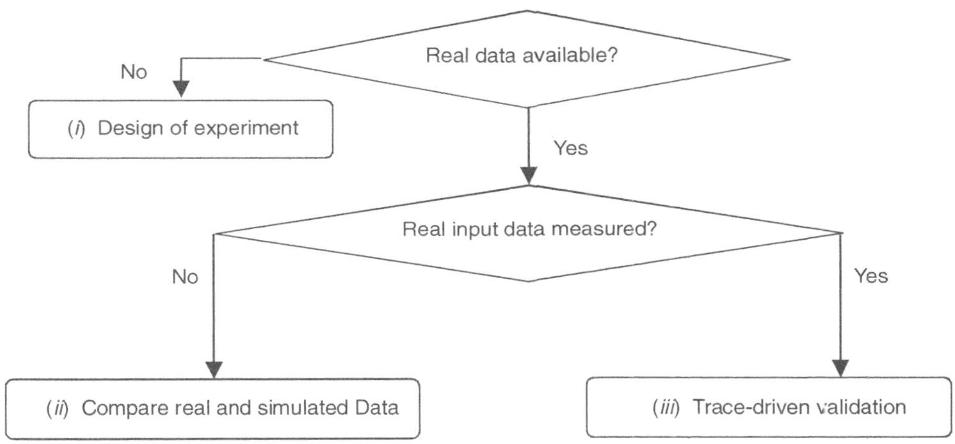

Fig. 6.5 Real data availability with three situations

To define *validation* as determining whether the conceptual simulation model is an accurate representation of the real system is the main task. Many types of validation are used in practice, but we focus on validation that uses *mathematical statistics*. After all, simulation means experimentation. And experimentation calls for statistical analysis, preceded by statistical design. Obviously, statistical analysis is only part of the whole validation process. However, if statistics are used, then the correct statistics should be used. One type of statistical validation compares data on the real and the simulated systems. Such a comparison makes much more sense if both systems are observed under similar scenarios; for example, a busy day at the real supermarket should not be compared with a slow day at the simulated store. Obviously, real data may pertain to input and output; for example, customers' arrival times and cashiers' service times at the supermarket are input, whereas customers' waiting times are output.

(*i*) In some applications, data on the real system are either completely missing or scarce. Examples are data on nuclear war, nuclear accidents, global warming or greenhouse effect. But, even if real data are missing, there is still *expert knowledge*.

For example, we all are experts in waiting at supermarkets, so we know that if more customers arrive per hour, then waiting times increase unless more cashiers become active. However, this knowledge is qualitative; to obtain quantitative knowledge, the system analysts develop a simulation model. In other words, the sign of the effect is known, not its magnitude. If the simulation model's input/output behavior violates this qualitative knowledge, the model should be seriously questioned: are there programming and conceptual errors? We propose a systematic, scientific method namely, design of experiments or DOE for selecting conditions or scenarios as input for the simulation model; and

(ii) In other applications, however, we are 'drown by the numbers'; examples are data on supermarket sales and on telecommunication operations. In general, data are abundant if systems are electronically monitored; examples are point of sale systems (POSS) and electronic data interchange (EDI). But, even if real output data are available, the corresponding real-world scenarios may not be measured. An example is a simulation model of the search for mines on the sea bottom, through sonar equipment: in practice it is virtually impossible to measure the temperature and the salinity of the sea water, at all times and places. In those cases only the outputs of the real and the simulated systems can be compared.

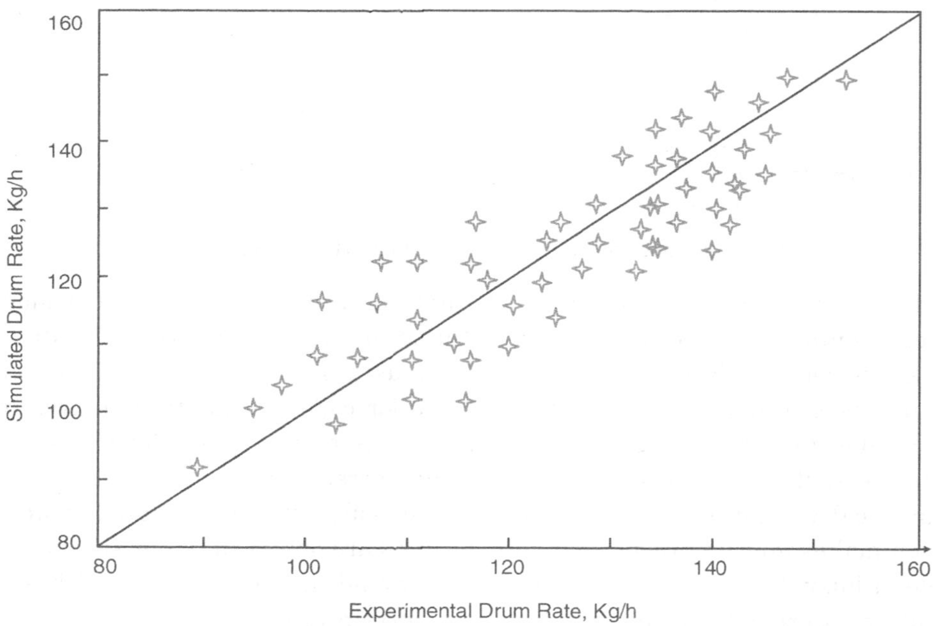

Fig. 6.6 Wrong analysis of trace-driven simulation

(iii) Finally, the most powerful validation is possible if both input and output of the real system are measured. In so-called *trace-driven* simulation, analysts feed

real input data into the simulation program, in historical order. After running the simulation program, analysts compare the time series of simulated output with the historical time series of real output. But, what is wrong with the following analysis of trace-driven simulation? Make a scatter plot with real and simulated outputs, fit a line to the scatter plot, test whether that line has unit slope and passes through the origin zero intercept (see figure 6.6).

6.6.11 Simulation Runs

A simulation experiment consists of a set of simulation runs. During a simulation run, all factors remain constant. During the experiment, factors do change; that is, each factor has at least two levels or 'values' in the experiment. The factor may be qualitative, as the priority rules exemplified. Most practitioners change one factor at a time, and think that this is the scientific way to perform *what-if* analysis. Actually it is easy to prove that this method gives less accurate estimates of the factor's (main or first-order) effect. Moreover, it does not enable estimation of interactions among factors: what happens if two or more factors change simultaneously? DOE provides much better estimators.

DOE and its regression analysis treat the simulation model as a black box: the simulation model's input/output is observed, and the factor effects in the meta-model are estimated. This approach has advantages and disadvantages. An advantage is that DOE can be applied to all simulation models, either deterministic or stochastic. A disadvantage is that DOE cannot exploit the specific structure of a given simulation model. DOE is a classic topic in statistics. However, the standard statistical techniques must be adapted such that they account for the following simulation peculiarities:

(*i*) There are a great many factors in many practical simulation models. For example, the ecological case study (mentioned above) has 281 factors, whereas standard DOE assumes only up to fifteen factors. 'Screening' aims at finding a short list of really important factors.

(*ii*) Stochastic simulation models use pseudorandom numbers, which means that analysts have much more control over the noise in their experiments than they have in standard statistical applications. For example, to reduce that noise, analysts may use so-called common and antithetic numbers.

(*iii*) Randomization is of major concern in DOE outside simulation. In simulation, however, this randomization problem disappears: pseudorandom numbers take over.

The regression meta-model shows which factors are most important; that is, which factors have highly significant regression estimates in the meta-model. If possible, information on these factors should be collected, for validation purposes. If the significant factors are controllable by the users, then the estimated regression effects show how to change these factors to optimize the real system. DOE assumes that the area of experimentation is given. A valid simulation model, however, requires that the inputs be restricted to a certain domain of factor combinations. Simulation models are often used in *risk analysis*:

what is the probability of a 'disaster'? That disaster may be a nuclear accident, a financial mis-investment, etc. These disasters are unique events, whereas the supermarket simulation concerns repetitive events (*e.g.*, customer waiting times). Consequently, validation in risk analysis is very difficult. A better term may be *credibility*. A technical issue in risk analysis is that DOE selects extreme combinations of factor values, which typically have extremely low probability of realization. Instead, risk analysis samples from the whole domain of possible combinations, according to a pre-specified probability distribution. This sampling uses the Monte Carlo technique (sometimes refined to Latin hypercube sampling or LHS). Next, analysts improve the risk model's credibility by applying statistical techniques. For example, regression analysis and contingency tables may detect which factors have significant effects; next analysts—using their expert knowledge–should be able to explain why these factors are important.

Validation through mathematical statistics gives quantitative information on the quality of the simulation model. Statistical validation may use various testing procedures, depending on the type of data available for the real system. We distinguished the following three situations. (*i*) *No* real data : Then analysts can still generate simulated data. Their simulation experiment should be guided by DOE; an inferior approach changes only one factor at a time. Regression models provide approximations (meta-models) of the simulation's I/O transformation, and show which factors are important. (*ii*) Only data on real *output*: Real and simulated outputs may be compared through the Student *t*-test. Alternatives are distribution-free procedures, which unfortunately—are applied rarely. (*iii*) I/O data on real system: Real I/O data enable trace-driven simulation. The validation of trace-driven simulation, however, should not use a scatter plot with real and simulated outputs, fit a line, and test whether that line has unit slope and zero intercept.

6.7 EVALUATION OF SIMULATION EXPERIMENTS

This section describes a procedure for evaluating proposed startup policies that define the initial conditions and the truncation point in a simulation experiment. The evaluation procedure involves the tabulation of bias, variance, and mean square error of the sample mean over a fixed range of truncation points and initial conditions. For each policy, the tabulated values are averaged with respect to an empirical truncation-point distribution based on independent model runs. These results are used to construct confidence intervals for the steady-state mean with the same average length for all policies; the corresponding average confidence interval cover age can then be used to compare policies.

To illustrate the procedure, several well-known policies are evaluated for two finite-state Markovian queueing systems—single-server queue with a capacity of 15 and a machine-repair system with 3 repairmen and 14 machines. The results for both systems indicate that the best initial condition is the most frequently observed value (the mode) of the steady-state distribution of the number-in-system process, and that the judicious selection of an initial condition is more effective than truncation in improving the performance of the sample mean as an estimator of the steady-state mean. The following analysis can be adopted for evaluation of simulation experiments:

- *Performance Evaluation and What-If Analysis*: The *what-if* analysis is at the very heart of simulation models.
- *Sensitivity Estimation*: Users must be provided with affordable techniques for sensitivity analysis if they are to understand which relationships are meaningful in complicated models.
- *Optimization*: Traditional optimization techniques require gradient estimation. As with sensitivity analysis, the current approach for optimization requires intensive simulation to construct an approximate surface response function. Incorporating gradient estimation techniques into convergent algorithms such as Robbins-Monroe type algorithms for optimization purposes.

The study suggests that computer simulations fill a different role than traditional experiments; that the environment in which the simulations are implemented has a major effect on user's perceptions of his/her value; and that qualitative data can play a vital role in understanding the effect of changes in curriculum.

We recommend the following sequence for the evaluation of simulation models:

(1) *Validation*: the availability of data on the real system determines the proper type of statistical technique.

(2) *Screening*: In the simulation's pilot phase the important inputs are identified through a novel technique, namely sequential bifurcation, which uses aggregation and sequential experimentation.

(3) *Sensitivity or what-if analysis*: the important inputs are analyzed in more detail, including interactions between inputs; relevant techniques are Design Of Experiments (DOE) and regression analysis.

(4) *Uncertainty or risk analysis*: important environmental inputs may have values not precisely known, so the resulting uncertainties in the model outputs are quantified; techniques are Monte Carlo and Latin hypercube sampling.

(5) *Optimization*: policy variables may be controlled, applying Response Surface Methodology (RSM), which combines DOE, regression analysis, and steepest-ascent hill-climbing.

6.7.1 Verification and Validation Activities

A large number of matching measurements and simulation results, though increasing confidence, does not prove validity of the model however. A single mismatch between measurements and simulation results invalidates the model. For this reason, Popper has introduced the concept of falsification, the enterprise of trying to falsify or disprove a model. A model may state that water in a pot boils at 100°C. Many experiments may confirm this model, until either the pot is closed or is taking to a different altitude. A falsified model should not lead to an outright rejection of the model. Rather, it should lead to a refinement of the model's experimental frame on the one hand and to an attempt to expand the model to fit the current experimental frame. In the case of the water boiling in a pot, a restricted experimental frame would state that the pressure must be constant. Expending the model would express the relationship between boiling point and pressure and volume. Various kinds of validation can be identified; *e.g.*, conceptual model validation, structural validation, and behavioral validation.

Conceptual validation is the evaluation of a conceptual model with respect to the system, where the objective is primarily to evaluate the realism of the conceptual model with respect to the goals of the study. Structural validation is the evaluation of the structure of a simulation model with respect to perceived structure of the system. Behavioral validation is the evaluation of the simulation model behavior. An overview of verification and validation activities is shown in figure 6.7. It is noted that the correspondence in generated behavior between a system and a model will only hold within the limited context of the experimental frame. Consequently, when using models to exchange information, a model must always be matched with an experimental frame before use. Conversely, a model should never be developed without simultaneously developing its experimental frame. This requirement has its repercussions on the design of a model representation language.

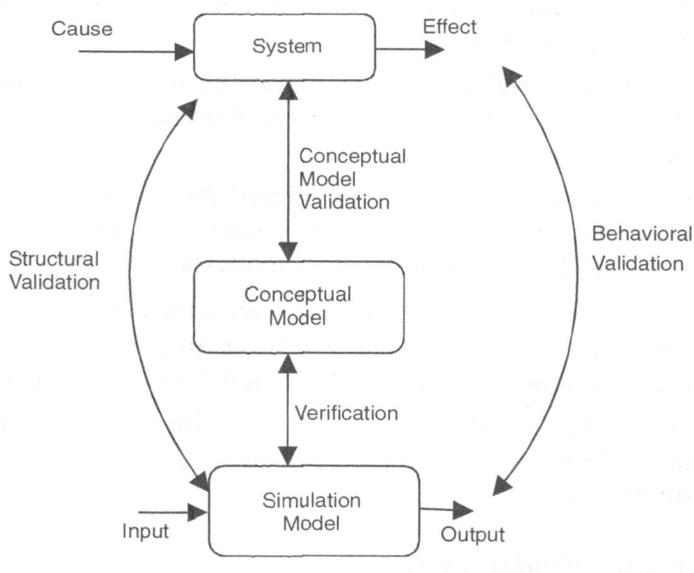

Fig. 6.7 Verification and validation activities

SUMMARY

The life cycle application of verification and validation is extremely important for successful completion of complex and large-scale modeling and simulation efforts. Assessing credibility throughout the life cycle is an onerous task. Applying the verification and validation techniques throughout the life cycle is time consuming and costly. In practice, under time pressure to complete a modeling and simulation effort, the verification and validation and documentation are sacrificed first. Computer-aided assistance for credibility assessment is required to alleviate these problems. More research is needed to bring automation to the application of verification and validation techniques. How much to test or when to stop testing depends on the modeling and simulation objectives. The testing should continue until sufficient confidence is achieved in credibility and acceptability of modeling and simulation results. The sufficiency of the confidence is dictated by the modeling and simulation objectives. Establishing a Simulation Quality Assurance (SQA) program within the organization conducting the modeling and simulation effort is extremely important for successful credibility assessment. The SQA management structure goes beyond verification and validation and is also responsible for assessing other model quality characteristics such as maintainability, reusability, and usability (human-computer interface). The management of the SQA program and the management of the simulation project must be independent of each other and neither should be able to overrule the other. Subjectivity is, and will always be, part of the credibility assessment for a reasonably complex simulation study. The reason for subjectivity is two-fold: modeling is an art and credibility assessment is situation dependent.

A set of *acceptability criteria* should be specified for each intended use of modeling and simulation application in the legal contract signed by the modeling and simulation sponsor and developer. Acceptance testing is typically conducted by an independent third party, *e.g.*, modeling and simulation certification agent, to judge if the modeling and simulation application meets the prescribed acceptability criteria. The acceptance testing commonly includes the assessment of many quality characteristics as well as the accuracy. Judging if the modeling and simulation application satisfies the acceptability criteria is a "confidence building" activity. The conclusion of the acceptance testing should also provide a confidence level such as "We are 95% confident that the modeling and simulation application satisfies the acceptability criteria for the stated intended use." However, it is usually very difficult to numerically define the confidence level; therefore, nominal characterizations such as exceptionally, exceedingly, highly, remarkably, or notably is used in place of the 95% numerical value. The confidence level can be more convincingly substantiated if a quality-centered approach is used in performing the acceptance testing. CMMI certification of the modeling and simulation application developer and the quality of the people tasked to develop the modeling and simulation application significantly affect the confidence level justification.

As validations are both an art and a science, requiring creativity and insight. But validation is a convoluted, multifarious and exasperating procedure, and is unavoidable as it is the evidence for the steadfastness and legitimacy of the model. Moreover, no single procedure can suit all the models. Statistical based validation techniques have been widely accepted among the management community. But the problem associated with this method is being able to determine the suitable type of statistical procedure, which in turn depends on the right type of data that is available for analysis. Moreover, the amount of deviation from the real system that is within the acceptable limits is uncertain. The chapter has given an insight on the widely approved validation schemes and techniques in practice.

The validation schemes can be applicable to quantitative (mathematical/computerized) as well as qualitative (conceptual) models. But reliability of the model can only be ascertained as the model passes more and more tests. Also, the decision of accepting a model as valid cannot be left to the modeler alone, inclusion of the client/practitioners in the validation procedure should be ascertained.

Simulation models are designed and used with a goal of learning about a process. Validation is the act of increasing to an acceptable level the confidence that an inference about a simulated process is correct for the actual process. There is no such thing as "the test". The experimenter selects a set of tests from the many possible-*a* standard decision problem of balancing the cost of testing against the cost of an incorrect inference. Three major classes of actions are finding models with face validity, testing assumptions and testing input-output transformations. Actions range from such highly technical approaches as spectral analysis to behaviorally oriented ones such as the "Turing test". Validation often becomes more tractable if simulation is viewed as one of several modes of investigation. Complementary research activities-related experiments, empirical analysis, analytic models, or prototypes-are widely used in the physical sciences to increase validity and appear equally appropriate for the management sciences. Some of the ideas and problems of validation are illustrated briefly.

In practice, validation has many forms, but we discussed on validation through mathematical statistics. Statistical validation may use various tests, depending on the type of data available for the real system. We discussed the following three situations:

(i) *No Real Data.* Even if there is no data on the input or output of the real system, the analysts can still generate *simulated* data. More specifically, the analysts should perform sensitivity analysis to find out whether the simulation model contradicts *qualitative, expert knowledge*. If the simulation's input/output behavior violates this knowledge, the model should be seriously searched for programming and conceptual errors. This sensitivity analysis should be guided by DOE including regression meta-models; an inferior approach changes only one factor at a time.

(ii) *Only Data on Real Output.* If there is data on the output of the real system, the means of real and simulated output distributions may be compared through the two-sample Student *t*-test. Alternatives are Johnson's modified *t* statistic (estimating the skewness of the output distribution), distribution-free statistics, and bootstrapping.

(iii) *I/O Data on Real System.* Real input data enable trace-driven simulation. The validation of this type of simulation, however, should not use a scatter plot with real and simulated outputs, testing whether the fitted line has unit slope and zero intercept.

To demonstrate the applicability of the various statistical methods, we summarized some case studies. Nevertheless, because validation involves the art of modeling and the philosophy of science, validation will remain controversial.

EXERCISE QUESTIONS

1. What do you understand by simulation experimentation? What is its need?
2. What do you mean by optimization in simulation experiments?
3. How experimental design for simulation is different from design of a software system?
4. What do you mean by sensitivity analysis in simulation experiments?
5. Explain the sensitivity of outputs on changing of inputs in a simulation experiment.
6. What do you understand by classical experimental design?
7. Why do we say that simulations are controlled experiments?
8. What is the importance of random numbers in simulation experiments?
9. Write short notes on the following:
   (*i*) simulation runs
   (*ii*) software agents.
10. What do you mean by validation and verification of simulation experiment ?
11. What is modeling and simulation product quality assessment ? What standards are followed for it ?
12. What do you understand by evaluation of simulation experiments ?
13. What are various methods for evaluation of simulation experiments ?
14. Explain various Validation Schemes for simulation experiments.
15. Explain validation scheme proposed by Khazanchi.
16. Write short notes on following:
    (*i*) Capability Maturity Model Integration(CMMI)
    (*ii*) Trace-driven simulation
    (*iii*) Scoring model approach
    (*iv*) Model Validation Process.

Chapter 7

PERT AND CPM

7.1 INTRODUCTION

Process Model simulation allows the activity times of a project to be represented by a variety of distributions and further the resulting project time may also be represented by a variety of distributions. This is a significant improvement over the traditional methods of CPM and PERT. Program Evaluation and Review Technique (PERT) takes the CPM network and adds distributions to represent the activity times of the project. CPM assumes the activity times to be constant, which is not likely in the real world. PERT assumes the activity times of the project to be distributed as Beta distributions and the resulting project time to be a Normal distribution. This is better than assuming them to be constant, but these assumptions are needlessly restrictive.

Complex projects require a series of activities, some of which must be performed sequentially and others that can be performed in parallel with other activities. This collection of series and parallel tasks can be modeled as a network. Network scheduling is typically performed in three phases—network creation, analysis, and development. Although the Critical Path Method (CPM) constitutes a well-established logic in network analysis, human intuition and experience are required for the creation and development of the network. Because of this, a variety of alternative CPM networks can be created in scheduling the same project. The use of the most desirable network can lead to a considerable reduction in the duration of the projects. Accurately identifying activities and linking them in an appropriate manner can achieve this. Many researchers insisted that network scheduling lacks efficiency in scheduling repetitive-unit projects. Because of this, many scheduling methods have been developed to model such types of projects. However, most are not network based and require a large amount of input data, although most leading scheduling software remains network based and field engineers desire network like forms of the schedule.

The *Program Evaluation and Review Technique* (PERT) is a network model that allows for randomness in activity completion times. PERT was developed in the late 1950's for the U.S. Navy*is* Polaris project having thousands of contractors. It has the potential to reduce both the time and cost required to complete a project.

In 1957 the Critical Path Method (CPM) was developed as a network model for project management. CPM is a deterministic method that uses a fixed time estimate for each activity. While CPM is easy to understand and use, it does not consider the time variations that can have a great impact on the completion time of a complex project.

Gantt chart or Bar chart is the most commonly adopted project-planning tool due to the ease of use and easily understood by project stakeholders, however this primitive tool falls short in reflecting the interdependencies of WBS (Work Breakdown Structure). Project Network Plan on the other hand is far more effective as its network diagrams can be developed systematically by converting WBS in the forms of nodes and arrows represented in graphical flowcharts for organizations to embrace as project management best practice.

In a project, an activity is a task that must be performed and an event is a milestone marking the completion of one or more activities. Before an activity can begin, all of its predecessor activities must be completed. Project network models represent activities and milestones by arcs/arrows and nodes respectively. PERT originally was an *activity on arc* or *activity on arrow* (AOA) network, in which the activities are represented on the lines and milestones on the nodes. Over time, some people began to use PERT as an *activity on node* (AON) network.

The PERT chart may have multiple pages with many sub-tasks. The following is a very simple example of a PERT diagram:

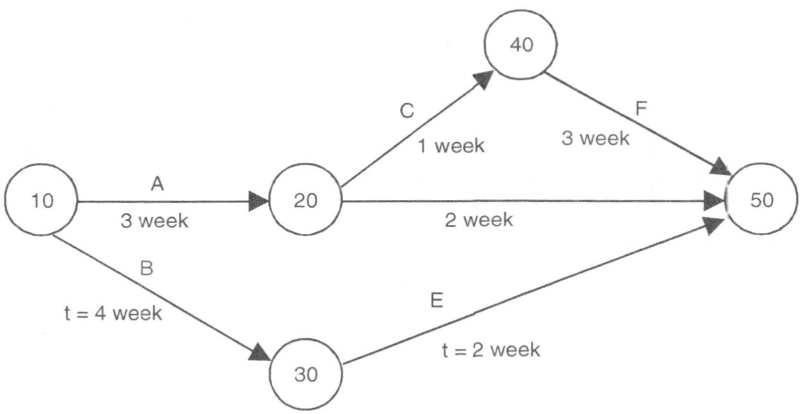

Fig. 7.1. A PERT Chart

The milestones generally are numbered so that the ending node of an activity has a higher number than the beginning node. Incrementing the numbers by 10 allows for new ones to be inserted without modifying the numbering of the entire diagram. The activities in the above diagram are labeled with letters along with the expected time required to complete the activity.

The Program Evaluation and Review Technique commonly abbreviated PERT is a model for project management invented by United States Department of Defense's US Navy Special Projects Office in 1958 as part of the Polaris mobile submarine-launched ballistic missile project.

PERT is basically a method to analyze the tasks involved in completing a given project, especially the time needed to complete each task, and identifying the minimum time needed to complete the total project. It was developed in the *i*50*is*, primarily to simplify the planning and scheduling of large and complex projects. It was able to incorporate uncertainty in the sense that it was possible to schedule a project not knowing precisely the details and durations of all the activities. This technique is used more in R&D-type projects where cost is not a major factor but time is.

7.2 WORK BREAKDOWN STRUCTURES (WBS)

The development of a project plan is predicated on having a clear and detailed understanding of both the tasks involved, the estimated length of time each task will take, the dependencies between those tasks, and the sequence in which those tasks have to be performed. Additionally, resource availability must be determined in order to assign each task or group of tasks to the appropriate worker. One method used to develop the list of tasks is to create what is known as a work breakdown structure.

A *work breakdown structure* (WBS) is a hierarchic decomposition or breakdown of a project or major activity into successive levels, in which each level is a finer breakdown of the preceding one. In final form a WBS is very similar in structure and layout to a document outline. Each item at a specific level of a WBS is numbered consecutively (*e.g.*, 10, 10, 30, 40, 50). Each item at the next level is numbered within the number of its parent item (*e.g.*, 10.1, 10.2, 10.3, 10.4). The WBS may be drawn in a diagrammatic form (if automated tools are available) or in a chart resembling an outline. The WBS begins with a single overall task representing the totality of work to be performed on the project. This becomes the name of the project plan WBS. Using a methodology or system life cycle (analysis, design and implementation) steps as a guide, the project is divided into its major steps. The first phase is project initiation; the second major phase is analysis, followed by design, construction, testing, implementation, and post-implementation follow-up. Each of these phases must be broken in their next level of detail, and each of those, into still finer levels of detail, until a manageable task size is arrived at. The first WBS level for the life cycle would be:

Table 7.1 WBS level

WBS number	*Task Description*
1.0	Project initiation
1.1	Draft project plan
2.0	Analysis phase
2.1	Plan user interviews
2.2	Schedule users interviews
3.0	Examination and test

4.0	Design
5.0	Test
6.0	Implementation
7.0	Post implementation review

Tasks at each successively finer level of detail are numbered to reflect the task from which they were derived. Thus, the first level of tasks would be numbered 1.0, 2.0, 3.0, and so forth. Each of their subtasks would have a two-part number: the first part reflecting the parent task and the second part, the subtask numbers itself, such as 1.1, 1.2, or 1.3. As each of these, in turn, decomposed or broken down into its component tasks, each component receives a number comprised of its parent number plus a unique number of its own.

7.3 PROJECT NETWORK PLAN

The two building blocks of project network plan comprising WBS as input and project network diagrams as output that represented by nodes (boxes) and arrows for a work package. The nodes depict activities whereas arrows show dependencies and project flows. Based on the required work package consists of a series of WBS, a detailed project schedule can be defined with the use of project network diagrams for the entire project.

Project network plan is an effective tool for project planning, scheduling, monitoring and control the work-in-progress. Network diagrams are developed based on a series of WBS in the form of nodes and arrows represented in graphical flowcharts. The nodes display critical information of early start, early finish, late start, late finish, duration and slack time of WBS; whereas the arrows direct project flows from start to finish in a sequential order with interdependencies among nodes and underlining the critical paths. The project network diagrams, apart from being the framework for project information system, can help project managers to make an informed decision on project status, potential risks and constraints. There are two approaches to which project network diagrams can be developed, namely the *activity-on-node* (AON) and *activity-on-arrow* (AOA), the brainchild of Dupont in 1950s to solve its maintenance-scheduling problem with resounding success. AON can be also found in many project software packages that convert Gantt chart into AON once built.

7.3.1 How to Develop an Effective Project Network Plan

Project time management is one of the nine knowledge areas of project management by Project Management Institute (PMI) which underlines the following processes to help develop project time schedule, these processes are also the basis for our project network plan development.

Definition of Activity

To identify specific activities that must be performed to produce the various project deliverables. This can be accomplished by consolidating all inputs on WBS, scope statement, historical information, constraints, assumptions and expert judgment. Using decomposition and templates as tools and techniques to produce activity list, supporting details and WBS updates.

Sequencing of Activity

To identify and documenting interactivity dependencies. This can be achieved by considering all aspects of activity list, product description, mandatory dependencies, discretionary dependencies, external dependencies and milestones. Tools and techniques may include Precedence Diagram Method (PDM), Arrow Diagram Method (ADM), conditional diagramming methods and network templates to generate project network diagrams and activity list updates.

Duration Estimating of Activity

To estimate the number of work periods that will be needed to complete individual activities. This is facilitated with the use of activity list, constraints, assumptions, resource requirements, resource capabilities, historical information, and identified risks. Tools and techniques that will help include the expert judgment, analogous estimating, quantitatively based durations, reserved time to provide the activity duration estimates, basis of estimates and activity list updates.

Development Schedule

To analyze activity sequences, activity durations, and resource requirements to create the project schedule. This can be accomplished with the inputs received on project network diagrams, activity duration estimates, resource requirements, resource pool description, calendars, constraints, assumptions, leads and lags, risk management plan and activity attributes. Tools and techniques that may be useful are the mathematical analysis, duration compression, simulation, resource leveling heuristics, project management software, coding structure to generate project schedule, supporting details, schedule management plan and resource requirement updates.

Schedule Control

Tools and techniques include schedule change control system, performance measurement, additional planning, and project software to define schedule updates, corrective action and lessons learned. Nonetheless, developing an effective project network plan entails a concerted effort from project team members of project manager, engineers and other project stake holders who are the subject experts and knowing the required time taken for the respective WBS of work package with reference to contracted scope and technical complexity.

Constructing a comprehensive project network diagram in a graphic format seems tedious. However it is necessary to present a realistic project schedule and this task is usually performed by project managers in conjunction with team members but once built, it serves as a resource for project team to track the project status and if slippage is imminent. Essentially, there are basic rules to observe while building a project network diagram:

1. Project network flow is typically starts from left to right.
2. A WBS cannot begin until all preceding connected WBS have been completed.
3. Arrows on networks indicate precedence and flow. Arrows can cross over each other.
4. Each WBS should have a unique identification number
5. A WBS identification number must be larger than that of any WBS that precedes it.
6. No looping is allowed.
7. No conditional statements are allowed.
8. A common start node can be used to indicate a clear project beginning on the network.

7.4 VARIOUS METHODS OF PROJECT PLAN

In comparing the Gantt chart method, which does not provide clarity on WBS interdependencies, project network diagram method on the other hand offers unique information display on project flows and WBS interdependencies in a graphical format. Gantt chart even though primitive can be easily understood and popularized by software available in the market. In construction industry where the project network diagram method is common supported by high-end project management software for planning and control of hundreds or thousands of WBS that must be accounted from project initiation towards project closing. Many automation providers might not be aware the usefulness of project network diagram method that can help to plan and control projects more effectively ranging from small to large scale projects. In process automation, most project owners require vendors and service providers to submit only the Gantt charts based on Microsoft Project to outline critical milestones, because the automation package is generally less significant as compared with the total project packages as far as the project owner is concerned. Nonetheless, it must not be an excuse for automation providers to ignore project network diagram method that is also beneficial for root cause analysis; help visualizing entire project requirements and containing project costs overrun and milestones slippage, as a best practice for project management in any organizations of today*i*s automation business.

Process model simulation allows the activity times of a project to be represented by a variety of distributions and further the resulting project time may also be represented by a variety of distributions. This is a significant improvement over the traditional methods of CPM and PERT. Program Evaluation and Review Technique (PERT) takes the CPM network and adds distributions to represent the activity times of the project.

Below is a PERT chart that shows the development of a system.

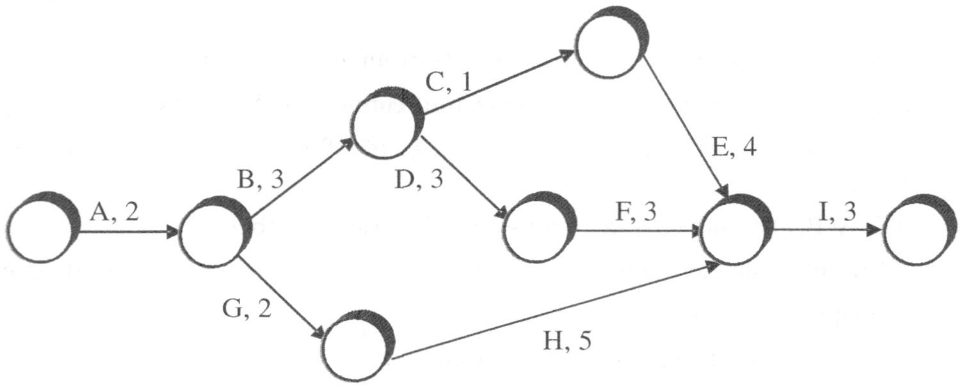

Fig. 7.2 A PERT Chart to show development of a system

Here are the some points to think over before we discuss anything else.

- The CIRCLES mark the beginnings and ends of TASKS to be done in the project, these are also called NODES.
- The ARROWS are the tasks themselves. They are identified by letters A to I. In a real PERT chart, the actual names of tasks would be used instead of letters. The lengths of the arrows does not relate to their length in time.
- The NUMBERS after the task names are the DURATIONS of the task. The time interval may be anything from picoseconds to years. Let us assume these timings are in days.

Important point to remember:

- The ARROWS are tasks, not the circles (nodes).
- When a node has two or more tasks branching from it, it means those tasks can be done concurrently (at the same time.)
- When a node has incoming arrows, it means the incoming task must be completed before progress may continue to any arrows heading away from the node, *e.g.* task A must be completed before tasks B or G may begin.

Task *A* is the first task and takes 2 days. When it is done, tasks *B* and *G* can begin. If we follow the task *G* line, it takes 2 days to reach task *H* which takes 5 days. Task *H* leads to the final task, *I*. Total time for following this path is 2 + 2 + 5 + 3 = 12 days. The path would be described as *A*, *B*, *G*, *H*, *I*.

When task *G* began, so did task *B* (with another team of workers). When task *B* finished, after 3 days, there is another opportunity to run some tasks concurrently. So after *B*, tasks *C* and *D* began at the same time.

If we follow task *C*, it takes 1 day to reach task *E*, which leads to the final task *I*. Total time for this path was 2 + 3 + 1 + 4 + 3 = 13 days.

If we followed task *D*, which takes 3 days, it leads to task *F* (also 3 days) before reaching the final task, I. Total time for this path is 2 + 3 + 3 + 3 + 3 = 14 days.

Note that tasks E, F and H must all be finished before task I can begin.

You will have noticed that there are several paths through from task A to task I. Each of these paths takes a different amount of time.

Now the question is what is the shortest possible time for the project to take (without leaving any tasks out)?

The answer is 14 days (the longest possible path). It sounds odd that the shortest time is the longest path, but considers another example. You are getting ready for school. At the kitchen table, you have to have breakfast while you finish your maths homework. You have to finish both before you can leave. Breakfast takes 12 minutes. Maths takes 20 minutes. What is the shortest time you would need to leave? *Twenty* minutes, because both tasks must be finished. Just because one task finishes before the other, you cannot leave yet. So in the chart above, the shortest project time would be 14 days.

That is the CRITICAL PATH of the project: the sequence of tasks from beginning to end that takes the longest time. No task on the critical path can take more time without affecting the end date of the project. In other words, none of the tasks on the critical path has any SLACK.

SLACK is the amount of extra time a task can take before it affects a following task. In the breakfast example above, the breakfast could take another eight minutes before it affected the leaving time, so it has eight minutes' slack.

Tasks on the critical path are called CRITICAL TASKS. No critical task can have any slack (by definition).

Before attempting to use these tools, the project's information must be assembled in a certain way. The following preceding steps can include basic description. The project planning process consists of:

1. Setting the project start date
2. Setting the project completion date
3. Selecting the project methodology or project life cycle to be used
4. Determining the scope of the project in terms of the phases of the selected project methodology or project life cycle
5. Identifying or selecting the project review methods to be used
6. Identifying any predetermined interim milestone or other critical dates, which must be met.
7. Listing tasks, by project phase, in the order in which they might be accomplished.
8. Estimating the personnel necessary to accomplish each task
9. Estimating the personnel available to accomplish each task
10. Determining skill level necessary to perform each task
11. Determining task dependencies:

- Which tasks can be done in parallel
- Which tasks require the completion of other tasks before they can start
  - project control or review points.
  - performing project cost estimation and cost-benefit analysis.

7.4.1 PERT

A PERT chart is a tool that facilitates decision making; a PERT chart does not make decisions. A PERT chart displays interconnected events (each of which is an important milestone), conventionally represented as numbered circles as in the diagram above. The first draft of a PERT chart will number its events sequentially in 10s (10, 20, 30, etc.) to allow the later insertion of additional events. Two consecutive events in a PERT chart are linked by activities, which are conventionally represented as arrows in the diagram above.

A PERT chart presents a graphic illustration of a project as a network diagram consisting of numbered *nodes* (either circles or rectangles) representing events, or milestones in the project linked by labeled *vectors* (directional lines) representing tasks in the project. The direction of the arrows on the lines indicates the sequence of tasks. In the diagram, for example, the tasks between nodes 1, 2, 4, 8, and 10 must be completed in sequence. These are called *dependent* or *serial* tasks. The tasks between nodes 1 and 2, and nodes 1 and 3 are not dependent on the completion of one to start the other and can be undertaken simultaneously. These tasks are called *parallel* or *concurrent* tasks. Tasks that must be completed in sequence but that do not require resources or completion time are considered to have *event dependency*. These are represented by dotted lines with arrows and are called *dummy activities*. For example, the dashed arrow linking nodes 6 and 9 indicates that the system files must be converted before the user test can take place, but that the resources and time required to prepare for the user test (writing the user manual and user training) are on another path. Numbers on the opposite sides of the vectors indicate the time allotted for the task.

The PERT chart is sometimes preferred over the Gantt chart, another popular project management charting method, because it clearly illustrates task dependencies. On the other hand, the PERT chart can be much more difficult to interpret, especially on complex projects. Frequently, project managers use both techniques.

The events are presented in a logical sequence and no activity can commence until its immediately preceding event is completed. The planner decides which milestones should be PERT events and also decides their "proper" sequence. A PERT chart may have multiple pages with many sub-tasks.

PERT is a variation on Critical Path Analysis (CPA) that takes a slightly more skeptical view of time estimates made for each project stage. To use it, estimate the shortest possible time each activity will take, the most likely length of time, and the longest time that might be taken if the activity takes longer than expected. This helps to bias time estimates away from the unrealistically short time-scales normally assumed.

Key points:

Critical Path Analysis is an effective and powerful method of assessing:

- What tasks must be carried out
- Where parallel activity can be performed
- The shortest time in which you can complete a project
- Resources needed to execute a project
- The sequence of activities, scheduling and timings involved
- Task priorities
- The most efficient way of shortening time on urgent projects.

An effective Critical Path Analysis can make the difference between success and failure on complex projects. It can be very useful for assessing the importance of problems faced during the implementation of the plan. PERT is a variant of Critical Path Analysis that takes a more skeptical view of the time needed to complete each project stage.

Terminology related to PERT Charts

A PERT event: is a point that marks the start or completion of one (or more) tasks. It consumes no time, and uses no resources. It marks the completion of one (or more) tasks is not "reached" until all of the activities leading to that event have been completed.

A predecessor event: an event (or events) that immediately precedes some other event without any other events intervening. It may be the consequence of more than one activity.

A successor event: an event (or events) that immediately follows some other event without any other events intervening. It may be the consequence of more than one activity.

A PERT activity: is the actual performance of a task. It consumes time, it requires resources (such as labour, materials, space, machinery), and it can be understood as representing the time, effort, and resources required to move from one event to another. A PERT activity cannot be completed until the event preceding it has occurred.

Optimistic time (O): is the minimum possible time required to accomplish a task, assuming everything proceeds better than is normally expected.

Pessimistic time (P): is the maximum possible time required to accomplish a task, assuming everything goes wrong (but excluding major catastrophes).

Most likely time (M): is the best estimate of the time required to accomplish a task, assuming everything proceeds as normal.

Expected time (T_E): is the best estimate of the time required to accomplish a task, assuming everything proceeds as normal (the implication being that the expected time is the average time the task would require if the task were repeated on a number of occasions over an extended period of time).

$$T_E = (O + 4 \times M + P) / 6$$

***Critical Path*:** is the longest possible continuous pathway taken from the initial event to the terminal event. It determines the total calendar time required for the project; and, therefore, any time delays along the critical path will delay the reaching of the terminal event by at least the same amount.

Lead time: is the time by which a *predecessor event* must be completed in order to allow sufficient time for the activities that must elapse before a specific PERT event is reached to be completed.

Lag time: is the earliest time by which a *successor event* can follow a specific PERT event.

Program evaluation and review technique (PERT) charts depict task, duration, and dependency information. Each chart starts with an initiation node from which the first task, or tasks, originates. If multiple tasks begin at the same time, they are all started from the node or branch, or fork out from the starting point. Each task is represented by a line that states its name or other identifier, its duration, the number of people assigned to it, and in some cases the initials of the personnel assigned. The other end of the task line is terminated by another node that identifies the start of another task, or the beginning of any slack time, that is, waiting time between tasks. Each task is connected to its successor tasks in this manner forming a network of nodes and connecting lines. The chart is complete when all final tasks come together at the completion node. When slack time exists between the end of one task and the start of another, the usual method is to draw a broken or dotted line between the end of the first task and the start of the next dependent task.

A PERT chart may have multiple parallel or interconnecting networks of tasks. If the scheduled project has milestones, checkpoints, or review points (all of which are highly recommended in any project schedule), the PERT chart will note that all tasks up to that point terminate at the review node. It should be noted at this point that the project review, approvals, user reviews, and so forth all take time. This time should never be underestimated when drawing up the project plan. It is not unusual for a review to take 1 or 2 weeks. Obtaining management and user approvals may take even longer.

When drawing up the plan, be sure to include tasks for documentation writing, documentation editing, project report writing and editing, and report reproduction. These tasks are usually time-consuming; so do not underestimate how long it will take to complete them.

PERT charts are usually drawn on ruled paper with the horizontal axis indicating time period divisions in days, weeks, months, and so on. Although it is possible to draw a PERT chart for an entire project, the usual practice is to break the plans into smaller, more meaningful parts. This is very helpful if the chart has to be redrawn for any reason, such as skipped or incorrectly estimated tasks.

Many PERT charts terminate at the major review points, such as at the end of the analysis. Many organizations include funding reviews in the projects life cycle. Where this is the case, each chart terminates in the funding review node.

Funding reviews can affect a project in that they may either increase funding, in which case more people have to make available, or they may decrease funding, in which case fewer people may be available. Obviously more or less people will affect the length of time it takes to complete the project.

7.4.2 Steps in the PERT Planning Process

Identifying Activities and Milestones

The activities are the tasks required to complete the project. The milestones are the events marking the beginning and end of one or more activities. It is helpful to list the tasks in a table that in later steps can be expanded to include information on sequence and duration.

Determining Activity Sequence

This step may be combined with the activity identification step since the activity sequence is obvious for some tasks. Other tasks may require more analysis to determine the exact order in which they must be performed.

Construction of the Network Diagram

Using the activity sequence information, a network diagram can be drawn showing the sequence of the serial and parallel activities. For the original activity-on-arc model, arrowed lines depict the activities and circles depict milestones. If done manually, several drafts may be required to correctly portray the relationships among activities. Software packages simplify this step by automatically converting tabular activity information into a network diagram.

Estimation of Activity Times

Weeks are a commonly used unit of time for activity to be completed, but any consistent unit of time can be used, for example, hours or days. A distinguishing feature of PERT is its ability to deal with uncertainty in activity completion times. For each activity, the model usually includes three time estimates:

- *Optimistic time* — generally the shortest time in which the activity can be completed. It is common practice to specify optimistic times to be three standard deviations from the mean so that there is approximately a 1% chance that the activity will be completed within the optimistic time.
- *Most likely time* — the completion time having the highest probability. Note that this time is different from the *expected time.*
- *Pessimistic time* — the longest time that an activity might require. Three standard deviations from the mean are commonly used for the pessimistic time.

PERT assumes a beta probability distribution for the time estimates. Example of a beta probability distribution with minimum value a; maximum value b; and most likely value m, is shown in figure 7.3.

A new approach was developed for determining the beta distribution given a, b, and m. For a beta distribution, the expected time for each activity can be approximated using the following weighted average:

Expected time = (Optimistic + 4 × Most likely + Pessimistic) / 6

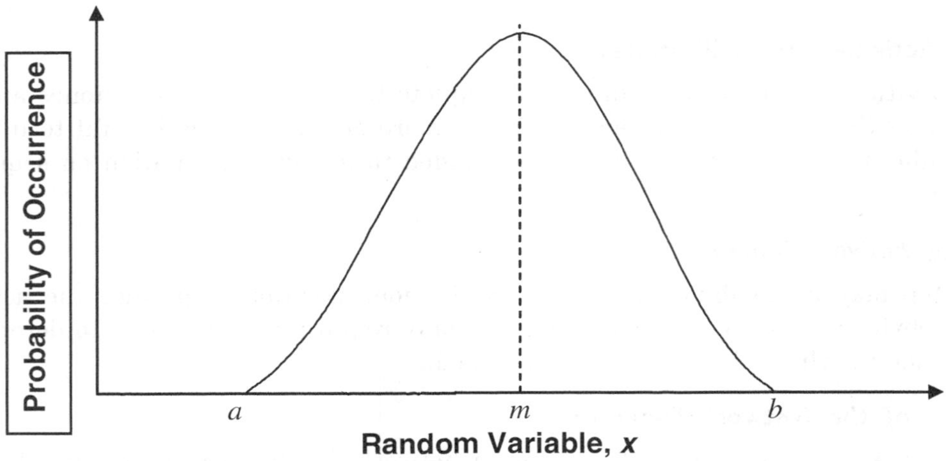

Fig. 7.3 Beta Probability Distribution

This expected time might be displayed on the network diagram. To calculate the variance for each activity completion time, if three standard deviation times were selected for the optimistic and pessimistic times, then there are six standard deviations between them, so the variance is given by:

$$\tilde{A}^2 = [(\text{Pessimistic} - \text{Optimistic})/6]^2$$

7.4.3 Benefits of PERT

PERT is useful because it provides the following information:

- Expected project completion time.
- Probability of completion before a specified date.
- The critical path activities that directly impact the completion time.
- The activities that have slack time and that can lend resources to critical path activities.
- Activity starting and end dates.

7.4.4 Limitations of PERT

The following are some of PERT's limitations:

- The activity time estimates are somewhat subjective and depend on judgment. In cases where there is little experience in performing an activity, the numbers may be only a guess. In other cases, if the person or group performing the activity estimates the time there may be bias in the estimate.
- Even if the activity times are well estimated, PERT assumes a beta distribution for these time estimates, but the actual distribution may be different.

- Even if the beta distribution assumption holds, PERT assumes that the probability distribution of the project completion time is the same as of the critical path. Because other paths can become the critical path if their associated activities are delayed, PERT consistently underestimates the expected project completion time.

The underestimation of the project completion time due to alternate paths becoming critical is perhaps the most serious of these issues. To overcome this limitation, Monte Carlo simulations can be performed on the network to eliminate this optimistic bias in the expected project completion time.

7.4.5 Implementing PERT

The first step to scheduling the project is to determine the tasks that the project requires and the order in which they must be completed. The order may be easy to record for some tasks while difficult for others. Additionally, the time estimates usually reflect the normal, non-rushed time. Many times, the time required to execute the task can be reduced for an additional cost or a reduction in the quality.

In the following example there are seven tasks, labeled A through G. Some tasks can be done concurrently (A and B) while others cannot be done until their predecessor task is complete (C cannot begin until A is complete). Additionally, each task has three time estimates: the optimistic time estimate (a), the most likely or normal time estimate (m), and the pessimistic time estimate (b). The expected time (T_E) is computed using the formula $(a + 4m + b)/6$.

Table 7.2 Activities/Task List with their Predecessors

Activity	*Predecessor*	*Opt.* a	*Norm.* m	*Pess.* b	T_E $(a + 4m + b)/6$
A	—	2	4	6	4.00
B	—	3	5	9	5.33
C	A	4	5	7	5.17
D	A	4	6	10	6.33
E	B, C	4	5	7	5.17
F	D	3	4	8	4.50
G	E	3	5	8	5.17

A network diagram can be created by hand or by using software such as Microsoft Project. There are two types of network diagrams, activity on arrow (AOA) and activity on node (AON). Activity on node diagrams are generally easier to create and interpret. To create an AON diagram, it is recommended (but not necessary) to start with a node named start. This "activity" has a duration of zero (0). Then you draw each activity that does not have a predecessor activity (A and B in this example) and connect them with an arrow. Next, since both C and D list A as a predecessor activity, their nodes are drawn with arrows coming from A. Activity E is listed with B and C as predecessor activities, so node E is drawn with arrows coming from both B and C, signifing that E cannot begin until both B and C have been completed. Activity F has D as a predecessor activity, so an arrow is drawn connecting the activities. Likewise, and arrow is drawn from E to G. Since there are no activities that come after F or G, it is recommended (but again not necessary) to connect them to a node labeled finish.

A network diagram created using Microsoft Project (MSP) is shown in figure 7.4. Note the critical path is in solid lines.

Note: All times listed are in work days (Monday - Friday, 8 AM to 5 PM with a one hour lunch break). Once this step is complete, one can draw a Gantt chart or a network diagram. Critical path is represented by vertical pattern on horizontal bars and slack is the black lines connected to the non-critical activities (shown by diagonal pattern).

ID	Task	Predecessors	Duration (Days)
1	Start		0.00
2	A	1	4 .00
3	B	1	5.33
4	C	2	5.17
5	D	2	6.33
6	E	3, 4	5.17
7	F	5	4.50
8	G	6	5.17
9	Finish	7, 8	0.00

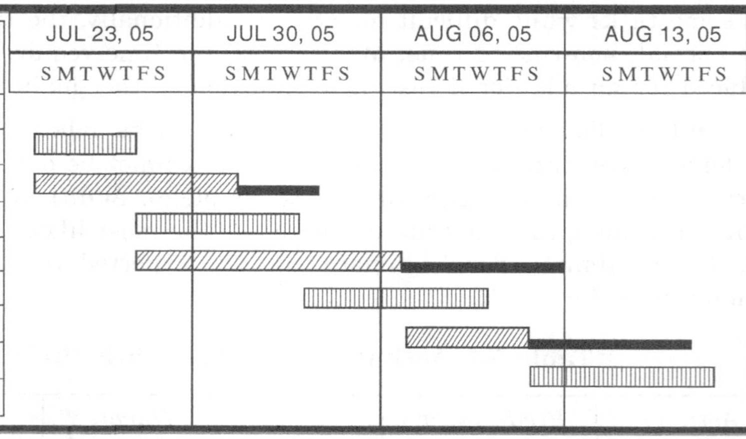

Fig. 7.4 Gantt Chart or a Network Diagram

Early start	Duration	Early Finish
	Task Name	
Late Start	Slack	Late Finish

Fig. 7.5 Task Name Types in PERT

A node like this one can be used to display the activity name, duration, ES, EF, LS, LF, and slack. By itself, the network diagram pictured above does not give much more information than a Gantt chart; however, it can be expanded to display more information. The most common information shown is:

1. The activity name
2. The normal duration time

3. The early start time (ES)
4. The early finish time (EF)
5. The late start time (LS)
6. The late finish time (LF)
7. The slack

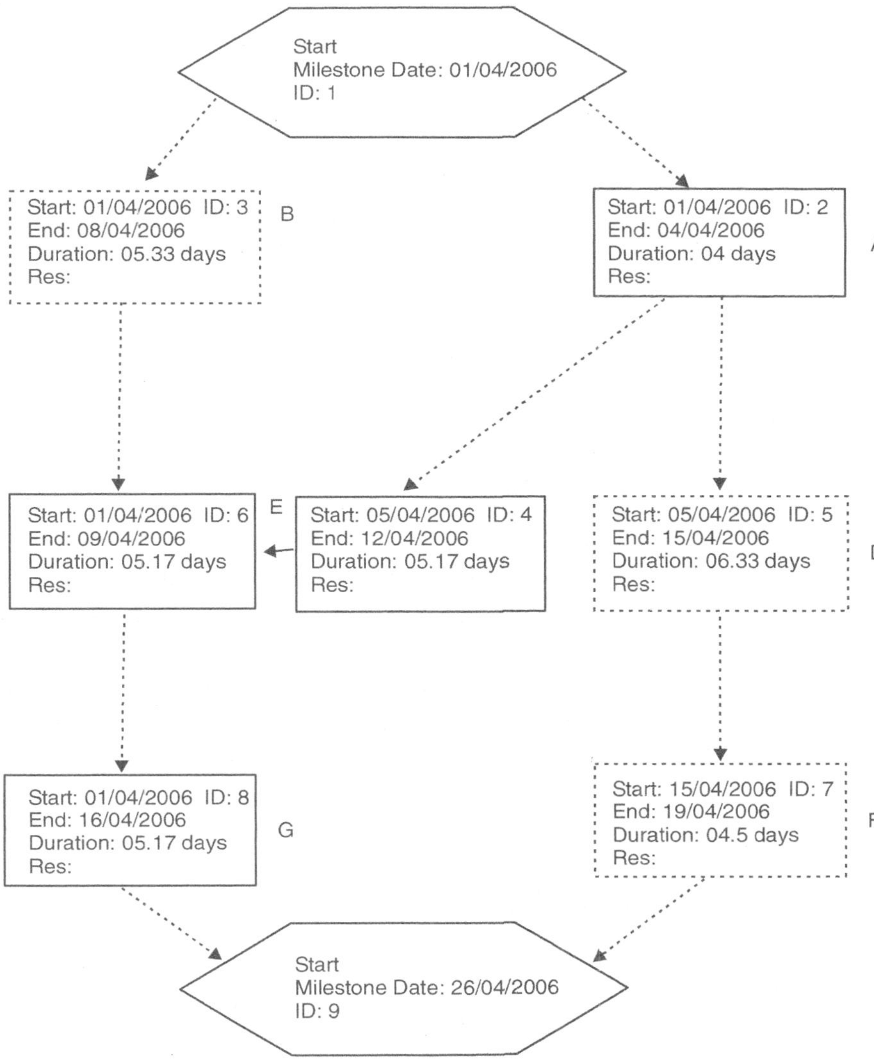

Fig. 7.6 Task Flow Diagram of above Network Diagram

In order to determine this information it is assumed that the activities and normal duration times are given. The first step is to determine the ES and EF. The ES is defined as the maximum EF of all predecessor activities, unless the activity in question is the first activity, which the ES is zero (0). The EF is the ES plus the task duration (EF = ES + duration).

1. The ES for start is zero since it is the first activiy. Since the duration is zero, the EF is also zero. This EF is used as the ES for A and B.
2. The ES for A is zero. The duration (4 work days) is added to the ES to get an EF of four. This EF is used as the ES for C and D.
3. The ES for B is zero. The duration (5.33 work days) is added to the ES to get an EF of 5.33.
4. The ES for C is four. The duration (5.17 work days) is added to the ES to get an EF of 9.17.
5. The ES for D is four. The duration (6.33 work days) is added to the ES to get an EF of 10.33. This EF is used as the ES for F.
6. The ES for E is the greatest EF of its predecessor activities (B and C). Since B has an EF of 5.33 and C has an EF of 9.17, the ES of E is 9.17. The duration (5.17 work days) is added to the ES to get an EF of 14.34. This EF is used as the ES for G.
7. The ES for F is 10.33. The duration (4.5 work days) is added to the ES to get an EF of 14.83.
8. The ES for G is 14.34. The duration (5.17 work days) is added to the ES to get an EF of 19.51.
9. The ES for finish is the greatest EF of its predecessor activities (F and G). Since F has an EF of 14.83 and G has an EF of 19.51, the ES of finish is 19.51. Finish is a milestone (and therefore has duration of zero), so the EF is also 19.51.

Barring any unforseen events, the project should take 19.51 work days to complete. The next step is to determine the late start (LS) and late finish (LF) of each activity. This will eventually show if there are activities that have slack. The LF is defined as the minimum LS of all successor activities, unless the activity is the last activity, for which the LF equals the EF. The LS is the LF minus the task duration (LS = LF - duration).

- The LF for finish is equal to the EF (19.51 work days) since it is the last activity in the project. Since the duration is zero, the LS is also 19.51 work days. This will be used as the LF for F and G.
- The LF for G is 19.51 work days. The duration (5.17 work days) is subtracted from the LF to get a LS of 14.34 work days. This will be used as the LF for E.
- The LF for F is 19.51 work days. The duration (4.5 work days) is subtracted from the LF to get a LS of 15.01 work days. This will be used as the LF for D.
- The LF for E is 14.34 work days. The duration (5.17 work days) is subtracted from the LF to get a LS of 9.17 work days. This will be used as the LF for B and C.
- The LF for D is 15.01 work days. The duration (6.33 work days) is subtracted from the LF to get a LS of 8.68 work days.

- The LF for C is 9.17 work days. The duration (5.17 work days) is subtracted from the LF to get a LS of 4 work days.
- The LF for B is 9.17 work days. The duration (5.33 work days) is subtracted from the LF to get a LS of 3.84 work days.
- The LF for A is the minimum LS of its successor activities. Since C has a LS of 4 work days and D has a LS of 8.68 work days, the LF for A is 4 work days. The duration (4 work days) is subtracted from the LF to get a LS of 0 work days.
- The LF for start is the minimum LS of its successor activities. Since A has a LS of 0 work days and B has a LS of 3.84 work days, the LS is 0 work days.

The next step is to determine the critical path and if any activities have slack. The critical path is the path that takes the longest to complete. To determine the path times, add the task durations for all available paths. Activities that have slack can be delayed without changing the overall time of the project. Slack is computed in one of two ways, slack = LF - EF or slack = LS - ES. Activities that are on the critial path have a slack of zero (0).

- The duration of path A-D-F is 14.83 work days.
- The duration of path A-C-E-G is 19.51 work days.
- The duration of path B-E-G is 15.67 work days.

The critical path is A-C-E-G and the critical time is 19.51 work days. It is important to note that there can be more than one critical path (in a project more complex than this example) or the critical path can change. For example, let us say that activities D and F take their pessimistic (*b*) times to complete instead of their expected (TE) times. The critical path is now A-D-F and the critical time is 22 work days. On the other hand, if activity C can be crashed to one work day, the path time for aceg is reduced to 15.34 work days, which is slightly less than the time of the new critical path, beg (15.67 work days). Assuming these scenarios do not happen, the slack for each activity can now be determined.

- Start and finish are milestones and by definition have no duration, therefore they can have no slack (0 work days).
- The activities on the critical path by definition have a slack of zero; however, it is always a good idea to check the math anyway when drawing by hand.
- $LF_A - EF_A = 4 - 4 = 0$
- $LF_C - EF_C = 9.17 - 9.17 = 0$
- $LF_E - EF_E = 14.34 - 14.34 = 0$
- $LF_G - EF_G = 19.51 - 19.51 = 0$
- Activity B has a LF of 9.17 and a EF of 5.33, so the slack is 3.84 work days.
- Activity D has a LF of 15.01 and a EF of 10.33, so the slack is 4.68 work days.
- Activity F has a LF of 19.51 and a EF of 14.83, so the slack is 3.84 work days.

Therefore, activity B can be delayed almost 4 work days without delaying the project. Likewise, activity D or activity F can be delayed 4.68 work days without delaying the project (alternatively, D and F can be delayed 2.34 work days each).

7.4.6 Critical Path Method (CPM)

The CPM was developed in the 1950s by DuPont, and was first used in missile-defense construction projects. Since that time, the CPM has been adapted to other fields including hardware and software product research and development. Various computer programs are available to help project managers use the CPM.

The essential technique for using CPM is to construct a model of the project that includes the following:

1. A list of all activities required completing the project (also known as Work breakdown structure),
2. The time (duration) that each activity will take to completion, and
3. The dependencies between the activities.

Using these values, CPM calculates the starting and ending times for each activity, determines which activities are critical to the completion of a project (called the critical path), and reveals those activities with "float time" (are less critical). In project management, a critical path is the sequence of project network activities with the longest overall duration, determining the shortest time possible to complete the project. Any delay of an activity on the critical path directly impacts the planned project completion date (*i.e.,* there is no float on the critical path). A project can have several, parallel critical paths. An additional parallel path through the network with the total durations shorter than the critical path is called a sub-critical or non-critical path.

These results allow managers to prioritize activities for the effective management of project completion. Originally, the critical path method considered only logical dependencies among terminal elements. Since then, it has been expanded to allow for the inclusion of resources related to each activity. This capability allows for the exploration of a related concept called the critical chain, which determines project duration based upon both time and resource dependencies.

Since project schedules change on a regular basis, CPM allows continuous monitoring of the schedule, allows the project manager to track the critical activities, and ensures that non-critical activities do not interfere with the critical ones. In addition, the method can easily incorporate the concepts of stochastic predictions, using the Program Evaluation and Review Technique.

Currently, there are several software solutions available in industry today that use the CPM method of scheduling. However, the method was developed and used (for decades) without the aid of computers (with pencil and paper).

A Critical Path Method is a project management tool used to formulate a time frame for a project in order to determine where potential delays are most likely to occur. The process includes a step-by-step process that provides the developer with a visual representation of potential bottlenecks throughout the course of the project.

The CPM was originally designed as a method of organizing and tracking the numerous activities regarding the Polaris missile defense program. However, a CPM is useful with many projects and makes the planning process easier.

The critical path method (CPM) is a step-by-step technique for process planning that defines critical and non-critical tasks with the goal of preventing time-frame problems and process bottlenecks. The CPM is ideally suited to projects consisting of numerous activities that interact in a complex manner. In applying the CPM, there are several steps that can be summarized as follows:

- Define the required tasks and put them down in an ordered (sequenced) list.
- Create a flowchart or other diagram showing each task in relation to the others.
- Identify the critical and non-critical relationships (paths) among tasks.
- Determine the expected completion or execution time for each task.
- Locate or devise alternatives (backups) for the most critical paths.

7.4.7 CPM Charts

Critical Path Method (CPM) charts are similar to PERT charts and are sometimes known as PERT/CPM. In a CPM chart, the critical path is indicated. A critical path consists that set of dependent tasks (each dependent on the preceding one), which together take the longest time to complete. Although it is not normally done, a CPM chart can define multiple equally critical paths. Tasks, which fall on the critical path, should be noted in some way, so that they may be given special attention. One way is to draw critical path tasks with a double line instead of a single line.

Tasks, which fall on the critical path, should receive special attention by both the project manager and the personnel assigned to them. The critical path for any given method may shift as the project progresses; this can happen when tasks are completed either behind or ahead of schedule, causing other tasks which may still be on schedule to fall on the new critical path.

By Completing a CPM the following will be known:

1. The total time to complete the project.
2. The scheduled start and finish dates foe each task pertaining to the projects completion.
3. The tasks that are "critical" to the project and must be completed exactly as scheduled.
4. The "slack" time available in non-critical tasks, as well as how long they can be delayed before they affect the project finish date.

Creating a CPM

Creating a CPM can be quite easy when these simple steps are followed:

1. List the activities to be considered in approximate order.
2. Number the events, estimate the time required for each, and determine the antecedents.
3. Arrange the events in a CPM diagram showing the numbered events, time required, and antecedent relationships with connecting lines.

4. Determine the *earliest* times for starting and ending the events.
5. Determine the *latest* times for starting the events.
6. Determine the critical path.

Step I List of Activities

First of all for each activity, show the earliest start date, estimated length of time it will take, and whether it is parallel or sequential. If tasks are sequential, show which stage they depend on. The chart representation in tabular form is shown in table 7.3 (see below):

Table 7.3 Task List: Planning a custom-written computer project

S.N.	*Task*	*Possible start*	*Length*	*Type*	*Dependent*
1.	High level analysis	Week 1	5 days	Sequential	
2.	Selection of hardware platform	Week 1	1 day	Sequential	1
3.	Installation and commissioning of hardware	Week 3	2 weeks	Parallel	2
4.	Detailed analysis of core modules	Week 1	2 weeks	Sequential	1
5.	Detailed analysis of supporting utilities	Week 1	2 weeks	Sequential	4
6.	Programming of core modules	Week 4	3 weeks	Sequential	4
7.	Programming of supporting modules	Week 4	3 weeks	Sequential	5
8.	Quality assurance of core modules	Week 5	1 week	Sequential	6
9.	Quality assurance of supporting modules	Week 5	1 week	Sequential	7
10.	Core module training	Week 7	1 day	Parallel	6
11.	Development of accounting reporting	Week 6	1 week	Parallel	5
12.	Development of management reporting	Week 6	1 week	Parallel	5
13.	Development of management analysis	Week 6	2 weeks	Sequential	5
14.	Detailed training	Week 7	1 week	Sequential	1-13
15.	Documentation	Week 4	2 weeks	Parallel	13

The start week shows when resources become available. Whether a task is parallel or sequential depends largely on context. All activities should be written in a list. For this example, we will use the activities listed below in determining the critical path of getting ready for a day.

Table 7.4 Task to be analyzed by CPM

Task
Wake up
Shower
Get ready
Dress
Eat
Make bed
Review to do list
Brush teeth
Drive to work
Step 2 Analyze List

Step 2 Analyze List

Critical Path Analyses are presented using circle and arrow diagrams. In these, circles show events within the project, such as the start and finish of tasks. Circles are normally numbered to allow you to identify them.

An arrow running between two event circles shows the activity needed to complete that task. A description of the task is written underneath the arrow. The length of the task is shown above it. By convention, all arrows run left to right. An example of a very simple diagram is shown below:

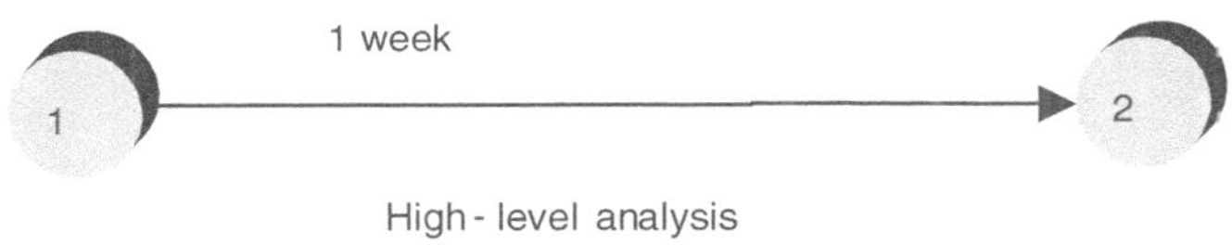

Fig. 7.7 Simple arrow and circle diagram

This shows the start event (circle 1), and the completion of the 'High Level Analysis' task (circle 2). The arrow between them shows the activity of carrying out the High Level Analysis. This activity should take 1 week. One activity cannot start until another has been completed; we start the arrow for the dependent activity at the completion event circle of the previous activity. An example of this is shown in figure 7.8 below:

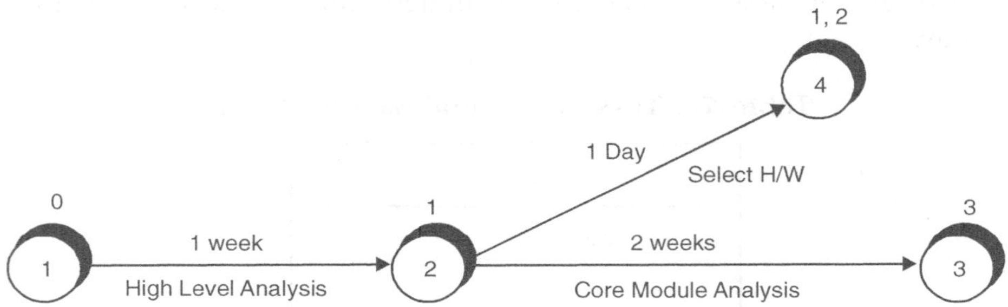

Fig. 7.8 Circles and arrow diagram showing two activities that cannot be started until the first activity has been completed

Here the activities of 'Selecting Hardware' and 'Core Module Analysis' cannot be started until 'High Level Analysis' has been completed. This diagram also brings out a number of other important points:

- Within Critical Path Analysis, we refer to activities by the numbers in the circles at each end. For example, the task 'Core Module Analysis' would be called 'activity 2 to 3'. 'Select Hardware' would be 'activity 2 to 4'.
- Activities are not drawn to scale. In the diagram above, activities are 1 week long, 2 weeks long and 1 day long. Arrows in this case are all the same length.

In the example above, you can see numbers above the circles. These show the earliest possible time that this stage in the project will be reached. Here units are whole weeks. A different case is shown below:

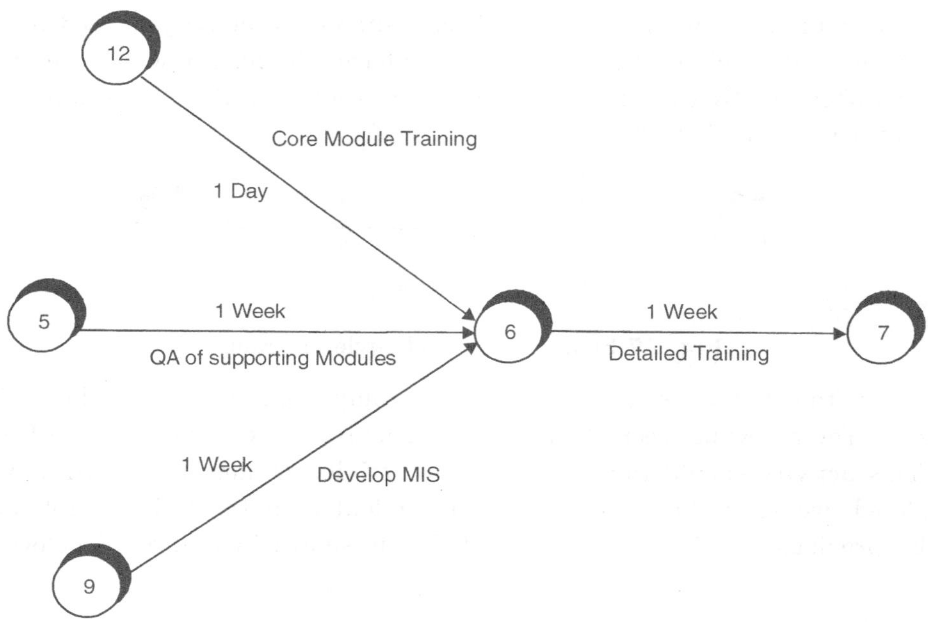

Fig. 7.9 Circle and arrow diagram showing an activity (6 to 7) that cannot start until other activities (12 to 6, 5 to 6, and 9 to 6) have been completed.

Here activity 6 to 7 cannot start until the other three activities (12 to 6, 5 to 6 and 9 to 6) have been completed. As an example, see figure 7.10 for the full circle and arrow diagram for the computer project

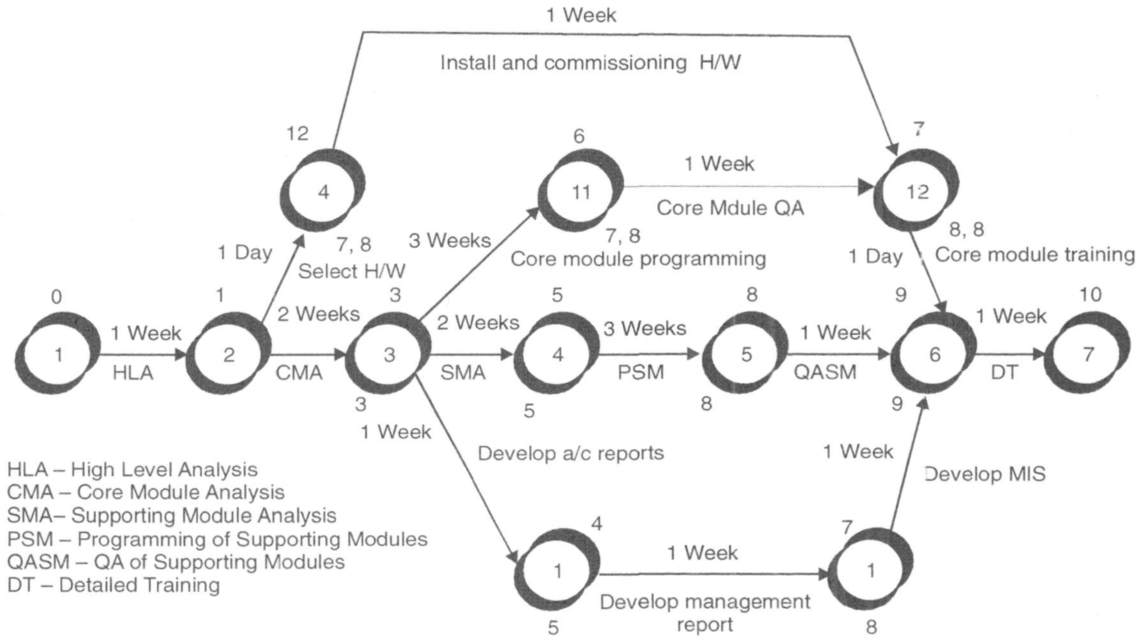

Fig. 7.10 Critical Path Analysis for a software Project

This shows all the activities that will take place as part of the project. Notice that each event circle has a figure below it as well as a figure above. This shows the latest time that it can be reached with the project still being completed in the minimum time possible. You can calculate this by starting at the last event (in this case number 7), and working backwards.

You can see that event 4 can be completed any time between 1.2 weeks in and 7.8 weeks in. The timing of this event is not critical. Events 1 to 2, 2 to 3, 3 to 4, 4 to 5, 5 to 6 and 6 to 7 must be started and completed on time if the project is to be completed in 10 weeks. This is the 'critical path' — these activities must be very closely managed to ensure that activities are completed on time. If jobs on the critical path slip, immediate action should be taken to get the project back on schedule. Otherwise completion of the whole project will slip.

7.4.6 Crash Action

You may find that you need to complete a project earlier than your Critical Path Analysis says is possible. In this case you need to take action to reduce the length of time spent on project stages. You could mound resources into every project activity to bring down time spent on each. This would probably consume huge additional resources. A more efficient way of doing this would be to look only at activities on the critical path.

As with Gantt Charts, in practice project managers tend to use software tools like Microsoft Project to create CPA Charts. Not only do this ease make them easier to draw, they also make modification of plans easier and provide facilities for monitoring progress against plans. Microsoft Project is reviewed at the top of our left hand title bar.

In this step, each process is ordered in the approximate order of completion. All processes are also given an estimated amount of time required to complete the task and all predecessor processes are also recorded. For example, the following table shows that in order to eat breakfast the person must have already dressed them and gotten ready for the day.

Table 7.5 Scheduled tasks and their completion time

S. No.	*Task*	*Time (Minutes)*	*Predecessor*
1	Wake up	5	-
2	Shower	10	1
3	Get ready	20	2
4	Dress	10	2
5	Eat	15	3, 4
6	Make bed	5	1
7	Review to do list	10	5
8	Brush teeth	5	5
9	Drive to work	20	6, 7, 8

Step 3 Creating the Diagram

In this step we arrange the events on a CPM diagram showing the events with numbered boxes and the antecedent relationships with connection lines. There are many methods of constructing a CPM diagram, but we choose to use boxes instead of circles. Each area of the boxes is explained in the box below. Also, some diagrams prefer to include the time of the project on the relationship line, but we believe the method below is thorough and precise.

Example Box:

ID (ID #)	**ES** (Earliest Start Time)	**EF** (Earliest Finish Time)
ID (Task duration)	**LS** (Latest Start Time)	**LF** (Latest Finish Time)

Step 4 Earliest Start Times

In this step we determine the earliest times for the starting and ending events. Event 1 can be started immediately, but events 2 and 6 cannot begin until event 1 is completed, 5 minutes later. Similarly, event 9 cannot begin until events 6, 7, and 8 are finished. Since event 9 must wait for all three of these activities to be completed, its finishing time will be the length of its task added to its starting time, which will be equal to the largest early finish time of the directly preceding events. The example of our CPM diagram with the earliest start times and earliest finish times can be seen below.

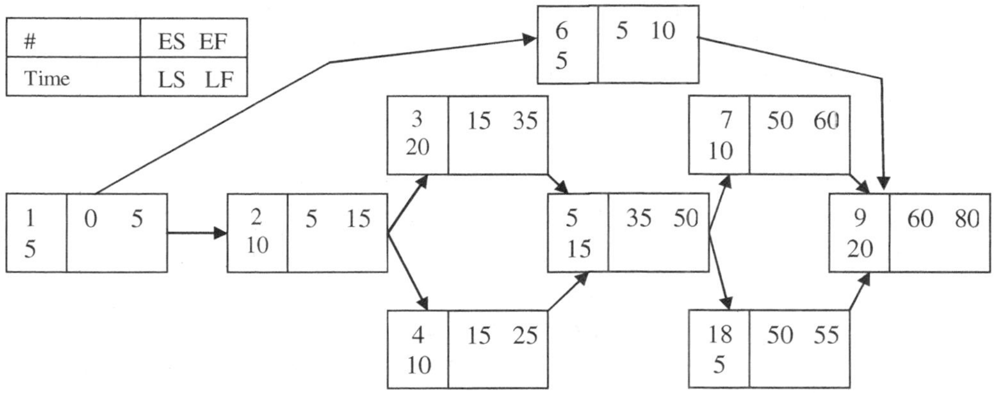

Fig. 7.12 Activities with ES and EF

Step 5 Latest Start Times

Determine the latest times for the ending events. This is completed by working backwards through the diagram. In each case, the latest starting time of an activity is equal to the earliest starting time of the activity directly following it minus the time required for the current project. In our example, as shown below, activity 5 has a latest starting time of 35 (50-15).

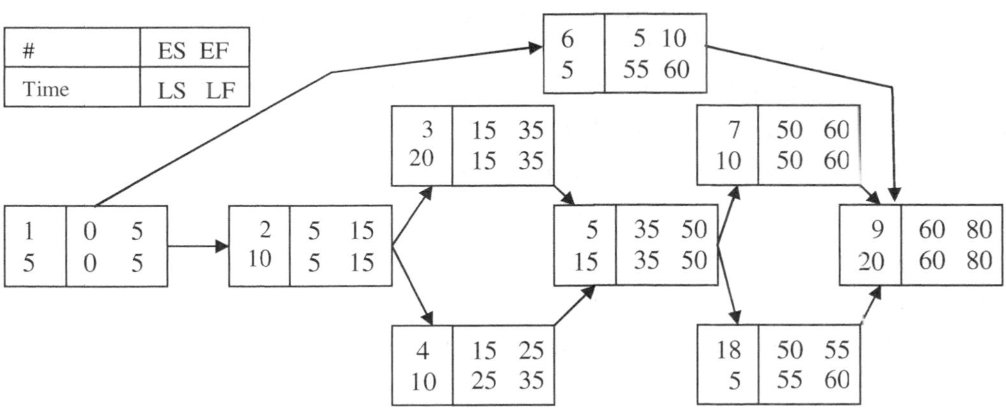

Fig. 7.13 Activities with ES, EF, LS, and LF

Step 6 Finding the critical path

If the earliest time that an event can be started is the same as the latest that it could be started (ES = LS), then the timing of that event is critical. The critical path is found by connecting the critical events, and is shown by double lines on the diagram. One must be aware that it is possible to have two separate critical paths. All other activities that are not part of the critical path have "slack" time, or time that an activity can be delayed without affecting the completion time of the project. Below is the completed diagram with the critical path.

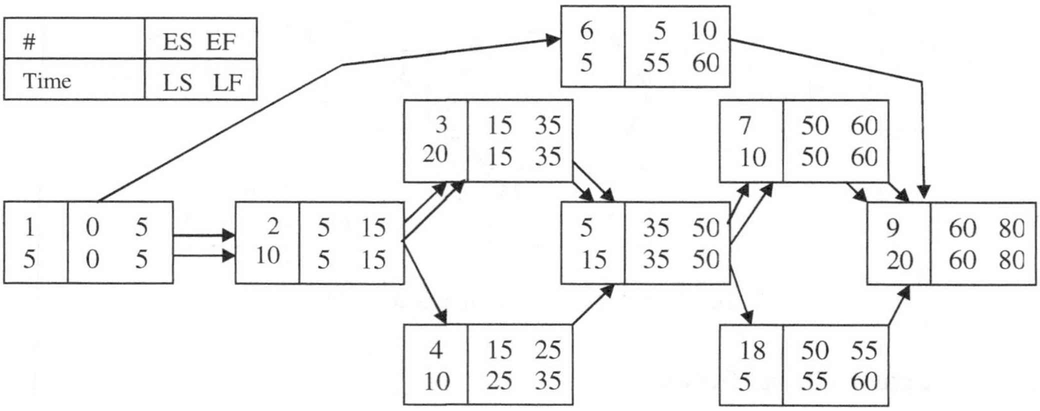

Fig. 7.14 Completed diagram with the critical path

Advantages of Using a CPM

- Helpful for scheduling, monitoring, and controlling projects.
- A project manager can determine actual dates for each activity and compare what should be happening to what is taking place and react accordingly.
- The activities and their outcomes can be shown as a network.

Displays dependencies to help scheduling.

- Evaluates which activities can run parallel to each other.
- Determines slack and float times.
- Widely used in industry.
- Can define multiple, equally critical paths.
- CMP determines the project duration, which minimized the sum of direct and indirect costs.

Disadvantages of Using a CPM

However, there are drawbacks of this technique, as estimations are used to calculate times; if one mistake is made the whole analysis could be flawed causing major upset in the organization of a project.

- CPM's can be complicated, and complexity increases for larger projects.
- It does not handle the scheduling of personnel or the allocation of resources.
- The critical path is not always clear and needs to be calculated carefully.
- Estimating activity completion times can be difficult.

Determining the Critical Path

Adding the times for the activities in each sequence and determining the longest path in the project determine the critical path. The critical path determines the total calendar time required for the project. If activities outside the critical path speed up or slow down (within deadline) the total project time does not change. The amount of time that a non-critical path activity can be delayed without delaying the project is referred to as *slack time*.

If the critical path is not immediately obvious, it may be helpful to determine the following four quantities for each activity:

- ES - Earliest Start time
- EF - Earliest Finish time
- LS - Latest Start time
- LF - Latest Finish time

These times are calculated using the expected time for the relevant activities. The earliest start and finish times of each activity are determined by working forward through the network and determining the earliest time at which an activity can start and finish considering its predecessor activities. The latest start and finish times are the latest times that an activity can start and finish without delaying the project. LS and LF are found by working backward through the network. The difference in the latest and earliest finish of each activity is that activity's slack. The critical path then is the path through the network in which none of the activities have slack.

Note: The slack of an event is a measure of the excess time and resources available in achieving this event. Positive slack would indicate *ahead of schedule*; negative slack would indicate *behind schedule*; and zero slack would indicate *on schedule.*

The variance in the project completion time can be calculated by summing the variances in the completion times of the activities in the critical path. Given this variance, one can calculate the probability that the project will be completed by a certain date assuming a normal probability distribution for the critical path. The normal distribution assumption holds if the number of activities in the path is large enough for the central limit theorem to be applied.

Since the critical path determines the completion date of the project, adding the resources required to decrease the time for the activities in the critical path can accelerate the project. Such a shortening of the project sometimes is referred to as *project crashing*.

7.4.8 Update as Project Progresses

Make adjustments in the PERT chart as the project progresses. As the project unfolds, the estimated times can be replaced with actual times. In cases where there are delays, additional resources may be needed to stay on schedule and the PERT chart may be modified to reflect the new situation.

7.4.9 Why Critical Path Analysis and PERT Charts

Basically Critical Path Analysis and PERT Charts are used for planning and scheduling more complex projects. Critical Path Analysis and PERT are powerful tools that help you to schedule and manage complex projects. They were developed in the 1950s to control large defense projects, and have been used routinely since then.

As with Gantt Charts, Critical Path Analysis (CPA) helps you to plan all tasks that must be completed as part of a project. They act as the basis both for preparation of a schedule, and of resource planning. During management of a project, they allow you to monitor achievement of project goals. They help you to see where remedial action needs to be taken to get a project back on course.

The benefit of using CPA over Gantt Charts is that Critical Path Analysis formally identifies tasks which must be completed on time for the whole project to be completed on time, and also identifies which tasks can be delayed for a while if resource needs to be reallocated to catch up on missed tasks. The disadvantage of CPA is that the relation of tasks to time is not as immediately obvious as with Gantt Charts. This can make them more difficult to understand for someone who is not familiar with the technique.

A further benefit of Critical Path Analysis is that it helps you to identify the minimum length of time needed to complete a project. Where you need to run an accelerated project, it helps you to identify which project steps you should accelerate to complete the project within the available time. This helps you to minimize cost while still achieving your objective.

7.4.10 CPM vs. PERT

Both CPM and PERT (Program Evaluation and Review Technique) provide the user with project management tools to plan, monitor, and update their project as it progresses. There are many similarities and differences between the two, however.

Similarities between PERT and CPM

- Both follow the same steps and use network diagrams
- Both are used to plan the scheduling of individual activities that make up a project
- They can be used to determine the earliest/latest start and finish times for each activity

Differences between PERT and CPM

- PERT is probabilistic whereas CPM is deterministic
- In CPM, estimates of activity duration are based on historical data
- In PERT, estimates are uncertain and we talk of ranges of duration and the probability that an activity duration will fall into that range
- CPM concentrates on Time/Cost trade off.

7.4.11 AON Network with Forward Pass and Backward Pass

Activity-on-Node (AON) method is also known as precedence diagram method for network construction in which an activity is represented by a node. Arrows between the nodes on the AON network represent the dependencies among activities. The arrows indicate how the activities are related and the sequence in which things must be accomplished. The length and slope of the arrow are arbitrary and set for convenience of drawing the network. Inside the box it contains identified activities and identification numbers for network construction and analysis.

Forward Pass Method—Earliest Times

The forward pass starts from the first project activity A and traces each path through the network to reach the last project activity. When tracing along the path, activity times are added gradually. The longest path denotes the project completion time for the plan is called the critical path. As shown in figure below, the early start (ES) time for activity A is zero. The early finish (EF) for activity A is (ES + Dur = EF or 0 + 3 = 3). Activity A is also the predecessor for activities B, C and D thus the earliest these activities can begin is upon completing activity A after 3 workdays which is also the ES times for activities B, C and D. The EF times for activities B, C and D are 8, 9 and 6 workdays respectively. The ES for activity E, a merge activity is 9 workdays as all preceding activities of B and C must be completed before activity E. Since activity C finishes in 9 workdays and also controls the ES for activity F. The ES for activity G can also be determined accordingly. The EF of 18 workdays for activity E is also the ES for activity H which adds up the duration of 3 workdays to become 21 workdays to complete the work package from kick off meeting to design freeze stage. It must be noted that Forward Pass requires three things when computing early activity times:

1. Add activity times along each path in the network (ES + Dur = EF).
2. Carry the early finish (EF) to the next activity where it becomes its early start (ES) unless.
3. Next succeeding activity is a merge activity. In this case is to select the largest early finish number (EF) of all its immediate predecessor activities.

In this, project network diagrams can help to track and monitoring work progress more readily based on individual nodes albeit attention must be directed on software definition which is the critical path in this case example to ensure the design freeze package can be completed in time for design freeze meeting. Forward pass method is normally used to determine time taken required to complete a work package if deadline for the project is not given.

Backward Pass Method—Latest Times

The backward pass begins with the last project activity and traces each path in a reversed order through the network to reach the first project activity A. When tracing along the path, activity times are subtracted gradually until it reaches zero as late start (LS) for activity A. As shown in figure below that the late finish (LF) for activity H is 21 workdays and LS of 18 workdays (LF - Dur = LS or 21-3 = 18). The LS for activity H becomes the LF for activities E hence G. The LS for activities E and G becomes 9 workdays (18 - 9 = 9) and 13 workdays (18 - 5 = 13) respectively. The LS for activity G is the LF for activity F with its LS of 11 workdays. Activities B and C are burst activities tied to activities E and F. The LF for activity B is controlled by the LS of activities E and F, as a result the LS for activity E is 9 workdays hence LF for activity B and C are having 9 workdays. We can now determine for activity A, the LF is 3 workdays and LS is 0 workdays (3 -3 = 0). The backward pass, there are three things need to be remembered:

1. Subtract activity times along each path starting with the project end activity (LF Dur = LS).
2. Carry the LS to the next preceding activity to establish its LF, unless
3. The next preceding activity is a burst activity; in this case you select the smallest LS of all its immediate successor activities to establish its LF.

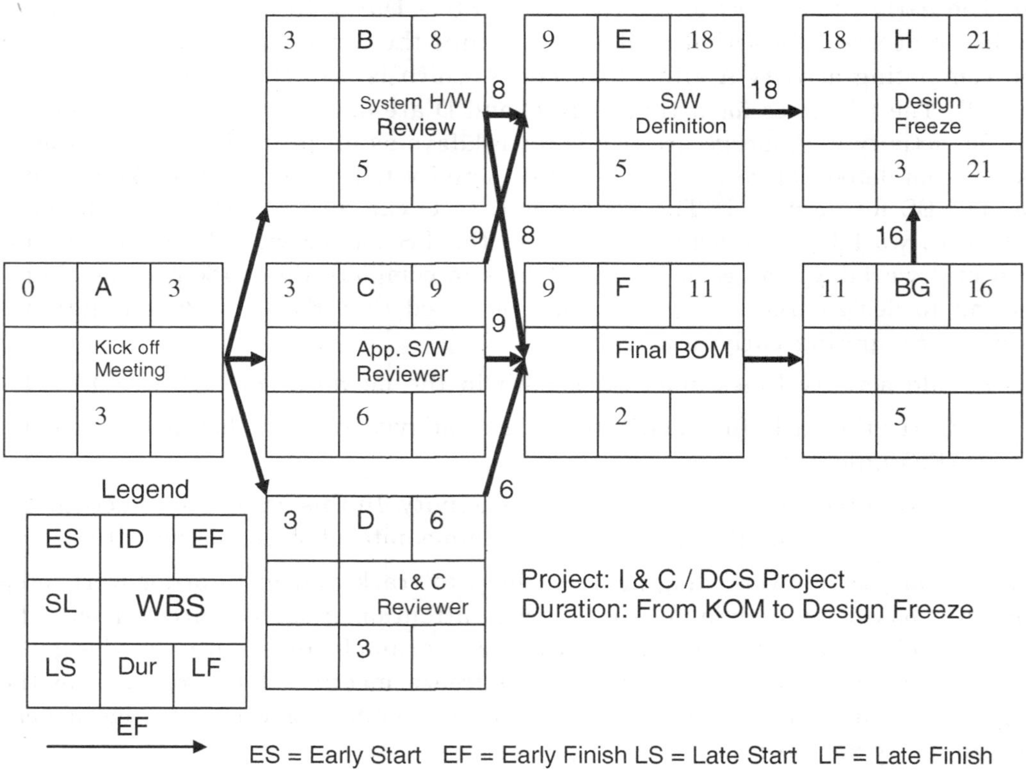

Fig. 7.15 AON Forward Pass Method

With the backward pass method of calculation, it verifies and confirms this work package can be completed in 21 workdays from kick off meeting until design freeze stage. Thus, backward pass method is useful in a situation where a project deadline is given, but to establish if WBS must be adjusted to meet the required deadline.

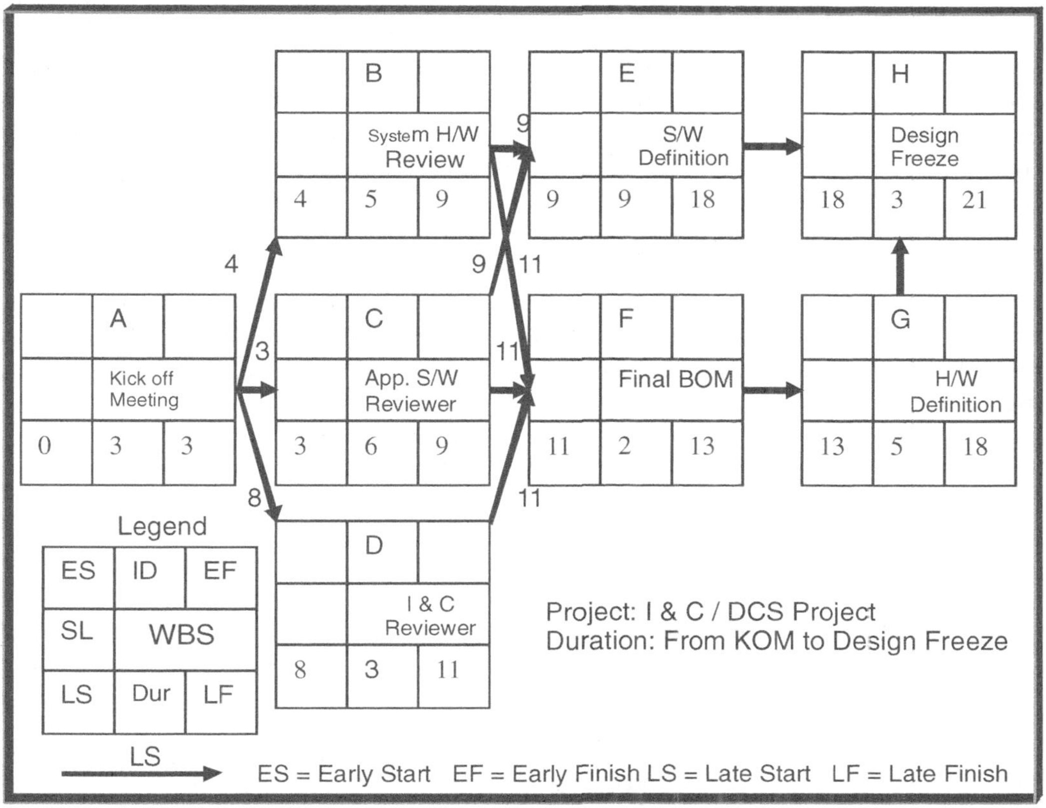

Fig. 7.16 AON Backward Pass Method

7.4.12 AOA Network with Forward Pass and Backward Pass

Activity-on-Arrow (AOA) method is also known as arrow diagram method. CPM (critical path method) or PERT (program evaluation and review technique) utilizes arrows and nodes as network building blocks however its arrows represent individual activities that require time. The length and slope of arrows have no significance on the network. A node represents an event with a small circle depicting points in time but do no consume time. Each activity on the network has a start node as event 1 and an end event node with a large number without repeating the numbers. Dummy activities are used to maintain a logical sequence of network dependencies when two or more parallel activities are having the same beginning and ending event nodes.

Forward Pass Method—Earliest Times

The forward pass in AOA uses the same concepts found in the AON procedure. The key difference lies in the use of events to set early and late start and finish times for activities. As shown in figure 7.17 a sequence of events, activities and durations for early start times and finish times. Also near each event is a box for recording event times and slack purpose. Event 1 is a start event with early start time (ES) at zero and early finish

(EF) is 3 workdays (ES + Dur = EF or 0 + 3 = 3), which is placed at the arrow-head of activity A. The earliest event 2 to occur is after activity A of 3 workdays, is also the ES for activities B, C and D of 8, 9 and 6 workdays respectively. The ES for dummy activity X from event 3 to event 4 is 9 workdays and its EF is also 9 workdays (9 + 0 = 9). Despite the dummy activity has zero duration; it must be included in the forward and backward pass computations. For event 4 and event 5 both are the merged events that required selection among activities merging into these events. Event 4 has activity B and X, which is the dummy activity, the largest EF for these two activities, is 9 workdays for event 4. Likewise for event 5 is controlled by activities D and Y, since activity Y has the largest early finish of 9 workdays, it establishes the ES for event 5 and activity F. Hence, the EF for activities E and G are 18 and 16 workdays respectively. The ES for activity H is 18 workdays plus the duration of 3 days to arrive at 21 workdays as EF at event 8 under the work package.

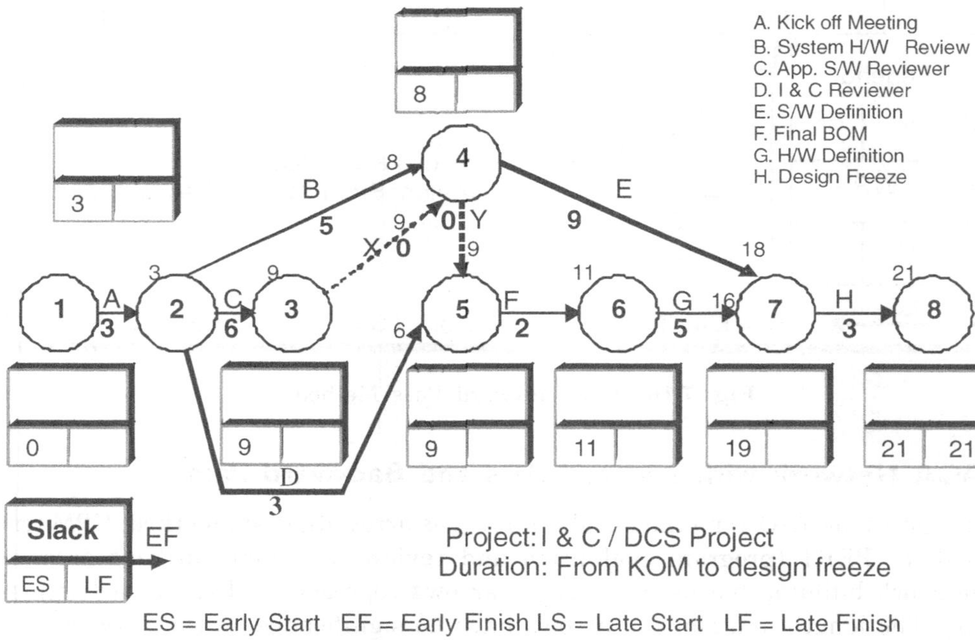

Fig. 7.17 AOA Forward Pass Method

Backward Pass Method—Latest Times

The backward pass procedure is similar to that of AON procedure as shown in figure 7.17 with last event 8 of 21 workdays as late finish (LF) to begin and subtracting the duration to arrive at late start (LS) of 18 workdays at the tail of the arrow of activity H in the reversed order. The LS for activity H becomes the LF for event 7. This procedure continues until event 4 which is a burst event. The LS for activity E is 9 workdays and for activity Y is 11 workdays respectively. The smallest time is 9 workdays as LF for event 4. The next burst event is event 2 where the LS for activities B, C and D are 4, 3 and

8 workdays respectively. Activity C controls the LF for event 2 with 3 workdays and to end activity A at event 1 with time zero.

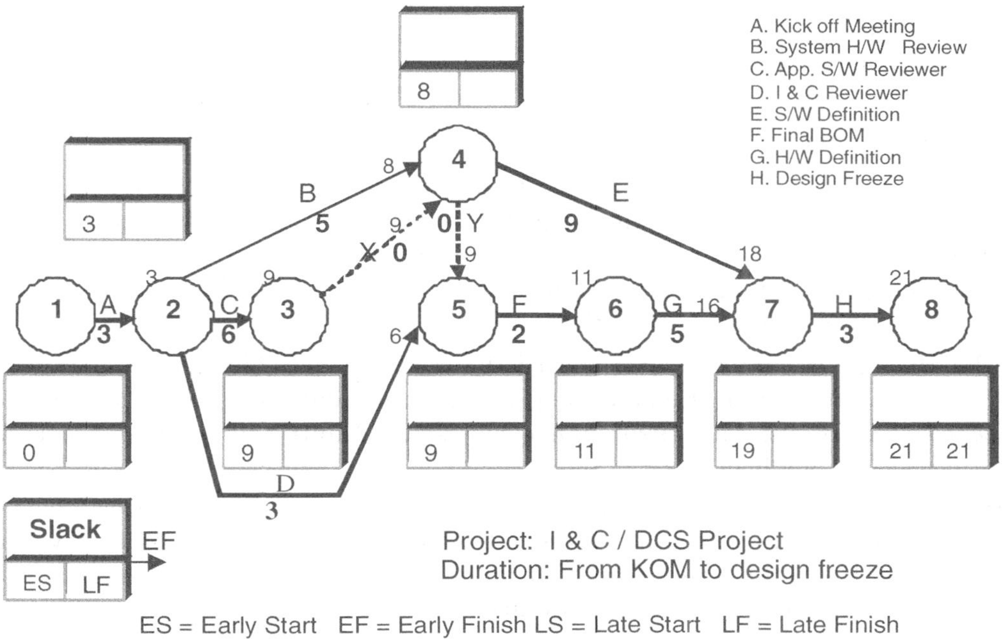

Fig. 7.18 AOA Backward Pass Method

7.4.13 Project Planning and Control Tools

There are hundreds of commercialized project planning and control tools in the market and they can be grouped into four main categories:

1. Entry level for beginners who wish to learn the basics and interdependencies of WBS chart and PERT chart that can be downloaded from websites as free trial versions; they are extremely useful for starters on small projects;
2. Mid level for project managers who have the fundamentals in project planning and control to leverage on various features these tools provide such as the Microsoft Office enterprise project management solution 2007. MS project is by far the most commonly adopted project management tool from small, mid and large-scale projects;
3. High level applications designed for project managers and project planners for specific applications and industries. It offers a wide range of options for senior executives, functional managers and other project stakeholders to collaborate in large-scale projects.
4. Advanced level meant for highly complex projects using four dimensional simulation models to organize blueprints, schedules and cost reports into a database that

integrates 3D drawings with time dimension apart from schedules, costs, and resources. These tool scan visualize the progress scenario for project analysis prior to project initiation which is critical for construction industry. It also supports drawing files created in AutoCAD or MicroStation, and schedules created by Microsoft Project.

7.4.14 Gantt Chart

A Gantt chart is a popular type of bar chart that illustrates a project schedule. Gantt charts illustrate the start and finish dates of the terminal elements and summary elements of a project. Terminal elements and summary elements comprise the work breakdown structure of the project. Some Gantt charts also show the dependency (*i.e.*, precedence network) relationships between activities.

In the 1980s, personal computers eased the creation and editing of elaborate Gantt charts. These desktop applications were primarily intended for project managers and project schedulers. In the late 1990s and early 2000s, Gantt charts became a common feature of web-based applications.

Although now considered a common charting technique, Gantt charts were considered quite revolutionary at the time they were introduced. In recognition of Henry Gantt's contributions, the Henry Laurence Gantt Medal is awarded for distinguished achievement in management and service to the community.

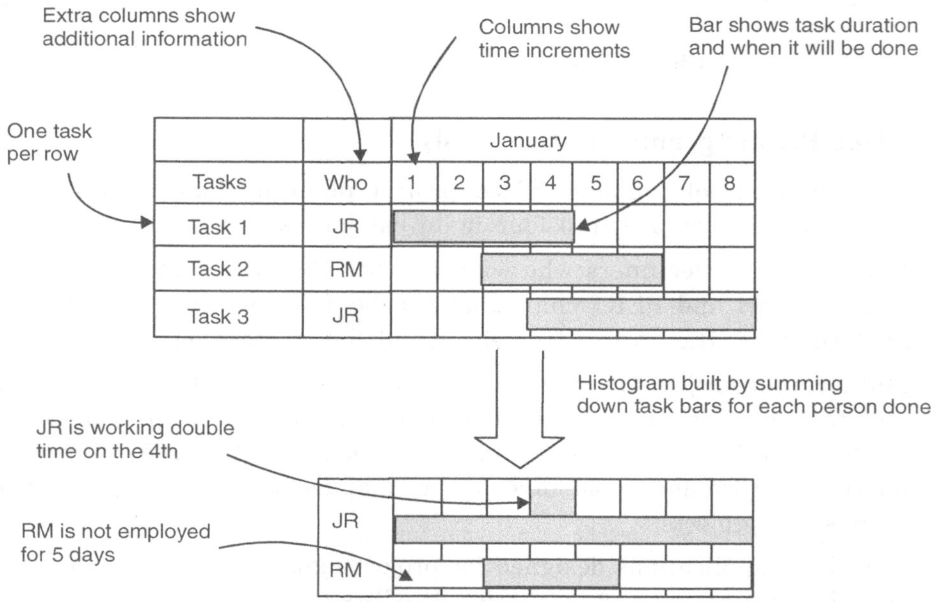

Fig. 7.19 A Gantt Chart

A Gantt chart is a matrix, which lists on the vertical axis all the tasks to be performed. Each row contains a single task identification, which usually consists of a number and name. Columns indicating estimated task duration, skill, head the horizontal axis level needed to perform the task, and the name of the person assigned to the task, followed by one column for each period in the project's duration. Each period may be expressed in hours, days, weeks, months, and other time units. In some cases it may be necessary to label the period columns as period 1, period 2, and so on.

The graphics portion of the Gantt chart consists of a horizontal bar for each task connecting the period start and period ending columns. A set of markers is usually used to indicate estimated and actual start and end. Each bar on a separate line, and the name of each person assigned to the task is on a separate line. In many cases when this type of project plan is used, a blank row is left between tasks. When the project is under way, this row is used to indicate progress, indicated by a second bar which starts in the period column when the task is actually started and continues until the task is actually completed. Comparison between estimated start and end and actual start and end should indicate project status on a task-by-task basis.

The following Gantt chart contains simple horizontal Bar Chart, where bars represent the actual calendar time which is planned for each task. The scale used for the time depends on the overall size of the project and the estimation increment used.

Advantages and limitations

Gantt charts have become a common technique for representing the phases and activities of a project work breakdown structure, so a wide audience can understand them. A common error made by those who equate Gantt chart design with project design is that they attempt to define the project work breakdown structure at the same time that they define schedule activities. This practice makes it very difficult to follow 100% Rule. Instead the WBS should be fully defined to follow 100% Rule, and then the project schedule can be designed.

Although a Gantt chart is easily comprehended for small projects that fit on a single sheet or screen, they can become quite unwieldy for projects with more than about 30 activities. Larger Gantt charts may not be suitable for most computer displays. A related criticism is that Gantt charts communicate relatively little information per unit area of display. That is, projects are often considerably more complex than can be communicated effectively with a Gantt chart.

Gantt charts only represent part of the triple constraints of projects, because they focus primarily on schedule management. Moreover, Gantt charts do not represent the size of a project; therefore the magnitude of a behind-schedule condition is easily miscommunicated. If two projects are the same number of days behind schedule, the larger project has a larger impact on resource utilization, yet the Gantt does not represent this difference.

Although project management software can show schedule dependencies as lines between activities, displaying a large number of dependencies may result in a cluttered or unreadable chart. Because the horizontal bars of a Gantt chart have a fixed height, they can misrepresent the planned workload (resource requirements) of a project. Another disadvantage of the Gantt chart is that dependencies between tasks are not shown, which can lead to tasks being ordered wrongly. This can be addressed by using an Activity Network beforehand, to calculate realistic start dates for each task. Other items from the Activity Network including slack time, tasks on the critical path, and milestones may also be displayed on the Gantt.

7.5 HOW TO USE THESE TOOLS

As with Gantt Charts, the essential concept behind Critical Path Analysis is that you cannot start some activities until others are finished. These activities need to be completed in a sequence, with each stage being more-or-less completed before the next stage can begin. These are sequential activities. Other activities are not dependent on completion of any other tasks. You can do these at any time before or after a particular stage is reached. These are non-dependent or parallel tasks.

SOLVED EXAMPLES

Example 7.1 *Which tasks are on the critical path of the PERT chart below?*

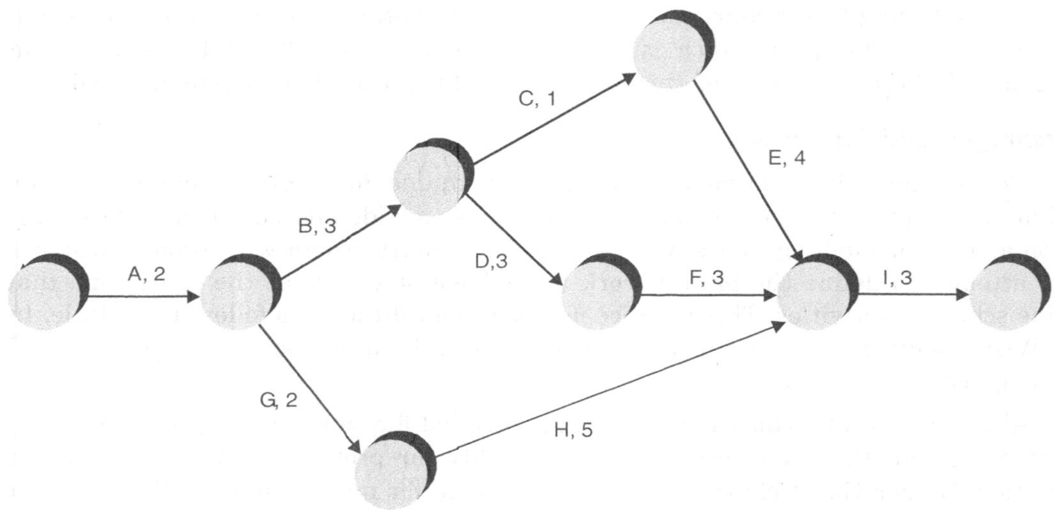

Fig. 7.20 A Critical Path of example 7.1

Solution. The tasks A, B, D, F, and I are on the critical path of the PERT chart

Example 7.2 *What is the slack time for tasks C, D and G?*

Solution. Slack time for task C: let us isolate that bit of the PERT chart.

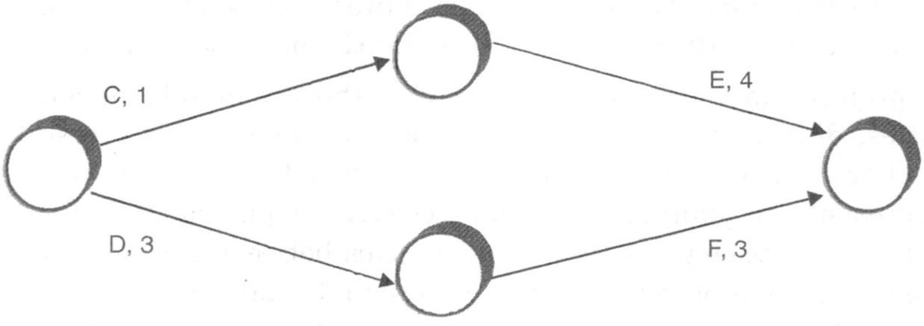

Fig. 7.21 A Critical Path of example 7.2

To work out the slack time for a task, backtrack from the task to the node where the task split off from other concurrent tasks. In our case, it is the node directly before task C. Also look forward to the node where task C and the other concurrent tasks (D, F) join up again with C.

In the chart below, the beginning node is represented by star and the ending node is represented by double circle.

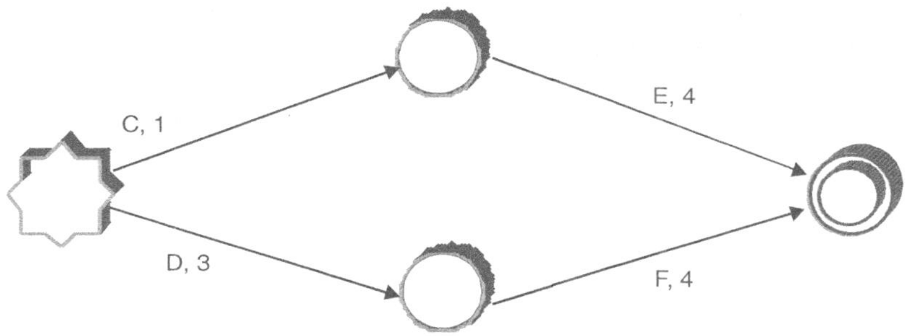

Fig. 7.22 Modified Critical Path

The top pair of tasks (C, E) is being done at the same time as the bottom pair of tasks (D, F). Together, C and E take 1 + 4 = 5 days. Together, D and F take 3 + 3 = 6 days, so tasks C, E will finish 1 day before D, F finish. Therefore, either task C or task E could take one extra day to finish without disturbing the task that comes after the green node.

That is the SLACK time for task C (it equally applies to task E: but remember the slack time is shared between them. They cannot both take another day without causing delays.)

So, the slack time available to task C is ONE DAY.

Example 7.3 *What is the slack time for task D?*

Solution. This is easy, when you remember that task D is on the critical path. By definition, critical tasks have NO SLACK: they cannot run overtime without affecting the ending date of the project. So, the easy answer for this is THERE IS NO SLACK for task D.

Example 7.4 *What is the slack time for task G?*

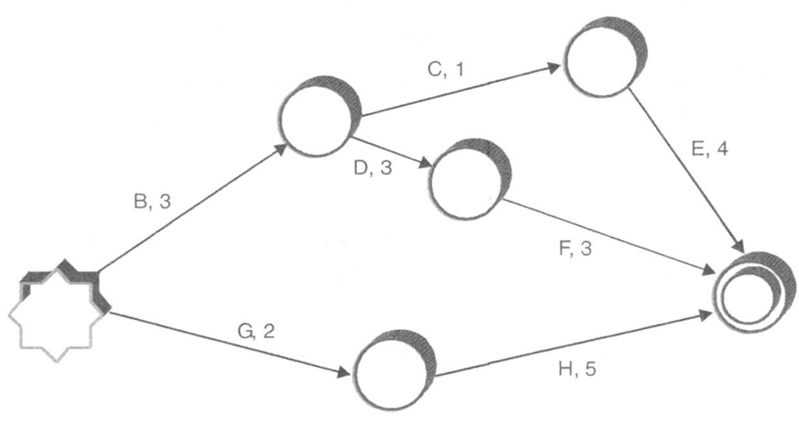

Fig. 7.23 Critical Path of example 7.4

Solution. Tasks G, H take a total of 7 days. Meanwhile, tasks B, C, E take 3 + 1 + 4 = 8 days and tasks B, D, F take 3 + 3 + 3 = 9 days. So, task G could run an extra 2 days before it caused delays, since it had to wait for tasks B, D, F to finish anyway.

So the answer would be, the slack time for task G is 2 days.

Example 7.5 *The person working on task C tells the project manager he cannot start work until one day after the scheduled starting date. What impact would this have on the completion date of the project? Why?*

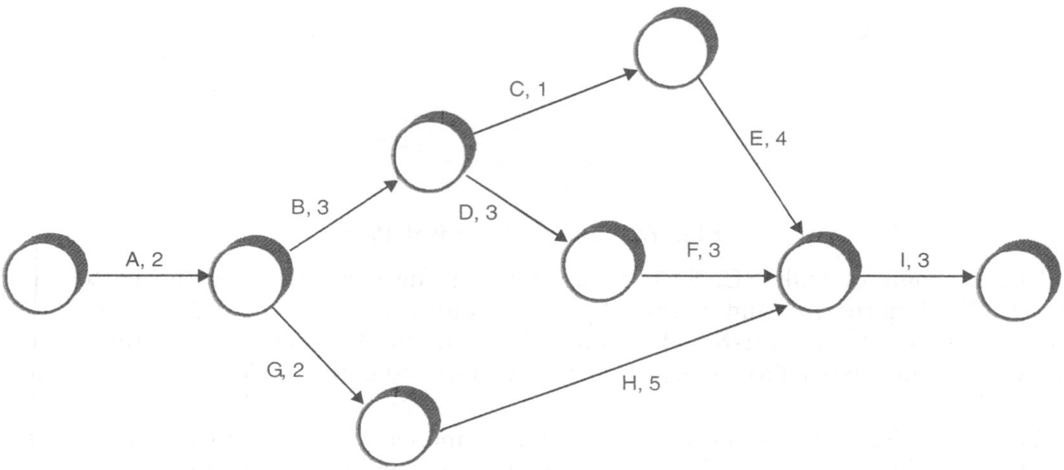

Fig. 7.24 Critical Path of example 7.5

Solution. Task C starting one day late is not significant to the ending date of the project. It would cause task E to start a day late (because task E is dependent on task C finishing first), but remember earlier we found that task C had ONE DAY OF SLACK. Therefore, if task C started a day late, it would merely use up its day of slack and no disruption would be felt by the time task E finished and the other concurrent tasks joined up to begin task I. So the answer is: task C finishing one day late would have no impact on the completion date of the project because it has one day of slack it could use.

Example 7.6 *The project manager decides to reduce the time needed for tasks D and F by one day each. How effective will this reduction be in achieving his aim of maintaining the original finish time for the project?*

Solution. Keep in mind that tasks D and F were chosen because they were on the critical path, and the only way to affect the finishing date is to affect critical tasks. Let us modify the PERT chart to show the new timeline if the manager shortened the time needed for tasks D and F.

If the chart given by figure 7.23, is modified as following:

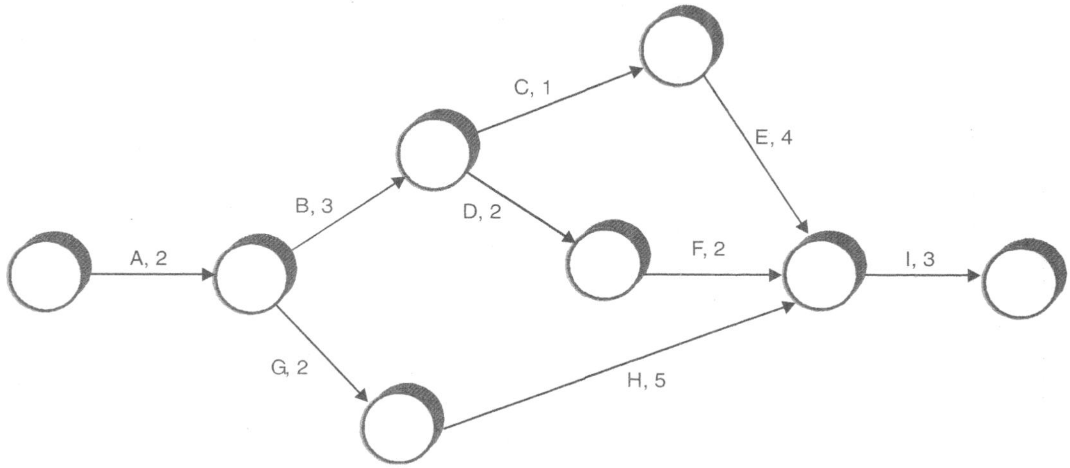

Fig. 7.25 Critical Path of example 7.6

Have a think: what has changed?

By reducing tasks A, B, D, F, I by a total of 2 days (to 12 days) means it is no longer the critical path. It is no longer the longest route from start to finish. In other words, it has been demoted. What is the new critical path?

The path A, B, C, E, I is now the longest at 13 days so it becomes the new critical path.

The project manager has reduced the old critical path from 14 to 12 days, but the new critical path still takes 13 days. So, the project will now finish ONE day earlier than originally.

Reducing both tasks D and F by one day each was unnecessary because after a 1 day reduction, the tasks were no longer critical. To reduce the overall project time further, the manager would have had to shift his attention to the new critical path, and try to reduce the times of the new critical tasks.

So, an answer could be: Reducing tasks D and F each by one day would only shorten the project by one day since after a 2 day reduction, tasks D and F are no longer on the critical path. To further shorten the project time, the project manager would have to shorten tasks on the new critical path A, B, C, E, I.

EXERCISE QUESTIONS

1. Give a comparative study of PERT, CPM and Gantt Charts.
2. Explain the advantages and disadvantages of Gantt charts.
3. What do you understand by Forward pass and backward pass in activity networks?
4. What is the contribution of PERT, CPM and Gantt charts in system simulation?
5. A project has characteristics given by following table:

Activity	*Preceding activity*	*Duration (Week)*
A	None	5
B	A	2
C	A	6
D	B	12
E	D	10
F	D	9
G	D	5
H	B	9
I	C, E	1
J	G	2
K	F, I, J	3
L	K	9
M	H,G	7
N	M	8

Determine the following:

(*i*) PERT network for this project.

(*ii*) Find various paths and the critical path as well as the project completion time.

(*iii*) Prepare the activity schedule showing the ES, EF, LS, and LF.

6. A company planning a project to introduce a new product, has listed the following necessary activities:

Activity	*Preceding activity*	*Expected time (Week)*
A	None	6
B	None	3
C	A	5
D	A	4
E	A	3
F	C	3
G	D	5
H	B, D, E	5
I	H	2
J	I, G, F	3

Determine the following:

(*i*) Draw the critical path network for the project and determine the critical path and its duration.

(*ii*) If the start of the activity B is delayed 2 weeks, activity E by 1 week and activity G by 2 weeks, how the total project time will be affected?

7. For a project consisting of several activities, the duration and required resources for carrying out each of the activities and their availabilities are as following:

Activity	*Equipment*	*Resources required Operators*	*Duration (in Days)*
1-2	X	30	4
1-3	Y	20	3
1-4	Z	20	6
2-4	X	30	4
2-5	Z	20	8
3-4	Y	20	4
3-5	Y	20	4
4-5	X	30	6

Resources available = Number of Operators = 50

Equipment X = 1, Y= 1, Z = 1

Determine the following:

(*i*) Draw the network, identify critical path and compute the total float for each of the activities.

(*ii*) Find the project completion time under the given resource constraints.

Chapter 8

SIMULATION LANGUAGES

8.1 INTRODUCTION

We are finally ready to describe or program the model in a language acceptable to the computer to be used. Well, over a hundred different simulation languages are commercially available. In addition, there are literally hundreds of other locally developed languages in use in Companies and Universities. We have three generic choices, namely: Build the model in a general-purpose language, build the model in a general-purpose simulation language, use a special purpose simulation packages.

Although general purpose programming languages such as FORTRAN, C++, Visual Basic, or Pascal can be used they very seldom are anymore. Using one of the general or special purpose simulation packages has distinct advantages in terms of ease, efficiency and effectiveness of use. Some of the advantages of using a simulation package are reduction of the programming task, provision of conceptual guidance, increased flexibility when changing the model, fewer programming errors, automated gathering of statistics.

The goal of any simulation package is to close the gap between the user's conceptualization of the model and an executable form. Simulation packages divide themselves more or less into two categories, namely (*a*) general purpose simulation languages, and (*b*) special purpose simulators. In the first category are those which can solve almost any discrete simulation problem. Among these are such systems as ARENA, AweSim, GPSS, SimScript II.5, Extend etc. Some systems are used for the simulation of manufacturing and material handling problems. Packages such as SimFactory, ProModel, AutoMod, Taylor II, and Witness fall into this category. Others are designed for conducting Business Process Reengineering studies. These include BPSimulator, ProcessModel, SIMPROCESS, etc. Still others are for healthcare delivery (for example MedModel), or communications networks (for example COMNET II.5).

Early effort in a simulation study is concerned with defining the system to be modeled and describing it in terms of logic flow diagrams and functional relationships. But eventually one is faced with the problem of describing the model in a language acceptable to the computer to be used. Most digital computers operate in a binary method of data representation, or in some multiple of binary such as octal or hexadecimal. Since these are awkward languages for users to communicate with, programming languages have evolved to make, easier to converse with the computer. Unfortunately, so many general and special purpose programming languages have been developed over the years, that it is a nearly impossible task to decide which language best fits or is even a near best fit to any particular application.

8.2 SIMULATION LANGUAGES

Over 170 programming languages were in use in the United States in 1972 and today there are even more. Consequently, the usual procedure is to use a language known by the analyst, not because it is best, but because it is known. It should be stated that any general algorithmic language is capable of expressing the desired model; however, one of the specialized simulation languages may have very distinct advantages in terms of ease, efficiency and effectiveness of use. It is not the intention of this chapter to teach how to program in any of the languages described, nor to discuss implementation techniques. What we do hope to accomplish is to make the reader aware of the characteristics of some of the more popular languages, their strengths and weaknesses. The major differences between special purpose simulation languages in general are classified as : (1) the organization of time and activities, (2) the naming and structuring of entities within the model, (3) the testing of activities and conditions between elements, (4) the types of statistical tests possible on the data and (5) the ease of changing model structure.

A computer simulation language describes the operation of a simulation on a computer. There are two major types of simulation: continuous and discrete-event simulation languages. Though there are several modern languages that can handle combinations of continuous and discrete-event simulation languages. Most languages also have a graphical interface and at least simple statistical gathering capability for the analysis of the results. An important part of discrete-event languages is the ability to generate pseudo-random numbers and variates from different probability distributions.

8.3 CONTINUOUS SYSTEM SIMULATION LANGUAGES

Continuous simulation languages developed in late fifties as simulators of analog computers. Simulation of analog computers is based on creating an analog electronic system whose behavior is described by the same mathematical model (with the help of differential equations) as the system being investigated. Interconnecting standard blocks based mostly on operational amplifiers modified to act as integrators, adders, and other functional units creates the electronic system. Then the user performs experiments with this electronic system by applying suitable inputs and recording the voltage at certain output points (for example, oscilloscope, and plotter). The changing voltage represents a time function that is the same as the function that describes the changes in the original system whose physical nature may be totally different (for example, mechanical displacement, temperature, etc.). The main problem of analog computers is an analog implementation of certain operations like multiplication, generation of some functions, generation of delays and others.

Digital computers perform all these functions very easily and today continuous simulation is performed only to them. Nevertheless there is one operation where the analog computers are better, is integration. Digital computers use numerical integration that is generally slower and less accurate compared with the integration of an analog integrator. Some special applications based on fast response use therefore the so-called Hybrid computers, which contain analog and digital parts connected by analog to digital and digital to analog converters. The digital part does everything except integration. It computes inputs of integrators, which are then converted by digital to analog converters to analog signals inputted to analog integrators. Their outputs are treated in the opposite way. The digital part also controls the interconnection of the analog part, which might thus change during computation.

Continuous simulation languages can be viewed as the model essentially as a set of differential equations. We have a specific kind of continuous simulation language named Advanced Continuous Simulation Language (ACSL), which supports textual or graphical model specification.

8.3.1 Advanced Continuous Simulation Language (ACSL)

The Advanced Continuous Simulation Language, or ACSL (pronounced as axle), is a computer language designed for modeling and evaluating the performance of continuous systems described by time-dependent, nonlinear differential equations. It is a tongue of the Continuous System Simulation Language (CSSL), originally designed by the Simulations Council Inc (SCI) in 1967 in an attempt to unify the continuous simulations field.

ACSL is an equation-oriented simulation language consisting of a set of arithmetic operators, standard functions, a set of special ACSL statements, and a MACRO capability which allows extension of the special ACSL statements. ACSL is intended to provide a simple method of representing mathematical models on a digital computer. Working from an equation description of the problem or a block diagram, the user writes ACSL statements to describe the system under investigation. An important feature of ACSL is its sorting of the continuous model equations, in contrast to general purpose programming languages such as Fortran where program execution depends critically on statement order.

Typical Applications

Applications of ACSL in new areas are being developed constantly. Typical areas in which ACSL is currently applied include control system design, aerospace simulation, chemical process dynamics, power plant dynamics, plant and animal growth modeling, toxicology models, vehicle handling, microprocessor controllers, and robotics.

8.3.2 Classification of Continuous Simulation Languages

Block–oriented simulation languages: These languages are based on the methodology of analog computers. The system must be expressed as a block diagram that defines the interconnection of functional units and their quantitative parameters. "Programming" means entering the interconnection of the blocks and their description. Then the user adds statements and/or directives that control the simulation. If the system is described as a set of equations, they must be converted to a block diagram. This conversion is a simple straightforward process. The typical blocks available in most continuous block oriented languages are integrators, limiters, delays, multipliers, constant values, adders, holders, gain (coefficient) and other. For example GPSS is the Block oriented simulation languages.

Expression-oriented continuous languages: These languages are based on writing expressions (equations) that represent the mathematical model. So the system simulated must be expressed by a set of equations. Then the user adds statements and/or directives that control the simulation. Some languages enable both block and expression based ways of system definition. Simulation control means selection of: the integration method (because some languages offer more), the integration step, the variables (outputs of blocks) that should be observed, the intervals for collecting data for printing and/or plotting, scaling of outputs (that may be also done automatically), duration of the simulation runs, number of repetitions and the way certain values are changed in them, etc. SimScript is the best example of expression oriented simulation languages.

8.4 DISCRETE SYSTEM SIMULATION LANGUAGES

Discrete-system simulation languages can be viewed as the model as a sequence of random events each causing a change in state of the system being simulated.

8.4.1 Classification of Discrete Simulation Languages

Broadly there are four types of discrete simulation languages.

Flowchart-oriented languages: These are represented by the language GPSS (General Purpose Simulation System), which exists in many versions on various computers. The user must view the dynamics of the system as a flow of the so called transactions through a block diagram. Transactions are generated, follow a path through a network of blocks, and are destroyed on exit. In blocks transactions may be delayed, processed, and passed to other blocks. Blocks are in the program represented by statements that perform the activities of the model.

Activity-oriented languages: These are not based on explicit scheduling of future activities of the system. For each activity the user describes the condition under which the activity can take place (that also covers scheduling if the condition is reaching certain time). The algorithm of the simulation control repeatedly increases time and tests conditions of all activities. The disadvantage of this approach is obvious, it is necessary to evaluate all conditions in every step, which may be very time-consuming. On the other hand it is conceptually very simple and the algorithm can be easily implemented in general high level languages (there are simulation languages based on this approach, but not widely used).

Event-oriented languages: These are based on direct scheduling and cancelling of future events of the system. The approach is very general. The user must view the dynamics of the system simulated as a sequence of relatively independent events. Every event may schedule and/or cancel other events. The system routine must keep record of scheduled events. That is why every event is represented by the so called Event notice that contains the time, the event type, and other user data. Event notices are kept in the so called *Calendar,* where the event notices are ordered by the scheduled time. After completion of an *Event routine,* the system removes the event notice with the lowest time from the calendar, updates the model time by its time, and starts the corresponding routine. This is repeated until the calendar becomes empty or the program stops because of other reason. Scheduling means inserting event notices to the calendar by the scheduled time, cancelling removes them. The approach based on explicit expressing of events is called Discrete Event Simulation. A typical representative of this group of languages is the language SIMSCRIPT, but its version II.5 supports also process oriented simulation.

Process-oriented languages: These are based on the fact, that events are not independent. An event is typically a consequence of other previous events. In other words it is often possible to define sequences of events that may be viewed as entities of a simulation model at higher level of hierarchy. A sequence of events is called *Process*. Unlike events process has a dimension in time. Process based abstract systems are very close to reality, which is always made of various objects that exist and act in parallel interfering with each other. Process way of viewing system dynamics is thus very natural. Mostly a process models an activity of a real object. It is believed, that process oriented discrete simulation is the best way how to create discrete simulation models. Typical representatives of this group of languages are MODSIM, SIMSCRIPT II.5, and the system class simulation of the SIMULA language.

8.5 GPSS (GENERAL PURPOSE SIMULATION SYSTEM)

The first version of the GPSS language was introduced by IBM in October, 1961. Thus, it has been in continuous, world-wide use for over 40 years. There are very few programming languages of any kind for which this is true. GPSS introduced the transaction-flow modeling paradigm. Under this paradigm, active "consumer" objects, called transactions, travel through a block diagram representing a system, competing for the use of "passive server" objects. This modeling paradigm is extremely general and has been adopted in a large number of simulation languages. Terminology differs from language to language. Transactions may be called items, entities, tokens, etc., but the basic architecture is the same: active objects compete for passive resources while travelling through a diagram representing a system.

GPSS was designed by Geoffrey Gordon as a tool for use by non-programmers. It is interesting to note that over 40 years later, "no programming required" is still featured as a virtue in advertisements for simulation software. Historically, GPSS models were developed by drawing block diagrams and manually typing character-based representations of blocks. Over time, the sizes of GPSS models grew well beyond what Geoffrey Gordon had ever anticipated. While drawing a 100-block diagram is relatively easy, drawing a 5000-block diagram is difficult. As users began developing larger and larger models, and as they became more comfortable with typing in blocks without first having drawn them, GPSS came to be viewed as a true programming language.

8.5.1 GPSS/H

GPSS/H was the first placed into commercial service in November, 1977. Over the ensuing years, it has become well-known for its speed and dependability. In GPSS/H, the transaction flow world view has been extended with many advanced features to make an extremely powerful and flexible tool capable of handling large, complicated models with ease, yet still providing exceptionally high performance. GPSS/H has been a very successful product. Its success is the result of both the superiority of its original design and subsequent years of improvement and enhancement. Most of the enhancements developed for GPSS/H have been improvements to it as a programming language.

Since it is a simulation *language*, GPSS/H requires some programming-style effort, but it does so within the intuitive modeling framework Gordon designed to be readily used without extensive programming experience. It is well suited for modeling both simple systems and large, complex systems. Although many new simulation tools have been introduced over the past decade, they have often been designed for specific classes of applications. In strong contrast, GPSS/H continues to be one of the most *general, flexible*, and *powerful* simulation environments currently available. GPSS/H is in use around the globe modeling manufacturing, transportation, distribution, telecommunications, hospitals, computers, logistics, mining, and many other types of queuing systems.

Representing a System in GPSS/H. In a GPSS/H model a transaction can represent a patient, a telephone call, a truck, a data packet, or any other type of individually identifiable entity that has a *behavior*. As a model executes, many transactions can flow through the model simultaneously—just as many objects would move through the real-world system being modeled. In addition, while flowing through the model, multiple transactions can execute the same GPSS/H model statements at the same instant in simulated time without any intervention by the modeler. The execution of a process-interaction simulation model is thus similar to a multi-threaded computer program. This differs greatly from the single-threaded, sequential execution of most general-purpose programming languages, and is a good reason why such languages are usually poor tools for writing simulation models.

Many simulation projects focus on the optimal use of system resources such as people, machines, conveyors, computers, physical space, and so on. In a GPSS/H simulation model, transactions compete for the use of these system resources. As transactions flow through the process representation, they automatically queue up when they can't gain control of a necessary resource. The modeler does not have to specify the transaction's waiting time or its queuing behavior for this to occur. Hence, the passage of time in a GPSS/H model can be represented *implicitly,* as in the case of a part waiting for a machine to become free, or *explicitly*, as in the case of a part being processed by a machine.

A GPSS/H model, like most real-world systems, may consist of multiple processes operating at the same time. Furthermore, each such process may affect the other processes in the system. For example, two parallel manufacturing processes may converge to a single inspection point where they are competing for a single resource, *e.g.*, an inspector. GPSS/H provides the capability for multiple parallel processes to interact with each other automatically. Transactions ("objects") may be sent between processes; they may control or share common resources.

Ease-of-Use. The presence or absence of a single characteristic such as a "visual interface" for building models is insufficient to determine a tool's ease-of-use. Whether a tool is "easy to use" depends upon the combination of *general characteristics* and *specific* *features* that are *heavily used* when real-world models are built. Moreover, the ease-of-use that is claimed for almost all simulation tools can mean many things—that the tool is easy to learn, easy to use once learned, easy to use when modifying models, easy to use when building simple models, or easy to use when building large, complex models. Rarely is a product equally good at all of these, but equally rarely is the prospective user informed about which "ease-of-use" is being claimed.

A simulation language's ease-of-use is rarely constant over the duration of a simulation project. The ease-of-use of a tool that is optimized for developing small models may diminish as a model gets larger and larger, and more details of system operation have to be incorporated into a model. Conversely, a tool that requires a bit more study to master may be harder to use in the early stages of a project, but offer downstream rewards when it is able to meet modeling requirements for a large, complex system. Scalability of technology is an important contributor to ease-of-use. GPSS/H has excellent scalability. It is able to handle very large models (10's of thousands of blocks).

Model Validation and Debugging. The GPSS/H Interactive Debugger provides invaluable assistance for rapid model development and verification. Prior to the advent of GPSS/H in 1977, most simulation tools featured batch-oriented, non-interactive debugging. To debug a model, one typically generated a large trace file and very carefully proofread the trace file to verify model correctness.

In GPSS/H, simple debugger commands are used to control a model's execution and to examine its status. Functions are provided to "step" through the model, to set breakpoints and traps that interrupt model execution based on multiple criteria, and to return to a previously saved state of the model. Almost all data values can be examined, including local data, global data, transaction attributes, entity statistics, and array data values. The debugger provides a "windowing" mode that displays source code, model status, and interactive user input as the model runs. A modeler can interrupt a long-running model at any time and use the debugging features to make sure that everything is running correctly before resuming execution. The GPSS/H debugger has almost no effect on execution speed. Because of this, many modelers use the debugger as their everyday run-time environment for GPSS/H.

General Purpose Simulation System is a discrete time simulation language, where a simulation clock advanced in uniform discrete steps. A system was modeled as transactions entered the system and were passed from one service to another. This is particularly well suitable for problems such as a factory. It was popular in the late 1960s and early 1970s but is little used today. GPSS is less flexible than simulation languages such as SIMULA and SIMSCRIPT II.5 that model a system with discrete events that are not constrained by a uniform time step.

The GPSS language as it exists today is the result of more than twenty years of evolution. While GPSS has its roots in the early days of mainframe computing, its basic ideas have proven suitable for application to today's problems using modern computing environments. The popularity of GPSS is due, in part, to its power of expression. A short, easily understood GPSS model would require many pages of FORTRAN coding to accomplish a similar goal. The GPSS user is free to concentrate on the important issues in the model being developed since the language itself collects statistics, produces tabulated results and performs a host of mundane tasks one would prefer not to deal with. The purpose of this brief article is to present some basic terminology and concepts which will enable the person meeting GPSS for the first time to understand the broad range of applications, power and ease of use that this language brings to the simulationist.

GPSS provides a set of abstract components of various types and a set of operators called blocks which perform certain actions on the individual components. The transaction is the component which moves through a sequence of blocks that has been designed to model the system being studied. The state of the components of the model determines the details of how a block of a given type will operate. For example, a block which permits a transaction to take control of a piece of equipment will not allow the transaction to proceed if the equipment is already at maximum capacity.

Several different types of equipment components are available in GPSS. A facility is an entity which is either available for use or is in use by at most one transaction at a time. Storage is similar but has a capacity which may be specified to suit the needs of the model builder. Finally, a logic switch is a simple ON/OFF element which may be set and tested to modify the path of a transaction through the blocks of the model.

GPSS provides an underlying control mechanism which is transparent to the user but which ensures that competition between transactions (for use of a facility, for instance) is consistently arbitrated and that transactions are moved through the blocks of the model in an orderly and efficient way. This control mechanism also administers the GPSS clock which provides the time-base for models.

The GPSS clock is also an abstraction. It measures time in clock units. A clock unit is interpreted appropriately by the person designing the model. In the factory model a clock unit could correspond to a second or a minute, while in the communication network the finer resolution of a one-millisecond clock unit would be more suitable. Function entities are provided to describe various types of numeric relationships. They may be used to produce random variates from theoretical or empirical probability distributions. They may also be used to modify transaction behavior depending on system-wide, entity or transaction attributes. Variable entities can be used to perform arithmetic calculations in all implementations of GPSS. The greater flexibility of GPSS/VX and GPSS/C versions permits arithmetic expressions to be entered wherever a constant is permitted. Certain modeling situations may take advantage of the set concepts embodied in the group entity-type. Other situations will benefit from the use of COUNT and SELECT blocks which permit a number of entities to be examined in a single operation.

GPSS provides entities known as save-values and matrix save-values which are numeric storage locations available for use or reference by all transactions. In addition, each transaction has a set of private numeric attributes called parameters which may be used to hold a variety of information as required by the user, such as a part number code or the size or weight of an item represented by a transaction.

A rich set of *Standard Numerical Attributes* (SNA's) provide a convenient notational way to access components of a model. For instance, Q$BOXOFFICE represents the current contents of the queue entity named BOXOFFICE. This SNA may be used wherever a numeric value is allowed. A simple balking situation could be represented by the block

TEST L Q$BOXOFFICE,FN$BALK,GOAWAY

which allows transactions to pass through if the current length of the BOXOFFICE lineup is less than the value returned by the function BALK, and otherwise re-directs them to the block GOAWAY. BALK may be written to return a random variate from any desired probability distribution; or it may return a value varying with the time of day in the model or a value dependent on the number of packages (represented by a transaction parameter) the theatre patron is carrying.

Simulation Software's GPSS products all feature interactive debugging capability which allows setting breakpoints in the model, single-stepping and examining attributes of model entities. Each implementation has additional innovative tools designed to make debugging a much shorter task. Features such as conditional breakpoints and animated displays optimize the model-development process, while internally-compiled code and optimizations shorten the run-times for production model runs.

8.5.2 A Simple GPSS Model

The following brief example models a bank with a individual queues for each of five tellers. The transactions are customers and facilities are used to represent the bank tellers.

```
1. SIMULATE
2. LINES EQU 1(5),Q,F
3. ARRIVE FUNCTION RN5,BE
4. GENERATE 20,FN$ARRIVE
5. SELECT MIN 1,LINES,LINES+4,Q
6. QUEUE P1
7. SEIZE P1
8. DEPART P1
9. ADVANCE 90,20
10. RELEASE P1
11. TERMINATE 1
12. START 100
13. END
```

The following is a line-by-line description of the model:

1. SIMULATE is a control statement.
2. EQU defines LINES as the name of the first of a group of 5 corresponding queues and facilities—the lineups and tellers.
3. Defines ARRIVE as the name of a function transforming a random number between 0 and 1, into a value from a built-in exponential (BE) distribution—

a commonly-used in simulating arrival processes. The random number is taken from the fifth built-in stream of such numbers (RN5).

4. The customers arrive an average of 20 seconds apart with a random variation determined by sampling the function ARRIVE is defined in the previous line.
5. Set parameter 1 of each entering transaction to the number of the queue with the MINimum length.
6. Join the queue whose number is now in parameter 1.
7. When the corresponding facility is available take possession of it.
8. Now leave the lineup, recording the delay time in the queue statistics.
9. Delay for an average of 90 seconds with a variation of 20 seconds either way, representing time for the banking to be done. The delay is chosen randomly with uniform probability in the 70 to 110 second range. The facility remains in use for this period. The random number used to determine the actual delay time is taken from the first random number stream, thus the arrival times and delay times are statistically independent.
10. Free the facility for use by the next transaction.
11. Destroy the transaction. Count 1 completes customer cycle.
12. Run the model until 100 customers have reached the TERMINATE block.
13. END marks the last line of the model.

Syntax in GPSS

Block Entities. The GPSS block entity is the basic structural element of a GPSS simulation program. It is useful to think about a GPSS model by considering its Block diagram as implemented in a simulation program. The model is the connected network of block symbols that correspond to the positions of block entities (lines of GPSS code) in the simulation. The types of Blocks are identified by names, usually written in upper case, that suggest their function, such as GENERATE, SEIZE, and TERMINATE. Each type of block is associated with an action in the simulation. All Blocks have a set of operands that are written sequentially after the Block type and separated by commas. The sequential positions of these operands are referred to by capital letters (A,B,C,...) of the alphabet in their usual order. Blocks can optionally be given unique labels suitable to the model they represent. The syntax of a Block statement is then

Label BLOCKTYPE A,B,C,... ;comment

Operands may be blank, in which case a default value is used. If all trailing Operands are blank they may be omitted altogether.

System Numerical Attributes. System Numerical Attributes, or SNAs, are simulation "state variables" that are available for use throughout a simulation. They return numeric or string values, and may be used in GPSS Statement operands and in Expressions. They are best considered with the entities they describe.

Transactions. A Transaction is a GPSS object with a set of attributes. Attributes are called **Parameters** in GPSS. Transactions are created either one at a time or in batches in GENERATE Blocks and pass from Block to Block in a simulation acting on, and being acted upon by, the Blocks they pass through, and possibly by other GPSS Entities. A single Transaction may consist of several individual entities, such as more than one person being "served" by an elevator. Common ways to describe how Transactions behave in a GPSS simulation is to use phrases such as "Transactions enter, pass through, are contained in, acquire, own, and/or are in contention for various Blocks." Also Block types, which are usually verbs, can have case suffixes as in "a Transaction SEIZEs a Facility", where SEIZE is a Block type. This terminology is patterned after the idea that an entity, represented as a Transaction, actively deals with various types of servers, as in a single server queuing system. Each Transaction in the model is contained in exactly one Block, but most Blocks may contain many Transactions. Each Transaction enters one Block, then the next, and so on, until it is TERMINATEd or the simulation ends. Transactions occasionally must wait in or before a Block until conditions are favorable for entry into the that Block. The Blocks a transaction passes through are written in successive lines of a GPSS simulation unless they encounter a TRANSFER Block which may send them to another Block not in the sequence. A GENERATE Block creates Transactions for future entry into the simulation; it has 5 operands (A,B,C,D,E):

A = Mean inter generation time or Function representing the distribution of inter generation times

B = Inter generation time half range (for uniformly distributed inter generation times) or Function Modifier.

C = Start delay time.

D = Maximum number of transaction to be created at this GENERATE Block.

E = Priority level.

It helps to think that the first transaction created by a GENERATE Block is actually created right before the GENERATE Block and then enters the GENERATE Block. From then on, every time a Transaction enters a GENERATE Block, the next Transaction is created. This new, next Transaction does not enter the GENERATE Block right away. Instead, it is placed on the Future Events Chain according to the arrival time interval specified by the GENERATE Block. The Future Event Chain (FEC) is a list of events to be executed later than the current simulation clock time. They are removed from the FEC in time sequence. The Current Events Chain (CEC) is the set of Transactions that still have Blocks to be entered at the current system clock time. Transactions are taken from the front of the Current Events Chain, one at a time, to enter as many Blocks as possible. When there are no more Transactions on the Current Events Chain, GPSS World will advance the system clock. ASSIGN Blocks are used to place or modify a value in a Transaction Parameter; if the Parameter does not exist it is created. Their syntax is:

ASSIGN A,B,C

where,

A = Parameter number of the Active Transaction. It is not optional. Plus/minus sign after the number indicates that the value of the Operand B is to be added or subtracted to the original Parameter value.

B = The operand must be Name, Number, String, Parenthesized-expression, SNA, or SNA*Parameter.

C = Function number. It is optional.

Related SNA

P *Parameter* or **Parameter* (where *Parameter* is the number or the name of a Transaction Parameter): Parameter value. P *Parameter* returns the value of Parameter *Parameter*. (note: *e.g.*, P1 or *1 or P$NAME will yield the value in the Parameter 1 in the first two cases and the Parameter called NAME in the final case.). An important Parameter of each Transaction is its Mark Time, the time the transaction entered the simulation or when it passes through a MARK Block with no A Operand. The time from the last Mark Time to the current clock time can be retrieved from the M1 SNA. The current simulation time can be assigned to a transaction by a MARK Block. Its syntax is

MARK A

Where A = Parameter number. It is optional. If A is absent the current time is kept in a virtual Parameter called the Mark Time.

Facilities

A *Facility* is an entity that has several attributes, the most important of which is ownership. A Facility is automatically created when the first transaction reached a block that uses a Facility. Facilities do not have to be defined/declared by a Command.

There are several GPSS Blocks which can be used with Facilities:

- SEIZE Blocks attempt to take ownership of a Facility.
- RELEASE Blocks relinquish ownership of a Facility.
- PREEMPT Blocks attempt to take ownership of a Facility, possibly displacing the existing owner.
- RETURN Blocks relinquish ownership of a Facility.
- FAVAIL Blocks place a Facility in the available state.
- FUNAVAIL Blocks place a Facility in the unavailable state.

Except for PREEMPT and FUNAVAIL, these Blocks all take a single Operand A, which is the label of the Facility to be SEIZEDed, RELEASEed, RETURNed, and/or made available. FUNAVIAL has up to 8 Operands; it is not used frequently enough to be considered in this document. The PREEMPT Block has 5 Operands:

A = Facility name or number.

B = PR for Priority Mode or if omitted Interrupt Mode.

C = Block name or number for the new destination of the Transaction presently owning the Facility.

D = Parameter number of the preempted Transaction to receive residual time if preempted Transaction is removed from FEC.

E = When RE the preemption is in the Remove Mode, which Removes preempted Transaction from contention for the Facility. If RE, you must specify a destination in Operand C.

Transactions acquire ownership of a Facility by successfully entering a SEIZE or PREEMPT Block (a PREEMPT Block has the power to displace the existing owner of the Facility). A Facility is restricted to be owned by a single Transaction, in which case it is said to be busy, or it may not be owned at all, in which case it is said to be idle. If a Transaction cannot acquire ownership, it comes to rest on a Facility Transaction Chain. A Facility has several waiting lines for Transactions that are waiting for some Facility-oriented event to occur. Each Facility has a Delay Chain for normally waiting Transactions, a Pending Chain for Interrupt Mode preemptions that were not allowed, and an Interrupt Chain for previously preempted Transactions. Transactions waiting on a Delay Chain, a Pending Chain, or an Interrupt Chain are said to be "in contention" for the Facility. Each Transaction which owns a Facility must eventually give up ownership by entering a RELEASE or a RETURN Block. Since a contending Transaction will generally become the owner of the Facility, contention for a Facility carries the obligation of eventually releasing the Facility. Those Transactions which fail in their attempt to enter a SEIZE Block come to rest in priority order on the Delay Chain of the Facility. When a Facility is freed by an owning Transaction, the next owner is chosen from occupants of the Facility's Transaction chains. The pending Interrupt Mode preemptors are chosen first, followed by previously preempted Transactions, followed by Transactions waiting normally in priority order on the Delay Chain.

A Facility may be available or unavailable. When it is available, Transactions acquire and give up ownership of the Facility normally. When the Facility is unavailable, ownership is not given to newly arriving Transactions. FAVAIL Blocks are used to place a Facility in the available state, and FUNAVAIL Blocks are used to place it in the unavailable state. Any Transactions present at the Facility at the time it was made unavailable are disposed of as specified in the FUNAVAIL Block operands. The symbol Entnum stands for a Facility number of name. The SNAs associated with Facilities are:

- F *Entnum*—Facility busy. If Facility *Entnum* is currently busy, F *Entnum* returns 1. Otherwise F *Entnum* returns 0.
- FC *Entnum*—Facility capture count. The number of times Facility *Entnum* has been SEIZEd or PREEMPTed by a Transaction.
- FI *Entnum*—Facility *Entnum* interrupted. If Facility *Entnum* is currently preempted by a Transaction in an Interrupt Mode PREEMPT Block, FI*Entnum* returns 1. Otherwise FI*Entnum* returns 0.
- FR *Entnum*—Facility utilization. The fraction of time Facility *Entnum* has been busy. FR*Entnum* is expressed in parts-per-thousand and therefore returns a real value between 0 and 1000.
- FT *Entnum*—Average facility holding time. The average time Facility *Entnum* is owned by a capturing Transaction.
- FV *Entnum*—Facility in available state. FV*Entnum* returns 1 if Facility *Entnum* is in the available state, 0 otherwise.

Storage

A Storage Entity is associated with a number of storage units which are allocated and returned by Transactions. Storage entities must be by defining/declaring them with a STORAGE Command.

Name Storage A

Name is a required label for this entity. A is required and is total storage capacity; this is often interpreted as the number of units of the Storage that are available to Transactions. There are several GPSS Blocks that can be used with Storage Entities:

- ENTER Blocks attempt to increase the contents of (place tokens in) a Storage Entity.
- LEAVE Blocks decrease the contents of (remove tokens from) a Storage Entity.
- SAVAIL Blocks place a Storage Entity in the available state.
- SUNAVAIL Blocks place a Storage Entity in the unavailable state.

The ENTER and LEAVE Blocks take two Operands, the first is required and indicates the Storage to be ENTERed or LEAVEd while the second is the number of units of the Storage capacity to be used or discarded by the Transaction. If only one unit of Storage capacity is to be used or discarded, the second Operand can be omitted. SAVAIL and SUNAVAIL need only the A Operand which is the Storage to be made available or not. When a Transaction ENTERs a Storage Entity, it utilizes or occupies one or more storage units (given by the B Operand) of the Storage Entity. A Transaction is denied entry into an ENTER Block if its storage demand cannot be met. Such a Transaction comes to rest on the Delay Chain of the Storage Entity. Then it must wait until other Transactions free enough storage by entering LEAVE Blocks.

Storage capacity may be released by any Transaction, even if it had not previously ENTERed the Storage Entity. However, if more capacity is released than was declared in the STORAGE Command an Error Stop occurs.

When a Transaction enters a LEAVE Block and gives up one or more storage units, other Transactions are sought which can have their storage demands satisfied. A "first-fit-with-skip" discipline is used to schedule Transactions which are waiting. This means that each Transaction on the Delay Chain is tested for fit in the Storage Entity, starting with the highest priority. If a fit is found, the Transaction is removed from the Storage Delay Chain, allowed to enter the ENTER Block, and placed on the CEC behind its priority peers. Then the next Transaction on the Storage Delay Chain is tested. ENTER and LEAVE Blocks are used to update the statistics associated with a Storage Entity and several SNAs are available which return derived statistics. The SNAs associated with Storage Entities are:

- R*Entnum*—Unused storage capacity. The storage content (or spaces available for use by "tokens") available for use by entering Transactions at Storage Entity *Entnum.*
- S*Entnum*—Storage in use. S*Entnum* returns the amount of storage content (or "token" spaces) currently in use by entering Transactions at Storage *Entity Entnum.*
- SA*Entnum*—Average storage in use. SA*Entnum* returns the time weighted average of storage capacity (or "token" spaces) in use at Storage *Entity Entnum.*

- SC*Entnum*—Storage use count. Total number of storage units that have been acquired from Storage *Entity Entnum*.
- SE*Entnum*—Storage empty. SE*Entnum* returns 1 if Storage *Entity Entnum* is completely unused, 0 otherwise.
- SF*Entnum*—Storage full. SF*Entnum* returns 1 if Storage *Entity Entnum* is completely used, 0 otherwise.
- SR*Entnum*—Storage utilization. The fraction of total usage represented by the average storage in use at Storage Entity Entnum. SR*Entnum* is expressed in parts-per-thousand and therefore returns a real value between 0 and 1000, inclusively.
- SM*Entnum*—Maximum storage in use at Storage *Entity Entnum*. The "high water mark".
- ST*Entnum*—Average holding time per unit at Storage *Entity Entnum*.
- SV*Entnum*—Storage Entity in available state. SV*Entnum* returns 1 if Storage *Entity Entnum* is in the available state, 0 otherwise.

Queue Entities and Queue Blocks

Queue Entities are used primarily for the collection of statistics such as the current count, total entries, and the count-time product of a *Queue Block*. They keep track of transactions that are blocked from entering Facilities and Storages because the Storage is full. Similar to Facilities, Queues are created when the first entity reaches a block that used the Queue. The GPSS Blocks that can be used with Queue Entities are:

- QUEUE Blocks increase the content of a Queue Entity.
- DEPART Blocks reduce the content of a Queue Entity.

These Blocks have two Operands: A is the name or number of the Queue and B is the number of entities being QUEUEd or DEPARTing the Queue.

The usual procedure is to "sandwich" a SEIZE, PREEMPT, or ENTER Block between QUEUE and DEPART Blocks. Notice that the transaction does not DEPART from the all jobs Queue until after it has successfully SEIZEd the Maintenance repairman facility. The SNAs associated with Queue Entities are:

- Q*Entnum*—Current Queue content. The current count value of Queue *Entnum*.
- QA*Entnum*—Average Queue content. The time weighted average count for Queue *Entnum*.
- QC*Entnum*—Total queue entries. The sum of all Queue entry counts for Queue *Entnum*.
- QM*Entnum*—Maximum Queue contents. The maximum count of Queue *Entnum*.
- QT*Entnum*—Average Queue residence time. The time weighted average of the count for Queue *Entnum*.
- QX*Entnum*—Average Queue residence time excluding zero entries. The time weighted average of the count for Queue *Entnum* not counting entries with a zero residence time.

- QZ*Entnum*—Queue zero entry count. The number of entries of Queue *Entnum* with a zero residence time.

Frequency distributions of these statistics can be accumulated by the use of QTABLE Commands that initialize queue time frequency distribution tables. The syntax of a QTABLE command is:

NAME QTABLE A,B,C,D

where,

A = Entity Label of the Queue Block.

B = Upper Limit of the first frequency class.

C = Size of frequency class.

D = Number of frequency classes.

ADVANCE Blocks

The only Block that can advance time in a GPSS simulation is the ADVANCE Block. When a Transaction arrives at an ADVANCE Block it is delayed by a specified amount of simulated time and then proceeds to the next Block. An ADVANCE Block calculates a time increment and places the entering Transaction on the Future Events Chain (FEC) for that amount of elapsed simulated time. Its syntax is:

ADVANCE A,B

where,

A = The required mean time increment.

B = The optional time half-range or, if a function, the function modifier.

The time increment can be calculated in several ways. If only the A Operand is specified, it is evaluated and used as the time increment. If the A and B operands are present, and B does not specify a function, both A and B are evaluated numerically and a random number between A-B and A+B, inclusively, is used as the time increment. If B is an FN class SNA, called a Function Modifier, the evaluating B is multiplied by the result of evaluating the A Operand; the product is used as the time increment. If zero is calculated as the time increment (ADVANCE 0), the entering Transaction is placed on the Current Events Chain in front of priority peers. Such a Block behaves as a null operation.

Function Entities

GPSS Function Entities are used to return a value derived from some argument, such as a random number. Actually, any SNA may be used as an argument. A Function is defined by a FUNCTION Command followed by one or more Function Follower Statements.

NAME FUNCTION A,B; comment

The A operand of the FUNCTION Statement specifies the argument, and the B operand is the catenation of the Function type and the number of data pairs to appear on the Function Follower Statements. It is the numbers, names, and/or SNAs in the Function Follower Statements that complete the definition of the function entity. There are 5 different types of function entities:

- Type C—Continuous valued Function. Performs a linear interpolation. A random argument is a special case.
- Type D—Discrete valued Function. Each argument value or probability mass is assigned an separate value. A random argument is a special case.
- Type E—Discrete, attribute valued Function. Each argument value or probability mass is assigned an SNA to be evaluated. A random argument is a special case.
- Type L—List valued Function. The argument value is used to determine the list position of the value to be returned.
- Type M—List valued Function. The argument value is used to determine the list position of the SNA. This SNA is evaluated and returned as the result of the function.

A Function used in operand 'B' of an ADVANCE or GENERATE Block is called a "Function Modifier". The double precision floating point result of the function is multiplied by the evaluated 'A' operand. The result is then used as the time increment required by the Block. The SNA associated with functions is:

FNEntnum—Function. Result of evaluating Function Entnum.

TRANSFER Blocks

A TRANSFER Block causes the active Transaction to jump to a new Block or Command location that is not necessarily the next sequential Block. It is one way to allow non-sequential operation in a simulation. A Transfer Block has 4 operands (A,B,C,D):

A = One of 9 Transfer Block modes.

B = Block number or location.

C = Block number or location.

D = Block number increment for ALL Mode

Unconditional Mode: A is blank. The active transaction always jumps to the location specified by the B Operand. A Transaction is never refused entry by a TRANSFER Block. If a Transaction becomes blocked by refusal of the destination Block it remains in the TRANSFER Block.

Fractional Mode: A is a probability (number between 0 and 1). The active transaction jumps to the location specified by the C operand with probability A and to the location specified by the B operand with probability 1 - A. If B is blank the transaction goes to the next sequential Block (NSB). This is the most common use of a Transfer Block.

BOTH Mode: When the A Operand is BOTH the Block specified by the B Operand is tested. If it admits the transaction, then the location specified by the B Operand is the next transaction destination. Else the Block at the C Operand is tested. If this Block admits the transaction, then the location specified by the C Operand is the next transaction destination. If neither block admits the transaction, the Transaction waits at the TRANSFER Block until one of the Block specified by the B or C Operand admits it.

ALL Mode: When the A Operand is ALL, all the Blocks between that specified by the B Operand and the C Operand are tested in sequence. The first Block to admit the transaction will be the transactions destination. If no Block admits the Transaction, it stays in the TRANSFER Block until it can enter one.

PICK Mode: When the A Operand is PICK, the destination of the transaction is chosen randomly from the sequence of Blocks between those specified by the B Operand and the C Operand inclusively.

Function Mode: When the A Operand is FN the destination is chosen by evaluating a function entity, specified in B, and adding an optional increment specified in C. If C is not specified, the location specified by the B Operand is the location of the new destination.

Parameter Mode: When the A Operand is P the active Transaction jumps to a location calculated from the sum of a Parameter value named or numbered in the B Operand and the value of Operand C. If C is not specified, the Parameter value is the location of the new destination.

Subroutine Mode: When the A Operand is SBR he Active Transaction always jumps to the location specified by the B Operand. The location of the transfer Block is placed in the Parameter specified in Operand C. To return from the subroutine, use a TRANSFER Block in Parameter Mode as shown above.

Simultaneous Mode: When the A Operand is SIM the Active Transaction jumps to one of two locations depending on the Delay Indicator of the Transaction. If the Delay Indicator is set, the Transaction jumps to the location specified by the C Operand and the Delay Indicator is reset (turned off). If the Delay Indicator is reset (off), the Transaction jumps to the location specified by the B Operand. The Delay Indicator of a Transaction is set when the Transaction is refused by a Block. The Delay Indicator remains set until the Transaction enters a Simultaneous Mode TRANSFER Block.

Test Blocks

A TEST Block compares values, normally SNAs, and controls the destination of the Active Transaction based on the result of the comparison. It is another way to allow non-sequential operation of the simulation. The syntax of a Test Block is:

TEST O A, B, C

where,

O = Relational operator. It shows the relationship of Operand A to Operand B for a successful test. The operator must be E, G, GE, L, LE, or NE. Also sometimes referred as an auxiliary verb that is usually separated from the verb TEST by a single space whereas the Operands are usually separated from the verb by a tab.

A = Test value.

B = Reference value.

C = Destination Block number.

The relational operator is required. It may be E, G, GE, L, LE, or NE. The usual use of the Test Block is as follows:

If the test is successful the next Block to which the transaction is transferred is given by the C Operand; if not the Transaction proceeds to the next sequential Block. The successful tests are defined as follows:

E = the value of Operand A must be equal to the value of Operand B.

G = the value of Operand A must be greater than the value of Operand B.

GE = the value of Operand A must be greater than or equal to the value of Operand B.

L = the value of Operand A must be less than the value of Operand B.

LE = the value of Operand A must be less than or equal to the value of Operand B.

NE = the value of Operand A must be unequal to the value of Operand B.

Commands

Commands are GPSS statements that are immediately executed when a Transaction gets to the command. Some Commands are used to direct or modify the compilation and/or the execution of the simulation without having a Transaction arrive at the Command. They have the same syntax as Blocks.

8.5.3 GPSS World

GPSS World is based on the seminal language of computer simulation, GPSS, which stands for General Purpose Simulation System. This language was developed primarily by Geoffrey Gordon at IBM around 1960, and has contributed important concepts to every commercial discrete event Computer Simulation Language developed ever since. GPSS World is a direct descendent of GPSS/PC, an early implementation of GPSS for personal computers. Since it was introduction in 1984, GPSS/PC and its successors have saved thousands of users millions of dollars. Now, the Windows implementation of GPSS World extends these capabilities into an Internet aware environment.

GPSS World is designed to deliver answers quickly and reliably, with the least effort, achieving the highest reliability of results. Consistent with these objectives, visualization of running simulations is highly stylized and a default statistical treatment is built in. This approach means that animations are "free" requiring no additional effort to produce, but are not photo-realistic. GPSS World's forte is transparency, not photo-realism. Third party animation systems are available which can provide pictorial animations based on GPSS World simulations.

GPSS World was designed to address these issues. Its visual nature allows the internal mechanisms of models to be revealed and captured. Its interactivity allows one to explore and manipulate simulations. Its built-in data analysis facility can calculate confidence intervals and an Analysis of Variance easily. And now, it can even create and run sophisticated screening and optimization experiments automatically, with relatively little effort from you. Most systems can be modeled in any of several ways using GPSS World. Usually only a small subset of the features available is needed to be used. However, the greatest proficiency requires familiarity with all that GPSS World has to offer.

GPSS World is object oriented. Its inhabitants include Model Objects which are used to create Simulation Objects. Simulation Objects, in turn, are used to play out simulations and create Report Objects. Finally, Text Objects can be used as Include-files to support code sharing and a user source code library and they are often used as files which can be read from or written to by the simulation.

In Version 4 of GPSS World, the PLUS Language has been extended for definition of Experiments. This powerful feature permits programmable control and can even be based on simulation results. Thus, completely automatic operation is possible including the exploration of response surfaces. PLUS Experiments, which are invoked by the CONDUCT Command, can be used to control the running of simulations over a parameter space. Experiments can be created with minimal involvement on your part. GPSS World now includes two new powerful experiment generators that can be accessed through the Edit Menu of the Main Window. The Screening Experiment Generator will create a fractional factorial experiment under your direction, and insert its PLUS source code into your model. Similarly, the Optimizing experiment generator will insert a sophisticated response surface exploration experiment that searches for minimum or maximum yields. The CONDUCT Command necessary to initiate the experiments is by default loaded into a Function Key. To execute a Screening or Optimizing Experiment and analyze the results, all you have to do is press a button.

GPSS World has comprehensive discrete and continuous modeling capabilities. The tightly knit continuous modeling feature allows for easy transition between the continuous and the discrete phases. From the continuous phase thresholds can be established that trigger the creation of Transactions for the discrete phase. Conversely, the INTEGRATION Block and INTEGRATE Command, control the processing in the continuous phase.

Several new GPSS Blocks have been added to cover the control of integrations, Transaction rescheduling, changes to Assembly Sets, user-defined PLUS Blocks, and Data Streams. Data types now include integer and real numeric values, as well as strings. Each type is automatically coerced to the required form, as needed. The new data type "UNSPECIFIED" now is available to indicate the absence of valid data, such as that from a missing run of an experiment. Even matrix structures have been improved. They can now incorporate up to 6 dimensions. The new multiway ANOVA Library Procedure analyzes data from a "Result Matrix", which is nothing more than a GPSS Matrix Entity where the yields of an experiment have been stored in a conventional way.GPSS World is easy to operate. A full screen text editor can be used in any of the Text Windows. Even the Journal Window and Reports can be customized and annotated.

GPSS World provides for a set of snapshots, as well. These are advanced features intended for professionals who need detailed knowledge of microstates of the simulation. Static snapshots can be taken of any Transaction, the Future Events Chain, the Current Events Chain, or the membership of the Numeric and Transaction Groups. GPSS World is highly interactive. All Model Statements can be used interactively.

Simulations can communicate with the outside world. You can now use five new GPSS Blocks and/or PLUS Procedures to manipulate Data Streams. They are OPEN, CLOSE, READ, WRITE, and SEEK. The last of these, SEEK, provides for direct access into a database. Data Streams have many purposes. You can use them to access data files, to create Result Files and custom reports, to access internal data directly. There are now PLUS Library Routines with the same names that perform nearly the same functions. That means that complex I/O operations can now be handled inside User-created PLUS Procedures. GPSS World simulations can even communicate with other products by direct invocation. The PLUS Procedure Library now contains the Call(), Call_Integer(), Call_String(), and the Call_Real() procedures which can invoke external functions existing on your system in executable files (*i.e.*, EXE and DLL files).

The analysis of results is easy in GPSS World. It has facilities that support the capture and printing of graphical windows. The Journal Window records the activities associated with the Simulation Object. An automatic Report numbering system ensures the safe keeping of each Standard Report. The new ANOVA Library Procedure can perform a complete multiway Analysis of Variance when passed a Result Matrix. That is all there is to the generation of an ANOVA table and a set of Confidence Intervals. And now, the Automatic Experiment Generators can create sophisticated screening and optimizing experiments based on dialog-window input. The basic analyses of these experiments are done automatically and reported in the Journal Window.

8.5.4 GPSS World Concepts

GPSS World is populated by 4 kinds of objects. Model, Simulation, and Report Objects form the 3 basic types that are used in all GPSS World simulations. Typically, a Model is developed by editing the statements in a Model Object. Then, a Create Simulation Command is issued, thereby creating a Simulation Object structured according to the statements in the Model. Simulations are run by sending those GPSS Commands, or by including commands in the Model Object, itself. Normally, when a simulation completes, a Report Object is created automatically.

Overall control of multiple simulation runs can be handled within this framework by including a PLUS Experiment in the Model Object. (PLUS is the "Programming Language Under Simulation" that can be used to define procedures and experiments.) Then, a CONDUCT Command can be sent to the Simulation Object to control a series of simulation runs, and deal with the results.

The Text Object completes the four types of GPSS World Objects. These are named in INCLUDE Statements to aid the development of large simulations, and for a few other handy uses such as the creation of a source code library. In addition, Text Objects are often used by Simulation Objects, when OPEN, CLOSE, READ, WRITE, and SEEK operations are performed.

All GPSS World Objects can be saved at any time, in any state, and reopened in a later session. This includes Simulation Objects, which can be run any number of times from a saved state, thereby facilitating debugging and demonstrations. With some careful planning, Simulation Objects can be saved in the middle of complex Experiments, to complete the simulation runs at a later time.

All GPSS World Objects except Text Objects contain data in addition to the basic ASCII text. This is why one can use an external text editor to edit a Text Object, but not any of the others. Model, Simulation, and Report Objects contain Bookmarks for easy navigation, and a list of attribute values called Settings, which can be modified and are inherited by child objects. When a Simulation Object is created it begins with a copy of the Settings of the Model that created it. The same goes for Report Objects which inherit their settings from the parent Simulation Object. In addition, Model Objects remember all the Translation errors encountered the last time you tried to Create a Simulation Object from it. That way one can make some corrections and save the rest for later.

Model Objects. A Model Object contains primarily a sequence of Model Statements and a set of built-in values called Settings. In addition, a set of Bookmarks and a circular Result List of syntax errors are part of the Model Object. When a Simulation Object is created by translating the Statements in a Model, it inherits all the Settings from the parent Model Object. The *Command / Create Simulation* menu command in the Main Window is used to create a new Simulation Object.

Model Statements. A Model is the set of all statements contained in a Model Object and all its Include-files. A Model Statement can be either a GPSS Statement, or a PLUS Procedure definition. GPSS Statements, in turn, can be either Block Statements or Commands. Model Statements define a Simulation Object when it is first Translated, and they can be sent as interactions to an existing simulation.

Commands are either *Queued* or *Immediate*. Actually, all Commands except HALT and SHOW are Queued. Each Simulation Object has a special chain called a Command Queue that holds all Queued Commands received by the Simulation Object. Commands are taken off the Command Queue, one after the other, for execution.

The HALT Command is a special case. It is an Immediate Command, and therefore is not placed on the simulation's Command Queue. However, when a HALT is executed, all remaining Commands are removed from the Command Queue and discarded. This ensures that all action on behalf of the simulation ceases when a HALT is received. Normally, a HALTed simulation is resumed by sending it a CONTINUE Command.

Multiple Model Files. Usually, a Model is the set of Statements in a single Model Object, and optionally, any number of plain text files, called Text Objects. It is sometimes useful to place a sequence of one or more Statements, PLUS Procedures, and/or PLUS Experiments into one or more separate Text Objects in order to modularize the model.

Text Objects, which are plain text files, can be named in INCLUDE Statements in the Model Object. Doing so causes all Statements in the Text Object to be inserted in place of the INCLUDE Command when the Simulation Object is created. Text Objects may themselves may contain INCLUDE Statements, to a maximum nesting level of 5. INCLUDE Commands can be used interactively, as well as within Models. They can even be loaded into Function Keys, thereby invoking a complex sequence with a single keystroke.

A Model is built from the Statements in exactly one Model Object and optionally any (nonnegative) number of Text Objects, which are mentioned in INCLUDE Statements encountered during the Translation of the Model. Only the Model Object can have Settings associated with it, which can be accessed through the Main Window's *Edit / Settings* menu command. These Settings are inherited by all Simulation Objects Created from that Model

Object. To prevent the occurrence of multiple Settings, Model Objects may not be used in INCLUDE Statements, only Text Objects.

Report Objects. One of the strongest features of GPSS has always been its Standard Reports. With essentially no effort from the model developer, a simulation run automatically reports on all the GPSS Entities defined in the model when the simulation's Termination Count reaches zero. There are a variety of ways of customizing these reports by Editing the Settings in the Simulation Object.

Text Objects. A Text Object is simply a way to represent a plain text file in GPSS World. Their primary use is as the target of INCLUDE Commands. This allows a shared set of Model Statements to be accessed easily from a Model Object. You can even load an INCLUDE Statement into a function key. In that way, a complex Command list and/or PLUS Procedure in a text file can be sent to a Simulation with a single keystroke. Text Objects turn up in other places, as well. Data Streams allow a Simulation to read and write data from text files, and to create Result Files for later analysis. As you might expect, these files are all represented as Text Objects.

Architecture. At the interface level, GPSS World is an implementation of the Document/View architecture common to Windows applications. Objects can be opened with multiple views, modified, and saved to persistent memory according to highly intuitive action sequences on the part of the user. The familiar main window menu and the disabling of inappropriate menu commands guide the user to his/her objective with minimal distractions. Internally, GPSS World has been designed to take advantage of close interactivity even in a multitasking virtual memory environment. This is discussed next.

The Multithreaded-design of GPSS World allows it to run multiple simulations and experiments simultaneously. Not only is screen update, user input, disk Input/Output, printing, and simulation done concurrently, but any number of simulations can be run at the same time, as well.

Interactivity. GPSS World maintains a high level of interactivity with simulations. Any Model Statement can be sent to an existing Simulation Object, using the Command item on the main menu of the Model Window, Accelerator Keys, or by using Model Settings to load function keys with customized Commands. Custom Command Dialog for statements not on the drop down menu, and using an INCLUDE command. Even INCLUDE Commands can be loaded into Function Keys, thereby supporting iterations of any complexity invoked by a single keystroke.

Block Statements, when used interactively, cause the Active Transaction to attempt to enter a temporary block, which is then discarded. This mode is called Manual Simulation Mode and it is useful during Experiments, providing all the functions available inside the simulation. PLUS Procedure and Experiment Statements case a user-defined procedure or experiment to be registered in the simulation's Procedure Library. Any existing Procedure item of the same name and type is replaced. Commands, except for HALT and SHOW, when received by an existing Simulation Object, are placed on the simulation's Command Queue to be executed in turn. HALT and SHOW are Immediate Commands, and are executed immediately when first received by the simulation. In addition, HALT removes all waiting Commands from the Command Queue. CONDUCT Commands initiate a PLUS

Experiment that takes over control of the Simulation Object. Experiments can base decisions on results and invoke a statistical analysis; however interactivity is reduced during an Experiment.

Turing Machine Program in GPSS. GPSS Code Listing is given below for Turing machine.

```
;GPSS/PC Program File B TURING.GPS
10 *
20 STRING MATRIX ,10,5
30 ACCEPT FUNCTION RN3,C2 0.0,0/1.0,10
40 STATE1 FUNCTION RN1,C2 0.0,0/1.0,10
50 STATE2 FUNCTION RN2,C2 0.0,0/1.0,10
60 GENERATE ,,,100
70 TEST LE 5,FN$ACCEPT TRAP ;null string
80 IN_Q1 TEST LE 5,FN$STATE1 GO_Q2
90 CHECK1 TEST LE 5,FN$ACCEPT TRAP
100 *
110 MSAVEVALUE STRING+,1,2,1
120 TRANSFER ,IN_Q1
130 IN_Q2 TEST LE 5,FN$STATE2 GO_Q1
140 CHECK2 TEST LE 5,FN$ACCEPT TRAP
150 *
160 MSAVEVALUE STRING+,1,4,1
170 TRANSFER ,IN_Q2
180 GO_Q2 MSAVEVALUE STRING+,1,1,1
190 TRANSFER ,IN_Q2
200 GO_Q1 MSAVEVALUE STRING+,1,3,1
210 TRANSFER ,IN_Q1
220 TRAP MSAVEVALUE STRING+,10,5,1
300 TERMINATE 1
```

At first glance, no differences between the number of function choices seems to offer no conclusion. But, insight into how the Turing algorithm was manipulated into this analysis seeps out:

- The functions are basically sequential.
- The functions:
    1. Accept at q_1 or q_2,
    2. Change states,
    3. Go to trap state-implying nondeterminism

- The machine logic (*defined as controlled by LEFT or RIGHT*) was determined by the program not by the tape. Perhaps, if this program 'constructs' were changed around, a difference in function calls would be noticed.

8.6 SIMULA

Object Oriented Simulation (OOS) can be considered as a special case of Object Oriented Programming (OOP). Some principles of OOP like existence of a varying number of instances of interfering objects have been in standard use in simulation environment for a long time, often using other terminology. The SIMULA language (used to be called SIMULA 67) is the first true object oriented language. SIMULA 67 was introduced in 1967. Many implementations of SIMULA will not yet have all the features given in the 1984 standard, although they will probably have more than those defined in 1967. Being rather old, it still has most (and all important) mechanisms and principles of OOP. With the exception of Beta programming language, other broadly used OOP languages are conceptual subsets of the SIMULA language whose standard was defined in 1967. Some things like classes, inheritance, virtual methods, etc. have been defined in SIMULA long time before they were rediscovered by the OOP boom in the 1980s.

SIMULA has been criticized that on one side there is a high-level sophistication of the language itself combined with rather limited simulation capabilities except time control on the other side. Lack of supporting simulation tools like transparent collection of statistics, more advanced queues than the basic lists available in the system class Simset, report generation, etc. is caused by the fact that the language has been formally frozen in 1968. This decision was controversial. The advantage is that there is only one SIMULA with minimal differences between implementations. On the other hand future development was made difficult. SIMULA is thus more an OOP background for the creation of simulation tools than a complete user-friendly simulation environment. Probably the best known one of such tools is DEMOS. 'DEMOS' is not a subclass of the system class Simulation and thus the users cannot use processes of Simulation. The process-oriented discrete simulation is the most advanced and the most natural way of creating simulation models.

A SIMULA program is made up of sequences of instructions known as blocks, which act independently to varying degrees, but which are combined to produce the desired overall effect. The simplest programs contain only one block, known as the program block. All other blocks follow the same basic rules, so let us have a look at the single block program,

```
begin
integer intvar;
comment The first SIMULA program written for this chapter;
intvar:=3;
OutInt(intvar,4);
OutImage
end
```

8.6.1 SIMULA Data Types

SIMULA contains all common facilities of high level third generation languages.

Value Types

Integer Short Integer

Real Long Real

Boolean Character

Reference Types

Object Reference Declaration: Ref (Object Identifier) (None is the trivial value)

Text Constants: "A", "Simula", Notext

Text is conceptually a class instance, which has its attributes and methods.

Methods

Boolean Procedure Constant; (returns True if constant value)

Text Procedure Main; (returns Main string—the text is a part of Main)

Integer Procedure Start; (returns Starting position in Main)

Integer Procedure Length; (returns Number of characters)

Integer Procedure Pos; (returns Current position)

Procedure SetPos(i); Integer i; (sets Changing position)

Boolean Procedure More; (returns True if Pos <= Length)

Character Procedure GetChar; (returns Character from Pos)

Procedure PutChar(c); Character c; (returns Storing character to Pos)

Text Procedure Sub(i, n); Integer i,n; (returns Substring at i of length n)

Text Procedure Strip; (Removes right spaces)

De-editing Methods

Integer Procedure GetInt; (Reads integer)

Long Real Procedure GetReal; (Reads real value)

Integer Procedure GetFrac; (Like GetInt, ignores spaces)

Editing methods

Procedure PutInt(i); Integer i; (Writes integer value)

Procedure PutFix(i, n); Integer i,n; (Writes decimal value)

Procedure PutReal(r, n); Long Real r; Integer n; (Writes in scientific format)

Text generation

Text Procedure Blanks(n); Integer n; (Returns n blanks)

Text Procedure Copy(T); Text T; (Returns a copy of T)

Arrays

Examples of arrays declared in blocks (*n, m, a, b* are global variables):

```
Integer Array MyList (1:100);
Array Matrix (1:n, 1:m); (Implicit type is real)
Character Array Buffer(1: If a>b then a else b);
```

8.6.2 SIMULA Statements

Example of an assignment statement is given below:

```
Res := 3
Count := Last
Count := Last + 1
Message := "PLEASE TYPE YOUR NAME"
Next := Average*Number + 2
```

The use of spaces before and after the assignment operator has no effect on the correctness of the statement. This applies to all "operators" in SIMULA.

Structured statements. Following are some examples:

```
Begin
Statement1;
Statement2;
...
End;
If Condition then statement;
If condition then statements... else statements... ;
```

Simple use of an if statement is

```
begin
    integer Int1;
    Int1:=InInt;
    if Int1=2 then OutText("YES");
    else OutText("NO");
    OutImage
end
```

This program will read in a whole number and compare its value against 2. If it is equal to 2 then the program will print YES, otherwise a blank line will be printed.

Switch statement example is as following:

```
Switch Target := L1, L2, L3, ... ;
Goto Target( Index_expression );
```

```
L1: ...
L2: ...
```

The while loop is written as:

While condition do statement1; statement2; ... ;

For example,

```
begin
!comment Read and Total a stream of Positive numbers, ending when a negative
!number is found;
    integer Total,Next;
    Next := InInt; ! Read in an integer;
    while Next>=0 do ! Only perform the next statement if condition is true;
    begin
        Total := Total + Next; ! Update total;
        Next := InInt; ! Read in the Next integer;
    end; ! Go back to the start of the while loop;
    OutInt(Total,8); ! When the condition fails, print the total;
    OutImage
    end
```

This is a simple program and it is explained by its comments. Let us look at the syntax of the *while* loop statement, which may be used wherever any simple statement may be used.

For (very general) Example:

```
Begin
Integer i;
For i:= 1, 13, 20 step 10 until 40, 70, i+1 while i lt 76,
    100 step 50 until 250, 1000, 1500 do OutInt(i,5);
End;
```

Output: 1 13 20 30 40 70 71 72 73 74 75 100 150 200 250 1000 1500

8.6.3 SIMULA Procedures

Parameter Passing Modes. An example is given below:

Comment. Example procedure with two input and one output parameters: (Displays a right indented text)

```
Begin
    Procedure RightText(T, N, FitsIn); Text T; Integer N;
        Name FitsIn; Boolean FitsIn;
    Begin
```

```
            Integer I;
            FitsIn := N >= T.Length;
            For i:=1 step 1 until N-T.Length do OutText(" ");
            OutText(T)
        End of RightText;
        RightText("Short", 30); OutImage;
        RightText("And the long one", 30);
End of Program;
```

Output:

```
        Short
        And the long one
```

Let us consider a case when, Functions = Type Procedures

Example—Integer function with two input parameters: (Computes the greatest common divisor)

```
    Begin
        Integer Procedure GCD(M, N); Integer M, N;
        Begin
        While M<>N do
            If M<N then N := N - M else M := M - N;
        GCD := M
        End of GCD;
        Integer A, B;
        OutText("Enter an integer number: "); OutImage; A := InInt;
        OutText("Enter an integer number: "); OutImage; B := InInt;
        OutText("Greatest Common Divisor of your numbers is ");
        OutInt(GCD(A,B), 4); OutImage;
End of Program;
```

Note that, a function may be called as if it were a typeless procedure.

Simula Classes. Simula classes contain four parts as shown in figure 8.1, below

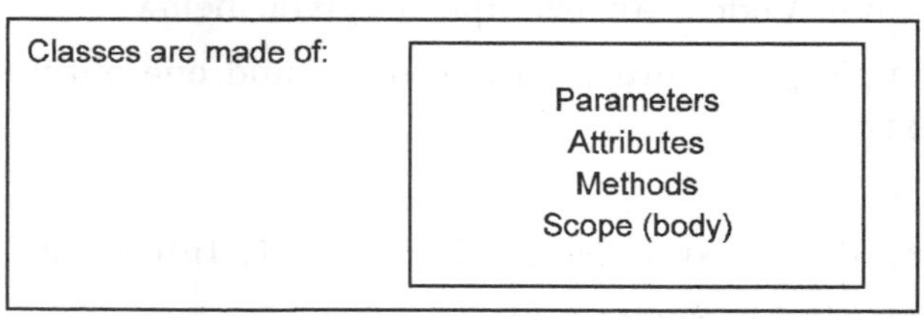

Fig. 8.1 Four parts in SIMULA classes

Declaration: Following example shows declaration of class, attribute, and method.

```
Class Rectangle (Width, Height); Real Width, Height;
                                          ! Class with two parameters;
      Begin
      Real Area, Perimeter; ! Attributes;
      Procedure Update; ! Methods;
      Begin
          Area := Width * Height;
          Perimeter := 2*(Width + Height)
      End of Update;
      Boolean Procedure IsSquare;
          IsSquare := Width=Height;
      Update; ! Life of rectangle started at creation;
      OutText("Rectangle created: "); OutFix(Width,2,6);
      OutFix(Height,2,6); OutImage
End of Rectangle;
```

Object generation. Here we discuss an example of object generation.

```
Ref(Rectangle) R; (Class reference variables)
Ref(LocRectangle) LR;
...
R :- New Rectangle(50, 40);
```

LR :- New LocRectangle(20, 30, 100, 200); (Note that also parameters for the parent class are given).

Activities involved in the above object generation: Memory allocation, reference stored to LR, copying values to all parameters (parent class first), Starting the body of the parent class, then the subclass.

Prefixing blocks. Let us assume a program with the following structure:

```
Begin
      Class A(P); Integer P;
      Begin LifeA1 Inner; LifeA2 End;
      Part1
      A(3) Begin
          Block body
      End;
      Part2
End;
```

Activities involved in the execution of the above prefixed block: Creating a class instance of A, copying values to its parameter(s), starting the body of the class, which includes execution of the block code.

So in the above program the sequence of operations is this:

Part1 LifeA1 Block body LifeA2 Part2

Prefixed block is conceptually *a class instance without a name* that has:

- parameters of the prefix class
- more attributes (class attributes + local block variables)
- more methods (class methods + local block procedures)
- more complex life rules (class body + block body).

The points to be noted here:

1. Block prefixing mechanism is not very useful in case of simple classes. The possible use is import of class declarations (parameters, attributes, and methods) into the block. It is supposed to be used mainly with the main classes (see the next chapter), that represent modules created by OOP principles. Prefixing a block by a main class (like for example Simulation) may import whole programming environments or special purpose SIMULA based languages.
2. In SIMULA programs there is no explicit memory de-allocation because the Garbage Collector recovers automatically the memory occupied by not referenced class instances.

Let us consider the nested classes in SIMULA. SIMULA PACKAGES = NESTED CLASSES

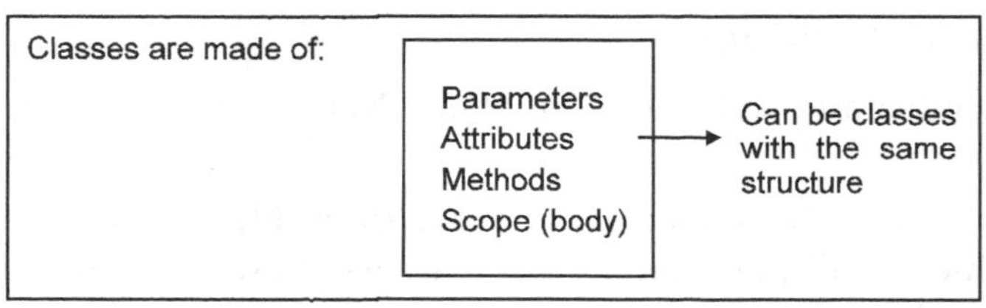

Fig. 8.2 Nesting in SIMULA classes

Classes that contain declaration of local classes are called main classes. Next example code defines a main class called Geometry.

```
! The program defines the main class "Geometry". ;
! It represents a theory with terms "point, rectangle, circle, and line".;
Class Geometry;
Begin
    Class Point(X,Y); Real X,Y;
    Begin
        Procedure Print; Begin ... End;
```

```
        Procedure Shift(Dx, Dy); Real Dx, Dy; Begin ... End;
        Print; ! scope of the point;
    End of Point;

    Class Rectangle(RecName, Width, Height);
        Text RecName; Real Width, Height;
    Begin
        Real Area, Perimeter;
        Procedure Update; Begin ... End;
        Procedure Show; Begin ... End;
        Update; Show; ! Scope of the rectangle;
    End of Rectangle;

    Class Circle(Radius, Center); Real Radius; Ref(Point) Center;
    Begin
        Procedure Shift(Dx, Dy); Real Dx, Dy; Begin ... End;
        OutText("Circle created at "); ! Scope of the circle;
        Center.Print;
    End of Circle;
    Class Line(M,N); Ref(Point) M,N; ! Line defined by two points m and n;
    Begin
        Real Slope;
        Slope := ... ; ! Scope of line;
    End of Line;
    !Variables declared in geometry: ;
    Ref(Point) Origin, A, B;
    Ref(Line) X,Y;

    !Life of geometry: ;
    Origin :- New Point(0,0); ! Creating the origin;
    A :- New Point(1,0); B :- New Point(0,1);
    X :- New Line(Origin, A); ! Creating the axes;
    Y :- New Line(Origin, B);
    OutText("*** Geometry initialized ***"); OutImage;
End of Geometry;
```

Next program is using the main class Geometry. Note how the classes declared in Geometry are used to declare subclasses specialized to the problem being solved. Later it is possible to declare and use reference variables qualified into both imported and locally declared classes. This is the fundamental idea of SIMULA based packages or user defined languages (what is the difference?)

```
External Class Geometry;
Geometry Begin
    ! Subclasses declaration in the prefixed block;
    Point Class Color_Point(C); Character C; Begin ... End;
    Rectangle Class Square; Begin ... End;

    ! Variables declaration in prefixed block;
    Ref(Color_Point) A1;
    Ref(Point) C, D;
    Ref(Circle) K;
    Ref(Line) E, F;
    Ref(Rectangle) R1;
    Ref(Square) S1;

    ! Block of the body;
    C :- New Point(5,6);
    D :- New Point(20,30);
    A1 :- New Color_Point(3, 4, 'G');
    K :- New Circle(10, C);
    E :- New Line(C, D);
    F :- X;
    K.Shift (1,1);
    R1 :- New Rectangle("Rec_R1", 5, 4);
    S1 :- New Square("Square_S1", 4, 6);
    S1.Show;
End of prefixed block;
```

8.6.4 SIMULA Standard Packages

Here we are giving the methods available for SIMULA. Attributes are available for Environmental constants (MaxInt, MaxReal, ...). Methods are available for:

- Basic arithmetical operations (Mod, Abs, ...)
- Basic text and character handling (Copy, Blanks, UpCase, ...)

- Mathematical functions (Sin, Exp, ...)
- Extreme functions (Max, Min)
- Random numbers (Draw, Uniform, Normal, Histo, ...)
- Compiler information (SourceLine, SIMULAId)
- Others (Error, Upper/LowerBound of arrays, Date, Time, ...)

Basic Input/Output

All input and output operations are represented by methods of file objects. A common ancestor called File (see figure 8.3) that implements facilities common to all files. Its subclasses are *ByteFile* and *ImageFile* (text file—"image" is its text buffer). Both are further specialized according to the access method (input, output, direct access). OutFile has one more descendent *PrintFile* that implements page oriented text output. Note that Simula does not have typed files made of for example records. This type of files can be implemented by byte files.

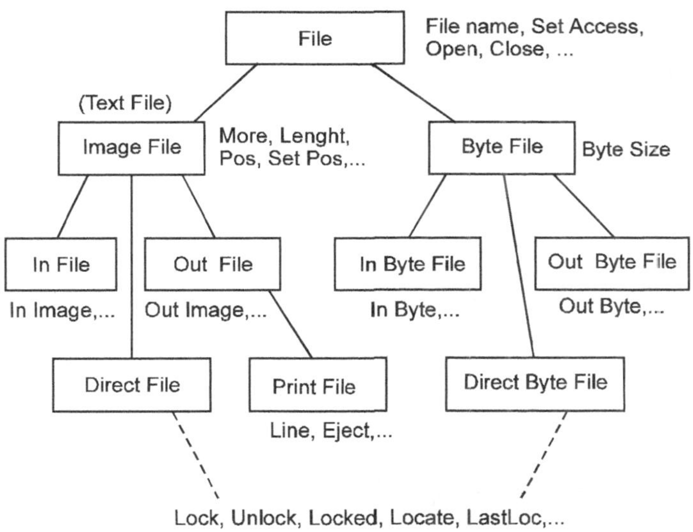

Fig. 8.3 Hierarchy of SIMULA file classes

Program frame. All system facilities in SIMULA are conceptually implemented as classes with certain attributes, methods and local classes. User programs are written as if they were inserted into the following frame. Note that the life rules of the class BasicIO create and open the system files before starting the user code. After its termination the system files are closed. The user code is inserted into a double Inspect statement. It means, that methods of system files (like for example GetInt, OutImage, etc.) need not be preceded by the file name.

Begin

Class Environment; ...

Environment Class BasicIO ... ;

```
        Begin
            Ref(InFile) SysIn; Ref(OutFile) SysOut; ...
            Class Simset ... ;
            Simset Class Simulation ... ;
            Procedure Terminate_Program;
            Begin ... ; GoTo STOP End;
            ...
            SysIn :- New InFile ( ... );
            SysOut :- New PrintFile ( ... );
            SysIn.Open ( ... );
            SysOut.Open ( ... );
            Inner; ! Starting of the user program;
            STOP: SysIn.Close ( ... );
            SysOut.Close ( ... )
        End BasicIO;
BasicIO Begin
        Inspect SysIn do
        Inspect SysOut do
Begin ! User program starts here;
        User statements
        End; ! Last line of user program;
End;
End;
```

8.6.5 Simulation Example Using SIMULA

1. A multi-channel queueing system (Active Customer approach). Figure 8.4 shows the system being simulated. It is an abstraction of for example a bank where the customers wait in one queue for any of the tellers. The interval between arrivals is random, uniformly distributed between 1 to 3 minutes. All servers have the same random service time, which is normally distributed with the mean value 8 minutes and the standard deviation 2 minutes. The simulation should find the average time a customer spends in the system. (Note that an analytical model of the above system is not available). Simulation of similar systems in SIMULA (exactly in the system class *Simulation* of SIMULA) always starts by identification of processes. One process is obviously the generator of customers—it will repeatedly generate a customer, record its arrival time, and wait a random delay. To express the dynamics of the system, there are two logical approaches. First is based on active customers and passive servers. The opposite approach—active servers, passive customers is shown in the next example. An *active customer* has *life rules* represented by the following steps:

1. If there is a free server, proceed. Wait in the queue otherwise.
2. Seize a server; generate random delay that represents the service time.
3. Release the server.
4. If there is a waiting customer (if the queue is not empty), remove it from the queue and activate it. (The activated customer will start its step 2.)
5. Update statistics.

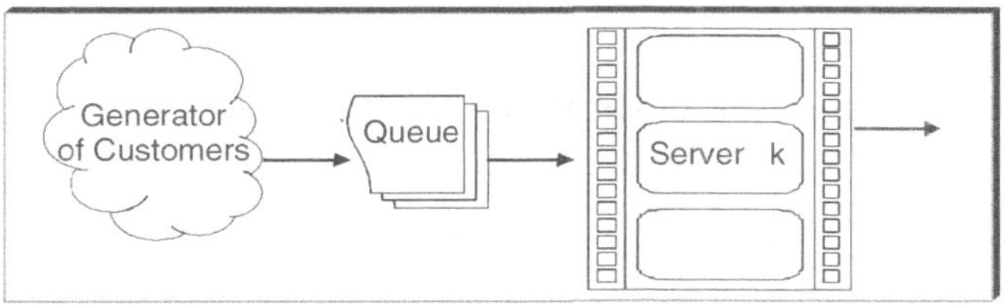

Fig. 8.4 Queuing system made of one queue and more servers

The following program is a simulation model of the above system. Here note that the primary objective was to show the logic of the model in a program as simple as possible. Real simulation models of course prompt for all variable parameters and provide more results (like for example average and maximum queue length, etc). In the following program there are two processes that exist during the whole experiment: the generator and the main program (block prefixed by Simulation), that just waits until the experiment is over and then displays the result. Then there are a varying number of customer processes, which exist temporarily. After updating statistics the customers terminate. Note the use of standard functions to generate random delays. There are standard functions in Simula for most commonly used distributions. All are given an integer variable as a seed to be used by the random generator. So all random values may use separate streams of random numbers or share a common one.

```
! Active customer approach;
Simulation Begin
      Real TrialDuration; ! Experiment length in [min];
      Ref(Head) Queue; ! The declaration of queue;
      Integer Servers; ! Total number of servers;
      Integer BusyServers; ! Total numbers of working servers;
      Integer TrialSeedG, TrialSeedS; ! Seeds of random generators;
      Long Real TotalTime, TimeSpent; ! Variables for statistics;
      Integer CustomersOut; ! Number of served customers;
      Real MinInt, MaxInt; ! Uniform interval between the arrivals;
      Real SMean, SStd; ! Normal service duration;
      Process Class Generator;
      Begin
```

```
        While true do begin
        Activate New Customer(Time); ! Time is the current (arrival) time;
        ! Interval between arrivals: ;
    Hold(Uniform(MinInt, MaxInt, TrialSeedG));
    End While;
End of Generator;
```

Process Class Customer(Arrival); Real Arrival;

```
Begin
Ref(Customer) Next;

    If not Queue.Empty or (BusyServers >= Servers) then
    Wait(Queue); ! Customer has to wait in the Queue;
        ! Service can start: ;
    BusyServers := BusyServers + 1; ! Seize a server;
        ! This is the teller service: ;
    Hold(Normal(SMean, SStd, TrialSeedS));
    BusyServers := BusyServers - 1; ! Release the server;
    If not Queue.Empty then begin
        Next := Queue.First;
        Next.Out; ! First customer from Queue served;
        Activate Next after Current;
    End If;
    CustomersOut := CustomersOut + 1; ! The Statistics;
    TotalTime := TotalTime + (Time - Arrival);
    End of Customer;
```

! The MAIN program body: ;

```
    TrialSeedG := 7; TrialSeedS := 23; ! Seeds for random variables;
    MinInt := 1; MaxInt := 3; ! Min and Max intervals;
    SMean := 8; SStd := 2; ! Random normal servers;
    OutText("Enter the number of Servers : "); OutImage;
    Servers := InInt; ! Initial numbers;
    TrialDuration := 600; ! Other variables initialized to 0;
    Queue :- New Head; ! Create an empty queue;
    Activate New Generator; ! This starts the experiment;
```

```
        Hold(TrialDuration); ! Experiment duration;
        TimeSpent := TotalTime/CustomersOut;
        OutText("Average time spent in the system: ");
        OutFix(TimeSpent, 3, 10); OutImage;
        InImage
End of program;
```

(2) A multi-channel queueing system (Active Server approach). The system being simulated is the same, as in the previous case—see figure 7.4. The difference is the active server, which repeatedly serves customers from the queue until the queue is empty. Then the server passivates. Customers at first activate all idle servers and then go into the queue. This is of course not very efficient, but simple. Customers are activated by servers after completing the service. In the rest of their lives the customers just update statistics. The main program creates and activates all servers, but they immediately passivate, because the queue is empty. Then the main program activates the generator and waits until the experiment is over.

```
! Active server approach is used in this program;
Simulation Begin
 Real TrialDuration; ! Experiment length [min];
 Ref(Head) Queue; ! The queue;
 Integer Servers; ! Total number of servers;
 Integer TrialSeedG, TrialSeedS; ! Seeds of random generators;
 Long Real TotalTime, TimeSpent; ! Variables for statistics;
 Integer CustomersOut; ! Number of served customers;
 Real MinInt, MaxInt; ! Uniform interval between arrivals;
 Real SMean, SStd; ! Normal service duration;
 Ref(Server) Array ServBank(1:10); ! Maximum number of servers is 10;
 Integer i;
 Process Class Generator;
 Begin
 While true do begin
 Activate New Customer(Time);
 ! Interval between arrivals: ;
 Hold(Uniform(MinInt, MaxInt, TrialSeedG));
 End While;
 End of Generator;
 Process Class Server;
```

```
Begin
Ref(Customer) ServedOne;

While true do
If not Queue.Empty then begin
ServedOne :- Queue.First;
ServedOne.Out; ! First from Queue served;
Hold(Normal(SMean, SStd, TrialSeedS));
Activate ServedOne after Current
end
Else
Passivate;
End of Server;

Process Class Customer(Arrival); Real Arrival;
Begin
For i:=1 step 1 until Servers do
If ServBank(i).Idle then
Activate ServBank(i) after Current;
Wait(Queue);

! The Service is finished: ;
CustomersOut := CustomersOut + 1; ! Statistics;
TotalTime := TotalTime + Time - Arrival;
End of Customer;

! The MAIN program body: ;
TrialSeedG := 7; TrialSeedS := 23; ! Seeds for random variables;
MinInt := 1; MaxInt := 3; ! Define Min and Max intervals;
SMean := 8; SStd := 2; ! Random normal servers;
OutText("Enter the number of Servers : "); OutImage;
Servers := InInt; ! Initial numbers;
TrialDuration := 600;
Queue :- New Head;
For i:=1 step 1 until Servers do begin
```

```
    ServBank(i) :- New Server;
    Activate ServBank(i) ! Create and activate all servers;
    End For;
    Activate New Generator; ! Starting of the experiment;
    Hold(TrialDuration); ! Experiment duration;
    TimeSpent := TotalTime / CustomersOut;
    OutText("Average time spent in the system: ");
    OutFix(TimeSpent, 3, 10); OutImage;
    InImage
  End of program;
```

8.6.6 SIMULA Nested QPS

A quasi-parallel system (QPS) in SIMULA is basically a block (typically but not necessarily a prefixed one), whose body creates some objects that together with the main block made up the system of quasi-parallel co-routines. Because SIMULA (unlike for example Pascal) is a true block oriented language, block (that generally means a QPS) can occur at any place in the code as a statement. It means that a QPS can contain local (nested) QPS's, which can also contain local QPS's, etc. This simple rule gives a way to create incredibly complex structures with consequences, which so far have not been fully utilized and not even understood. The next program outlines a possible use of a nested QPS in the chess control.

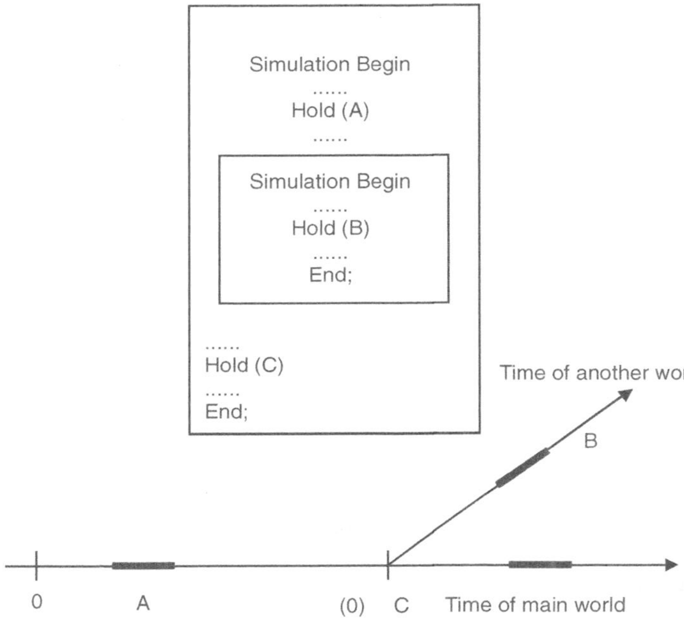

Fig. 8.5 The Basic idea of Nested Simulation

Nested Simulation Example: Let us consider a queuing network whose part is optimized by repeated nested simulation. Above figure shows the system being simulated. It is an abstraction of for example a bank where the customers at first wait in one queue for a teller. After being served by a teller, a customer is served by a cashier. There is another queue, where the customers wait for cashiers. The random interval between arrivals and the random service times of tellers and cashiers are known. Let's assume, that there is a certain number of clerks, that can work both as tellers and as cashiers. The management of the bank wants to check the way the clerks are allocated as tellers and as cashiers during a typical shift made of three periods: busy, idle, and a very busy one with different intervals between arrivals of customers. To find the best allocation policy, a nested simulation can be used in this way: at the beginning of each period, the internal repeated simulation will test the behavior of the first stage for various numbers of tellers (obviously the range is from 1 to the total known number of clerks). Using results from these internal simulation experiments, the management will choose the number of clerks who will work as tellers, the others will work as cashiers. To make the program simple, the decision is done by the user, who is given the results of internal simulation and then prompted to enter the number of tellers and the number of cashiers. The decision criterion is the average time spent in the first stage. The policy as such is also evaluated by the average time spent in the whole system.

The following program is an outline of the simulation program. Note, that the internal block prefixed by *Simulation* is performed repeatedly three times for all possible numbers of tellers. It contains declaration of classes similar to the outer ones. The difference is a simpler behavior of the customer, because there is only one service stage. There is also no further nesting in this system. Basically the internal simulation is similar to the example given in the chapter on the system class Simulation (active customer approach).

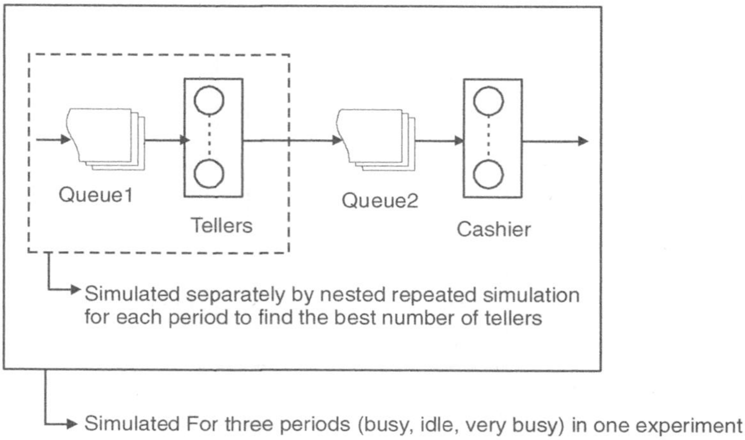

Fig. 8.6 Queueing network made of two multi-channel servers

Simulation Begin

Declaration of global variables

Process Class Generator; Begin ... End;

```
Process Class Customer; Begin ... End;

Initialize the global experiment

For Period:=1 step 1 until 3 do begin
For Trial:=1 step 1 until MaxClerks do
Simulation Begin

Declaration of internal global variables
Process Class Igenerator; Begin ... end;
Process Class Icustomer; Begin ... End;
Perform and evaluate one inner experiment
End of internal simulation;

Show results of internal experiments;
Select the best numbers of tellers and cashiers;
Perform a part of outer experiment for this period

End For;
Evaluate the global experiment
```

End of program;

The next program is the nested simulation model with the above structure.

Here we see NESTED Simulation in SIMULA class. The example is a model of a banking system. Customers are first served by tellers, then by cashiers. The input rate changes in three periods: there is a busy period, then an idle period and again a busy one. For each period the repeated inner simulation experiment simulates the first queue for the particular input rate and for various numbers of servers. Then it shows the results and prompts the user for the number of tellers and the number of cashiers. Tellers always finish a service that has already started. The simulation should find the time customers spend in the bank (average and maximum) for various numbers of clerks in the three periods.

Simulation Begin

```
! Global variables: ;
Integer Period,Trial; ! Period, Trial number;
Real Array MinInt,MaxInt(1:3); ! Define Min and Max intervals;
Real Array Duration(1:3); ! Duration of periods [min];
Ref(Head) Queue1,Queue2; ! The two queues;
```

```
Integer MaxClerks, Tellers, Cashiers; ! Total numbers;
Integer BusyTellers, BusyCashiers; ! Numbers of working clerks;
Real S1Mean, S1Std, S2Mean, S2Std; ! Random normal servers;
Integer SeedG, SeedS1, SeedS2; ! Seeds of the random generators;
Long Real TotalTime, MaxTime; ! Variables for statistics;
Integer CustomersOut; ! Number of served customers;

Process Class Generator;
Begin
While true do begin
! Interval between arrivals: ;
Hold(Uniform(MinInt(Period),MaxInt(Period),SeedG));
Activate New Customer(Time);
End While;
End of Generator;

Process Class Customer(Arrival); Real Arrival;
Begin
Ref(Customer) Next;
Real Spent;

If (not Queue1.Empty) or (BusyTellers >= Tellers) then
Wait(Queue1); ! Has to wait in the Queue1;
! Service starts here;
BusyTellers := BusyTellers + 1;
Hold(Normal(S1Mean, S1Std, SeedS1)); ! This is teller service;
BusyTellers := BusyTellers - 1;

If (not Queue1.Empty) and (BusyTellers < Tellers) then begin
Next :- Queue1.First;
Next.Out; ! First from the Queue1 served;
Activate Next after Current;
End If;

If (not Queue2.Empty) or (BusyCashiers >= Cashiers) then
```

```
Wait(Queue2); ! Has to wait in Queue2;
! Service can start;
BusyCashiers := BusyCashiers + 1;
Hold(Normal(S2Mean, S2Std, SeedS2)); ! This is the cashier service;
BusyCashiers := BusyCashiers - 1;

If (not Queue2.Empty) and (BusyCashiers < Cashiers) then begin
Next :- Queue2.First;
Next.Out; ! First from Queue2 served;
Activate Next after Current;
End If;

CustomersOut := CustomersOut + 1;
Spent := Time - Arrival;
TotalTime := TotalTime + Spent;
If Spent > MaxTime then MaxTime := Spent;
End of Customer;

Procedure Report; ! Experiment evaluation;
Begin
OutText(" *** Report on external simulation ***"); OutImage;
OutInt(CustomersOut,6); OutText(" customers ready at time ");
OutFix(Time,2,10); OutImage;
OutText("Average time in system: ");
OutFix(TotalTime/CustomersOut,2,10); OutImage;
OutText("Maximum time in system: ");
OutFix(MaxTime,2,10); OutImage;
End of Report;

! The MAIN program body;

SeedG := 11; ! Seeds of random variables;
SeedS1 := 13;
SeedS2 := 17;
MinInt(1) := 1; MaxInt(1) := 4; ! Defining Minimum and Maximum intervals;
MinInt(2) := 2; MaxInt(2) := 9;
```

```
MinInt(3) := 1; MaxInt(3) := 3;
Duration(1) := 120; ! Duration of periods;
Duration(2) := 240;
Duration(3) := 120;
MaxClerks := 6;
S1Mean := 6; ! Random normal servers;
S1Std := 1;
S2Mean := 8;
S2Std := 2;
Queue1 :- New Head;
Queue2 :- New Head;
Period := 1;
Activate New Generator;

For Period:=1 step 1 until 3 do begin

Real Array TimeSpent(1:MaxClerks);
OutText(" *** Results of internal simulation *** Period ");
OutInt(Period,1); OutImage;
OutText(" Tellers Average time spent"); OutImage;

For Trial:=1 step 1 until MaxClerks do
! ****************************************************** ;
Simulation Begin
! Internal Global variables: ;
Real TrialDuration; ! Internal experiment [min];
Ref(Head) Queue; ! The queue;
Integer Servers; ! Total number;
Integer BusyServers; ! Numbers of working clerks;
Integer TrialSeedG,TrialSeedS; ! Seeds of the random generators;
Long Real TotTime; ! Variables for statistics;
Integer CustOut; ! Number of served customers;

Process Class IGenerator;
Begin
While true do begin
```

```
Hold(Uniform(MinInt(Period),MaxInt(Period),TrialSeedG));
Activate New ICustomer(Time); ! Interval between the arrivals: ;
End While;
End of IGenerator;

Process Class ICustomer(Arrival); Real Arrival;
Begin
Ref(ICustomer) Next;

If not Queue.Empty or (BusyServers >= Servers) then
Wait(Queue); ! Has to wait in the Queue;
! Service can start;
BusyServers := BusyServers + 1;
Hold(Normal(S1Mean, S1Std, TrialSeedS)); ! Teller's service;
BusyServers := BusyServers - 1;

If not Queue.Empty then begin
Next :- Queue.First;
Next.Out; ! First from Queue served;
Activate Next after Current;
End If;

CustOut := CustOut + 1;
TotTime := TotTime + Time - Arrival;
End of ICustomer;

! Internal MAIN program body;

TrialSeedG := 7; ! Seeds for random variables;
TrialSeedS := 23;
Servers := Trial;
TrialDuration := 600;
Queue :- New Head;
Activate New IGenerator;
Hold(TrialDuration); ! Internal experiment duration;
TimeSpent(Trial) := TotTime/CustOut;
OutInt(Trial,13);
```

```
OutFix(TimeSpent(Trial),3,23); OutImage;

End of internal simulation;
! ********************************************************** ;

OutText("Enter the number of tellers : "); OutImage;
Tellers := InInt;
OutText("Enter the number of cashiers : "); OutImage;
Cashiers := InInt;
Hold(Duration(Period));
Report;
OutText("Press Enter to Continue."); OutImage; InImage;
End For;
End of program;
```

This is the output of the simulation model together with the numbers entered. The total number of clerks are 6, the numbers allocated as tellers and cashiers are inputted by the user. Note the maximum time spent in the system. It is kept reasonable until the third period, where it raised to 63.93 minutes (note that the total average service time is 6+8=14 minutes). So it is clear, that in the third very busy period one more clerk would considerably improve the system's behavior. This hypothesis was tested by another simulation run with the same data except one more cashier in the third period (four tellers, three cashiers). It gave these results: average time spent in the system 19.67 (21.84 for 2 cashiers), maximum time spent in the system 36.58, which is the expected improvement. So the outcome of the simulation is a suggestion to the management to allocate one more cashier in the third very busy period, otherwise the system behaves well with 6 clerks.

```
*** Results of internal simulation *** Period 1
                 Tellers      Average time spent
                    1              181.404
                    2               52.691
                    3                6.132
                    4                5.979
                    5                5.972
                    6                5.972

Enter the number of tellers : 3
Enter the number of cashiers : 3
```

```
*** Report on external simulation ***
42 customers ready at time 120.00
Average time in system: 18.52
Maximum time in system: 25.95
Press Enter to Continue.
*** Results of internal simulation *** Period 2
        Tellers     Average time spent
          1              36.620
          2               6.090
          3               6.045
          4               6.038
          5               6.038
          6               6.038

Enter the number of tellers : 2
Enter the number of cashiers : 4

*** Report on external simulation ***
91 customers ready at time 360.00
Average time in system: 17.29
Maximum time in system: 27.16
Press Enter to Continue.
*** Results of internal simulation *** Period 3
        Tellers     Average time spent
          1             205.290
          2             103.226
          3               7.937
          4               5.993
          5               5.974
          6               5.972

Enter the number of tellers : 4
Enter the number of cashiers : 2

*** Report on external simulation ***
119 customers ready at time 480.00
```

Average time in system: 21.84

Maximum time in system: 63.93

Press Enter to Continue.

8.6.7 Disadvantages of SIMULA

SIMULA has never became a widely spread commonly used language. There are various reasons to explain this fact. Even though the reasons all depend on each other, the following is an attempt to group them from various points of view.

Language features drawbacks:

- Limited file access facilities (typed files).
- Missing data types (records, sets).
- No advanced parallelism and real time support is available.
- No GUI support is available.
- Long executable files for short programs.

OOP features drawbacks:

- No multiple inheritances are available.
- No OOP interfaces are available.

Simulation drawbacks:

- No automatic collection of statistics is available.
- No report generator is available.
- No useful specialized facilities (resources) are available.

8.7 SIMSCRIPT

SIMSCRIPT II.5 modeling and simulation programming language is used world wide for building portable, high-fidelity, large-scale simulation and modeling applications. Its easy-to-use functionality features interactive graphical user interfaces, presentation graphics and animated graphics with embedded code which provides a wide range of programming options. The syntax of SIMSCRIPT II.5 is very English-like and self-documenting like other high level languages. Identifiers may be arbitrarily long and the user may tailor the appearance of the source code if desired. This not only helps others to better understand the code, but helps reduce further development and maintenance costs. Transient military personnel or newly assigned civilian simulation users are quickly able to develop sufficient proficiency to read, comprehend, and program in SIMSCRIPT II.5 with an abbreviated learning curve thanks to its English-like syntax.

8.7.1 Main Features of SIMSCRIPT

SIMSCRIPT II.5 is an easy-to-use and powerful simulation language with English-like syntax. In addition to the standard features of general-purpose high-level languages, it provides a timing mechanism and concurrent process management. Features like: entities, attributes, sets, events, processes and resources facilitate an easy mapping of real-world physical processes to computer based simulation models. Entities are user-defined objects, which can be dynamically instantiated, scheduled and destroyed during a simulation run. Entities represent components of a real-world system being modeled. Their properties are defined by attributes, while processes and events capture their behavior. Processes run concurrently, they can activate or interrupt each other and can be queued for limited resources. As simulation time progresses, statistical measures of changing quantities, such as queue lengths can be automatically collected and reported. During simulation run, a number of checkpoints can be created and simulation can be restarted from any one of them, facilitating multiple what-if scenarios.

SIMSCRIPT II.5 has built-in graphical capabilities that allow representation of entities by animated icons. Graphical icons are created off-line with Icon Editor, or by importing bitmaps. Users can create realistic graphical representations by displaying a geographical map, airport or factory layout in a background, while the entities are displayed in a foreground. Input parameters can be interactively entered through dialog boxes, while the model variables can be displayed dynamically, by using line or bar graphs, trace plots, pie charts, dials, and level meters.

Input or output of the model can be stored in a database. SIMSCRIPT II.5 provides SDBC (SIMSCRIPT Data Base Connectivity) APIs for major database systems on the market: Microsoft Access, SQL Server, Oracle, IMB DB2 and IBM Informix.

SIMSCRIPT II.5 models are portable across a variety of platforms. They are also open, and can easily be interfaced with libraries written in C/C++ or FORTRAN.

SIMSCRIPT II.5 simulation models are built using SIMSCRIPT II.5 Simulation Studio, an integrated programming development environment, which includes all the necessary tools for building non-graphical and graphical simulation models:

- SIMSCRIPT II.5 Compiler and Symbolic Debugger
- Graphical Editors for Icons, Graphs and Dialog Boxes
- Syntax Color Coded Text Editor
- SDBC—SIMSCRIPT II.5 Data Base Connection
- Automatic Project Builder and Help System
- Statistical Package
- On-Line Programming Manuals

SIMSCRIPT II.5 : Software package is fully supported worldwide by the CACI Products Company. It includes software updates, training, and technical support. Jump-start model building consultations are also available from experienced simulation specialists. CACI has been the leading simulation solutions provider for 40 years. Contributing to the wide acceptance and success of SIMSCRIPT II.5 modeling are:

Design: A powerful worldview, consisting of Entities and Processes, provides a natural conceptual framework with which to relate real objects to the model.

Programming: SIMSCRIPT II.5 is a modern, free form language with structured programming constructs and all the built-in facilities needed for model development. Model components can be programmed so they clearly reflect the organization and logic of the modeled system. The amount of program needed to model a system is typically 75% less than its FORTRAN or C counterpart.

Debugger: A well-designed package of program debug facilities is provided. The required tools are available to detect errors in a complex computer program without resorting an error. Simulation status information is provided, and control is optionally transferred to a user program for additional analysis and output.

Evolution: This structure allows the model to evolve easily and naturally from simple to detailed formulation as data becomes available. Many modifications, such as the choice of set disciplines and statistics are simply specified in the Preamble.

Documentation: You get a powerful, English-like language supporting a modular implementation. Because each model component is readable and self-contained, the model documentation is the model listing; it is never obsolete or inaccurate.

An Example of a SIMSCRIPT is given below:

"Solving an analytic equation arising from optimization of a coherent reliability system with 3" homogeneous components

```
Preamble
Define V as a real 1-dimensional arrays
Define I, N as integer variables
End

Main
      Open 3 for output, Name = "PROG.OUT"
       Use 3 for ouTPUT
       LET N=50
       Reserve V(*) as N
       LET V(1)=1.
       For I = 1 to N-1
       DO
       LET U=V(I)
  LET PPRAM=-9./((1+U)**2) + 9./((2.+U)**2) + 1./U**2
      LET V(I+1)=V(I)+PPRAM/I
   LOOP
PRINT 1 LINE WITH V(N) AND PPRAM THUS
OPTIMAL RATE IS: ****.*****, DERIVATIVE IS: ***.*****
END
```

The output

OPTIMAL RATE IS: 0.76350, DERIVATIVE IS: -0.00000

What is New in SIMSCRIPT II.5? New SIMSCRIPT II.5 Release 4.0 includes the new redesigned compiler, with several enhancements:

- Increased Execution speed for most very large simulation models.
- More efficient Ranked Sets, especially convenient in communication networks simulations.
- Stronger type checking, and extensive error reporting to speed-up model development
- Increased maximum size for arrays, entities and text variables.

Development Studio (SimStudio), Command line-interface, SIMSCRIPT graphics and SIMSCRIPT Data Base Connectivity (SDBC) are the same as in the previous SIMSCRIPT II.5 Release 3.0. SIMSCRIPT II.5 Release 4.0 is available on 32-bit PC Windows platforms and 64-bit AMD64 processors Opteron and Athelon with 64-bit Linux RedHat Enterprise 4. 64-bit version of SIMSCRIPT II.5 provides the following benefits:

- Increased address space
- Support for large files
- 64-bit pointers and 64-bit integers
- 64-bit Simulation Graphics
- 64-bit Data Base Connectivity

SIMSCRIPT II.5 Simulation Studio (SimStudio) : SIMSCRIPT II.5 Simulation Studio (SimStudio) is a programming development environment which provides support for projects with hierarchical directories. It has more intuitive GUI, modern look-and-feel, and incorporates SIMSCRIPT II.5 Syntax Color-Coded Text Editor and all Graphical Editors for SIMSCRIPT II.5 Graphics. SimStudio is available on all supported SIMSCRIPT II.5 platforms. SimStudio has structured organization of project directories and supports multiple routines in a file. New source file organization can easily be connected to a Configuration Management system of your choice.

SIMSCRIPT II.5 Simulation Graphics : SIMSCRIPT II.5 Simulation Graphics is based on Java environment for enhanced portability. Current SIMSCRIPT Models, which use Simulation Graphics II, only need to be re-linked with the new graphics libraries. New SIMSCRIPT II.5 Graphics uses JPG format, so bitmaps in .bmt and .xwd format have to be converted to JPG format. New SIMSCRIPT II.5 Graphics includes the new redesigned Interactive Graphical Editors integrated with the SimStudio. They have standard look-and-feel as other PC Windows applications, improved menu and dialog editing capabilities, more intuitive GUI and are easier to use.

SIMSCRIPT II.5 Data Base Connectivity (SDBC) : SIMSCRIPT II.5 Data Base Connectivity (SDBC) provides well-defined SIMSCRIPT II.5 Application Program Interfaces (APIs) to the major database systems on the market: Microsoft Access, SQL Server, Oracle, IBM DB2 and IBM Informix. SIMSCRIPT II.5 Data Base Connectivity User's Manual has details how to use it and SDBC Release and Installation Manual explain how to set-up and use it.

SIMSCRIPT II.5 Integrated Development Tools are used world wide for building portable, high-fidelity, large-scale simulation and modeling applications with excellent interactive graphical user interfaces and animated graphics.

Typical SIMSCRIPT II.5 : Its major applications include: telecommunications, network analysis, transportation, manufacturing, inventory control, health care, military operations, war gaming and logistics planning.

8.8 SIMULATION PACKAGES

There are several things that make an ideal simulation package. Some are properties of the package, such as support, reactivity to bug notification, interface, etc. Some are properties of the user, such as their needs, their level of expertise, etc. For these reasons asking which package is best is a sudden failure of judgment. The first question to ask is for what purpose you need the software? Is it for education, teaching, student-projects or research?

Animation in systems simulation is a useful tool and a user friendly tool must posses it. Most graphically based software packages have default animation. This is quite useful for model debugging, validation, and verification. This type of animation comes with little or no additional effort and gives the modeler additional insight into how the model. This type of animation comes with little or no additional effort and gives the modeler additional insight into how the model works. However, it augments the modeling tools available. The more realistic animation presents qualities that intend to be useful to the decision-maker in implementing the developed simulation model. There are also, good model management tools. Some tools have been developed which combined a database with simulation to store models, data, animations, and results. However, there is not one product that provides all of those capabilities.

Examples of some simulation packages are CSIM18, JSSim(JavaScript Simulation), Warped, BaseSim, OpEMCSS, TomasWeb, DEx, SimulAr, ACSL Sim, DESIRE, FreeMat, Scicos, etc.

8.9 SIMULATION BY SIMULINK AND MATLAB

It is the leading language for technical computing, DSP, control design, etc. SIMULINK provides a graphical interface to some of the MATLAB functions, thus enabling the user to graphically design models and control systems. MATLAB is a high-performance language for technical computing. It integrates computation, visualization, and programming in an easy-to-use environment where problems and solutions are expressed in familiar mathematical notation. Typical uses include

- Math and computation
- Algorithm development
- Data acquisition
- Modeling, simulation, and prototyping

- Data analysis, exploration, and
- Visualization Scientific and engineering graphics
- Application development, including graphical user interface building

MATLAB is an interactive system whose basic data element is an array that does not require dimensioning. This allows you to solve many technical computing problems, especially those with matrix and vector formulations, in a fraction of the time it would take to write a program in a scalar non-interactive language such as C or FORTRAN. MATLAB has evolved over a period of years with input from many users. In university environments, it is the standard instructional tool for introductory and advanced courses in mathematics, engineering, and science. In industry, MATLAB is the tool of choice for high-productivity research, development, and analysis. MATLAB features a family of add-on application-specific solutions called toolboxes. Very important to most users of MATLAB, toolboxes allow learning and applying specialized technology. Toolboxes are comprehensive collections of MATLAB functions (M-files) that extend the MATLAB environment to solve particular classes of problems. Areas in which toolboxes are available include signal processing, control systems, neural networks, fuzzy logic, wavelets, simulation, and many others.

The MATLAB system consists of five main parts:

Development Environment. This is the set of tools and facilities that help you use MATLAB functions and files. Many of these tools are graphical user interfaces. It includes the MATLAB desktop and Command Window, a command history, an editor and debugger, and browsers for viewing help, the workspace, files, and the search path.

The MATLAB Mathematical Function Library. This is a vast collection of computational algorithms ranging from elementary functions, like sum, sine, cosine, and complex arithmetic, to more sophisticated functions like matrix inverse, matrix eigen-values, Bessel functions, and fast Fourier transforms.

The MATLAB Language. This is a high-level matrix/array language with control flow statements, functions, data structures, input/output, and object-oriented programming features. It allows both "programming in the small" to rapidly create quick and dirty throw-away programs, and "programming in the large" to create large and complex application programs.

Graphics. MATLAB has extensive facilities for displaying vectors and matrices as graphs, as well as annotating and printing these graphs. It includes high-level functions for two-dimensional and three-dimensional data visualization, image processing, animation, and presentation graphics. It also includes low-level functions that allow you to fully customize the appearance of graphics as well as to build complete graphical user interfaces on your MATLAB applications.

The MATLAB Application Program Interface (API). This is a library that allows you to write C and FORTRAN programs that interact with MATLAB. It includes facilities for calling routines from MATLAB (dynamic linking), calling MATLAB as a computational engine, and for reading and writing MAT-files.

8.10 IMPORTANT SIMULATION LANGUAGES

ACSL Sim : ACSL (a language for simulation of continuous system) developed by AEgis Research into ACSL Sim, a tool for the simulation of continuous systems.

DSDS+ : The Data Systems Dynamic Simulator Plus (DSDS+) is a discrete-event-based simulator that eases the difficulties associated with simulation of high-data-rate, end-to-end systems.

JiST : JiST is a high-performance discrete-event simulation engine that runs over a standard Java virtual machine. It is a prototype of a new general-purpose approach to building discrete-event simulators, called virtual machine-based simulation, which unifies the traditional systems and language-based simulator designs. JiST is developed by Cornell Research Foundation, Inc. and it is free for non commercial uses.

MathCore : MathCore AB offers two main products: MathCore C++, an add-on to the well known Mathematica environment that compiles a subset of Mathematica into highly efficient C++ code. MathCode C++ provides a platform for rapid development of simulations and other expensive computations. MathModelica is an implementation of Modelica in Mathematica. MathModelica permits object oriented design of physical systems for simulation and visual programming using a graphic editor. MathModelica integrates documentation, runnable code, graphic connection diagrams and mathematical formulae in Mathematica notebooks.

MODSIM III : A language for simulation both objects and process oriented. MODSIM was recently sold to Compuware. CACI has migrated MODSIM users to SIMSCRIPT.

Parsec : Parsec a C-based simulation language, is used for sequential and parallel execution of discrete-event simulation models. It can also be used as a parallel programming language.

Pasion : Pasion is an object-oriented simulation language. The language has a process/event structure. Pasion source code is translated in Pascal, compatible with Delphi v3 or later. It can be used to model Queueing models, Continuous processes and allows the use of the Bond graphs paradigm.

SIMPLE_1 : SIMPLE_1 supports modeling discrete and continuous systems world views using a network modeling orientation. Features of the language include the ability of the user to declare variables and statistics requirements, perform input/output operations on files and to animate simulation results in real time easily utilizing built in language features. SIMPLE_1 utilizes a repetitive approach to run control to facilitate goal seeking modeling and run length definition based on model behavior.

SimPy : SimPy (Simulation in Python) is an object-oriented, process-based discrete-event simulation language based on standard Python and released under the GNU GPL. It provides the modeler with components of a simulation model including processes, for active components like customers, messages, and vehicles, and resources, for passive components that form limited capacity congestion points like servers, checkout counters, and tunnels. It also provides monitor variables to aid in gathering statistics. Random variates are provided by the standard Python random module. SimPy comes with data collection capabilities, GUI and plotting packages. It can be easily interfaced to other packages, such as plotting, statistics, GUI, spreadsheets, and data bases. SimPy is under active development by an international development team.

WinSAAM : The WinSAAM modeling system is a Windows-based version of the SAAM and Consam modeling systems. It has been developed under the auspices of the Laboratory of Experimental and Computational Biology, of the Division of the Cancer Biology and Diagnosis, of the National Cancer Institute. It is provided freely for use in scientific research.

XMLlab : XMLlab is an XML-based simulation authoring environment. The proposed description language allows to describe mathematical objects such as systems of ordinary differential equations, systems of non-linear equations, partial differential equations in two dimensions, or simple curves and surfaces. It also allows describing the parameters on which these objects depend. The simulation is written in XML, according to the DTD file, and then transformed into a Scilab-executable file.

8.11 WEB BASED AND DISTRIBUTED SIMULATION

Forio : Forio brings web-simulation a step forward since it lets the user enter his/her own model, using a scripting language and then it provides web-based tools to design the user interface. The simulation engine resides on the Forio web server. The main focus is on business simulations and they are geared towards operational issues (*e.g.*, development of market strategy).

GridSim : The primary objective of the GridSim project is to investigate effective resource allocation techniques based on computational economy through simulation. Millions of resources and thousands of users with varied requirements must be simulated. The scalability of systems, algorithms, efficiency of resource allocation policies and satisfaction of users is studied. GridSim is a research project based on SimJava. In the near future it will be more and more difficult to draw a line between web simulation and traditional simulation. Web simulation must allow the simulation and interaction of distributed entities.

JSIM : JSIM is a Java-based simulation and animation environment supporting Web-Based Simulation. In JSIM, simulation models may be built using either the event package or the process package (Process-Interaction Paradigm). In addition, a graphical designer (model package) allows process models to be rapidly built graphically. The QDS package (Query Driven Simulation) under development controls the storage, retrieval and execution of simulation models as Java Beans and utilizes JDBC to access databases. It also stores model inputs and outputs. Finally, JSIM has three foundation packages: queue, statistic and variate.

Silk : Silk is a Java-based modeling tool for the simulation, study and improvement of industrial systems. Silk is a modeling tool which merges the process-description modeling methodology within an object-oriented language.

STARDIS : STARDIS uses an object-oriented, event based approach to model real world entities and their communications. All the relevant discrete activities involved in the real world system are encapsulated in STARDIS entities using a mixture of rules written in structured English, and, if required, more complex routines written in a high level computer language.

8.12 MODELING AND SIMULATION OF ENVIRONMENTAL RESOURCES

This new category aims to list software tools for modeling and simulation of environmental systems such as water catchments, reservoirs, ecosystems, etc. Most probably it will evolve in a dedicated home page in the near future.

ICMS : The Integrated Catchment Management System (ICMS) is developed to facilitate the rapid development and delivery of catchment science to catchment managers. It implements a 'layered' approach to development, and delivery, through the use of four components. These are: ICMSBuilder—the central engine; Models embedded in the ICMS MDL (model libraries)—proprietary, free-ware and newly developed models; ICMS Projects-suites of linked models, and their data; ICMS Views—DLLs which provide tailored views of Projects

Tarsier: The Tarsier modeling framework is a modular collection of Windows software that enables fast development and deployment of a wide variety of environmental computing tools. These tools include simulation models, data storage and analysis tools, and visualization systems. The system supports many structures for the organization of quantitative environmental information, including: girded maps, networks, time series, and simple lists of geographic locations. Upon these are built analytical tools covering topics such as interpolation, statistics, sampling, and data transformation. At the top level are modules that implement a variety of simulation models, from cellular automata to stream pollutant routing models to large-scale spatial catchment hydrology models.

SEMOLA : SEMoLa (Simple, Easy to use, MOdelling LAnguage) is a non procedural meta-language to build simulation models for continuous/event driven, deterministic/stochastic systems, developed at the Agricultural and Environmental Sciences Department, University of Udine (Italy). While it is very generic, it has been successfully used to model biological, ecological and agricultural systems, at different scale and complexity level. The SEMoLa language is integrated in a simulation environment that simplifies the tasks of model building, simulation and documentation; moreover it provides calibration, validation, data management, neural network building, unit verification features and others.

Ecolego : Ecolego is a tool for modeling dynamic systems and to perform risk assessments using model simulations. It requires the Simulink toolbox of the MATLAB platform. The graphical user interface helps the user to define and manage building blocks, parameters, species and simulation settings. Ecolego also helps to create reports, to plot simulation results, to perform probabilistic simulations and sensitivity analysis. Even though Ecolego can be used to simulate any species and dynamic system, it has been specially designed to fulfill specific needs in the field of radio ecological risk assessment. It is platform independent and it runs under Mac OSX, Linux and Windows.

8.13 FACTORS IN SELECTION OF DISCRETE SYSTEM SIMULATION LANGUAGES

A selection process for Discrete Event Computer Simulation (DECS) software is discussed from a theoretical perspective. A survey of practitioners is conducted to examine identified components of simulation software and identify which attributes are considered to be of primary importance in the software selection process. The results of the study indicate a number of factors relevant to a decision on which type of software might be selected to conduct a given project. Based on data obtained from practitioners, a set of recommendations that are generalized to a variety of DECS package evaluation procedures are made by the authors.

8.14 SIMULATION LANGUAGES VS. PROGRAMMING LANGUAGES

Following are the major differences between simulation languages and general programming languages:

1. Simulation languages can be used for only simulating a system or a model, while general programming languages can be used for any purpose.
2. Although we can use general purpose language for system simulation but the programmer may face problem of lengthy coding, but in case of simulation languages a wide variety of tools are available to avoid lengthy coding.
3. Most of the simulation environment have graphical user interface but only few general purpose languages have graphical user interface. For example, C/C++, Java, Pascal, FORTRAN has no graphical user interface.

SUMMARY

Within the past several years, significant developments in simulation software have taken place: new simulation languages have been developed; new software packages have been developed for use in conjunction with simulation for purposes other than building models; new features have been added to existing languages; vendors new to the simulation community have marketed implementations of existing software packages; simulation environments, comprising integrated collections of simulation software tools have been built. As a consequence of these developments, those readers whose perceptions of simulation software are several years old should consider themselves out of date. Enormous amounts of time and energy are presently being expended on research and development of simulation software. Thus, we can expect dramatic changes to take place in the near future. Simulation software of the 1990's will be as far removed from present software as present software is removed from building models "from scratch" in languages such as FORTRAN.

In this chapter we have described new techniques for simulating systems with complex structures by use of a digital computer, as well as the requirements of tools (simulation languages) to cope with the problem in a user-friendly way. Emphasis is given to a general applicability of the software, that is, the described software is meant to be able to handle broad classes of problems in a sub-optimal way rather than to be able to treat any specific application problem in a truly optimal manner. The increased software robustness and the highly reduced costs in coding any application problem compensate, however, for the sacrifice of efficiency in executing a particular simulation project. Although many problems of numerical mathematics and information processing which are discussed in this chapter had to be considered and solved, the approach to them has been from the viewpoint of an engineer rather than from that of a mathematician.

EXERCISE QUESTIONS

1. What do you understand by simulation languages? Give the differences between continuous and discrete system simulation languages.
2. What is advanced continuous simulation language? What are its major features?
3. Give a comparative study of SIMULA and SIMSRRIPT.
4. Explain the object oriented features of SIMULA language.
5. Give the differences between simulation packages and simulation languages.
6. write short notes on following-
   (*i*) Online Simulation
   (*ii*) Visual Simulation Tools
   (*iii*) Distributed Simulation Tools
7. Explain the main functions of the following-
   (*i*) MATLAB
   (*ii*) Ecolego
8. Explain the factors used in the selection of a simulation language for a particular system simulation.
9. Explain the differences between simulation languages and general purpose programming languages.

INDEX

A

B

C

D

E

F

N

O

P

Q

R

S

T

U

V

W